*Corruption and Reform
in the Teamsters Union*

THE WORKING CLASS IN AMERICAN HISTORY

A list of books in the series appears at the end of this book.

Corruption and Reform
in the Teamsters Union

DAVID WITWER

University of Illinois Press

URBANA AND CHICAGO

Library of Congress Cataloging-in-Publication Data
Witwer, David Scott.
Corruption and reform in the Teamsters Union / David Witwer.
p.   cm. — (Working class in American history)
ISBN 0-252-02825-2 (acid-free paper)
1. International Brotherhood of Teamsters, Chauffeurs,
Warehousemen, and Helpers of America—History. 2. International
Brotherhood of Teamsters, Chauffeurs, Warehousemen, and Helpers
of America—Corrupt practices—History. 3. Teamsters—Labor
unions—United States—History. 4. Truck drivers—Labor unions—
United States—History. 5. Labor unions—United States—History.
I. Title. II. Series.
HD6515.T22I589   2003
331.88'11388324'0973—dc21   2002013118

Contents

Acknowledgments

I am happy to have the chance to acknowledge the people and institutions who have helped to make this book into a reality. A number of archivists and librarians have provided valuable aid. These include Kenneth J. Cobb and his staff at the New York City Municipal Archives, Harry Miller at the Wisconsin State Historical Society, Wendy Richter at Ouachita Baptist University, and Carmella Lee at the Paul Hall Library of the Harry Lundberg School for Seamanship. The librarians at the New York Law Institute generously granted me access to the stacks there, which contained a critical collection of trial transcripts. The Interlibrary loan staff at the Rockefeller Library at Brown University, and, more recently, Marlene Neece and other members of the staff of the Snowden Library at Lycoming College, helped me track down hard-to-find publications. At the International Brotherhood of Teamsters, General President Ron Carey and General Secretary-Treasurer Tom Sever gave permission to conduct research in the Teamster Papers. The National Labor Relations Board, and in particular their staff at the Newark office, set a model of speed and hospitality in fulfilling my Freedom of Information Act request.

I have been privileged to receive financial assistance from a variety of institutions. At Brown University, the history department's Jonathan R. Lax Fellowship helped fund early work on the dissertation upon which this book is based. Other funding received in that period included a dissertation grant in Law and Social Science from the National Science Foundation and a Littleton-Griswold Research Grant from the American Historical Association. At Lycoming College, several Professional Development Grants helped allay the cost of summer research trips. The National Endowment for the Humanities provided a summer stipend, and I benefited enormously from a year-long visiting fellowship at the Shelby Cullom Davis Center for Historical Studies at Princeton University.

A number of people provided hospitality, support, inspiration, and guidance that helped make this work not only a better book but also a much more enjoyable enterprise. From my days as a graduate student at Brown University I owe a debt of gratitude to John and Nancy Richards, Rich Canedo, Lucy Barber, Rik Kleinfeldt, and Charlie and Bill Fishbein. My dissertation committee included John L. Thomas and Naomi Lamoreaux, both of whom exemplify all that is the best in academia, as teachers, scholars, and friends. At Lycoming College, I acknowledge the support and encouragement of colleagues and friends: John Piper, Robert Larson, Richard Morris, Phil Sprunger, and Liz Yoder. The other fellows at the Davis Center during the 1998–99 year became valued acquaintances and played an important role in helping me to refine my ideas about corruption. They include Robert Gregg, Yemi Akinseye-George, Virginie Coulloudon, Gabriella Etmektsoglou, Vinod Pavarala, and the director of the center, William Chester Jordan. Melvyn Dubofsky, who led a National Endowment for the Humanities Summer Seminar in 1996, has become an important supporter and friend. Robert Zieger, David Brody, and an anonymous reader at the University of Illinois Press provided comments and suggestions that proved very useful in revising this work. Mary Giles did an excellent job of copyediting the manuscript. James T. Patterson was my dissertation advisor at Brown University. Those who have had the privilege of working with Jim know that there is no better mentor. I owe him a great deal, and this book would have been impossible without his support, guidance, and friendship. Finally and most important, I thank my wife, Catherine Rios, who has been my most dependable reader, partner, friend, and inspiration. This work is dedicated to her for all of the ways she has contributed to this book and, more important, enriched my life.

Introduction

This history of corruption and reform in the Teamsters Union provides a new way of looking at the problem of union corruption. Previous studies have treated the phenomenon of labor corruption in isolation, reviewing a series of criminal cases or notorious scandals but failing to situate those events in the broader context of a union's history or the social and political climate of the times. Such analyses made labor corruption a union problem and turned studies of it into de facto critiques of particular segments of the labor movement if not organized labor in general. In this literature the Teamsters Union loomed large, and its history, when presented, seemed to amount to little more than a series of convicted officials whose misdeeds received no criticism from a cynical and acquiescent membership.[1]

In contrast to such accounts, this study places the history of corruption within a larger narrative of the Teamsters Union's growth and development. Chartered by the American Federation of Labor in 1899, the Teamsters eventually became the largest union in the country. The organization evolved in response to changes in the transportation industry as motor trucks replaced horse-drawn wagons and later the interstate highway system fed the growth of long-haul trucking. The union addressed real needs for members, winning shorter hours, better wages, and improved working conditions. The average member's experience had little to do with the occasional acts of malfeasance by scattered union officials but instead was shaped by his or her local contract. Similarly, most Teamster officials served at the local level, engaged in no nefarious dealings with organized crime, and spent the bulk of their time busily responding to the needs and concerns of local members. On a day-to-day level, the crucial issues revolved around the work place. Only by taking into account this quotidian context can we understand the reaction of rank-and-file Teamsters to the scandals in their union.

Similarly, this study departs from previous works by addressing the multiple meanings given to the word *corruption*. It draws on the ideas of Daniel Rodgers, whose study of "political words" explored how certain "powerfully expansive words" come to have contested meanings. These key words framed debates about long-standing contentious issues in American history, and opposing sides in these debates mobilized the various meanings in order to sway public opinion.[2] In twentieth-century American history, labor corruption functioned as such a political word. Critics of organized labor wielded a broad definition of corruption, one that involved more than simply acts of bribery or extortion and at times included union activities that were technically legal. This broad, anti-union sense of the word *corruption* referred to cases where union leaders used aggressive organizing techniques that appeared to give them authority over the economy and society at large. In this way the label of corruption often amounted to a charge of irresponsible power. This particular understanding of the word might be called a political interpretation of corruption.

When groups opposed to the growth of organized labor raised the issue of union corruption, they mobilized this broader understanding of the term. They did so with particular vehemence in those periods when organized labor was making significant gains. This strategic use of the issue of corruption became particularly important if organized labor had gained a measure of political security. At such times, the usual dynamics of American labor history, where unions typically faced a hostile state, had shifted. In Progressive Era Chicago and in Franklin Roosevelt's New Deal Coalition, for example, organized labor enjoyed more hospitable political and legal environments. During these periods, anti-union forces drew on the issue of labor corruption and promoted a broader understanding of the term to undercut the political position of organized labor and to corrode the legal status of union organizing tactics. The result of these efforts amounted to a kind of crisis of corruption, one artificially created and stage-managed to promote an anti-union political agenda. Given the prominence and strategic power of the Teamsters, they usually played a key role in such crises. In this history, those crises occurred in three waves, first in the mid-1900s, then in the 1930s, and finally in the 1950s, all periods of dramatic union growth.

This history of union corruption thus offers an important contribution to a growing body of scholarship on labor law. Works by Christopher L. Tomlins and others have described how anti-union forces sought to undercut the growth and power of organized labor by engineering a latticework of constrictive legal language and judicial rulings.³ This study demonstrates that a broad definition of corruption played a part in a similar process. Corruption charges tarred sympathy strikes, secondary boycotts, and other union practices as illegitimate, and in a climate of crisis those tactics became illegal.

Teamster members understandably viewed charges of corruption made against this political backdrop with a measure of skepticism. But that does not mean that they simply discounted the issue of corruption. On the contrary, throughout the union's history members viewed corruption as a significant problem. Allegations about the union's aggregation of power might have left them unmoved, but other problems, such as fraud, bribery, organized crime's influence, and the denial of democratic rights, generated concern and on occasion spurred reform efforts. Behind the members' attitudes on these issues stood a general understanding of what their union should be doing. In contrast to observers who saw Teamsters as simply grasping cynics, members described their union's mission in terms laden with morality and tradition. Monetary issues played a part in this mission, but members' concerns embraced a wider array of benefits, usually lumped together under the general rubric of dignity and decency.

For members, corruption referred to cases of dishonest leaders who failed to represent the membership and thus undercut the union's ability to protect the members' dignity. In a typical instance, a local member in New York City wrote in 1942 that the organized crime connections of his local's leadership allowed them to defy the wishes of the membership. That led to misconduct. In return for bribes from employers, according to this member, local officials overlooked the violation of contract provisions, and men worked for less than scale, a condition known as "working under the hat." Explaining the situation in a letter to a newspaper columnist, "A Chauffeur" wrote, "The men must work under the hat and the boss hires less men than the contract calls for." Muzzled in their local, members needed someone to restore democracy. "If these officials were thrown out, maybe us chauffeurs could get steady work + decent conditions."⁴

The priorities of the membership shaped the ways in which they reacted to charges of corruption against their officers. An official who dutifully struggled for the interests of the membership but ran afoul of the political interpretation of corruption by engaging in aggressive organizing or strike tactics often remained popular with the members. The same priorities that moved members to support controversial leaders, however, also generated opposition when leaders betrayed the goals of the union. In either case, given the conflicting charges and countercharges, the opinions of the membership tended to be anything but monolithic. Like everyone else in America, Teamster members reacted to scandal in a variety of often contradictory ways. Still, the complexity of those reactions amounted to much more than cynicism and apathy.

On occasion, misconduct sparked reform efforts within the union. Given the fact that the Teamsters, like other unions, naturally constituted a one-party state, reform always proved a difficult task. The nature of these difficulties, however, varied, depending on the position of the reformers and the level of organization they targeted. Members of a local union trying to unseat their officers faced different obstacles and used different tactics than insurgents waging a campaign to change the national leadership. This long history of reform, largely ignored by previous studies on the Teamsters, illustrates the fact that many members took the issue of corruption quite seriously. It also demonstrates the organizational constraints that hampered reform. Over the course of the union's history, those constraints have grown worse.

This study also addresses the recurring connection between certain portions of the Teamsters Union and organized crime. Such connections did exist, but their nature and history have long been the subject of caricature and exaggeration. The decision of some union leaders to cooperate with members of organized crime must be taken out of isolation and placed within the context of the political and business environments in which the union operated. Union officials rarely played the central role in introducing organized crime to a particular industry; rather, they adapted the union to a preexisting business environment. Previous studies often have explained organized crime's influence by referring to the ideological grounding of particular union leaders or the moral predisposition of their members. Many have asserted that business unionism, the emphasis on simple bread-and-butter goals, left Teamsters ill-prepared to make the tough choices necessary to hold organized crime at bay.[5] This work, however, argues that ideology and individual morality had little to do with the presence of organized crime.

In sum, this study aims to supply a new understanding of union corruption, one situated within a comprehensive history of the Teamsters Union. The three sections of the book each focus on a particular crisis of corruption: the early 1900s, the 1930s, and the late 1950s and early 1960s. For each section, a preliminary chapter explains the background history of the Teamsters Union and the changing economic environment in which it operated. Succeeding chapters in each section center on the actual crisis of corruption and then the reaction within the union to that crisis. The conclusion briefly traces the union's history from the resignation of James R. Hoffa in 1971 to the government-supervised election in 1991 that saw the selection of a reform slate led by Ron Carey. The result is a historical narrative of the union, the first in more than a generation, along with a multifaceted investigation of the history of union corruption.

PART 1

The Opening Decade

At the close of the nineteenth century, teamsters formed a union to guard their dignity as changes in the teaming industry increasingly relegated them to the status of permanent wage laborers. The new union enjoyed dramatic growth in the first few years of the new century, but its strategic power also made it a leading target of an employer counteroffensive. A bitter strike in Chicago in 1905 marked a critical moment in that counteroffensive. In an effort to undercut the political strength of the Teamsters, the Employers' Association of Chicago promoted an investigation into union corruption that discredited the union's leadership and cast a shadow on the union's power. In the years that followed the Chicago strike a reform movement emerged within the union. When the union's incumbent president Cornelius Shea stacked the deck against electoral opposition, these reformers turned to secession, setting up a rival union. That tactic eventually forced Shea to allow a fair vote, and in that contest Daniel Tobin, a reformer, won election to the presidency in 1907. The victory of reform, however, proved only partial as corrupt elements within the union turned to secession in order to shake off Tobin's authority.

1. Building a Teamsters Union

It began with a desire for dignity. In 1905 the Teamsters of San Francisco opened their organization's new constitution and bylaws with a "Declaration of Principles" to explain their aims. Front and center among those principles was the stated desire to "regulate our affairs as a union and as individuals so as to make our occupation what it has a right to be—an honest and an honorable means of earning a decent and respectable livelihood." This stress on decency and respect appeared elsewhere in the document, too. The union's third principle called for members to demand "the right to be treated in a decent and respectable manner by our employers at the same time being conscious of corresponding duties to them."[1]

Calls for respectability and decency reverberate throughout the rhetoric of the early Teamsters Union. Indeed, the story of the birth and early growth of the Teamsters Union centers on the struggle of men engaged in a rough occupation who organized both for better material conditions and for a sense of what they saw as dignity. The rise of their organization brought them a measure of dignity and power in the new twentieth-century city, yet it also drew criticism. As part of a new wave of labor organizing by the American Federation of Labor, the Teamsters Union became the focus of a potent new antiunion movement that emerged around 1902. Critics, who charged that organized labor exercised excessive power, frequently cited the Teamsters as an example of a tyrannical, and, as these critics phrased it, corrupt, union. The sources of these charges lay as much in the nature of the teamsters' role in urban America as in any type of policies or practices engaged in by the union.

Tarred with controversy right from the start, the origins of this labor organization date from the turn of the century. Union organization stemmed from changes in the teamsters' occupation that occurred in the last quarter of the nineteenth century and from the evolving nature of the teaming industry. The national union that began in 1899 and expanded dramatically during the next decade reflected the distinctive qualities of the teamsters' trade. The Teamsters Union addressed the needs of working teamsters and, in some ways, of the teaming business.

The Teamster Occupation

By the end of the nineteenth century, commercial growth had transformed American cities, in turn fueling dramatic changes in the teaming industry. As railroad traffic increased and cities expanded, the business of hauling goods grew in size and scale. Teamsters formed both the first and the final links in the transportation chain. They brought goods to and from railroad depots, freight yards, and shipping docks; they also ferried people around the growing city. Most urban residents were too poor to own and maintain their own carriages. They depended on teamsters to transport them to locations not served by public transportation or for travel on occasions (such as weddings and funerals) when public transportation lacked the proper character.[2] Living in an increasingly urban world, Americans needed more teamsters. The 1860 U.S. census listed seventy-seven thousand teamsters nationwide, by 1890 that number had risen to 360,000, and by 1900 more than a half-million men worked as teamsters.[3]

Stated simply, these half-million men, who were defined as teamsters, drove a range of different kinds of wagons, from hacks and express wagons, the equivalent of taxicabs and delivery vehicles, to huge freight wagons known as "trucks" or "drays." Trucks were often massive vehicles pulled by huge draft horses working in teams of two, three, four, and at times as many as eight. The horses stood five feet tall at their shoulders and often weighed up to 1,600 pounds. When loaded, a truck held between eight and twelve tons.[4]

The census, along with many observers, described the occupation of teaming as unskilled. Those more closely connected to the working life of a teamster, however, questioned such a classification. As one team owner noted, "To drive such a team through the labyrinths of other teams and among the cars in winter weather and escape crash and wreck requires capacity." In fact, teaming demanded both craftlike skills and clerical abilities. A good teamster knew how to manage horses. He could get his team to pull heavier loads and deftly maneuver them in the most difficult situations. "The man who can take a team of horses and get the work out of it while at the same time keeping it in good condition and spirits, and keeping clear of accident in the crowded streets of the city deserves commendation," observed one team owner. "He will," the owner continued, "have his hands full."[5] When he was out making deliveries, a teamster served as the main contact between his employer and the customers. Thus he often had to be able to read and write. In many cases he served as a combination record-keeper and salesman. He built the business up by bringing in new customers, and he smoothed over day-to-day problems to keep old customers happy.[6]

Although skill and literacy were often required, the physical rigor of the work, combined with the exposed and often contentious workday, created an emphasis among teamsters on toughness. Whether a milkman or a coal hauler, every teamster spent the bulk of his day, good weather or bad, up on a wagon behind the horses, or he might be hefting the goods he delivered from the back of the wagon to their place of consignment. It was, all agreed, hard and demanding work. For that reason a team owner observed that a "competent teamster" required not only "memory, accuracy and forethought" but also "endurance."[7]

Working teamsters turned this necessity into a virtue and celebrated their toughness as evidence of their manhood. Referring to teamsters, one journalist noted, "Physical strength counts for much with them."[8] Their readiness to fight was celebrated. A writer in 1904 observed of the teamster, "His whole waking life was an endless fight for precedence. In the South Water Street jam [an open fruit and vegetable market in Chicago] the police gave up making arrests, for there were fights every hour, while at the bridges, markets and railway stations, wherever the tangle was the thickest, the teamster amply makes good the name which the County Hospital doctors have given him—'the roughest, toughest, scrapper of the working classes.'"[9] Luke Grant, a Chicago newspaper reporter, described how teamsters union officials reflected the toughness of the men who they represented. "The walking delegate of a union of printers is apt to be diplomatic, ready with intelligent arguments and courteous in his address. On the other hand, the walking delegate of a union of teamsters is apt to be rough in his manner, profane in his language, and more ready to settle an argument by physical force than by skillful diplomacy."[10]

Toughness provided a badge of manhood, and it also reflected a more bleak reality of a job that, before the union arrived, usually involved painfully long hours. The hours were long because a teamster was responsible for maintaining his horses and outfit (wagon and harness) and because he worked for as long as there were deliveries to make. Typically, he would arrive at the stables by 5 A.M. to water, feed, and hitch the horses. Deliveries were made all day, and then at the end of the day he returned to the stable, where, before leaving, he watered, fed, and groomed the horses. Often a teamster would not get home until 9 or 10 at night. As one union flier put it, "The Philadelphia Driver gets very small wages, long long hours of labor, and the story is told that he meets himself coming to work in the morning when he is going home at night." A teamster worked such hours six days a week. On Sundays, when there were no deliveries, the teamster came in to clean and oil the harness, grease the wagon axles, and, once again, feed and water the horses. For all of this he received between $8 and $12 a week. When John R. Commons, the pioneering labor economist, looked at the teamsters in 1905, he noted that before the union arrived hours varied greatly. "In general," though, he concluded, "they ranged from seventy to one hundred hours a week, according to the seasons and kinds of teaming."[11]

Men willing to take on this kind of grinding work day were mostly immigrants, the sons of immigrants, or African Americans. According to the 1900 census, African Americans made up about 13 percent of all teamsters, and first- and second-generation immigrants from Europe and Canada accounted for another 44 percent. In southern cities African Americans played a much larger role, ranging from a quarter to more than 90 percent of the Teamster workforce. Similarly, both blacks and immigrants figured more significantly in larger cities, those with populations of more than fifty thousand.[12]

Perhaps reflecting the public perception of their job, working teamsters complained about the way others treated them. Their pronouncements have a tone of injured pride. One of the founders of the Teamsters Union, Al Young, observed in 1903, "We have to stand more abuse than any other craft in existence. We have to stand the abuse of every shipping clerk in every office, as well as the abuse of everyone who has the charge of the freight we handle."[13] They resented the petty indignities practiced upon them. Testifying before the New York Board of Mediation in 1898, drivers for the New York Cab Company complained about having to provide their dispatcher with gifts of rum and cigarettes in order to get the more lucrative calls. What comes through here is a concern about one's dignity. In 1896, worried that accepting tips might injure their dignity, a coachmen's association in New York City debated the appropriateness of tipping for several hours at one of its meetings. As one of the teamsters present explained the issue, "By accepting tips we lose our dignity and become objects of charity. We lower ourselves and our business."[14]

They fretted over such slights because they saw their social status steadily eroding. As the nineteenth century came to a close, commercial growth created more teamster jobs, but at the same time the possibility of upward mobility faded. Testifying before a congressional committee in 1883, New York teamster Thomas B. McGuire recalled a time when all drivers could hope to become employers themselves one day. "Men who embarked in trucking twenty years ago have become wealthy, to my own knowledge, have become the owners of houses and other property, and are doing a vast business, some of them having from fifteen to twenty trucks." By the time McGuire testified, however, the competition these large firms provided, with their economies of scale and efficient equipment, made it impossible, he argued, for someone just starting out to break into the business unless he had an amount of start-up capital much larger than a typical driver could hope to possess.[15]

Doomed to be employees in a job others would not choose to do, teamsters questioned whether they could still consider themselves men. Sometimes they used the term *slave* to describe the debased status they feared. Thomas McGuire explained the lowly status of livery drivers, "For instance, a man who can afford to lease a large stable, and can manage to get men at starvation wages, and put them on a hack and put a livery on them, with a gold band and brass buttons, to show that they are slaves—I beg pardon; I did not intend to use the word slaves; there are no slaves in this country now—to show that they are merely servants."[16] In Chicago in 1905, a teamster remembered the sense of shame he formerly felt in his job. "I was slave for five years," he recalled, "I worked three hundred and sixty-five days in the year, twelve to fourteen hours a day."[17] At other times they compared themselves to the animals with whom they worked. Thus when teamsters described working such long hours that they ended up sleeping in the same stables as their horses, they were complaining not just about the hours but also about their status differing little from that of the horses.[18] Later the analogy involved machinery. A union flier in 1913 asserted, "The Team Driver . . . must be allowed to live and not merely exist, he must get decent treatment and not be worked as a machine, for he is human."[19] The national union's constitution embodied this status concern in 1899 when it explained that the purpose of the union was "to rescue our craft from the low level to which it has fallen, and by mutual effort to endeavor to place ourselves on a foundation sufficiently strong to resist further encroachments."[20]

Teamsters faced the new century with misgiving. Many more men worked at the occupation, but now they saw themselves as permanent employees doomed to work under increasingly degraded conditions. Union organization, which came at the end of the century, offered assistance on issues such as wages and hours, but that was not the union's only appeal. To men worried about their status in society, a union offered significant psychological benefits. In the union's world of brotherhood, all members (including immigrants and African Americans) partook of a shared sense of dignity and respect, and the labor organization fought to defend those issues as much as it championed the need for better pay and shorter hours.

The Business of Teaming

The changing nature of teamsters' working lives helped spur the creation of a union organization and shaped the form the labor organization would take, but so, too, did the structure of the teaming businesses where these men worked. By the turn of the century, teaming had diverged in two very different directions. Especially in smaller towns, small owner-operators continued to exist, while in larger cities team owners, essentially operating medium-sized businesses, predominated. In both cases, though, the business of teaming was bedeviled by excessive competition, a problem that union organization helped solve.

Observers at the time frequently commented on the size and scale that urban teaming companies had assumed in the final decades of the nineteenth century. Small businesses increasingly had become sizable operations. J. S. Hilliard bought a Boston teaming business in 1861 that consisted of thirteen horses and two wheel carts. When he died in 1901, his firm owned more than a hundred horses and did "the transfer business of three coast wise steamship lines, as well as railroad transfer, dry good delivery, boiler and iron works for some of the largest firms in the city." All told, his firm hauled between seven hundred and nine hundred tons per day.[21] This change in scale also involved livery stables, which had become corporate operations backed with large amounts of capital.[22] The largest firms were the express companies, which were, in fact, national corporations. Wells Fargo Express, which operated along the largest stretch of the country's railroad mileage, earned $17 million in gross receipts for 1905. American Express showed a capitalization of $18 million in 1907.[23]

Still, it would be a mistake to believe that the average team owner, even in cities, had become a corporate capitalist. Most occupied a simpler, less impressive economic niche. Of the fifty-nine stables in Chicago signed up with Local 705 of the Teamsters Union in 1911, the largest employed fifty drivers. The average team owner in this group employed twelve teamsters.[24] That was apparently a fairly representative sampling. In San Francisco, one study has found that the average team owner had seven drivers working for him, and trucking firms that joined the union in Philadelphia averaged about fifteen teamsters.[25] Except for the express companies, team owners ran businesses that served their own local markets.

These team owners existed in a fiercely competitive business environment. Compared to other forms of enterprise, teaming was a relatively easy business to get into, and so many did. A heavy wagon might cost $500, and a good team of horses might go for another $1,000 to $1,500, but secondhand and second-rate equipment would come cheaper and that could be enough to get one started, if the team owner could get the business.[26] To do that he underbid competitors, hauled more goods more cheaply, and lost money if he had to in the short term, figuring that once he had the customers he could make it back. Writing in 1906, a Philadelphia team owner reviewed the history of the business in his city: "Coming down to the present, the conditions of the teaming trade in Philly were the same as in most other places. Cut-throat competition was the order of the day."[27] In Wheeling, West Virginia, a team owner claimed that other team owners "will sooner give the merchant the wagon for nothing than let his competitors do the hauling."[28]

In such a business environment, attempts to find some way to limit the competition were endemic but usually not successful—before the union came along. From the 1870s on, team owners had been forming associations that set schedules of standardized hauling rates for their members to charge. Typically, such schemes failed when individual team owners found it difficult to resist the urge to pick up a few new customers by underbidding the organization's established rate.[29]

This cutthroat business environment, along with the teaming industry's scale and local-market orientation, shaped the teamsters' union that emerged in the early twentieth century. Team owners, like other employers, resisted union organization from fear of paying higher wages and concern about the constraints a union contract imposed on their control over employees. When the union offered a way to control competition, however, employer resistance decreased. The business of teaming then invited a particular kind of union organization.

A National Union Emerges

As the business of teaming evolved in the late nineteenth century, more and more teamsters gathered into unions, initially forming independent, local organizations. Out of these scattered locals, the American Federation of Labor (AFL) coaxed together a national teamsters' union. The new organization soon distinguished itself by accepting owner-operators for members, along with recent immigrants and African Americans, thus reflecting the diversity of the occupation it sought to organize. Based in an industry still very locally oriented, the union's national leadership maintained a tenuous hold over the scattered local affiliates. But this fragile, diverse, and still relatively new organization did make a difference. It helped local teamsters battle for better working conditions, and it championed their efforts to imbue their occupation with the decency and dignity for which the drivers hungered.

The AFL stood as a kind of godparent to the new Teamsters Union. Since its formation in 1886 the AFL assiduously encouraged union organization all across the country. A key part of the AFL's efforts involved forming new national unions out of the scattered local organizations that existed in a variety of trades, among them the teamsters.[30] At the turn of the century, such local independent teamster organizations were common. As one union official put it, "You can scarcely go in a city or town of any size in America that has not an independent teamsters organization."[31] In 1898 the AFL brought together seven of these local teamster leaders at the organization's annual convention in Kansas City and put their names on a charter for a national teamsters' union. They called it the Team Drivers' International Union (TDIU).[32]

The new national union grew quickly. By May 1901 the TDIU included 270 local unions and claimed a membership of more than thirty thousand.[33] The TDIU achieved this rapid growth by organizing new local unions and by bringing many of the preexisting independent local unions into affiliation with the national union. Because of the nature of the teamster's occupation, however, this rapid growth also brought conflict, especially over who should be allowed membership in the union.

Owner-operators dominated many of the independent local unions, especially in smaller towns where the scale of the teaming business was still quite small. At first the new TDIU welcomed these owner-operators, many of whom were small employers. The union's early constitution required only that a member be "engaged in driving" and did "not own or operate more than five teams."[34] Experience showed, however, that many of the small-town locals dominated by such employers became "boss organizations" and were more concerned with protecting employers' interests than drivers'.[35] Tension over the issue led to a secession movement in 1901 when a group of delegates at the annual TDIU convention demanded that all employers be banned from membership. When they lost the vote, these delegates walked out and formed a rival organization, the Teamsters' National Union (TNU). The breakaway TNU began encouraging other TDIU locals to secede, and, under pressure, the TDIU's leadership changed its constitution to ban employers while continuing to accept owner-operators.[36] With the key issue dividing the two teamster factions removed, an amalgamating convention occurred in Niagara Falls, New York, in 1903, and the reconstituted union chose the name it still bears: the International Brotherhood of Teamsters (IBT).[37]

Although the reborn national union had resolved a basic membership issue, secession movements would continue to dog the union. Each secession stemmed from a variety of political and personal issues within the union, but the trend also reflected the continued local character of the teaming trade. Unlike stove molders or woodworkers, team owners did not produce goods that might be shipped to another market in another town. Because a team owner could not shop around and find lower wages in various towns, teamsters in different towns had less reason to coordinate wage demands through a national union.[38] A system of benefit funds run at the national level might have provided a tie between the local unions and the national union. The low wages of most teamsters, however, made such a benefits system difficult to institute.[39] National officers were never able to raise the union's dues high enough to set up the sort of sick and unemployment funds that unions such as the Cigar Makers so effectively used to bind their organization together. By the fall of 1901, the national union did provide strike pay.[40] The fund from which such money came remained relatively small, however, and the national union did its best to discourage locals from counting on it.[41] As a result, no strong ties held local unions or their members to the national organization, and secession remained an inviting option for disgruntled local unions.

The union pulled back from its willingness to grant membership to employers, but at the same time it chose to accept immigrants and African Americans as members. The decision became important as the Teamsters Union established local unions in larger urban centers and cities of the South. Organizing in big cities raised the question of whether to accept immigrants, especially those from Southern and Eastern Europe who formed the largest share of the most recent wave of immigration. In the South, African Americans composed a major part of the teamster workforce, and so their membership status, too, became an issue as the union grew.

The union's policy of interracial unionism stood in stark contrast to many other AFL affiliates of the period, and it stemmed from Teamster officials' single-minded emphasis on building the strength of their organization. Although a number of labor organizations in and out of the AFL practiced various forms of ethnic and racial exclusion, the Teamsters organized recent immigrants as well as African American drivers.[42] Given the prevailing racial attitudes of the day, the union's efforts to organize African American workers were especially remarkable. By 1912 they composed about one-seventh of the union's membership, making it one of the most integrated labor organizations of its time. Even if it was open to African Americans, however, the IBT was no ideal, egalitarian paradise devoid of racial discrimination. At the local level, their treatment varied, with separate segregated locals existing in the South and integrated locals occurring in the North. In spite of the union's professed racial equality, white Teamster leaders shared the racist views of the period, and a variety of forms of discrimination occurred within the organization.[43] What can be said, in sum, is that the desire to build a strong union in an industry with a diverse workforce checked the worst racist predilections of the white Teamster leadership.

The union's willingness to open its ranks helped it grow dramatically in larger urban areas, but so, too, did its ability to provide big-city team owners with a way to stabilize competition. The most important example of such cooperative organization occurred in Chicago, which became the center of the International Brotherhood of Teamsters. Other accounts suggest that a similar pattern of organization took place in several other large cities during the same period.

In Chicago, the union grew through an arrangement both opportunistic and pragmatic between two men: Al Young and John C. Driscoll. Young, who drove a coal wagon, in 1899 organized his fellow drivers into a local union that he then affiliated with the Team Drivers' International Union. In 1901, frustrated with what he saw as the employer orientation of the national organization, he pulled his local out of the TDIU. Eventually, he set up the rival union, the Teamsters National Union.[44] As he organized this successful secession movement he also began to work with Driscoll, a former ward-level politician active in the Democratic machine in Chicago.[45]

Together, Young and Driscoll set up a collusive arrangement in Chicago's coal-hauling industry. Driscoll helped organize a Coal Team Owners' Association and became its agent. In January 1902 he brokered an agreement between the Coal Team Owners and Young's Teamsters Union that raised the base rate of wages of the drivers from $8 a week to $15 and at the same time reduced their weekly hours. In return, the Teamsters Union agreed to help the Coal Team Owners double the rates they charged for hauling coal. What had been a conflict of interest between union and employer became a coincidence of interests. The team owners agreed to employ only union members, and the union promised that its people would be allowed to work only for association members. A team owner who hauled coal could belong to the Coal Team Owners' Association only so long as he followed its schedule of rates to charge. In effect, if a team owner tried to haul coal in Chicago for less money than what the Coal Team Owners' Association had set as the minimum, he would find Al Young and his Teamsters Union harassing his non-union wagons and interrupting his business. To the benefit of both parties, the agreement proved very effective. Teamsters made more money, and team owners made more money, too.[46]

Through the spring and early summer of 1902, Driscoll set up similar arrangements for the other types of teaming. A Furniture Movers and Expressmen's Association formed and signed closed agreements with the Van Drivers' Local and the Express Drivers' Local. The Commission Team Owners' Association settled up with the Commission Drivers' Union. Truck owners set up the Chicago Team Owners' Association, which dealt with Local 705, the Truck Drivers' Local. In this way, and with very little conflict, most Chicago teamsters were brought into the union. Rates went up, as did wages. Driscoll served as secretary to five of these associations. By the summer of 1902 Young found himself at the head of a thirty-thousand-man Teamster organization in Chicago.[47]

This kind of collusive organization occurred in other large urban areas. In his account of the Teamsters Union's growth in San Francisco, Jules Tygiel describes how the Draymen's Association in that city came to terms with Teamsters Local 85 in September 1900. The association raised teamster wages from 45 to 100 percent for the various teamsters and helpers included in the union's contract. Hours were cut, and Sunday work was eliminated. "In exchange for this," Tygiel explains, "the teamsters pledged to work only for firms belonging to the Draymen's Association. In this way, the owners hoped to use the union to coerce recalcitrant drayage establishments to join their organization, enabling them to eliminate wage differentials and regulate competition."[48] Teamster organizers in St. Louis and Philadelphia made references to employers who sought to emulate the system that existed in Chicago.[49]

Clearly, not all Teamster locals benefited from involvement in such associations. Reports from organizers traveling in the field contain numerous accounts of employers who fought tooth and nail against union organization. Sometimes the Teamsters Union won these contests, and quite often it lost. Nor did the fact that a collusive agreement existed in a particular industry in one city mean that such agreements occurred in all other cities. In Chicago, the Coal Teamsters remained tightly bound to the Coal Team Owners' Association for decades. When the IBT tried to organize coal teamsters in Indianapolis in August 1911, however, no such arrangement emerged, and the unionization effort failed.[50] Why team owners in Indianapolis avoided the arrangement embraced by their counterparts in Chicago and San Francisco remains unclear. What is apparent is that the union's strength centered in those large cities where such agreements were reached. Chicago, with more than thirty thousand Teamsters Union members, became the heart of the IBT.[51]

In Chicago and elsewhere, the union brought dramatic improvements to drivers' lives. In 1905 John R. Commons carefully traced the union's victories in reducing members' arduous work schedules, which had previously ranged from seventy to one hundred hours a week. Milk drivers, for instance, had typically labored between eighty and one hundred hours a week. Thanks to their new union contracts, they worked about fifty-two hours a week by 1905. In general, Teamsters Union contracts stipulated that work done before 6 A.M. or after 6 P.M. would qualify for overtime pay, as would work on Sundays. Team owners responded to the new terms by more carefully scheduling delivery work so it would not require overtime and having stable hands do much of the horse care and maintenance work that teamsters once performed. While hours decreased, wages went up. Commons estimated that typical weekly wages before the rise of the union ranged between $8 and $12 a week. The union worked steadily to raise them. "The standard towards which all are aiming," Commons explained, "being $15 a week of six days, and the rate that the largest number have reached being somewhat less."[52]

Such changes in hours and wages mattered to teamsters, but so, too, did the changes in status that coincided with the material improvements. As Commons observed, the union pushed for contract language that would distinguish teamsters from common laborers. It sought, for instance, to have teamsters paid a weekly salary instead of by the load or by the hour. The change would help keep a man steadily employed and save him from having to "'hang around,' waiting for work," something that common laborers did, not craftsmen.[53]

Better wages and hours also made a difference because they allowed the teamster to lead a more respectable and decent life. References to family life embody some of those concerns. In Philadelphia, a union flier described how "One Philadelphia Driver managed to get home to his Sunday Dinner last week and one of his children said, 'Mamma who is that strange man.' His own children did not know him, as he left the house at 5 A.M. in the morning and got home at 8 o'clock at night and Sunday morning he spent at the stable."[54] To be respectable and decent meant fulfilling one's role in the family. To these working men it meant fulfilling the social expectations of being husbands and fathers. At the union's 1906 convention delegates debated whether to institute a special benefits program in order to attract southern African Americans as members. Referring to what really mattered to teamsters, though, one organizer asserted that no new benefits program was necessary: "If you show the colored man in the South that the International

Union is behind him and that it will help him educate his children and prevent his wife from looking into the washtub every day in the week."[55] A respectable man earned a decent enough living so his wife would not have to take in laundry to make ends meet.

The union gave these men a measure of respectability, and it would be a mistake to underrate how important that was to them. When a Chicago Teamster wrote an article on his union for *The Independent* magazine in 1905 he carefully emphasized the respectability and decency that came with union organization. He described the history of his own local union, the Department Store Drivers, and noted that in his local, "We exercise care in admitting men to our organization." He concluded, "The union not only regulated wages and working hours, but improved the class of men employed."[56] Writing to the union's journal to describe the achievements of his local in Des Moines, Iowa, W. S. Duckworth concluded, "A living wage scale was set, and to-day we are receiving $3.50 per day with shorter hours, which enables the wage earners and their dependents to live an honourable, upright life, enjoy the respect of their employers and last, but not least, be 'men among men.'"[57]

Although union members focused on the issue of respectability and decency, essentially questions of dignity for them, others viewed the rise of the Teamsters Union with very different concerns. The union's ability to win such changes for its members reflected the rise of the organization's power. Other segments of society looked at this new element in the urban landscape and saw a threat in the power that it wielded.

2. One Version of Corruption: Teamsters as Tyrants of the Street

In the spring and summer of 1905, the *Chicago Tribune* ran two front-page political cartoons that offered biting illustrations of the hostility and suspicion with which many people viewed the rise of a powerful Teamsters Union. The cartoon of April 29, 1905, pictures a husky teamster engaged in a sympathetic strike (fig. 1). A month later, on June 3, 1905, the cartoon emphasized the coincidence of the June 1905 uprising in Russia and a grand jury investigation of Teamster strike leaders in Chicago (fig. 2).

Both cartoons highlighted the theme of irresponsible power, whether of a dictatorship or an unprincipled grand duke. Teamster leaders were tyrants, these images say. Their dictatorial powers had crept beyond the realm of union affairs, and there lay the true menace conveyed by the images. The cartoons assert that Teamster leaders held it in their power to stop the flow of business activity in Chicago. A sign in the June cartoon explains that at the headquarters of these labor leaders one could find "strikes arranged on short notice," "commerce blocked," and "business ruined with neatness and dispatch." Some reporters captured the comparison and its argument by referring to the leader of the Teamsters Union as a "czar."[1]

During the first decade of the twentieth century, many people found the rise of the International Brotherhood of Teamsters a cause for alarm. While rank-and-file members of the Teamsters focused on the improvements brought to their lives by a powerful new organization, business leaders and their allies worried about the nature of the union's power. Their concerns reflected an often-forgotten reality: Men who drove horses and wagons, an age-old endeavor, played a critical role in the streets of the new twentieth-century city and with that critical role came influence for their union. Powerful business interests viewed this influence with trepidation. Organized into

Figure 1. From the *Chicago Daily Tribune,* April 29, 1905, 1.

Figure 2. From the *Chicago Daily Tribune,* June 3, 1905, 1.

employers' associations, businessmen in a string of cities confronted the Teamsters. Because the union's power did not spring from the traditional channels of electoral politics or accumulated capital, employers' associations argued that it was a new social threat, an emerging form of tyranny. The leaders of the Teamsters Union, according to this argument, were tyrants, corrupt not because they stole from members but because of the irresponsible nature of their power over commerce. Corruption for these employers referred to the state of affairs that existed when society's natural order—as they understood it—was overturned. Aggressive acts such as sympathy strikes, or actual violations of the law, such as extortion attempts, were the symptoms of this corrupt state of affairs.

Corruption, as a term, functioned in a way historian Daniel Rodgers has ascribed to certain "keywords" in America's political tradition. Its meaning was contested, broad, and shifting. Like the keywords upon which Rodgers focuses, corruption served less to name a universally agreed upon concept and functioned more as a tool. "Political words take their meaning from the tasks to which their users bend them. They are instruments, rallying cries, tools of persuasion."[2]

Employers took up the term *corruption* to argue against the growing power of labor organizations. They used it to try and manipulate people's perceptions of unions. Seeing the Teamsters as one of the most powerful unions of the day, they used the word to refer to that organization. But the theme of corruption loomed over much anti-union rhetoric of the day.[3] One employers' association pamphlet from the first decade of the twentieth century conveyed this sense that society had been corrupted by the rise of a newly militant organized labor: "The old time trade union was composed of able, skilled, and peaceful citizens, seeking mutual benefit with no thought of tyranny and crime. But as time went on, unprincipled men frequently obtained control and used their power for the oppression of the people"[4]

Moved by concern about the union's power, business interests challenged the Teamsters in a series of violent strikes. They depicted their struggles, however, not as an economic contest with unionized workers over wages and working conditions but rather as a campaign for reform. The fiercest battle, really a contest over the survival of the Teamsters Union, took place in Chicago in the spring and summer of 1905.

Unionized Teamsters and the Streets of the Early-Twentieth-Century City

Although often overlooked in later descriptions of the turn-of-the-century city, many contemporaries viewed the early Teamsters Union as a powerful force to be reckoned with. Most accounts of early-twentieth-century American cities emphasize the role of new technologies such as electric lights and streetcars, but in so doing they overlook the important role still played by horses, wagons, and their drivers.[5] In larger cities, unionized teamsters won strikes by blockading busy streets against non-union wagons. They could, at crucial times, appear to control access to the streets. Their apparent power eventually made the union a prominent target of the employers' counteroffensive.

Efforts to organize and maintain a union of teamsters drew much attention at the time because such efforts frequently involved bloody contests over access to the streets. Strikes were public events that took place in what we would now call public space. Moreover, Teamster strikes were often violent, and the violence took place in a city's main thoroughfares. To win a strike, Teamsters had to convince non-union wagon drivers not to take their wagons out on the street. Organizers did this by approaching these non-union wagon drivers in the street and cajoling, haranguing, or threatening them. When gentler methods failed, organizers would pull the non-union man from his wagon, often committing assault in the process. To give the surrounding crowd a better opportunity to harass the non-union driver, unionized teamsters often maneuvered their wagons in the street to block the path of non-union wagons.[6] As John R. Commons observed in 1905, "Actual or expected violence is looked upon by employers and teamsters as a matter of course. Blockades and obstruction, as well as violence, are effective."[7]

Both sides, it must be remembered, engaged in violence and sought a measure of control over the streets. Employers enjoyed certain advantages in these contests. They could pay for replacement drivers and hire private security firms to provide guards for their wagons. They could also claim the right to protect their property and on occasion receive police protection for the wagons.[8] Often enough these advantages were sufficient to defeat the union.[9]

But the union, too, enjoyed certain advantages in these contests, especially if it had already established a base of organization in a particular city. The nature of the teamsters' trade and the geography of the early-twentieth-century city made non-union wagons vulnerable. A heavily loaded wagon had to slowly traverse a maze of crowded streets and travel through districts where union pickets or strike sympathizers could await the opportunity to attack non-union drivers. Employers, who sought safety in numbers, organized non-union wagons into long convoys, with guards posted at intervals along them. Such convoys, however, could easily be blockaded by a single union teamster and his well-placed wagon. Teamsters Union leader Dan Furman described how well such a tactic fit the urban landscape in Boston in 1904.

Speaking to the Teamster convention that year, Furman said, "It is the opinion of your delegate that our forefathers had in mind the teamster when they made the streets as they are. One teamster can, by driving directly across any of the principal streets, block the entire traffic of that street, and for the life of me, I cannot see how a 'scab' could live in Boston in time of trouble."[10]

Once a strong organization had been established, the openness of the teamsters' working environment, the streets, made it relatively easy to keep the union intact. As Commons explained, "In the crowded streets, with thirty thousand teamsters organized, there is not much room for the unorganized." These non-union drivers could be and often were blockaded or attacked by their union counterparts. Union drivers were expected to follow a basic rule: "All members of this local shall at all times while on duty wear his union button in plain sight, so it can be seen by anyone."[11] A man not wearing a union button yet on a wagon could be singled out when opportunity arose.

It would be a mistake, however, to see the growth of the Teamsters as simply the result of a series of bitter street battles. The Teamsters Union frequently convinced employers—team owners—that they had something to gain from allowing employees to join the union. Indeed, in Chicago and elsewhere the union's strongest locals grew out of arrangements peacefully arrived at with team-owner associations that saw the union as a useful way to control a dangerous level of competition in the teaming industry. In such situations team owners stopped fighting the union and often worked peacefully with it.[12]

The toughest fights arose from attempts to build a local union in a previously unorganized city or when union teamsters were caught in the efforts of other workers. In the former case, where team owners chose not to cooperate and no substantial body of unionized drivers existed to lend support on the streets, organizing efforts usually failed. Often enough, however, the conflict had little to do with organizing teamsters. Unionized teamsters periodically aided other workers engaged in labor disputes, and when they did so teamsters faced not a compliant team owner but a fiercely anti-union business interest.

Although it brought them much trouble, the nature of their occupation meant that Teamsters found it difficult to stay out of the conflicts of other unions. In the course of making deliveries to different locations, union drivers occasionally encountered the picket lines of other unions. If drivers refused to cross those lines, they denied supplies to a strike-bound employer, probably crippling the business and greatly aiding the strikers' cause. But in refusing to cross such picket lines the driver broke the Teamsters Union's contract with the team owner, who himself was not involved in any labor dispute.

The team owner, who had conducted his labor relations in good faith, might find his business imperiled because he in turn had not fulfilled his hauling contract. Technically, the Teamster who honored a picket line in this way engaged in a sympathetic strike.[13]

Such sympathetic strikes could wreak havoc on employers. In Chicago in July 1902, freight handlers struck for recognition of their union. Rank-and-file Teamsters decided to honor the freight handlers' picket lines, and the movement of railroad freight in and out of Chicago ground to a halt. In two weeks Chicago businesses reportedly lost $10 million. At the end of those two weeks the leadership of the union asserted itself, and the Teamsters' influence swung the other way. Union officers, who felt the need to abide by their contracts with team owners, ordered rank-and-file Teamsters to cross the picket lines, and the freight handlers' strike collapsed.[14]

In this way the sympathy strike greatly expanded the power of the Teamsters. It gave them influence over employers who might not have a single teamster on their payroll. The union's ability to call a sympathy strike had become a way for it to control access to the public streets for most of Chicago's employers. Teamsters drew on this power to interject themselves in a range of labor disputes, often pressuring employers into arbitration that involved some form of union recognition. The sympathy strike made them the champions of organized labor in Chicago and in other cities such as San Francisco, where they were well organized.[15]

At the same time, dominance over the public space of the city eventually became the most widely cited bone of contention for employers who opposed the growth of the Teamsters Union. In 1903, New York City building contractors waged a costly effort to block the unionization of teamsters who delivered their building supplies. The contractors made it clear that they feared the Teamsters' growth would give union officials too much power. Contractors pictured this potential growth in union organization as an effort "to dictate as to whom, by whom, and in what manner material shall be delivered, thereby controlling the source of supply and closing the circuit of union domination in the building industry of this city."[16]

If they feared the ambitions of union leaders, businessmen and their allies also worried about the sympathies of rank-and-file Teamsters. Much to the frustration of businessmen, individual Teamsters often inserted themselves into the disputes of other workers. During a strike by streetcar workers in Chicago in November 1903 individual Teamsters plagued the City Railroad Company's efforts to operate its lines with replacement conductors and gripmen. Time and time again wagon drivers stopped their vehicles on streetcar tracks and blocked oncoming trains. As the trains ground to a halt, a crowd would gather to harry the company's replacement workers.[17] In the middle of the strike the *Chicago Tribune* asserted, "Yesterday the police had more trouble with the teamsters than with any other set of men."[18]

To contemporaries, the horse and wagon, and the men who drove them, appeared not as anachronisms but as powerful, even threatening, forces in early-twentieth-century cities. Because they delivered the material used to build downtown office buildings, the contractors who erected those structures feared the growth of the Teamsters Union. They could block the aspirations of the streetcar company as well as the progress of the occasional streetcar. Teamsters, in fact, seemed so powerful that they became the focus of an emerging employer counteroffensive.

The Employers' Counteroffensive

In their strategic use of the sympathy strike, the Teamsters in Chicago were part of a nationwide trend. From the turn of the century forward, organized labor began to use an effective variety of powerful organizing techniques, among them the sympathetic strike. In 1904 there had been ninety-three sympathy strikes nationwide, the greatest number since the failure of the great Pullman Strike in 1894. The sympathy strike, along with the closed-shop agreement and the boycott, helped create a period of dramatic growth for American trade unions.[19] From 1897 to 1904, union membership in America rose from 447,000 to 2,073,000.[20] That growth spurred an employers' counteroffensive that began around 1902. The need to resist "union domination" became the rallying cry of a wave of employer efforts to stem the tide of union expansion. The organizations formed by employers focused on organizing tactics like the sympathy strike, and quite often they targeted the Teamsters Union itself.

A change in attitudes had occurred. Business organizations such as the National Association of Manufacturers (NAM) and the National Erectors' Association, once willing to work with unions, began to favor confrontation.[21] On the local level Teamsters began to encounter businessmen and employers organized on a citywide basis to fight unions. This technique, which involved a series of coordinated lockouts, had been pioneered in 1901 by the Dayton Employers' Association. The Dayton group served as a model for other citywide employers' associations, including the Employers' Association of Chicago. A studied effort made to expand this kind of citywide organization led to the creation in the fall of 1903 of the Citizens' Industrial Association. Headquartered in Indianapolis, the group spearheaded a national antiunion campaign designed to re-create the Dayton model in communities across the country. It encouraged businessmen in each town and city to form a local employers' association and fight unions.[22] Local branches of this movement had various names—Employers' Association, Citizens' Alliance, or Citizens' Industrial Association—but they shared the same goals and techniques.

In their campaign to curtail the growth of unions, employers' associations aimed their attacks at the key organizing tactics of labor organizations: the boycott, the sympathy strike, and the closed-shop agreement. Employers designed their campaign to tap into traditional American values. The closed-shop agreement, they argued, abridged the treasured rights of the American mechanic to work at whatever job he chose. The sympathy strike, they added, involved a breach of contract and indicated that the word of union leaders was worthless. In general, as labor historians Selig Perlman and Philip Taft have pointed out, "Employers sought to convince the public that labor was both the aggressor and the oppressor. It was the employer who suffered from tyranny and oppression."[23]

Unions everywhere began to feel the heat of organized opposition, with the Teamsters becoming a favorite target. Preliminary contests between Teamster locals and the new anti-union groups occurred during 1903 and 1904 in St. Louis and other midwestern cities.[24] Inevitably, the contest centered on Chicago, where both sides had their strongest organizations. The largest concentration of Teamster members lived in Chicago, perhaps as many as thirty thousand of a total national membership of about forty-five thousand in 1905.[25] On the employers' side, the Citizen's Industrial Association was headquartered in Indianapolis, but the Employers' Association of Chicago was its most important affiliate and one of the strongest organizations of its kind in the country. Members included some of the city's largest employers, especially the new department stores.[26]

From its beginning, the Employers' Association of Chicago saw the Teamsters as its critical opponent. Writing on the formation of the association in February 1903, the trade journal *Iron Age* noted the group's early focus on the Teamsters. Explaining the motives of the new association, *Iron Age* observed, "For years the power of trades unions has been growing in that city [Chicago], until it is now regarded as the strongest labor center in the world. The Teamsters Union and their support of strikers in other lines have brought the matter to a crisis."[27] Dealing with that crisis meant confronting the Teamsters.

The two groups skirmished during a livery drivers' strike in December 1903, but that strike ended too quickly. It was not until the spring of 1905 that the Employers' Association received the opportunity to take on the Chicago

Teamsters. What became the Chicago Teamsters strike was the culmination of a crisis long in the making. The growth of the Teamsters Union had allowed the men who drove wagons to assert themselves more and more in the struggles of other workers. Employers who resented the power of the sympathy strike along with other labor organizing tools had formed national and citywide groups to curtail the growing power of labor unions. The Teamsters, because of the nature of their work, became a natural focus for these groups; Chicago, the center of strength for both organized Teamsters and organized employers, became the inevitable battleground.

The Chicago Teamster Strike of 1905

The Teamsters Union stumbled into a contest with the Employers' Association of Chicago (EA) in April 1905. The union presented the department store Montgomery Ward's and Company with an ultimatum in early April calling on the company to rehire striking members of the United Garment Workers' Union whom the company had replaced months earlier. When Montgomery Ward's refused the demand, the Teamsters declared that they would honor the Garment Workers' original picket line. No Teamster member would be allowed to deliver or pick up goods from the store.[28]

The Employers' Association quickly stepped into the conflict. In order to stop the union from singling out Montgomery Ward's, the Employers' Association encouraged all other State Street department stores to order their drivers to make the forbidden deliveries. As the men refused, they were laid off and replaced with non-union drivers recruited by the association. Through similar tactics, the Employers' Association also managed to involve grocery suppliers, firms that hauled lumber, and express companies. When the Garment Workers' Union pulled out of the strike in late April the dispute appeared to have come to an end, but the Employers' Association kept it going. The State Street department stores, backed by the association, refused to rehire any of the striking Teamsters. The association, in fact, pushed to involve even more employers in the conflict, and by May about 3,500 Teamsters were out on strike.[29] "The employers' associations and the employers generally have made up their minds that this must be a finish fight," *Iron Age* reported, "and they are determined to wipe out of existence a union which has been used as a club by all other unions to enforce its demands, dictating terms to employers who were dependent upon teams for the transfer of materials."[30] To move their goods through strike-bound streets, the Employers' Association chartered a new corporation, the Employers' Teaming Company, and bought the equipment and stock of strike-bound team owners.[31]

Publicly, the Employers' Association framed it as a contest over the free use of public streets and the abuse of the sympathy strike by the Teamsters Union. The Employers' Association insisted that the central issue at stake in the strike was the right of the public, especially merchants, to use the streets. According to a newspaper report on one meeting at the Employers' Association in late April, "The right to do business and to have uninterrupted traffic on the streets were the demands voiced by those who participated in the meeting, other matters pertaining to the strike being put aside as of minor consideration."[32] Theirs was reasonable reform effort, employers asserted.

In order to achieve this reform, break the strike, and tame the Teamsters Union, employers needed help from the city government to clear the streets of hostile strike supporters. The association hoped eventually to make as many daily deliveries with its new teaming company as had occurred before the strike. To do that, the replacement drivers needed to be able to travel securely throughout the city. Faced with hostile mobs and blockades, however, most of them stayed bunched together in protective convoys, moving slowly along a limited range of routes constantly guarded by police. Newspaper accounts of the strike justify the employers' belief that their most serious threat was not from organized, structured picketing but from an aroused working-class community that actively cooperated with and fought for the Teamsters Union.[33]

Crowds of working-class Chicagoans came out in support of the strikers because the Teamsters Union stood at the center of a dynamic new labor movement in the city, one distinguished by a remarkable degree of solidarity across occupations and strongly rooted in the community.[34] The sympathy strike, an important expression of this solidarity, had helped transform Chicago's unions. Since 1901 a wave of labor organizing in Chicago had established a new unionism quite different from the more conservative bureaucratic model exemplified by the older building trades unions.[35] In ways that echoed the goals and achievements of the earlier Knights of Labor, newer unions such as the Teamsters and the Teachers Federation had led the Chicago Federation of Labor (CFL) into aggressively using the sympathy strike and the boycott to organize unskilled workers. This new unionism in the CFL drew more women members; at the same time, it included large numbers of unskilled workers in previously unorganized industries such as laundries and restaurants. It threatened to organize not only locally based businesses that served a local market but also national concerns such as the meatpackers. The leadership of the new unions broke away from labor's previous ties to the Democratic Party's machine and joined a Progressive political insurgency whose immediate aim was public ownership of streetcar lines.[36] The foundation of this new unionism in Chicago rested on the ability of stronger unions to engage in job actions that supported weaker fellow unionists. The key expression of this support was the sympathy strike. The Chicago Teamsters strike of 1905 thus became a contest to determine whether the newer model of unionism would survive or whether it would give way to the more conservative model represented by the building trades.[37]

Finally, the strike also reflected a larger political struggle then taking place in Chicago. A Progressive political alliance had emerged that brought together labor organizations and middle-class reformers around the question of municipal ownership of streetcar lines. The Teamsters Union had played a critical role in that movement, whereas many of the city's business interests bitterly opposed it. Historian Georg Leidenberger has shown how the municipal ownership movement challenged the control that private business interests wielded over the city's streets in the form of profitable streetcar franchises. In April 1905, on the eve of the strike, supporters of municipal ownership won an important victory with the election of one of their own, Edward F. Dunne, as the city's new mayor. Dunne committed his administration to achieving municipal ownership.[38] So closely interwoven were the municipal ownership movement and the Teamster strike in terms of the themes and players involved that some observers saw them as part of the same contest. A few commentators even speculated that employers had initiated the strike immediately after Dunne's election in order to sidetrack the municipal ownership movement.[39]

Corruption Charges and the Issue of Irresponsible Power

Whether or not it had initiated the strike in order to stymie Mayor Dunne's efforts to achieve municipal ownership, the new mayor clearly did not suit the purposes of the Employers' Association. Having won election with the support of the city's unions, Dunne responded to the concerns of the association with skepticism. He ordered the police to provide strike-breakers with limited protection, but he refused to have working-class crowds driven from the streets. In the face of the business community's cries that only the militia could restore order, Dunne insisted that no emergency existed. His position proved decisive. Neither the state's governor nor President Theodore Roosevelt was willing to send troops into the city over Dunne's objections.[40]

Faced with an unsympathetic municipal government, employers turned to the legal system, where judges and prosecutors proved much more willing to be helpful. Injunctions that restricted picketing were soon issued and contempt proceedings begun. In addition, employers drew on the power of the State's Attorney's Office for Cook County by promoting a wide-ranging criminal investigation into the origins of the strike and the issue of labor corruption.[41] The tactic offered the association a powerful method for shaping public opinion. The reports generated by the investigation about the questionable origins of the strike and the corrupt nature of organized labor in Chicago placed employers on the moral high ground in the contest. The issue of corruption also raised concerns about the nature of the power that the Teamsters Union wielded.

Corruption surfaced as an issue a few weeks into the strike. On April 14, allegations appeared in Chicago's newspapers that certain Teamster leaders had been paid to stage the walkout.[42] Ten days later the Garment Workers Union pulled out of the conflict, complaining that a strike against Montgomery Ward's had never served its members' needs.[43] The charge of corruption, and the credence apparently given to it by the Garment Workers, provided justification for the Employers' Association to demand a wide-ranging inquiry into union corruption.

Prosecutors chose to cater to the interests of Chicago's employers, a decision that shaped the course of the investigation that resulted. Each month in Chicago a grand jury was impaneled to hear the presentation of evidence by the State's Attorney's Office. If the grand jury felt the evidence warranted doing so, they voted criminal indictments on charges suggested by the state's attorney. Early in the strike the employers moved to harness this judicial system. In mid-April, on the same day they filed for an injunction to limit picketing, a committee from the Employers' Association visited State's Attorney Steve Healey and urged him to have the April grand jury investigate the strike and labor conditions generally. Healey quickly agreed, and as time passed the prosecutor allowed the employers' role in the investigation to increase.[44]

In May the new grand jury had as its foreman A. A. McCormick, publisher of the *Chicago Evening Post,* an anti-union newspaper. His son-in-law managed one of the leading firms involved in the Employers' Association.[45] By the time of the June grand jury, attorneys from the Employers' Association were working hand in glove with the State's Attorney's Office in managing the investigation. For example, prosecutors met with the association's attorney at the close of each day's grand jury testimony to coordinate questions of investigative strategy, such as who would be called in to testify.[46] By mid-June, the State's Attorney's Office openly admitted that the goals of the grand jury proceedings included serving the needs of the employers. One item on the list of priorities given to the press by Assistant State's Attorney Fred Fake was to "restore normal industrial conditions to Chicago and make it unnecessary for manufacturers and other commercial enterprises to re-move from the city so they can do business on a fair and economical basis."[47]

The employers' efforts bore fruit in the form of a blossoming labor cor-ruption scandal. In turn, the prosecutor's decision to cooperate with the Employers' Association shaped media coverage of the labor dispute. Scan-dal and allegations of criminality offered exciting copy, and daily newspa-pers soon were filled with the reports, leaks, and discussion that surround-ed a very public set of grand jury investigations into labor corruption.

The resulting haze of scandalous allegations directed at union leaders that spring should not obscure what the employers had done. They deployed a broad definition of the term *corruption,* using it not simply as a descriptive device but as a kind of rhetorical tool. In other words, although it is true that arrangements between employers and union officials had taken place that both union members and the general public found illicit, it is also true that em-ployers' charges of corruption attempted to smear a much wider range of union activities with the taint of criminality. Allegations of graft proliferated in 1905 and undercut the legitimacy of organized labor. In the end, however, Teamster leaders were indicted not for extortion or bribery but on conspira-cy charges that stemmed solely from their leadership of a sympathetic strike.[48]

Employers raised the issue of corruption to score political points, but the tactic worked because a history of illicit arrangements between them and Chicago's labor leaders lent credence to their charges. In the recent past var-ious parties had paid for different Teamster local unions in Chicago to stage strikes against business rivals or companies that defied certain cartel arrange-ments. A reform movement within the union apparently put a stop to such proceedings in 1903. That year, the Teamsters Joint Council had forced the primary team owners' association, the Associated Teaming Interests, to fire John C. Driscoll, the group's secretary and a self-avowed strike-broker. The strike against Montgomery Ward's and Company, however, had the look of one of Driscoll's operations. It did not seem to be a straightforward sympa-thy strike. The garment workers in whose support the Teamsters ostensibly were striking had asked for help in January, and the Teamsters had turned them down.[49] The sudden change of heart in early April allegedly came as a result of an illicit payment. Who exactly was supposed to have paid for the strike against Montgomery Ward's is unclear, although varying accounts ex-isted. In one version, for instance, Sears and Roebuck bought the strike in order to injure its competitor.[50] In another version, conservative employers arranged the strike to embarrass a newly elected and reform-oriented mayor.[51]

In the end, the grand jury investigations that spring and summer came to no conclusions about the possible illicit origins of the strike. Instead, they focused on other matters. Despite the unions' decision in 1903 to oust Driscoll, he became the central figure in the employers' efforts to raise the specter of labor corruption. In June 1905 the state's attorney, working closely with the Employers' Association, arranged for Driscoll to testify about his past relations with a number of the city's union officials.[52] Leaked details of this testimony, along with Driscoll's informal discussions with reporters, became front-page news.[53]

The Employers' Association stage-managed the resulting corruption scandal. Working through the prosecutor's office, employers made sure that only labor leaders would be the subject of these damaging revelations. Driscoll himself noted that the State's Attorney's Office had scrupulously refrained from asking him substantive questions that might implicate any employers. Instead, he was asked only questions about union officials. As he explained to the *Chicago Tribune*, "They easily could have discovered who were the big employers who supplied me with money for my negotiations, and yet they accomplished nothing along that line."[54]

Indeed, members of the June grand jury reported that the scope of their investigation was strictly limited by forces they believed to be linked to the Employers' Association. One juror described his frustration to the *Chicago Record-Herald*, "We were almost at a point where indictments might be voted. Now a screw has been put in the investigation. Assistant State's Attorney Fake is doing his best to force someone to loosen up, and meantime we are more or less at a halt." The juror had no doubt about who had shut down the investigation. "It is evident to us where the cause of the check rests. A number of employers and their agents are behind the move. In fact, we can see that we ourselves are the victims of a conspiracy that results in suppressing facts."[55] The *Chicago Daily Tribune* referred to a report "that the Employers' Association, which had promised to aid in the exposure, was not working enthusiastically in any movement that might lead to indictments of employers for complicity in labor graft."[56]

Employers had no wish to see the grand jury investigation set loose to hunt for misdeeds in the city's labor relations. The results could prove as embarrassing to them as to their union opponents. At the employers' behest the grand jury veered away from uncovering actual instances where employers had arranged strikes with union leaders and instead centered on discrediting the union's leadership. State's Attorney Fred Fake explained in June that although the grand jury might very well not bring any indictments for corruption it would still accomplish an important goal. The investigation would, he said, "discredit grafting and dissolute labor leaders to such an extent that it no longer would be possible for them to secure office."[57]

The focus of this campaign soon came to be Cornelius Shea, president of the striking Teamsters Union. As the campaign developed, Shea was depicted as a model villain: corrupt, tyrannical, and profligate in his personal life. He was made the embodiment of irresponsible power in order to portray the apparent authority that his union wielded over the city's streets as dangerous.

The grand jury found no firsthand evidence that Shea had received bribes, but that did little to slow an investigation now focused less on criminal conduct and more on discrediting union leadership in order to curb union power.[58] In an effort to depict him as dissolute, the June grand jury spent a great deal of time looking into Shea's private life. Although married, he apparently had been seeing a nineteen-year-old waitress. To publicize that fact the State's Attorney's Office brought her in to testify before the grand jury. A similar motive led prosecutors to bring in three prostitutes from a brothel called the Kentucky Home, which Shea allegedly frequented.[59] Investigators claimed that they hoped the women could testify about "some of the confidences Shea has made in his moments of relaxation," but the main goal was publicity. As one investigator explained, "When it is known just how he spent the money he got for working the strike to suit the men who paid him, he and his confederates will lose their jobs, or they ought to."[60] In terms of publicity, the tactic worked. Scenting an exciting story and following the lead of the grand jury, newspapers provided plenty of coverage. The *Record-Herald* ran a photograph of the Kentucky Home with a caption that read, "The Kentucky Home in Indiana Avenue, said to have been the scene of wild orgies."[61]

The campaign to vilify Shea culminated when the June grand jury submitted its formal report in early July. Although they lacked evidence to indict him for bribery or extortion, the grand jury charged that "Shea [had] benefited by demands made for money [from] representatives of capital," charges "abundantly established by satisfactory evidence." Here they alluded to secondhand allegations that he had extorted money from "representatives of the packing industry to settle the stockyards strike." Perhaps because the biggest representatives of the meatpacking industry had strongly denied this allegation, the grand jury quickly moved on to other sorts of charges.[62] They referred to his personal conduct as evidence of his corruption. "That Shea has lived recklessly; that he has dined and wined, and been wined and dined, and that he has spent many hours and days and nights in company with profligates and disreputables is evidenced by competent proof." Finally, the grand jury rested upon the charge that Shea had assumed dictatorial power over the city of Chicago. They noted that some team owners who employed union men had been able to run their teams down strike-bound streets. These particular team owners had apparently acquired a special permit from the union's leaders. The grand jury suggested that such an arrangement smacked of militarylike power. "Why," they asked, "unless martial law prevailed, was such a permit asked for or given?"[63]

The amalgam of all these charges amounted to a model of a corrupt labor boss. Shea was described as immoral and unrestrained in his personal life while wielding the power of a dictator over the commercial life of the city. One passage in the report summed up the connection between these themes. "Cornelius P. Shea said to a prominent business man and a reliable witness 'that in the city of Boston [his hometown] I [Shea] cannot stop a jackrabbit, but here in Chicago I can put you out of business and I will if you don't do what I tell you to,' and this from a man who has confessedly been several times in jail, who has debauched his manhood, and brought public condemnation on the association of workingmen whose president he is."[64] He was, in other words, the very embodiment of irresponsible power. He was a man not in control of himself who had achieved great power over the streets of Chicago not through democratic election by the general public and not by the other acceptable means of accumulating capital.

This image of a corrupt labor boss was picked up and echoed by the media. Newspapers referred to "Boss Shea" or, even more often, to "Strike Dictator," terms that reminded readers of other examples of irresponsible power.[65] The cartoons described at the beginning of this chapter offered another way to portray this theme of irresponsible power. A magazine profile of Shea, entitled "Cornelius Shea, the Teamsters 'Boss' of Chicago," was printed at the height of the strike and assured readers that Shea had become the complete ruler of Chicago, supplanting the elected government. "Mayor Dunne still administrates the municipal government, but in the last analysis Shea is in control. At least the peace of the city hangs on his moods and whims."[66]

By depicting Teamster power in this way, employers and their allies could call for a particular kind of reform. Union members were urged to throw out their current leaders and elect a more conservative group that would forego use of the sympathetic strike. In the meantime, employers were justified in continuing their fight against the Teamsters Union. Only if the union was tamed would the streets be reclaimed from the tyrants of organized labor.[67] In the end, that version of reform—the employers' version—was only partly achieved.

Conclusion

The strike escalated through April and May, at times verging on class warfare. Chicago police flooded the streets of the city to offer protection to the wagons of the Employers' Association. At the beginning of the strike, the entire Chicago police force amounted to about 2,300 officers. By early May, the mayor had assigned 1,700 of those men to strike duty, escorting about nine hundred wagons operated by the association. When the strike further expanded in late May, the mayor initiated a recruitment campaign that brought in 208 new policemen. Stretching his manpower to its limits, Mayor Dunne even reassigned the city's dogcatchers to strike duty.[68] The presence of all of these police, however, did little to decrease strike violence in the streets. Before the strike's conclusion in late July, twenty-one people had been killed and 416 injured.[69] Jane Addams recalled that it was during this strike that "class bitterness rose to a dramatic climax."[70]

The strike finally ended in a draw, thus bringing to an unsuccessful close the effort of the Employers' Association to deliver a fatal blow to the Teamsters Union's power. Unable to win security for its non-union drivers, the association decided to come to terms with the Teamsters. For its part, unable to drive the association's wagons from the streets, the union accepted short-term defeat. The Teamsters dropped the strike against Montgomery Ward's and accepted the fact that many strikers would not be rehired by the companies on which they had walked out. Many replacement drivers would become permanent employees.[71] The Teamsters had also learned to avoid any further participation in sympathetic strikes, at least against members of the Employers' Association.[72] In the years that followed, the Teamsters Union became more bureaucratic and focused on winning benefits and avoiding acts of solidarity that might prove costly to the organization. Seven years later, for instance, the Teamsters refused to strike in sympathy with Chicago's freight handlers. Daniel Tobin, then president of the union, explained that the decision had been based on "the lesson we learned in 1905 when our organization was practically ruined."[73]

The Employers' Association sought to convert this immediate victory into a long-term trend by creating new work rules that forbade Teamsters from wearing a union button.[74] The association's concern over the issue stemmed from its realization that after the strike, once police had been reassigned to normal duty, non-union replacement drivers would be vulnerable to retaliation. They would have to go out onto streets where some thirty thousand Teamster members still wielded a great deal of day-to-day power. As one writer very sympathetic to the employers observed, "The fact that comparatively few of the teamsters, approximately one-seventh of those organized, were directly involved in the strike, makes it quite improbable that any far-reaching consequences should result. Non-union men will probably be gradually forced out, and the streets again taken over by the 'Brotherhood.'"[75] For employers, the union's power remained an unpalatable reality.

The strike and its attendant corruption scandal, however, had tarnished public perceptions of the Teamsters Union. The employers' strategy of emphasizing the disreputable lifestyle of Teamster President Shea worked. Indeed, exposures of Shea's private life had helped drive away some of organized labor's former allies. Settlement house reformers, who had sympathized with Chicago unions in earlier labor disputes, now criticized the irresponsible and immoral labor leadership whom they described as lording it over their membership and the entire city. Looking back at the recent strike and its scandals in a September 1905 article, Graham Taylor, a leader of the settlement house movement, exemplified that new attitude. Referring to the strike, Taylor wrote, "The teamsters have won nothing but shame. The leader and some of his colleagues have proved themselves personally to be shameless libertines, who transferred the headquarters of the strike to a notoriously disreputable house, whose courtesans gave evidence of their reckless profligacy." The fact that rank-and-file members of the union had not abandoned Shea when those revelations emerged only heightened Taylor's concerns. In language that echoed the June grand jury report, he explained, "The return of Cornelius P. Shea to the presidency of their international organization [national Teamsters Union], after the exposure of his shameless record is a deserved disgrace and most serious injury to their unions, which cannot fail to put the public on guard against them, and ought to arouse a revolt in their membership against such an administration of their affairs."[76] This new and more critical public perception of the union affected Chicago politics. The emerging political alliance between the Chicago Federation of Labor and middle-class liberals faded in the wake of the strike and its scandals.[77]

Finally, the strike left a lingering impression of how the power of the Teamsters should be conceived. It was now tagged as illegitimate—an example of corruption. As one author summarized his understanding of the union in the wake of the strike, "In Chicago, the teamsters' badge is still as it has been for years, to a considerable extent an insignia of criminal association. An irresponsible organization would take possession of the public highways, and has demonstrated that it is banded together to establish and maintain its domination at any cost."[78]

3. Corruption Viewed through Union Members' Eyes and Reform via Secession

In the wake of the Chicago Teamster strike of 1905, John Cummings, writing in the *Journal of Political Economy*, concluded that the strike and its aftermath had proven one thing above all else—the failure of union democracy. Drawing from press reports in the spring and summer of 1905, Cummings asserted, "The labor leaders were unquestionably and avowedly conspiring and single-minded in their motive to levy blackmail, but they were known to be such not only to their fellows in the organization, but to the whole community, in which their characters had been notoriously established for years." Because of this notoriety, union members who elected these men must have known that they were abetting crime. "If their fellows were not perfectly well informed," Cummings noted, "they were the only people in Chicago who were ignorant in the matter." Therefore, he argued, the crimes assigned to the union leaders were due to the weaknesses of democracy in the Teamsters Union and, by extension, in all modern labor unions. "It is, therefore, not as a conspiracy of blackmailers, but as a modern instance of the working of democracy in the industrial field, that the Chicago teamsters' strike takes on ominous aspects."[1]

Cummings raised an issue that numerous other observers have also written about since 1905. Essentially, it boils down to a question: What are we to think when ostensibly democratic unions elect and reelect leaders labeled as notoriously corrupt or, at times, even leaders convicted of crimes? In 1905 that puzzle had special reference to the Teamsters Union and to a few other labor organizations tagged as corrupt, such as certain of the building trades unions.[2]

Cummings, many of his contemporaries, and many observers since have asserted that Teamsters Union members were morally deficient. "In Chicago the teamsters' democracy was one which chose corrupt men for leaders, and which has chosen to continue these men in power," Cummings wrote. It seemed to him that rank-and-file Teamsters held a different view of morality, one that accepted criminality and generally held lower standards of appropriate behavior. In the worldview that Cummings suggested Teamsters held, "A man's earnings cease to bear any relation to his economic service. They are what he can seize upon, spoils wrested by force from an exploiting bourgeoisie."[3] In such a worldview, anything goes.

Cummings wrote from an anti-union perspective, but other observers who were in sympathy with unions offered explanations that echoed his argument of working-class moral deficiency. Hutchins Hapgood produced a sympathetic, if at times patronizing, portrait of the Chicago labor movement in 1907. Describing the morality of teamsters and other workers, Hapgood used expressions such as "child-like," "unthinking," and "simple." Explaining the view that workers held of a labor leader recently convicted of receiving a bribe in New York, Hapgood wrote, "The fact that such a man might 'steal' from the class whom they regard as robbing the workingmen in general, does not seem to them to be of any great moment."[4] Later observers have put forward similar views, depicting Cornelius Shea's reelection in 1905 as an example of the way in which a kind of moral "slackness" undercuts the effectiveness of union democracy.[5]

These arguments have two important flaws. First, they assume a universal understanding of what was meant by the term *corruption;* however its meaning was more contested than the arguments admit. To say that union members stood by in the face of corruption, therefore, begs the issue. To what behavior, we need to ask, did they object? How did they construe corruption? Second, the arguments overlook the reform efforts that took place in these years. The revelations of the June grand jury in Chicago and the general air of scandal that surrounded the Chicago strike of 1905 worried many within the union. Unnoticed by Cummings and other observers, several waves of reform swept through the union in the wake of the strike. These reform efforts drew on particular critiques of the existing administration, and they also used a powerful method to overcome the entrenched power of incumbent union officers. In the end, however, reformers achieved only a partial victory.

Corruption and Reform from the Union Perspective

"Corruption" was a contested term, but one meaning had more currency among the press as well as in the prosecutor's office and for the grand jury in Chicago in 1905. The working conclusion to which they came was that all payments from employers to union officials represented blackmail and thus a form of blatant corruption. The actual details did not always appear so neat, however. The prosecutors and the grand jury stumbled across cases in which some employers had conspired to use labor unions against other employers. For a time, there had even been talk of indicting a few of those employers. In the end, however, the prosecutor overlooked the complicated nature of employer-union relations and instead referred to "the dammable conditions that have existed ever since employers first displayed a willingness to be blackmailed."[6]

Corruption then became the condition that existed whenever money passed between an employer and a union official, and generally in such an exchange the employer was the victim and the union official was the victimizer. In the broadest sense, corruption existed when these labor leaders, irresponsible in their personal habits and in their exercise of power, could challenge the authority of more traditional bastions of society, the political and commercial leadership. Being able to demand blackmail constituted but one symptom of this corrupt system.

Union members and union leaders saw matters in a different light. Payments between employers and union officials could take place for a variety of reasons. In some instances such payments might serve illicit purposes, but in other cases they might actually play a role in building the strength of the union. For union members, the broader meaning of corruption described the failure of officials to conform to standards of dignity and decency that members hoped their organization would champion. They also used the term to refer to acts that betrayed the interests of the organization.

Cooperation vs. Corruption

The difference in understanding the nature of corruption became apparent during the spring and summer of 1905. The heart of the scandalous revelations that surfaced then had to do with a public retelling of the history of the Chicago Teamsters Union since 1902. Even then this was not new history. News reports and magazine articles had previously described how the union had been built, local by local, through a set of closed agreements between associations of team owners and particular local unions.[7] The main organizers of the arrangement had been Albert Young, leader of the Coal Teamsters Local Union, and John C. Driscoll, who had begun by organizing an association of coal team owners. When Driscoll talked to the press in June 1905, and when he testified before the grand jury, he reviewed this history and described a string of payments he had arranged between employers and Teamsters Union officials such as Albert Young. The grand jury referred to such payments as blackmail, but closer inspection reveals something far more complex.

Quite frequently, employers made payments through Driscoll to union officials in return for the union's efforts to strengthen a particular segment of the teaming industry. One incident, referred to in June 1905, involved a payment from the coal team owners, through Driscoll, to Young in February 1902. Young had led the Coal Teamsters in a sympathy strike against a set of downtown Chicago office buildings, stopping the delivery of all goods to those buildings. As he explained, it had been done at the request of the employers and also in the interests of the local union. "It was represented to me that if the coal teamsters would strike against the office buildings using fuel gas in the summer time two hundred more local teamsters could have employment." Young charged that in this case one of the largest coal dealers, Francis Peabody, had not paid a bribe but rather the strike benefits for the Coal Teamsters and several other local unions involved.[8]

The strike against office buildings created more business for coal dealers, but other strikes worked to strengthen industrial associations. For example, a local brewers' association arranged a strike against the St. Louis–based Anheuser-Busch Brewing Company when it set up shop in Chicago in 1903. According to Fritz Sontag, the Chicago manager of the company, the Teamsters made no demands on the business. Instead, Sontag explained, the strike was "inspired by the Chicago and Milwaukee Brewers' Association." He recalled that "a paper was presented to me to sign after the strike had begun which would have meant our going in with the [brewers'] association, and I was told that if I would sign, the strike would be called off in two minutes." He added, "The man who presented the paper was not a labor leader."[9]

As an outside brewing company coming into the Chicago area, Anheuser-Busch was being pressured into joining the local brewers' association. None of the reports specifically say why such pressure was applied, but probably the Chicago and Milwaukee Brewers' Association sought to control the level of competition in the local brewing industry. In their efforts to maintain the strength of their association, the brewers apparently turned to the local Teamsters Union. "We were asked," Albert Young explained, "to declare a strike of the Anheuser-Busch teamsters, so as to force the company to join the association." When the company still refused to join the brewers' association, Young noted, Teamster leaders turned down the request to continue the strike.[10] If money passed between the brewers and Teamster leaders, it might well have been to pay the strike benefits of men thrown out of work by the dispute. Such transactions highlight how organized groups of employers used the Teamsters to bolster their industries.

Although those cases were old news to Chicagoans, the June grand jury in 1905 did stumble on a continuing arrangement that involved Chicago's brick manufacturing industry. A highly competitive business environment had been stabilized in 1900 when thirty-five separate brick manufacturing plants merged to form the Illinois Brick Company (the "Brick Trust"). Small, independent brick manufacturing firms emerged in subsequent years and tried to gain business by underselling the trust. When they did so, however, they found themselves plagued by Teamster strikes. The trust apparently used the union to maintain a cartel arrangement in the brick industry. In going though the books of the Brick Trust, investigators found the existence of a $25,000 "labor fund."[11]

Organizations of employers who paid money for strikes were not being blackmailed. If anything, evidence indicates that these employers put great pressure on Teamster local unions to work with them. In 1908, for instance, employers in the Furniture and Expressmen's Association (an employers' group) became concerned that their organization had gradually lost its ability to enforce a standard schedule of hauling rates on the furniture moving business in Chicago. The employers brought back John Driscoll, whose services had languished since the grand jury hearings in 1905. Driscoll, at their request, quickly moved to force the local Teamsters Union to work with the Furniture and Expressmen's Association. When the local union leadership balked, Driscoll sponsored a rival local union and forced the drivers employed in the moving industry to join it.[12] Two decades later, the movers' association in St. Louis threatened to break its agreement with the Van Teamsters in that city unless the union acted with more diligence in declaring strikes against independent moving firms.[13]

Union leaders resented it when money paid by employers for these employer-inspired strikes was labeled as graft. Frank Ray of the Commission Wagon Drivers and Daniel Furman of the Truck Drivers both voluntarily went before the June grand jury in 1905 to explain that they had indeed received money from employers. They wanted it noted, however, that it had been in the form of compensation to their local unions for strike benefits.[14]

Still, such arrangements often led to problems because they drew union officials into entangling relationships with employers. The lines between appropriate and inappropriate actions on the union leaders' part blurred. How far could and should a local leader go to help employers in his industry? Conflicts of interest seem inevitable. In St. Louis, some officers in the Van Teamsters were criticized because "they would do any thing the bosses wanted them to do."[15] Legal problems could arise. Quite often the situation would leave the union leader involved in a conspiracy in restraint of free trade—an antitrust violation.[16] Moreover, when employers paid strike benefits through a union's leadership it could be the first step in a larger pattern in which union officials accepted payments from the bosses. According to one reported interview, Sam Parks, a building trades union official in New York City convicted on corruption charges, believed that accepting such strike benefits had been the beginning of his downfall. He asserted that it was "that habit of making money transactions with employers" that led to his eventual jail sentence.[17]

From the union's perspective, cooperation between a local leader and a group of employers did not necessarily constitute corruption. Nor did unionists apparently consider it corruption when a local union leader arranged to call strikes at the behest of a group of employers or accepted money from an employer to compensate his local for strike benefits.

Corruption by Betrayal

For unionists, corruption existed when leaders violated the organization's trust. An example of such corruption can be found in the affair that led Chicago trade unionists, including the Teamsters, to break with John Driscoll in 1903.

That year Driscoll sought to extend his range of operations into Chicago's meatpacking industry. Chicago meatpackers, as employers, had applied to join the Association of Teaming Interests, one of the groups Driscoll had created and which he served as secretary. To better look after the meatpackers' interests, Driscoll wanted to make sure that he had an inside line on the Packing Trades Council, an association of various unions representing workers in the meatpacking industry. Driscoll tried to hire an official in the council to work as his spy.[18] His efforts failed dramatically. The official he approached publicly denounced the bribery attempt and testified that Driscoll had bragged about having other union officials on his payroll. In response, the Chicago Federation of Labor (CFL) passed a resolution condemning Driscoll as "an enemy and a menace to the labor movement" who "has been using sums of money in an effort to reach officers of labor unions in this city." The resolution concluded, "We expose this Trickster in the Chicago Federation of Labor so that all unions may be warned to have nothing to do with him."[19] Driscoll's purported role as a facilitator and negotiator, it now became clear, had served as a cover for his efforts to control and subvert unions by buying off their leadership. In exposing his activities, the CFL tagged those union officials who had worked with Driscoll as corrupt because they had helped him betray their unions.

Efforts soon began to dislodge Driscoll and those Teamster officials most closely connected with him.[20] E. L. Turley, an official with the Department Store Teamsters, emerged as a rival to Albert Young, Driscoll's most powerful union associate. The reform faction that gathered around Turley helped him win election as secretary-treasurer of the national union in 1903 while Young was consigned to a lesser office.[21] Now distrustful of Driscoll, Teamster leaders prodded employers to remove him from the various employers' associations he had helped create. The truck drivers' local union, for instance, refused to negotiate with the truck owners' association until they fired Driscoll. By the spring of 1904, according to the *Chicago Tribune,* officials in the truck drivers' union had "repeatedly asserted that they would not enter into any arbitration, negotiations, nor frame any agreement with an organization of which Driscoll was an official." In April 1904, largely thanks to the union's prodding and in part because of the employers' own growing distrust of the man, Driscoll was forced to resign his post as secretary of the Associated Teaming Interests, the most powerful of the organizations he had created.[22]

By the time of the grand jury investigations in the summer of 1905, Teamster members viewed allegations that strikes had been bought and sold with a critical eye. Given the union's history, however, they did not dismiss them out of hand. In the midst of a bitter labor conflict unionists denounced the animus behind the charges of graft being made in the press and elsewhere. Charles Dold, head of the Chicago Federation of Labor, told union members, "The papers come out and charged graft to poison your minds and have you lose confidence in your [strike] committee."[23] In addition, many of the strikes covered by the grand jury's report had been part of what unionists would see as acceptable efforts to work with the organizations of employers for the good of the trade. Clearly, however, not all the transactions described belonged in that category. Driscoll and others had testified about making payments to Teamster leaders in return for these officials holding back or ending a sympathy strike. Such charges did not amount to proof beyond a reasonable doubt, but in their cumulative effect they stung. One Teamster wrote that the union had been badly hurt when "it was openly charged that some of these [Teamster] officers had been receiving money from certain employers, either for the purpose of calling a strike or to settle one. The only offset to these damaging stories lay in the fact that the paying employers were equally to blame."[24]

In the wake of the charges in June that strikes had been bought and sold, a certain measure of demoralization set in. Officials from other unions distanced themselves from the strike, and donations to the strike fund from members of other unions fell off.[25] Within the Teamsters, support for the strike of 1905 began to wane. The Joint Council had to begin sending squads out to enforce the union's rule about working members contributing $1 of their weekly pay to support the strike.[26]

Corruption through Disrepute

Charges that strikes had been bought and sold stung, but so, too, did publicity about Cornelius Shea's personal life. His profligacy—to use the language of the June grand jury—drew in a different way on the Teamster members' sense of what constituted corruption. Wagon drivers, who valued the respect and dignity won for them by their union, resented leaders whose indecent behavior cast disrepute on their union.

From the Teamsters' perspective, one of the most damaging revelations to surface was that Shea had socialized with John Driscoll in the years since 1903. The specific bribery allegations against Shea received due skepticism, but Teamster leaders and members could not accept his willingness to socialize with the notorious Driscoll, something that both men agreed had occurred. As in 1903, unionists suspected the loyalty of anyone who would choose to associate with such a "trickster." When the General Executive Board of the national Teamsters Union met in Chicago in mid-June, members reportedly denounced Shea because he had "associated with the man the better element had been fighting for years."[27]

Shea's personal conduct also became an issue. Beginning in mid-June 1905, the grand jury heard testimony about his visits to brothels. The investigation into this matter, and the testimony offered by women from the brothels, received a great deal of publicity in the press. Shea attempted to defend himself by pointing out that prominent employers visited the brothels as well, but many Teamsters rejected that defense.

The revelations hurt because they brought the union into disrepute. When he wrote about the scandals that emerged during the strike, one Teamster asserted, "But far the greatest blow our cause received was the discovery that some of our leaders were engaged in the most disreputable mode of life. They spent nights in low resorts and spent money freely in entertaining women of the vilest characters."[28] News reports suggest that many of the union's top officers felt the same way. A story on the General Executive Board's meeting noted the group's opposition to Shea and explained, "The public disclosures of Shea's way of life also have influenced the board. The members feel that the president of their union has brought disgrace down upon it. They believe he should be removed 'for the good and welfare of the union.'" One board member reportedly said after the meeting, "[Teamsters] know their union is being disgraced by Shea and they will support any legal attack on him."[29]

To understand the apparent strength of feeling on this issue one needs to remember the importance of dignity and decency to Teamster members. Although they joined the union for material benefits members also treasured the dignity which their organization brought to a low-status occupation. Part of their notions of dignity and decency involved conservative and gendered models of propriety. The union fit within these models of propriety because it allowed a man to fulfill his patriarchal roles in a virtuous, family-centered world. Members wrote of how the union's effort "enables the wage earners and their dependents to live an honourable, upright life, enjoy the respect of their employers and last, but not least, be 'men among men.'"[30] The shame of having officers live a disreputable life undercut one's enjoyment of an "upright life." There was, in fact, a specific clause in the union's constitution that referred to members who endangered this decency by bringing the union into disrepute. Section 40 of the constitution read, "The General Executive Board shall have full power to . . . try cases involving danger or *disgrace* to a Local Union, or the International Brotherhood, and to pass judgment on all cases appealed to it."[31] Through his conduct Shea had brought disgrace down upon the union.

In the summer of 1905, when Teamster members described a corrupt state of affairs, they meant something different from what the employers had in mind. Employers connected corruption to a perceived imbalance of power relations, situations where unions and union leaders held enough authority to challenge employers and political leaders. Teamsters, however, saw corruption as a betrayal of union interests. Such a betrayal did not occur immediately when a union official began cooperating with an employer or even if an official accepted money from that employer in the form of strike benefits. But a betrayal did occur when the official no longer worked for the good of the union—if, for example, he sold strikes and accepted money to call them off merely to line his pockets. Only part of this model of corruption, however, had to do with overt betrayal. For union members, behavior that brought their union into disrepute also constituted corruption. Here conservative notions of propriety underlay the usage of terms like dignity and decency. A decent man fulfilled the patriarchal model of dutiful husband and father. If their leaders violated such standards, then members worried that all Teamsters might very well be tarred with the same brush, and the hard-won dignity brought to them by the union might disappear.

The Reelection of Shea

On the one hand, concerns about corruption pushed many Teamsters that summer to question Shea's leadership; on the other hand, however, the membership's emphasis on dignity drew others toward continued support of him. These contradictory impulses existed at the same time in the same union and reflect the complex ways in which individuals react to scandal.

Some Teamsters distrusted Shea, but others viewed him as a champion. Different notions of masculinity provided grounds for either denouncing Shea as dissolute or hailing him as a virile, man's man. As historians of gender have noted, manliness functions as a kind of discourse, available for use in a range of different ways. At any one time several competing models of manliness exist. At the turn of the century, manliness meant, for many workers, respectability, independence, and self-control. But a competing identity, a kind of rough masculinity, celebrated physical strength, forcefulness, even sexual passion.[32] In this way, revelations that Shea visited brothels or had an extramarital relationship might well provide fodder for very different reactions. By all accounts he projected an image of toughness, one that seemed popular with many of the rank and file. Newspaper accounts in 1905 depict him as a powerful speaker who defiantly refused to have the interests of the striking drivers sacrificed for the sake of reaching a peace agreement with the Employers' Association.[33] His tough stand involved a celebration of the dignity of the striking drivers. A speech he reportedly made in late May exemplifies this militant tone. Referring to the Employers' Association, Shea said, "They may go out and get injunctions, they may create institutions to prostitute our manhood, they may contribute millions, they may blacklist our people, they may indict us all if the law is behind them, but we will not be downed for five minutes."[34]

He claimed, with some justification, that the attacks on him in the press and the indictments against him from grand juries stemmed from his leadership of the strike.[35] Other labor officials believed he was milking his status as a martyr to shore up his shaky political situation.[36] Whether that was true or not, the length and the bitterness of the strike, combined with the pressure applied on him personally by the employers and prosecutors, added to his appeal among some of the rank and file. Moreover, abandoning Shea at this time could be seen as abandoning his militant stance and in effect undercutting the strike.

At the union's annual convention in early August 1905, Shea narrowly escaped an opposition reform movement's effort to unseat him. The reformers made their case in difficult circumstances. Descriptions of the convention highlight the disorder of the proceedings and refer to delegates walking the floor openly armed with revolvers.[37] Moreover, as the incumbent Shea enjoyed political advantages in managing the convention, which he adroitly exploited. To bolster his cause, he and his supporters organized a kind of caucus that combined the qualities of a political party and a secret society; it was known by opponents as the "Vaseline Club."[38] The election itself took place on the fifth day of the convention, and although the votes were close, Shea's slate proved victorious. Shea himself won reelection by the narrow margin of 129 to 121. None of his opponents, the reform faction within the union, managed to win any national office.[39]

The outcome of the election can be read in a number of different ways, each of which offers some perspective on democracy in the Teamsters Union. The vote indicated that many Teamsters continued to see Shea as their embattled champion. As the ardent defender of the man on the wagon's dignity in the war against employers and a martyred target of employer aggression Shea clearly had his share of supporters. Edward Nockels, an official with the Chicago Federation of Labor, explained the results of the election by saying of Shea, "The world loves a fighter, and the labor world is no different from other bodies of men."[40]

Still, in spite of all of the benefits of incumbency, and in spite of the fact that the convention had begun only six days after the union's most bitter strike had ended, it had been a very close contest. The closeness of the votes cast by delegates chosen during the strike reveals the depths of their concern over the issue of dignity. Nor, Shea's critics observed, did the vote necessarily reflect the will of the membership. The political machinations of the Vaseline Club and the disorder of the proceedings had impeded a fair and open fight. In addition, only 126 out of the 516 International Brotherhood of Teamsters local unions had sent delegates to the convention. Locals in the West found the costs of sending a representative across the continent for a week prohibitive. Similarly, the mass of small-town locals with fifty or a hundred members also lacked the resources to send someone to cast their vote for them. [41]

Whatever the political maneuverings involved in Shea's victory, it is also true that his reelection reflects the fact that members brought to this contest a complex set of concerns. They did not see the issue of corruption in the same light as the employers. Instances of cooperation between union leaders and employers, even the acceptance of strike benefit funds from an employer, did not constitute corruption to members. That did not mean, however, that Teamsters approved of their leaders betraying the interests of their organization. Members, for instance, disapproved of leaders who abetted the buying and selling of strikes merely to line officials' own pockets. Many also disapproved of what they deemed disreputable behavior, which cheapened the image of their union and, by implication, tarnished their own claims to decency. In that charges of betrayal and loose morals circled around him, Shea drew criticism from many members and fellow leaders. Yet the opposition was far from unanimous. He was a tough leader waging a bitter strike, and Teamsters apparently saw him as a symbol of their dignity in the face of employer aggression. Still, to argue that the emotions aroused were complex is different from saying that Teamsters voted for him because they did not care about the worst charges made against him.

In the end, Shea won reelection, but a strong reform movement had begun to coalesce that was centered around the goal of finding some way to remove him from office. This opposition movement eventually developed the tactic of reform through secession.

Reform via Secession

Anti-union critics like John Cummings looked at the results of the Teamster convention of 1905 and asserted that union democracy had failed because members lacked the integrity necessary to police their own organizations. For such critics the issue was not the lack of democracy but that members chose not to vote responsibly. Opponents of Shea within the Teamsters, however, argued that he had stifled real democracy in the convention and therefore its outcome did not reflect the will of the members. To get around what they viewed as the autocratic structure of the union's government these reformers organized secession movements, one in 1905 and, following its demise, another in 1906.

The secession effort broke out soon after the close of the 1905 convention and had roots in dissatisfaction with the results of that gathering. In the wake of Shea's reelection, George Innis, one of the founders of the Team Drivers' International Union, set the foundation of a reform movement. Stubborn, sententious, perhaps even at times cranky, Innis's almost proprietary view of the union may well have moved him to wage a losing battle for reform. On the last days of the convention he proposed two amendments to the union's constitution that would, he argued, help correct some of the mistakes made at the meeting. Claiming that he had "heard accusations of graft ever since this Convention opened," Innis asked that a committee of three be appointed to examine the bills of the current officers and determine their legitimacy. The committee would make its report to the whole union and in this way "let the sunlight in on everything." He also proposed that the union adopt the referendum method of electing national officers. Nominations would occur at the convention, but actual elections would be decided by the votes of individual union members. Neither proposal passed.[42]

Those proposals embodied the central frustrations of Shea's opponents. The charges of graft, which hung over the affairs of the union, needed to be cleared up, many felt, and a vigorous internal investigation offered one way to do that. Critics within the union also argued that only a minority of locals actually sent delegates to the convention, rendering the bulk of the members, especially those in the many small-town locals, disenfranchised. Finally, they felt that Shea had manipulated the convention by packing it with his supporters and abusing his power as chair of the proceedings.[43]

Drawing on such misgivings, Innis launched a reform movement as soon as he returned from the gathering, focusing his initial efforts on locals in his hometown of Detroit. After hearing his version of the convention, the membership of these locals lined up strongly behind him. In addition, he arranged with the publisher of a local labor newspaper, the *Michigan Union Advocate*, to print on the back page of the weekly edition a column entitled "Teamsters' Weekly Review." Innis planned to use this column to convey his attacks on Shea to the rank and file. He hoped to send copies to all the local unions and to any individual member who requested one.[44]

In early September 1905, local unions began to receive a sort of reform packet from Innis in the name of a committee of twenty-four delegates who had attended the Philadelphia convention and protested its results. The packet included a set of written charges against Shea and four proposals on which local union members were to vote. Charges centered on Shea's conduct during the convention in Philadelphia and on alleged acts of malfeasance and mismanagement during his tenure in office.[45]

Innis criticized Shea for using the Vaseline Club and his power as chair to stifle debate and sabotage democracy at the convention. His criticism also focused on financial management of the union. According to Innis, Shea had "used the funds of our organization to further his personal and selfish ambitions." As president, Innis charged, Shea boosted his salary by claiming per-diem expenses for every day he had held office, weekends and holidays included. Meanwhile, under his leadership the union had plunged into a state of decline. When Shea took over in 1903, there had been 672 local unions and 61,448 members. Two years later 506 locals remained, and membership had fallen to 48,978. The union's financial reserves had sunk dangerously low, while the strikes for which these funds were spent, with only a few exceptions, had been lost.[46]

To oust Shea from office, Innis and his committee accompanied their written charges with a sort of do-it-yourself referendum. The committee asked local unions that received its package to read the charges to their membership and then vote on four specific propositions. One proposition involved voting to repudiate the recent election in Philadelphia. Voting yes on another proposition meant the local would withhold support from President Shea. Members also were to decide whether to approve the creation of a special committee of three that would assume control of the union from Shea while conducting an investigation of his conduct in office. Finally, the committee included a proposal to institute a referendum for deciding important union issues in the future.[47]

In the long run, the reform program aimed to create a more democratic union; in the short run, it set the stage for secession and a dual organization. The third question in the referendum asked, "Shall we withhold support from President Shea and his executive board pending an investigation?" Withholding support meant refusing to make the local union's share of per-capita payments to the national office.[48] Eventually, that money was to go to Innis and the reform committee to support national reform efforts.[49] They would become a de facto national headquarters for seceding locals, and when enough locals had signed with Innis he would have set up a new Teamsters Union. In effect, Innis led a secession movement whose greatest threat to the IBT was that it might become a dual organization. Writing to Samuel Gompers in November 1905, Shea complained "of the movement which has been started in Detroit which will ultimately lead to the creation of an independent organization."[50]

The reform movement enjoyed some early successes but soon faded. Initially, three of the strongest locals in Chicago responded positively to the reform package.[51] Among small-town locals in the Midwest, especially those which had not been able to send a delegate to the convention, Innis's message also found a ready audience.[52] The early victories, however, did not lead to bigger things. Most important, Innis never gained the financial base needed to promote his movement.[53] After the initial three Chicago locals responded positively, none of the other big-city local unions came on board. By late October Innis could no longer put out his newsletter, the *Teamsters' Weekly Review*.[54] His reform movement had stalled.

Meanwhile, Shea assumed the offensive, sending out the union's organizers to make his case at local meetings and pressuring the AFL to use its influence against seceding locals.[55] In Detroit the AFL expelled Innis's local from the city's central council, and Shea chartered a new local union to draw away Innis's membership.[56] Already stalled because of a limited financial base,

by January 1906 Innis's movement had crumbled before the aggressive counterattack. Innis himself faded from the scene, never again to play a role in the
union's history. Although his reform movement did not succeed, he had
developed a strategy and set of issues that the next reform movement could
draw upon, and the second wave of reform enjoyed far more success.

Secession in 1906: The United Teamsters of America

Shea's opponents turned to secession once again in 1906 after he railroaded
the union convention of that year. He had remained controversial, and his
opponents prepared to defeat him when Shea ran for reelection at the Teamsters' annual convention in August, held that year in Chicago. This time, they
might have thought, he would not have the Chicago strike around which to
rally support. In addition, the coalition against Shea had gained adherents
from among his former supporters. Al Young of the Chicago Coal Teamsters,
who had supported Shea in 1905, now came out against him.[57]

As the convention opened, it became clear that Shea had ensured reelection by denying the credentials of the biggest bloc arrayed against him. Forty delegates, all from the New York City local unions and all opposed to Shea,
were denied seats in the convention by the Credentials Committee, a group
appointed by Shea. The committee based its decision on a tangled dispute
that involved unpaid strike benefits and per-capita tax money that should
have gone from the locals to the national union.[58] The power to appoint convention committees gave incumbent union officers like Shea the ability to
use such a tactic. Because of that, opposition groups in the Teamsters and in
other unions found conventions to be far from level playing fields.[59] In spite
of the ruling, the New York locals sent their delegates, hoping to reverse the
decision. When the appeal failed, anti-Shea delegates walked out and formed
a rival convention.[60]

As Innis had done, the insurgents of 1906 complained that Shea had become a dictator. One of his leading opponents, N. W. Evans, asserted, "We
are like the peasants of Russia. We propose to down the 'czar' and allow the
duly elected representatives of the teamsters to have something to say about
the conduct of affairs." Anticipating a charge from Shea that he and his fellow secessionists were but disappointed office-seekers, Evans averred, "We
are not looking for office, but for an organization that will do something for
the team drivers of the country."[61]

In contrast to Innis's ill-fated attempt to rally the opposition, this secession movement caught fire and drew in a significant portion of the union.
More than a hundred delegates (some of whom were apparently from the

unseated New York delegation) signed a resolution against the administration of Shea, describing it as "a stench and abomination in the nostrils of organized labor."[62]

The official convention had begun with 244 accredited delegates, but by the opening of the third day only 166 remained.[63] News reports described twenty-one local unions with around fifteen thousand members being involved in the secession. And, again unlike Innis's movement, the secession included locals from major urban centers. Local unions in New York, St. Louis, and Chicago formed the core of the movement, along with locals from Detroit, Rochester, and Birmingham. Members of Innis's old faction, sometimes called the "Lily Whites," had struck a pragmatic alliance with forces loyal to Al Young.[64] The larger numbers involved in this reform action thus stemmed from the kind of political coalition that Innis had been unable to assemble. The success of the second group also must have had something to do with the clarity of their issue. This time around Shea clearly had subverted the democratic process. To ensure that he could win reelection, his Credentials Committee had disenfranchised one of the major regions of the country.

The rival convention met in a hall across town and set up a new national union: the United Teamsters of America (UTA). When representatives from the American Federation of Labor tried to resolve the division, UTA delegates made their position clear. As one leader put it, "Unless the American Federation of Labor can depose C. P. Shea and his entire executive board, we are in this movement to stick. There can be no harmony with that man at the head of the teamsters."[65] If Shea refused to step down, the leaders of the UTA planned to draw enough of the nation's teamsters into a rival organization to put the International Brotherhood of Teamsters out of business. "The American Federation of Labor will not have two teamsters' unions to deal with for long," said a UTA leader.[66]

A hard-fought struggle ensued. In the months that followed these rival conventions, the two teamster unions grappled for dominance in a struggle that left the IBT greatly weakened. Leaders of both sides visited local union meetings, trying to sway the membership to come over to their organization. The gatherings could become contentious, and *Roberts Rules of Order* frequently gave way to more direct forms of argument.[67] Eventually, the conflict invaded some workplaces, and the rival organizations engaged in bitter jurisdictional strikes to determine whose members would work at particular stables. One such strike, at the Pennoyer Stable in Chicago, lasted ten weeks, left thirty men in the hospital, and cost the IBT close to $20,000.[68] The same sorts of struggles broke out in other cities, and the only consistent winner was the employer.[69] As the *Team Owners' Review* put it, "Let the drivers fight it out among themselves while the team owner sits by and saws wood." Employers relished the disarray of the union and the chance to play one side against the other.[70] Even where the IBT and UTA did not come directly into conflict, rank-and-file teamsters suffered because of the dispute. Having spent $20,000 on the strike at Pennoyer, the national union had less money available to aid local unions that needed strike support.[71]

Money was in short supply anyway. The fight against the UTA—with its attendant expenses—had come at the worst possible moment for the national union. In the fall of 1906 the IBT needed every penny it could get to pay its legal fees. Shea and some of the top union leaders in Chicago were on trial for criminal conspiracy for their part in the strike against Montgomery Ward's and Company the previous year. Once more the Employers' Association played an active role, raising the stakes in the case by seeking a guilty verdict that would clearly establish the illegitimacy of the sympathy strike. With financial support from the association, the prosecution mounted an imposing case. The union was forced to expend substantial sums to match those legal efforts.[72]

The first trial in the case ended in a hung jury, but in the second trial the jury quickly returned a verdict of not guilty.[73] In the short run, the verdict offered Shea a certain amount of vindication. In the long run, however, it led directly to his downfall. The threat of conviction on criminal charges in 1906 had allowed Shea to rally support to his cause. He claimed that if he were ousted from office before the trial the jury would read that fact as a denouncement by his union, and it would very likely lead to a conviction. Moreover, as he pointed out, if that were the case, it would harm not only him but also the reputation of the union and the labor movement in general. With the trial over, that rationale for supporting Shea disappeared.[74] Meanwhile, the union hit rock bottom. Its funds had been drained to pay for the battles against the UTA and for legal expenses incurred during the trials. There existed no money to pay for national union organizers or even to support local unions out on strike.[75] Things could not get much worse, and as long as Shea remained in office it seemed unlikely that they would get any better. The UTA would never make peace with an organization led by Shea.

By the spring of 1907 some of Shea's strongest supporters began to line up in the opposition. When the convention came around in August these men backed a reform slate led by Daniel J. Tobin.[76] This time Shea took no active steps to disenfranchise his opposition. The danger of further feeding secession probably restrained him from using the type of tactics that had proved so successful in 1906. Even without using his extralegal powers, Shea's status as an incumbent proved helpful to him. In spite of the union's dreadful condition and his unsavory reputation, he still came close to winning reelection. Tobin beat him by a vote of only 104 to 92.[77] Without pressure from the UTA secession Shea might never have been ousted.

This time reform won out. Shea's defeat provides important lessons on how democratic reform of the period worked at the national level. For reformers, success required some type of organization outside the existing union structure. The experiences of opposition factions at the 1905 and 1906 conventions revealed the limitations of working within the union. An unscrupulous incumbent could shape nominally democratic forums to suit his purposes. At the convention, for instance, opposition could either be outmaneuvered or disenfranchised. Between conventions, insurgent factions faced serious retribution. Leaving the national structure, however, gave reformers freedom to express opposition with a measure of protection from retaliation. And if, as in the case of Shea, fear of secession restrained an office-holder from further improprieties, real internal democracy could finally have its day.

In other unions, secession movements played a similar role. The case of the United Garment Workers' Union (UGW) provides one parallel. Chartered by the American Federation of Labor to organize clothing manufacturers, it had fallen into the hands of a conservative and corrupt clique by 1910. The national leadership held strong anti-immigrant prejudices even as new immigrant groups came to predominate in the membership. Bitter strikes in the early teens energized a militant insurgent wing within the union. This faction came to the UGW's 1914 convention intending to elect a fresh group of national officers. Instead, they found that the national office had disenfranchised them: 110 delegates belonging to the opposition faction were denied seats at the convention, and those delegates represented sixty thousand union members. As had been the case at the 1906 Teamster convention, opposition delegates formed a rival convention and proclaimed their intention to supplant the existing organization. That convention of clothing worker delegates formed the nucleus of what soon became the Amalgamated Clothing Workers of America (ACWA). The old UGW survived the split but, failing to reform, it slid into relative obscurity. It was saved from extinction mainly by the intransigence of Samuel Gompers, president of the AFL, who refused officially to recognize the ACWA as a legitimate union.[78]

Gompers' stand against reform secession movements seems ironic given the fact that he had led a similar movement forty years earlier. As a young man he and his allies had found it impossible to obtain the changes they wanted in the existing Cigarmakers Union. Instead, they pulled out of the national organization and put together a new style of trade union based on open admittance and a structured benefit system. They rejoined the older national union only when it rewrote its constitution to include the changes they wanted.[79]

Secession and the Limits of Reform

If the story ended here it would offer a roseate picture of reform. Instead, there was twist. Both Shea and John Driscoll emerged again and led local Teamster groups. Daniel Tobin, the newly elected president of the IBT, found that because of the ease of secession there was little he could do to combat the local influence of such leaders.

Few questioned the reform orientation of Tobin in the years that immediately followed his election in 1907. Thirty-two years old when he became president, Tobin had come to the United States from Ireland seventeen years earlier when he was only fifteen. In his twenties he turned to driving a wagon in Boston. He became a union member around 1900 and a few years later won election to office in his local union. He proved well suited for the job. Tobin demonstrated his leadership capabilities during a bitter Boston Teamsters strike fought during the months preceding the convention in 1907. A picture of him from the year of his election shows a hearty-looking, dark-haired young man with a full mustache. His hair is oiled and neatly parted down the middle, and he wears a stiff collar and a tie. The picture shows an ambitious young man, but there remains beneath the grooming and the collar a tough, masculine teamster. Tobin was a hardened, street-smart unionist from a big city. Unlike his fellow Boston Teamster Cornelius Shea, however, he still apparently lived by a strict code of personal ethics. He was a dutiful family man who had a wife and six sons. No public charges of immorality or dishonesty ever blemished his personal reputation—a fact he mentioned with increasing frequency in later years.[80]

Turmoil marked his first two years in office. In 1908, acting at the behest of certain employers, Driscoll reasserted his influence within several locals in Chicago.[81] When Tobin made clear his opposition to Driscoll's presence, the locals seceded from the IBT.[82] In October 1908 fourteen local unions in Chicago with about eight thousand members pulled out of the International Brotherhood of Teamsters. Working with Driscoll, who once again represented the interests of employers seeking collusive agreements, the officers of these local unions set up a separate organization, the Chicago Teamsters Union.[83] They were now free from Tobin's restraint and control.

That same fall, Shea set up operations among certain locals in New York

City. Tobin charged that Shea and his supporters were calling arbitrary strikes in order to obtain by fraud money the national union sent out for strike funds.[84] When Tobin went to a meeting of one New York local in order to inform its membership of what was occurring, Shea's local allies assaulted him, beating him so severely that he nearly died from the resulting injuries.[85] Tensions mounted, and when the national union refused to pay certain strike benefits a group of the New York City locals seceded to form the International Brotherhood of Teamsters of New York and New Jersey.[86]

The secession movements showed the limits of the reforms won in 1907. Tobin could do little to effectively combat local leaders who allied themselves with Driscoll and now Shea. He issued fliers to rank-and-file members of seceding locals in Chicago but with little assurance of them reaching their targets.[87] To visit the locals themselves proved dangerous if not impossible, as his beating had taught him.[88] He might try to wage the same vigorous effort against the dual organizations that the IBT had conducted against the UTA in 1906. That effort, however, had proved very expensive and brought limited results.

Instead of fighting, Tobin led the IBT through the worst of the crisis and learned to appreciate the hidden benefits of such localized secession movements. In 1909 the union's membership fell from fifty to thirty thousand. "We are," Tobin wrote to members of the General Executive Board, "without any question at the most critical point in our organization."[89] Things soon began to improve. The atmosphere in New York changed dramatically when Shea was removed from the scene. In May 1909 he attacked the woman with whom he lived and stabbed her twenty-five times with a pen knife. She survived the attack, barely, and Shea was tried on charges of assault. In court he admitted having the attacked the woman. He claimed, however, that constant drinking had rendered him insane at the time he did so. The judge found him guilty and sentenced him to five to twenty-five years of hard labor.[90]

Without Shea, the secession movement in New York began to falter. Secessionists argued among themselves, and soon various factions made separate inquiries about the terms Tobin would demand for reaffiliation.[91] No such dramatic change affected the breakaway group in Chicago. By the end of the decade, however, Tobin could see a positive aspect to that secession. The locals that had left had always had bad reputations. They were, as he termed it, "local unions that were always identified with wrong doings." He expressed concern for their rank-and-file members but argued, "At the same time it was a glorious day for the International Brotherhood of Teamsters when some of the leeches and scoundrels left us, who were always using our organization for purposes that were discreditable to the entire labor movement."[92]

Conclusion

Although observers such as John Cummings focused on the seeming unlimited approval that Teamsters gave Shea in 1905, the actual history is more
complex. Teamster members did hold a different view of corruption, but it
was neither simple-minded nor particularly more permissive than that of
employers. Instead, this broad and contested term was used as a tool to serve
a different agenda, in this case the protection of the union's goals. Shea was
reelected in 1905, but his victory came in the face of a stiff opposition movement. Although his opponents found themselves outmaneuvered at the convention, they learned to push for reform through organized secession efforts.
The secession of 1906 enabled a reformer, Tobin, to defeat Shea in 1907. Secession, as it turned out, was a two-edged sword. It empowered reformers,
but it also limited the scope of reform because less idealistic union leaders
could also use it as a tactic.

PART 2

The 1930s

Under the leadership of Daniel Tobin the Teamsters changed dramatically. A strife-torn and financially strapped union of horse and wagon drivers evolved into a smoothly run organization with deep pockets, and most of its members drove motor vehicles by the 1930s. Yet there were continuities. Most important, although motor vehicles transformed elements of drivers' work, the basic core of the men's concerns remained constant. In a variety of ways, including celebrating the dignity of the Teamster, the union addressed those concerns.

During the 1930s the union gained notoriety for corruption. Organized criminal gangs, based in particular economic sectors, used Teamster locals to manage competition in certain industries and to levy extortion. The Teamsters suffered from such predations more than other unions because trucking played a pivotal role in industries most prone to this kind of criminal activity. The union also ran afoul of the broad meaning given to the term *racketeering* by critics of organized labor who used the word to denounce a range of aggressive union tactics. The Teamsters' strategic power made it a frequent target of such criticism, which mounted over the course of the decade in response to the growth of organized labor. Thus both criminal activity and political rhetoric made the union notorious. Although critics denounced Teamster leadership for its alleged complacency in the face of these corruption scandals, serious reform efforts did take place. The national headquarters had limited tools available for reform, and those often proved insufficient for dealing with organized criminals. At the local level, a number of factors, such as the size of the local or the nature of the collective bargaining environment, determined the success of rank-and-file reform efforts.

4. Tobin's Union in a Period of Transition, 1910–40

Like most people, Daniel Tobin embodied a series of contradictions. Jimmy Hoffa remembered him as a man who took pride in being able to drink until 4 A.M. and then rise at 8 the next morning to a day of making speeches and dominating meetings.[1] Another observer was struck by the way Tobin included moralizing articles on self-improvement in the union's official journal, urging members to shed their bad habits and look after their health.[2] He was a hell-raiser and a sententious moralizer as well as a skilled union politician and a narrow-minded crank. At one point he gravely intoned, "We are free from prejudice and we are not fanatics or bigots."[3] On another occasion he complained about opponents of immigration restriction who were "preaching to let in the starving millions of Slavonians, Polacks, the worst kind of Italians, the lowest kinds of Russians."[4]

Dave Beck, whose own career in the Teamsters was sponsored by Tobin, asserted that his mentor was a man who "couldn't organize his own mother. But, by God," Beck continued, "he did have the ability, as he proved, to hang on to people that could organize and give them opportunity when he was convinced that that was their objective and nothing else." Indeed, in spite of his quirks, or maybe because of them, Tobin inspired great loyalty not just in Beck but among a host of subordinates in the union.[5] It was that loyalty in addition to his administrative and political skills that for good or for ill kept Tobin in office from 1907 to 1952.

After winning election in 1907, Tobin struggled first to reform the union and then to protect that reform. He suffered for his efforts, but by 1910 he and the reform wing could claim a measured victory. Cornelius Shea had been ousted from power, and his allies on the General Executive Board were gone. The local leaders in San Francisco and New York City who had fled from the Shea-controlled union returned. In the end, to maintain reform Tobin found he had to sacrifice unity. He blocked John Driscoll's effort to reassert himself in the union's affairs and willingly paid the price of a new secession movement in Chicago.

Some twenty years later Tobin would face another crisis. During the 1930s organized criminal gangs began to seek control of both particular local unions and in some cases the national headquarters of the Teamsters. Tobin himself received death threats. Other top officers in the union were shot at, and several were killed. At the same time, ironically, he was reviled by critics who charged that his conservatism and complacency had allowed racketeers to take over the union. The reformer now appeared to be in need of reform, and the union he had worked so hard to clean up was labeled the most racket-ridden in the country.

Over the course of two decades that separated these crises much had changed in America and within the union itself. Presiding over the organization during this period of transition, Tobin could claim credit for some of the developments that had occurred. Thus, under his guidance the nearly bankrupt IBT became a model of financial stability and orderly government. He led a broadening of the organization's jurisdiction, taking in categories of workers who did not drive but whose presence bolstered the size and bargaining position of the union. Many other changes, however, resulted from the broader social and technological developments that swept across the United States in these years. A union of men who worked on horse-drawn wagons evolved into an organization made up of automobile and motor truck drivers. New patterns of residential development and emerging highway networks changed the work routines of members and strained older methods of union organization. Meanwhile, the Great Depression and the New Deal fed a revolution in union growth. As a result of all of these changes, by the 1930s the Teamsters Union had become much larger, much wealthier, and more occupationally diverse than it had been in 1907.

And yet there were important continuities as well. Tobin's own durable hold on his office highlighted the degree to which the top leadership remained unchanged over these years. In spite of the growth of early intercity trucking, the IBT had not yet devised a coherent policy to coordinate organizing and bargaining among its scattered locals. Finally, the character of the average Teamster's work remained constant in ways that belied the obvious technological changes. Faced with a hard, public, and independent daily routine, Teamster members still looked to their union to validate and protect their dignity. Under Tobin the union took that mission quite seriously.

The Rise of Motor Trucking

Daniel Tobin started driving a delivery wagon in the 1890s, and he lived to see the gradual disappearance of the horse-drawn vehicles that had first led him into the Teamsters Union. Writing in 1929, he could still remember his first look at an automobile in the streets of turn-of-the-century Boston. "When I first saw the automobile, or vehicle without horses or steam, running around the streets, I thought we had reached the pinnacle of our accomplishments. I never dreamed the day would come when I would drive an automobile from Boston to Indianapolis without changing tires." By 1930 Tobin estimated that 70 percent of Teamster members worked on automobiles or motor trucks, and horse-drawn vehicles were increasingly becoming anachronisms.[6] The change occurred gradually and on the whole with little disruption to the union, but it carried important implications for the structure of the organization.

The conversion to automobiles began slowly. In the first decade of the twentieth century team owners were often wary about experimenting with the new gasoline- and electric-powered vehicles then being introduced. Small businesses had to be careful in weighing the risks involved in making what for them would be a sizable investment, and not everyone declared the experiment a success. A few employers found the mechanical problems too bothersome and the maintenance costs too high and switched back to horses.[7] Better able to afford the risk, bigger companies took the lead and gradually integrated motor trucks into their existing transportation systems. American Express, for example, began its first trial purchases in 1907.[8]

Despite the risks and the initial costs, the greater efficiency of motor vehicles encouraged team owners to make the switch. In 1910 salesmen generally told team owners that "one good motor truck will replace three horse-drawn trucks in the same service."[9] Steadily improving technology gradually made that boast an understatement. By 1930 Tobin claimed that "the same amount of coal can now be delivered in our large cities with a five or seven-ton truck operated by two men, as was formerly delivered by seven sets of men and three horse wagons."[10]

As mechanical improvements to these motor vehicles accumulated, steadily heightening their efficiency and dependability, more team owners were willing to make the leap. In this meandering process of transformation, the beginning of the second decade marked a watershed. Up to 1910, about ten thousand motor trucks had been registered in the United States. By 1914 nearly a hundred thousand were registered, and in 1920 that number would rise to more than a million.[11] Woodrow Wilson helped celebrate the new motor age when in 1913 he became the first president to ride to his inauguration in an automobile.[12]

As motor trucks and automobiles played an ever-greater role in their jurisdiction, the Teamster leadership moved to address that change. This process of adaptation occurred in two ways. The union shifted its jurisdiction, and the leadership itself worked to learn about and adopt the new technology.

The union shifted its jurisdiction at its 1906 convention to include men who operated motor vehicles. Delegates approved a resolution to expand the union's jurisdiction so that it now took in "any man driving a team or operating an automobile."[13] Four years later the leadership recognized the growing importance of motor trucks by moving to put a new occupation, chauffeur, into the union's title. Once the American Federation of Labor granted formal approval in 1910, the union officially became known as the International Brotherhood of Teamsters, Chauffeurs, and Helpers.[14]

On a personal level, the national leadership urged local leaders to become familiar with new technology. In 1913 the General Executive Board ordered all local union officers to educate themselves about automobiles so they could intelligently represent the chauffeurs who now fell under their jurisdiction.[15] In at least one case, Local 553, a New York City Coal Drivers Local, officials went so far as to buy an automobile in order to train members in how to drive it.[16] The former teamsters who composed the leadership thus made the transition to the automobile age along with everyone else in the country. By 1913 locals began to buy cars for their officers' use in conducting union business, and in 1916 the IBT supplied Tobin and the other national leaders with automobiles.[17]

Most of the membership made the transition with comparatively little trouble. By and large, the men who operated the new motor trucks were the same ones who had earlier driven horses and wagons. Some employers, however, did express concerns about letting unskilled teamsters loose on their new and expensive machinery. One warned fellow employers that putting a teamster "in charge of delicate machinery would be like turning a bull loose in a China shop."[18] Most employers deemphasized such concerns, preferring to recruit drivers from among working teamsters rather than the more mechanically knowledgeable existing chauffeurs. As one employer explained, "An automobile driver may know more about the mechanism of the truck, but he is unfamiliar with the type of work demanded of a motor truck driver." He did not know how to handle freight and make deliveries in heavy traffic.[19] Indeed, traffic conditions made knowledge of horses a continued asset. As the owner of a fleet of five-ton motor trucks explained, "Speaking from considerable experience the writer would recommend the employment of former horse drivers; they become very efficient in two or three weeks driving with proper tuition; they know the rules of the road, and their acquaintance with the idiosyncrasies of horses is often valuable."[20] Some firms made a regular practice of starting all their men out as horse and wagon drivers; later, as they proved their ability, they would be promoted into chauffeuring positions.[21]

Although the union embraced the new technology and welcomed the drivers into the union, in the long run the growth of motor trucking created organizational tension; at the heart of the tension was the rise of intercity trucking. The idea of hauling freight between distant cities by motor truck surfaced early in the period, but for a long time it remained largely a pipe dream. Trial freight runs in 1911 highlighted the impracticability of such a business. The general manager of the Dayton Auto Truck Company did successfully manage to haul a load of soap bars on a three-ton truck from Chicago to New York City, but it took him thirteen days to make the trip.[22] That same year, a five-ton truck traveling over the primitive roads between Denver and San Francisco took five weeks to complete the journey.[23]

In the 1920s better roads and improved motor trucks changed the character of such trips from adventurous odysseys to increasingly profitable ventures. By 1932 the federal government had funded the construction of two hundred thousand miles of paved highways, and by the end of the 1930s the total amount of paved roads would double. At the same time, pneumatic tires, better transmissions, and improved brakes, along with advances in headlights and refrigeration, expanded the range and usefulness of trucks. More flexible in setting rates than railroads, trucking companies also offered commercial customers the benefit of door-to-door deliveries, eliminating the troublesome and time-consuming transfer points required in shipping by rail. Given these advantages along with the improved technology, motor trucking increasingly offered serious competition with railroads.[24] By the mid-1920s some firms had come to specialize in long-distance hauls.[25]

Intercity trucking had emerged, yet by the early 1930s it remained limited in volume and range. Indeed, it would be more accurate to describe it as primarily intraregional trucking. Railroads had lost about 10 percent of the intercity freight business to trucking companies by 1933, but most of it was in the short-haul end of the industry.[26] Sixty percent of all trucks in 1930 traveled fewer than a hundred miles a day.[27] The average intercity haul in the early 1920s was between forty and fifty miles, and by 1933 it had only risen to a hundred miles, still a far cry from the average intercity haul of 250 miles that developed in the 1950s.[28] Describing the trucking industry in the early 1930s, the U.S. Bureau of Public Roads asserted, "Truck traffic on rural highways is predominantly a short haul movement."[29]

Although intercity trucking had not yet achieved the presence and scope that it would after World War II, it had begun to shape American society. In 1933 the President's Research Committee on Social Trends observed that motor trucking had helped create a "modern economic regionalism." Trucks linked larger surrounding geographic areas to the economic sphere of America's cities. The committee found a new radius of about forty miles, the outer limit of what motor trucks could deliver to and return from in one day, where residents and businesses were now more tightly bound together in regular commercial exchanges. Within this zone, for instance, big-city department stores increasingly muscled aside small-town competitors. Shoppers from surrounding rural areas preferred the greater selection of the metropolitan stores, and now, thanks to the new technology, they could have their purchases delivered to their homes. Farmers in the forty-mile radius could engage in direct trade with the large urban market and truck produce into the city on a daily basis.[30]

In the 1920s and 1930s it was this new, intraregional trucking that the Teamsters Union had to confront. The IBT had been built originally on a foundation of localism, a foundation that itself reflected the character of the teaming industry. In larger cities a local union had jurisdiction over one branch of the teaming trade; in smaller towns, however, one local might cover several different kinds of teamster, from milkmen to coal haulers. But in both cases the union had always ruled that the local's jurisdiction would be strictly guided by a city's limits. In each city, locals made collective bargaining agreements independently and with no coordination with other locals in other cities. But in the 1920s, as truck drivers from neighboring cities began to travel into the jurisdictions of other local unions, that kind of independence began to make less and less sense. Truck drivers and IBT locals from different cities competed in a way that team drivers never had. Like everyone else, Teamsters found themselves affected by "modern economic regionalism."

Tobin and his generation of IBT leadership never found a systematic and effective response to the new situation. As early as 1926, Michael Casey, the leading Teamster official on the West Coast, put the problem before the General Executive Board. Casey reported on a trucking company that was running from Los Angeles to San Francisco. The company was willing to put its men into Casey's San Francisco–based Local 85 (there was no effective Teamster organization in Los Angeles), but some of the men involved lived in Los Angeles. In effect, that would extend Local 85's jurisdiction to another city. Casey wanted to know what the board's policy would be in such cases, but the board was unable to make a decision.[31] In succeeding years it issued contradictory rulings on such matters, never arriving at a positive overall response.[32]

Only at the end of the 1930s would Tobin and the other members of the General Executive Board slowly come to accept various regional forms of organization being developed on the local level in the Northwest, Upper Midwest, and in New England. The success of those tactics, regional conferences, and regional contracts convinced Tobin to promote them all across the country, but the change would not occur until after World War II. Regional forms of organization in the IBT were isolated experiments during the 1930s and viewed with some wariness by national officers who feared that they might be preludes to secession movements.[33]

Building a Stable Union Government and Broadening the Jurisdiction

The new economic regionalism of the motor age caught Tobin and the union flat-footed, but in other policy issues he proved quite adept at building and protecting the organization's strength. In the years that stretched from 1910 to 1940, Tobin carefully husbanded the resources of the IBT, keeping it out of dangerous conflicts and guarding the sanctity of its treasury. At the same time, he created a union governing structure that allowed for both stability and a measure of democracy. A canny conservative, Tobin hearkened to tried-and-true craft union ideals; at the same time, he steadily brought a range of different occupational groups into the IBT. In effect, he built an industrial union on the foundation of one particular craft's organizational strength.

When first elected to office in 1907, Tobin took command of a union that had been torn apart by dissension. Over the course of the next several decades he labored assiduously to restore unity and order to the organization. In doing so he worked with local union leaders, assuring them a responsible and secure place in the national organization. Indeed, the IBT is usually depicted in these years as nothing more than a confederation of semi-independent locals.[34] Closer scrutiny suggests, however, that Tobin, in spite of the limited formal authority of the national headquarters, managed to exercise great informal influence over the locals.

The constitution of the IBT set up democratically governed local unions as the foundation of the rest of the organization. Local members voted on who would lead them, and those leaders in turn conducted negotiations with employers, monitored the contract, and led strikes when necessary. As a practical matter, local officers also tended to be delegates to the union's national conventions. There they deliberated changes to the IBT's constitution and voted on the national officers of the organization, including Tobin. Only a relatively few formal ties bound the locals to the national. In return for paying a share of its members' monthly dues to the national organization, a local was entitled to receive fairly modest strike benefits. For its part, the national organization had the authority to make sure that locals obeyed the rules for governance and conduct set out in the IBT constitution.[35] Locals on occasion shook off such control by dropping out of the national organization. They lost access to the strike benefits, but in return they no longer had to share the membership's dues.[36]

Tobin sought to forge stronger formal links between the locals and the national organization but achieved only limited success. In 1908 the national union's General Executive Board won authority to appoint trustees or receivers over local unions deemed to be led by "dishonest or incompetent" officers or where the local organization was "not conducted for the benefit of the entire membership."[37] Tobin also tried to bind local members more tightly to the national organization by instituting a national system of benefits such as life insurance.[38] He argued that such a system would make local secession unlikely. His efforts were frustrated, however, by delegates at successive conventions who voted down his proposals, apparently because they objected to the increased dues they would require.[39]

These defeats illustrate the democratic qualities of the IBT during the decades before World War II. Under Tobin, conventions proceeded in an orderly fashion and provided a safe venue for opponents of the national leadership to express themselves. Delegates felt free to vote against Tobin's proposals, and although such defeats were rare they did on occasion involve significant issues.

In many ways, however, the public image of localism and democracy obscured Tobin's ability to manage the union from behind the scenes. By the 1920s, he was using his assistant, John Gillespie, as a floor manager at the conventions. Gillespie collected the votes necessary to win the measures Tobin wanted passed and made sure that proposals considered troublesome would be sent back to committee. Because Tobin chose all committee members, he could be certain that they would consign any unwanted proposal to oblivion.[40] Over time, conventions became less of a struggle for Tobin and less frequent as well. Beginning in 1915, the IBT met only once every five years. Between conventions, a network of officers on the international's payroll— vice presidents, organizers, and auditors known collectively as international representatives—exercised supervision and informal control over local unions. The international representatives stepped into local affairs at critical moments—for example, during strikes or negotiations. When they thought it necessary, they would move against local leaders and stage elections they felt confident would bring men they wanted to office. Prestige, experience, and personal contacts favored the international representatives in these contests; often, they were the ones who had originally organized the local in question.[41] On occasions where such efforts failed Tobin took stronger measures, such as revoking a local's charter or appointing an international representative as trustee of an obstinate local.[42]

The tricky part of this network of influence involved managing the international representatives. Tobin benefited from his ability to inspire loyalty and his willingness to search out and cultivate potential leaders. He was always on the lookout for new talent.[43] In 1940, for example, he put aside his political conservatism and actively recruited Farrell Dobbs, a Trotskyist Socialist from Minneapolis who had proven his ability in a very successful organizing campaign among intercity truck drivers. Although Tobin offered to make him a vice president in the union, Dobbs chose instead to abandon union organizing for the field of radical politics, leading the Socialist Workers Party from its headquarters in Greenwich Village.[44]

The episode illustrated Tobin's continued effort to cultivate the best new leadership he could find to reinforce a group of loyal international representatives upon which he had long depended. Michael Casey typified such long-term loyalists. A vice president based in San Francisco, he led the largest local in that city from early the 1900s until his death in 1937, and for decades he represented the national union on the West Coast.[45] Tobin recruited Dave Beck to serve the same function in the Northwest in 1926 after Beck had distinguished himself as a local union officer in Seattle.[46] Other representatives played a similar role in other regions, operating out of a particular city but supervising locals in the surrounding area.

Tobin depended upon the assistance of such regional leaders, but he remained the boss, setting their salaries and issuing instructions from the national headquarters in Indianapolis.[47] In this way an apparently decentralized, democratic union government actually contained an effective top-down mechanism for supervision and control. Tobin used that mechanism, among other things, to impose his conservative trade union philosophy on local unions.

In 1937 the secretary-treasurer of the newly chartered Local 434 of Watertown, Wisconsin, received a long letter from Daniel Tobin. He may not have known it, but this was a standard letter sent to all new locals. In it Tobin offered a catalog of warnings, most of which centered on ways for the local to avoid involving itself in a strike, any strike, especially long ones or those the local could not win. Tobin expected new locals to keep a low profile for the first year. They were to eschew confrontations with employers and instead focus on building a stable, financially strong, local organization that had signed up at least 85 percent of the industry's employees. Locals that chose to ignore this advice or that found themselves unavoidably caught up in a dispute were required to apply for, and receive, several levels of approval before they could hope to receive strike benefits from the national organization. In no case, Tobin warned, would sympathy strikes in support of other unions be sanctioned.[48]

Tobin's philosophy of labor unionism was a conservative one. As he wrote in the union's journal in 1915, "Our International Union is a business institution and it must be run on business lines or it cannot continue to exist."[49] Running the union as a business meant avoiding unnecessary and unjustified risks. It meant staying out of contests the union could not win. In 1923 Michael Casey, the Teamsters' West Coast organizer, asked the national office to back an organizing strike in Los Angeles. The men would likely lose the strike, the organizer explained, but the national union's support would show its good intentions and perhaps rally the local's morale. Tobin responded, "It would be poor business ability and judgement on our part to sanction a strike that might cost a whole lot of money—say from thirty to fifty thousand dollars—dumped onto a place where it would only help the men cut their own throats."[50]

Within the AFL, Tobin's conservatism was not unusual. As labor historian David Brody has observed, AFL leaders who experienced the destructive anti-union campaigns of the early 1900s came to place the needs and interests of their organizations ahead of any abstract duty to unionize unorganized workers.[51] Nor did Tobin believe it was useful to antagonize unionized employers needlessly or undercut their economic position through excessive demands. For that reason especially, Tobin opposed getting involved in sympathy strikes, which tended to hurt the "fair employers who had signed union contracts with our local unions."[52]

Avoiding the kind of risks that had gotten Cornelius Shea involved in a full-blown contest with the Employers' Association of Chicago allowed Tobin to keep the union's finances and membership on a course of steady improvement. In 1913 the union for the first time had more than $100,00 in its treasury, and he described that milestone in language redolent with vindication. "Five years ago," Tobin recalled, "we had nothing in the treasury." Two years later the membership climbed to 56,308, for the first time topping the IBT's reported size at the time of the original amalgamation in 1903.[53] Financially the organization made dramatic progress in the years that followed; its treasury contained more than $1 million by 1925, $2¼ million by 1935, and $6 million by 1940.[54] Membership grew as well; slow but steady gains brought the IBT up to ninety thousand by 1930.[55]

During the 1930s the IBT went on to achieve phenomenal growth, with membership reaching 450,000 by 1940, in part because of the larger political and social climate of the day but also because it had quietly broadened its jurisdiction to include a host of occupation groups.[56] There is a certain irony to this aspect of the union's history. Publicly, especially at union gatherings, Tobin championed the ideal of craft unionism (in which different occupational groups are organized into separate unions) against efforts to promote industrial organization (or gathering all workers in a particular workplace or industry into one union).[57] Under his leadership, however, the IBT did not become an exclusionary organization of skilled craftsmen. He had decided to limit Teamster efforts to groups that showed potential for organization. Part of that potential involved previous union experience, and part of it involved the workers' ability to support a local union. The IBT did not ban unskilled workers. Indeed, teamsters and truck drivers themselves were classed as unskilled workers.[58] Nor, in practice, did the union follow any kind of strict craft lines in choosing who it would bring into the organization.

Through the years, strategic considerations had led it to broaden its jurisdiction to include employees who worked alongside teamsters and truckers at stables, garages, factories, and other venues. In 1906 delegates at the union's convention, citing tactical benefits, voted to welcome stablemen.[59] Similar considerations led in 1919 to inclusion of all the various employees involved in the ice business, from the loaders and pullers in ice factories to the foremen, sub-foremen, and the sales force employed at retail ice stations. That same year, the Teamsters also opened their doors to a range of dairy workers, including bottle washers and bottle fillers.[60] Although those workers were often factory laborers, Tobin had come to see them as critical to the strength and survival of drivers' locals. During an ice-driver strike that he led in Cincinnati in 1915, Tobin wrote that laborers who worked inside ice plants "were of importance to the industry, and an absolute necessity to their [Teamsters] organization should they ever again become involved in trouble."[61]

As the motor age progressed the union claimed jurisdiction over a broad swath of emerging, garage-related occupations. Car washers, oilers, polishers, and tire removers were all eligible for membership, as were those mechanics who worked in small, private garages.[62] For all of his rhetorical opposition to industrial unionism, Tobin urged local leaders to keep the strategic needs of the union in mind and make vigorous efforts to organize these different occupation groups.[63]

At the local level, some leaders, apparently with Tobin's support, went further even than the union's already broad official jurisdiction. The 275 members of San Francisco Bakery Drivers Local 484 included sixty who worked as packers, receiving clerks, and loaders at various bakeries.[64] In 1923 the Boston Coal Drivers represented yardmen (referred to as "wharfmen"), who received the same union scale as teamsters who drove one-horse wagons.[65]

Ever pragmatic, Tobin was willing to ignore craft lines and even AFL jurisdictional boundaries in the interest of building strong local unions. Occasionally, that policy was spelled out. In 1938 Tobin's assistant, John Gillespie, instructed the leader of a laundry drivers' local to go ahead and organize a group of workers who properly belonged to the International Laundry Workers' Union. Gillespie emphasized that the organizational needs of the local should prevail. "Do not," he advised, "allow any union to organize any kind of an organization that will interfere with our drivers that is, where we have any form of jurisdiction such as we have in the laundry and dry cleaning business." The national headquarters, he noted, would take the heat for such a violation. "Whatever complaint there is from the International union [Laundry Workers] we will take care of from this office."[66]

Given his aggressive sense of the union's jurisdiction and his tactical view of its organizing priorities, Tobin did not need anyone to point out to him the benefits of unionizing intercity truck drivers. He expressed skepticism about organizing owner-operators ("gypsies") because he could see no effective way of policing their contracts.[67] But he strongly advocated organizing long-haul drivers who worked for intercity trucking firms. In 1927, referring to intercity drivers, Tobin wrote to the membership in the union's journal, "Many of these men are not organized, and we want to keep them before you through the journal until they are. Our individual members come in contact with them. Make it your aim to point out to these teamsters and chauffeurs the advantages of being within the organization and a real part of our organization."[68] Internal union correspondence indicates that organizers were busily engaged in bringing intercity drivers into the union as early as the mid-1920s.[69]

Tobin's willingness to take an expansive and pragmatic view of the IBT's jurisdiction did not, however, constrain him from fighting tooth and nail against other unions whose own strategic needs might lead them to bring a few drivers into their organizations. He took such challenges as a serious test of the IBT's mettle. Local leaders who failed to defend their jurisdictions with appropriate vigor received his scorn. In 1935 he wrote in the union's journal, "I despise the local union and its officers that sit still and are satisfied to have somebody come into their house and steal part of their possessions that rightfully belong to them, without offering a protest."[70] Instead, he urged local leaders to "fight with every ounce of energy" to protect the union's jurisdiction "from encroachment by any other union."[71] In vigorous contests with the Brewery Workers, the Amalgamated Meat Cutters, the Clerks, and later the CIO, Tobin quite happily championed the cause of craft unionism.[72] It served, however, as more of a useful argument to him than a consistent ideal. Indeed, as the 1930s progressed Tobin used the contest with the CIO to justify broadening the IBT's jurisdiction even farther beyond its original craft lines. In 1936 he cited the need to block the growing International Longshoremen's and Warehousemen's Union (ILWU), an important West Coast affiliate of the CIO, and moved to bring warehouse workers into the Teamsters.[73] Nine years later the same justification was used to bring cannery workers into the IBT.[74]

Tobin's stance on jurisdictional matters was intellectually inconsistent, but it offered practical advantages. Because he was not the dogmatic leader many accounts have suggested, the Teamsters were not a narrow and exclusionary union.[75] By the 1930s the union had long practiced the tactic of using the striking power of drivers to help organize a range of different occupation groups. In the New Deal era, when organizing became less difficult, the IBT's flexibility allowed it to expand at a rapid pace.

Teamsters at Work in the Motor Age

While the broadened jurisdiction left the IBT in a better position to build its membership, the heart of the union remained the drivers. The motor age had transformed some aspects of their work, but in its basic essentials the working life of a Teamster member continued to be defined by physical rigor and stress. Hard labor in a public setting, the arbitrary authority of the boss, and customers who were at once demanding and dismissive shaped the daily world of most drivers. To address those conditions the union under Tobin offered shorter hours and better wages, and it also championed the membership's quest for decency, dignity, and respect.

In 1915, Local 229 in Scranton, Pennsylvania, numbered about three hundred members, making it a typically sized local. Those three hundred members labored in five main occupations: taxi drivers, bakery wagon drivers, beef truck drivers, drivers who worked for the city, and coal and ice drivers. Of the five, coal and ice drivers constituted the single largest group, with 118 of the members working for ice delivery firms that also supplied coal in the winter.[76] By the mid-1930s home refrigerators would become increasingly common, but until then ice drivers remained an important constituency within the Teamsters Union. A look at their working day provides a window into world of the average Teamster in this transitional period.

What would be a long, hard day usually began early. In Detroit in 1919, icemen began loading their wagons at 6 in the morning. The typical ice driver in that era handled a residential route with between 180 and 220 customers. He might cover the route with an automobile, but it was also still quite common to use a one-horse wagon. The amount of ice he delivered varied according to the season, perhaps four thousand pounds a day in May and up to six thousand or more by July. It was a daily routine that required strength and endurance. At stops the iceman lifted hundred-pound blocks of ice from his truck or wagon using a pair of tongs as his only mechanical aid. Because most home iceboxes took twenty-five-pound or fifty-pound blocks, he used a pick, an axe, or a saw to cut hundred-pound blocks into smaller pieces. To avoid waste he made the division as close to the residence as he could. That meant hoisting the hundred-pound block onto his shoulder and hauling it to a building's doorway or even up several flights of steps. He repeated this process roughly two hundred times a day, putting in a ten-hour day, six days a week.[77]

The work demanded more than just strength. One had to be able to remember details and cultivate customers. Home iceboxes had different shapes, and a good iceman remembered each one on his route, carving the block to fit while he was outside the house to avoid splattering water and ice chips all over a customer's kitchen. Working on commission, he sought to keep customers happy. He brought a fifty-pound block through a crowded apartment and placed it in a cluttered icebox without disturbing the household. Customers were supposed to signal when they needed more ice by placing a card in their window, but people often forgot. A good driver kept track of a household's ice usage and knew when to come by, even if no card was in the window. Always on the lookout for new customers, he monitored new residents along his route and made it his business to offer his services to them. A man who lacked hustle would never make it as an ice driver. Companies started drivers out on a route with forty or fifty stops already provided but expected them to build that route to about two hundred stops through their own efforts. Those who could not do so lost their routes.[78]

Finally, at the end of the day, the iceman came back to the barn and went over his receipts for the day. Different companies used various methods of payment and systems of accounting, but all of them held the driver responsible for any shortages. Before he could check out, the foreman would review his records to make sure they came out right.[79]

Other kinds of Teamsters followed similar routines. Milkmen, coal haulers, and laundry delivery drivers all worked jobs that combined the duties of a salesman with a tough physical routine. For all of those drivers, like their turn-of-the-century counterparts, long hours were a common feature of the occupation. Harry deBoer, who worked as a coal hauler in Minneapolis in the early 1930s, recalled, "When bad weather came in, you'd work from early morning to past midnight."[80] The union sought to curtail such unreasonable demands, but driving remained an occupation that required endurance. A 1925 study by the Department of Labor reveals that unionized teamsters and chauffeurs worked significantly longer hours than other groups of unionized workers. While teamsters and chauffeurs who belonged to the union averaged 56.4 hours a week, the next-closest group, unionized bakers, worked on average only 47.4 hours. The average for all unionized trades was 45.5 hours of work a week.[81]

The long days were combined with another overriding feature of the teamster trade—these were men who scrambled, hustled, and hurried to make a living. Unemployment and underemployment loomed for drivers caught in a seasonal trade. Icemen and coal teamsters, often interchangeable, found their hours regulated by the weather. During his days as a coal teamster, Harry deBoer recalled, "The only time you worked was when the weather was cold. If the weather was nice, you could hang around the 'dog house,' they would call the place where you could keep warm."[82] Those who got work scrambled to keep it. Harry Boscoe drove a laundry delivery truck in suburban Minneapolis during the mid-1930s and remembered his efforts to make a living on commission-bound wages. "You had to get five more customers per week. You had to keep shuffling; besides the people you were dealing with, you had to call next door, trying to bring [in] more people." To stop before the route was finished was to risk losing customers and maybe even the job. "You worked until you got your truck empty or you just gave out for the day."[83]

What the work offered by way of compensation for grueling routines was a degree of independence. Drivers typically worked alone or with a helper, free from the constant supervision of a foreman. They jealously guarded this freedom, much to the consternation of employers who sought to assert greater control over their workforce. Ice companies that aimed to create greater discipline by issuing uniforms found that men often refused to wear them. Icemen also liked to drive their routes differently each day, and they stubbornly balked at efforts to take this control away from them in the name of efficiency.[84] Employers who tried to reassert control over how men operated their vehicles faced similar resistance. A variety of devices were manufactured to keep track of how fast trucks were driven or limit the driver's ability to go over a certain speed. But there were always a number of drivers who regularly disabled such devices.[85]

It is likely that independence mattered so much because it offered a portion of dignity and control in jobs otherwise lacking in such qualities. The arbitrary authority of the boss dominated the working life of a driver. The boss or his foreman determined who got work and who did not and what pay one would receive. The rationale for these decisions often struck the men as mysterious or capricious. Harry Boscoe remembered that all the drivers at the laundry where he worked made different wages and he never understood how they were set.[86] Jimmy Hoffa, who had begun working at a warehouse in the early 1930s, recalled that all his fellow workers referred to their foreman as the "Little Bastard." Emphasizing the humiliations that the foreman dished out to the men, Hoffa explained, "He thoroughly enjoyed screaming out commands and then cursing a man and threatening to fire him if he didn't move quick enough."[87] Twenty years earlier, a working teamster lamented a similar fate, adding only that he received equally bad treatment from the customers he served. A teamster, he asserted, "stands as a buffer between his employer and the dear, old public, takes the abuse of both and gets the thanks of neither."[88]

Under Tobin, the union responded to these concerns by making itself the champion of the teamster's dignity. Part of the campaign involved improving the material conditions of the membership. At the level of the local union, gains could be quite dramatic. In Scranton, Local 229 successfully organized the city's milk drivers in the late 1910s. At the time, milkmen worked ten to twelve hours a day, with no days off, and received, at times, as little as $45 a month. By 1927 the local boasted that the men worked nine-hour days, receiving every seventh day off along with a week's paid vacation. Pay had risen to about $130 a month.[89] Nationwide there were steady wage increases for all unionized teamsters and chauffeurs. From 1913 to 1925, according to the Department of Labor, wages rose by 123 percent.[90]

Union contracts offered other benefits. Sometimes these amounted to no more than an attack on the petty exactions of the employers. In 1924 chauffeurs in St. Louis won the right to "room and board where they please," and although they still had to wear uniforms the company was now required to provide them. Their contract also stipulated that drivers no longer were required to wash the company's cars.[91] Although local complaints might vary, the central benefit of the contract remained the same; it offered workers protection from the capricious behavior of foremen. Wages were standardized, and overtime payments were required for any extra work that might be imposed. Most important, contracts regulated the conditions under which a man might lose his job. The 1919 Detroit Icemen's contract read, "Causes for dismissal shall be intoxication while on duty, incompetency, dishonesty, neglect of duty." The union provided drivers who felt unfairly treated with an avenue of appeal that would eventually lead to a panel of arbitration.[92]

Beyond such contractual issues, the union played a symbolic role in championing a teamster's dignity. To some that might seem a trivial matter, but for Tobin it ranked equal to the more material questions of wages and hours. At the union's 1940 convention he summarized the IBT's achievements under his tenure and emphasized symbolic achievements first and increased wages second. He told delegates that the IBT was "an organization that has raised the employment of its members from a condition of slavery and contempt . . . to a position of notable citizenship, clean living, and respect in the eyes of the nation."[93]

As Tobin used the terms, dignity and the related concept of decency involved cultivating respectability and maintaining traditional (patriarchal) notions of masculinity. "Because an individual is a teamster or chauffeur," he told delegates at the union's convention in 1912, "is no reason why he cannot be a man."[94] The national officers of the union were held up as models of decent, respectable masculinity. They were described as faithfully married men who were dutifully raising families and engaged in no shameful excesses.[95]

By the 1930s, Tobin had come to use the pages of the union's official journal, which he had edited since he became president, as a forum in which to promote the standard of the decent Teamster. In 1936 he wrote, "This is a union labor publication and its columns are not only intended for organizing purposes but are intended to and expected and has always endeavored to raise up the standards of its membership, making better men if possible of our members because they are union men."[96]

During the 1930s the reputation for decency that Tobin cultivated, and the dignity it celebrated, came under attack. Critics maligned the union and impugned the integrity of its leadership. The organizational strengths that Tobin had helped the Teamsters achieve combined with the union's continued strategic role in the urban economy and made it a target. For organized crime, the union offered a lucrative new enterprise. For conservative critics of the New Deal and business groups that resented the growth of organized labor, the Teamsters offered a powerful symbol of the dangerously expansive power of trade unions.

5. "The Most Racketeer-Ridden Union in the United States": The Problem of Corruption in the Teamsters Union during the 1930s

Surveying union corruption in *Labor Czars: A History of Labor Racketeering* (1938), Harold Seidman wrote that the Teamsters Union had become "perhaps the most racketeer-ridden union in the United States today."[1] The verdict would stick with the organization. Some five decades later the President's Commission on Organized Crime listed the Teamsters as one of the "four international unions most frequently associated with organized crime."[2] Indeed, by mid-century the Teamsters had come to symbolize the problem of union corruption. If there is consensus that the union has a problem with corruption, there also exists general agreement that the origins of the problem lie somewhere in the 1930s.[3] As Steven Brill put it in his popular account of the union, "It was during these hard, violent times that many of the big-city Teamsters locals and joint councils made their first alliances with local gangsters."[4]

How and why did the Teamsters Union become notoriously corrupt during the 1930s? The answer to that question requires consideration of several others. What made the Teamsters more prone to charges of corruption than other labor organizations? How did organized crime come to play such a well-publicized role in its affairs? And, why has this corruption proved to be such an enduring problem?

Previous studies, seeking to answer those questions, have tended to fall into two categories. One group has placed the blame on the union, citing the ideology of union leaders or the problematic morals of membership. An opposing group emphasizes the critical role of the economic and political setting to which particular unions, among them the Teamsters, must adapt. Although they do not refer to themselves collectively in this way, the two camps can be labeled as "moralists" and "structuralists."

Moralists charged that greedy and indifferent Teamsters have ignored or condoned a broad range of criminal behavior; that, in turn, has allowed organized crime's influence in the union to flourish.[5] For example, in his history of labor corruption John Hutchinson placed blame on the ideology of business unionism as celebrated in the Teamsters and in other affiliates of the American Federation of Labor (AFL) that were also dogged by corruption. "Business unionism" refers to the belief that a labor organization should focus solely on gaining better wages and working conditions for its membership. Although leaders of the Congress of Industrial Organizations (CIO) had larger social and political goals, Hutchinson argued, business unionists in the AFL had substituted the profit motive for a moral compass. Thus, as he saw it, "in the presence of temptation or error the so-called business unionists could have used a stronger creed."[6]

For their part, structuralists downplayed the importance of individual conscience—or the lack thereof—and emphasized larger economic forces. In particular economic settings, sociologists have noted, collusive arrangements involving employers and union leaders have worked to stabilize the market. Businessmen operating in industries marked by easy market entry, tight competition, and high proportionate labor costs have traditionally turned to labor unions for help. Typically, the two parties conspired to control competition. Such arrangements, sociologists argue, combined with local demographic and political factors to create a pattern of endemic corruption for unions forced to operate in such sectors. Thus Daniel Bell, who asserted that "racketeers were able to enter only into small, unit-sized industries where chaotic competition prevailed," also found that "the greatest potential for racketeering is in the Teamsters union."[7]

The contours of this debate constrained the analysis of the issue of union corruption because questions of morality, ideology, and economics squeezed out consideration of other matters. In reality, charges of corruption included more than the malfeasance of a few labor bureaucrats, and a sense of crisis surged beyond the narrow economic confines where collusion proliferated. The larger historical context needs to be considered and along with it the tense relationship between America's labor organizations and the rest of society. Finally, the broader uses of the terms *corruption* and *racketeering* must be explored. In common parlance, both words describe instances of extortion, bribery, collusion, and miscellaneous violations of fiduciary trust, but in this period they also played a more political role.

Consideration of these issues offers a more complex understanding of how the Teamsters became notorious for corruption during the 1930s. Structural factors did play an important role in shaping patterns of collusion and inviting the presence of organized crime. Because critics of union growth broadened their use of the word *racketeering* to include a wide range of activities, however, charges of corruption came to indict the whole Teamster organization rather than only those elements entangled in arrangements with organized crime. For its part, the union faced two dilemmas. On the one hand, it had to deal with collusive arrangements and organized criminal activities that were, in a sense, natural to many of the economic fields within its jurisdiction. On the other hand, it faced a definition of corruption that came to include methods of organization long accepted as necessary and legitimate within the union.

Racketeering and Organized Crime

In 1931 the National Commission on Law Observance and Enforcement (the Wickersham Commission) noted, "The words 'racket' and 'racketeer' are recent additions to our language made necessary in order to describe types of crime and criminals which have become an increasingly important factor in the life of the country during recent years." The term *racketeering* was broadly used to describe a range of conspiracies to extort money from businesses, often under the pretext of controlling competition in a particular industry.[8] Although the Wickersham Commission dated the origins of racketeering to World War I, its report described a crisis that had only recently become acute. "All informed persons agree," it asserted, "that crime of this character [racketeering] is widespread, especially in the larger cities, and that it has come to pervade a substantial part of the national economic life."[9]

The term's popularization stemmed from fears about the growth of organized crime. In and of themselves, the activities included under the rubric *racketeering* were not new. Collusion between unions and businesses in particular industries dated at least as far back as the turn of the century. Extortion had long been practiced in those same sectors. The new element in all of this, however, was the role of organized crime. To contemporaries, it appeared that organized crime had expanded beyond its traditional sphere in urban vice districts and through racketeering stood poised to threaten the larger economic sphere.[10] In 1931 the *Saturday Evening Post* warned, "It is realized that, unless something drastic is done, every legitimate business will be paying tribute in one form or another to the underworld."[11]

Criminal gangs had long been a part of America's urban landscape, but their character evolved during the 1920s. Gangs came to hold the central position in the business of organized crime. Some of the changes stemmed from the effects of Prohibition, but a process of acculturation by newer immigrants was also at work. Gangs at the turn of the century played only a limited role in the commercial vice industry that constituted the heart of organized crime. Vice entrepreneurs ran the prostitution and gambling businesses that usually existed in segregated districts of large cities. Political machines, which controlled the police, oversaw a regular system of payments from vice entrepreneurs in return for the right to conduct business without undue harassment. Under this system, gangs occupied a peripheral position. Neighborhood gangs of youths and young adults, when not engaged in fighting each other over territorial disputes, sold their services to vice entrepreneurs and politicians. Gang members worked as bouncers or debt collectors and fought the regular battles at the ballot box that political machines at times required. They amounted to casual laborers. In the organizational structure of the time, gangs stood at the bottom of the pyramid in terms of power and revenue; politicians and vice entrepreneurs called the shots.[12]

Prohibition, which stretched from 1919 to 1933, worked to shift those arrangements. Bootlegging offered enormous profits and generated an unprecedented level of chaotic violence. Because violence had always been the specialty of gangs, their role in organized crime grew in importance during the 1920s. In effect, only gang leaders could offer protection from violent assault. As time passed, bootleggers either willingly attached themselves to gangsters for protection or found themselves forcibly supplanted. Similarly, other vice entrepreneurs in gambling and prostitution, also vulnerable to the sanction of violence, made regular payments to gangs. Political protection remained important, but the gangs of the 1920s, which had access to great amounts of money and the backing of ever-larger numbers of strong-arm men, dealt with representatives of political machines from a position of equal or even superior status.[13]

Meanwhile, the character and organization of the gangs themselves evolved. Street gangs based on neighborhood and ethnicity, what criminologists refer to as "cultural gangs," lack a formal structure and continuity of membership. People drift in and out of the cultural gang, and no clear chain of command exists. By the 1920s young men who were from immigrant backgrounds and had begun their careers in such gangs, people like Meyer Lansky, Charles Luciano, Al Capone, and Arthur Flegenheimer, more commonly known as Dutch Schultz, had moved on to found or join entrepreneurial gangs. Although these gangs often exhibited the sorts of ethnic and neigh-borhood commonalties that had existed in street gangs, the new groups had a tighter structure and focused solely on making money. Membership was by necessity active and permanent, and a formal chain of command existed, as did occasional examples of a kind of division of labor. The Italian American Mafia formally inaugurated in New York under Charles ("Lucky") Luciano is the best-known example of this new gang structure, but other entrepreneurial gangs emerged at roughly the same time. In Chicago, the sizable entrepreneurial gang that coalesced around Al Capone apparently lacked the ethnic exclusiveness and ceremonial trappings of Luciano's Mafia. Its Irish, Welsh, Italian, and Jewish membership did, however, cohere into an effective structure and chain of command. In New York's Lower East Side, Louis ("Lepke") Buchalter and Jacob Shapiro built a powerful entrepreneurial gang not on bootlegging but on a range of activities that included serving as mercenaries in labor disputes.[14]

Designed to make money, entrepreneurial gangs were structured to encourage members to search out new sources of revenue.[15] By the end of the 1920s that process of expansion began to affect organized labor. In Chicago, the expansion apparently came to involve labor unions around 1928. A gang of Irish Americans from the city's West Side, the Dead Shots led by George ("Red") Barker and William ("Three-Fingered Jack") White, reportedly used violence to gain influence in a series of local unions, all of which belonged to the breakaway group known as the Chicago Teamsters.[16] These locals had seceded from the national organization, the International Brotherhood of Teamsters (IBT), in 1908 and remained independent, existing side by side with IBT locals in Chicago. Somewhere along the way, probably in 1929, Barker and his gang seem to have reached an agreement with Al Capone, who reportedly offered them protection and assistance in return for a 25 percent share of their profits. By September 1930, a news report asserted that Capone and Barker planned to use the Chicago Teamster locals, which they dominated, to win control over the city's strategic Building Trades Council, a group that coordinated the various unions involved in the construction trades.[17]

Moving from the secessionist Chicago Teamsters, Capone and Barker turned their attention to the IBT in 1929. Their initial goal seems to have been limited to looting union treasuries. According to Roger Touhy, whose gang ran a bootlegging operation in the suburban Northwest area of Chicago, Capone's representatives approached him in 1929 about taking part in this activity. Touhy remembered that Capone's intermediary, Marcus ("Studdy") Looney, "brought a list of Chicago area unions . . . with the amounts of money in their treasuries." Looney showed particular interest in the IBT, noting that the local milk drivers had $1.3 million in savings and the national headquarters had $8 million. According to Touhy, "The Chicago mob planned to knock off the teamsters' locals one by one and finally to grab the treasuries." Touhy declined to take part, but he later found out that the campaign had been launched without him.[18]

Although the references are often cryptic, the national leadership of the Teamsters clearly felt themselves to be under assault. Minutes from the national organization's General Executive Board meeting on January 15, 1930, read, "One of the Vice-Presidents called the attention of the Board to the situation in Chicago where certain undesirables were endeavoring to break into our local unions. That situation was very carefully and thoroughly discussed by the General Executive Board."[19] Soon enough the undesirables reached out to the president of the Teamsters, Daniel Tobin, who apparently received several death threats in mid-February and took them very seriously.[20] In early March, Tobin wrote to a longtime colleague and friend, "The situation in Chicago is just the same, with the exception of the fact that I am not getting so many direct threats."[21]

Although Tobin escaped harm and would continue to lead the union until 1952, several other Teamster leaders did not fare so well. No complete count exists, but from 1928 to the mid-1930s at least a half-dozen local leaders in Chicago were killed and several others were seriously wounded.[22] Among those killed was Patrick Berrell, a vice president of the Teamsters Union who supervised the Chicago locals. One night in July 1932 a carload of gunmen caught Berrell as he was leaving a roadhouse and sprayed him and his bodyguard with machine-gun fire, killing them both.[23]

When Leslie Goudie replaced Berrell he received an armored car and two police bodyguards, but the union continued to be menaced. At one point in June 1933, expecting to meet a lawyer and another man, Goudie instead encountered three carloads of gunmen, one of whom pointed a machine gun in his direction and said, "You've taken Paddy Berrell's place. We want $300,000." Goudie was told to get the money from the Teamster national headquarters. A few weeks after the union refused, Henry Burger, an organizer for the national union, was ambushed one night while driving home. Burger received several gunshot wounds. One bullet lodged in his skull, while another shot shattered the kneecap of his wife, Ellen, who had been seated next to him in the car.[24]

At the same time that Teamster officials in Chicago were becoming targets, a similar sort of process seemed to be occurring in New York City. There Michael Cashal, the first vice president of the IBT, oversaw the local unions for the national office. He reported that organized crime groups had begun demanding that the IBT grant them charters to form their own local unions in particular industries. "The racketeers are getting desperate in this district," Cashal informed Tobin in June 1931:

> My job is getting real serious and dangerous one of the biggest in the game has two state charters Taxi cab drivers and Laundry Drivers and there are others looking for Charters in the Bakery line and in other lines and they are making all sorts of threats against me on account of refusing them charters, it is going to be a strenuous hard fight to keep them out, if any one writes you in reference to a charter refer him to the Joint Council and let him know they have to be [an] active worker in the craft they are seeking a charter for, I will do all in my power to keep them out, they will stop at nothing.[25]

The Complex Arrangements between Local Unions and Organized Crime

The expansion of organized crime into racketeering was often pictured as an invasion, but that metaphor tends to obscure the complexity of the change that occurred.[26] A closer look at the union's history in this period indicates that organized crime's influence tended to spread through a process more complicated than simple violent assault. The trope of invasion makes organized crime the sole agent in the change that occurred, when the reality involved a coalescence of interests. Some within the union firmly opposed making any arrangements with organized criminals. Others, for a variety of reasons, welcomed them. For their part, businessmen in particular industries also turned to gangsters for assistance. In certain settings, organized crime offered union leaders and businessmen a range of benefits. Not everyone found such arrangements palatable, and violence most often occurred to impose an unwonted consensus on such objectors. In other cases, violence stemmed not so much from an invasion by organized crime as a contest between rival groups.

In Chicago, for instance, some of the violence resulted from a conflict between gangsters in the Capone organization and a group of unionists allied to Roger Touhy. From the national headquarters, Teamster President Tobin noted that local officials, as tensions mounted in 1930, were making various arrangements with various gangsters. Writing to an associate in the spring of 1930, Tobin observed that in Chicago, "Three or four of [our] unions have associated with them very undesirable characters from the underworld. In one or two instances, as explained at the Board meeting, these people have forced themselves into the local and in other instances the local union offic-

ers were compelled to hire those kind of men for their own individual protection."[27]

Some local officials had gone to Touhy for help. Patrick Berrell, the top
Teamster official in the city, had moved his home into Touhy's territory, and
several other Teamster officials followed him. The change involved more than
just a new residence, because the officials took on some of the accoutrements
of the gangsters who had threatened them. A former member of the Bugs
Moran gang constantly accompanied Berrell, and the other Teamster leaders also brought with them a collection of well-armed bodyguards. In a way,
they became an armed camp. Even Touhy described the officials and their
entourages as a tough lot.[28]

The group came into renewed conflict with the Barker-Capone faction
over the milk industry. Local 753, the IBT's Milk Drivers' Local, had a long-
standing arrangement with a number of the city's largest dairies, which were
organized in the Pure Milk Association, to limit the amount of competition
in the Chicago milk industry. When a new dairy, the Meadowmoor Company, attempted to break into the market in 1932, Local 753 refused to provide
it with union drivers. When the company indicated that it would still enter
the market, its plant was bombed in mid-May of 1932.[29] A few days after that
bombing, Red Barker, Three-Fingered Jack White, and several of their associates visited the Milk Drivers' headquarters and explained that they would
be taking on the job of delivering Meadowmoor's milk. They spoke with
Berrell, and what exactly he told them remains a mystery.[30] Three weeks later, though, someone opened up with a machine gun from the window of a
second-floor apartment, killing Barker as he got out of his car to enter a
speakeasy he frequented. The timing of the murder suggests that it was in
response to Barker's visit to Local 753. Police later found that the apartment
where the machine gun was posted had been rented on June 7, two weeks after
the confrontation with Berrell.[31] Somewhat more incriminating was the fact
that the Teamsters were not surprised by Barker's death. A *Chicago Tribune*
reporter remembered that "an attorney for the union predicted the slaying
of Barker three hours before it occurred."[32] When Berrell was murdered a
month later, newspapers speculated that it was in revenge for Barker's death.[33]

Berrell's arrangement with Touhy illustrates some of the complexities involved in the ties between local union leaders and organized criminal groups.
Given the corruption and ineffectiveness of local police, union leaders could
expect little real protection from the law. Resistance to one gang, therefore,
might lead to a closer relationship with another. Given this access to violence,
the distinction between a union official and a gangster sometimes seemed
blurred. Organized crime had come to play a larger role in union affairs, but

union officers involved in the process were at times more than hapless victims.

The bonds between local Teamster officials and organized gangs, however, did not stem solely from fears of violence. Ambition, greed, good intentions, and pressure from employers all played a part in the arrangements that emerged. Within local unions and among employers, individuals viewed such alliances from a variety of perspectives. In cases where organized crime came to exert influence, it offered advantages that at least some in the union and among the employers found enticing. One way to understand the complex web of motives is to consider one particular case, that of Local 584, a local of milk drivers in New York City, where there exists a detailed, firsthand account of how the arrangement emerged. The case reveals how organized crime served a variety of interests.

The problems in Local 584 began with the election of a new business agent in early 1934. Following up on his campaign pledges, Charles Green initiated a campaign to organize the men who drove for the city's independent milk dealers.[34] About three hundred such dealers did business in the city, typically operating on a small scale; the largest employed about 120 people. Most of their customers were neighborhood stores.[35] Low capital requirements made it fairly easy to go into the business, and that ease of entry, in turn, assured fierce competition among dealers.[36]

The self-destructive nature of the competition had long invited attempts at collusion. In the mid-1920s Harry Danziger, an official at the city's Department of Health, had arranged an industry trade association that enforced a price schedule on dealers and barred them from stealing each others' customers. Those dealers who tried to remain independent of the association or refused to cooperate found their licenses revoked by the department.[37]

After Danziger's arrest for these activities, a former bootlegger named Larry Fay took up the same role during the late 1920s. He continued to use the Department of Health to back a collusive trade association, and in addition he fielded a team of organizers who personally convinced milk dealers and wholesalers to cooperate with his scheme. Clearly, some felt intimidated by the ex-convicts Fay employed, but many dealers acted out of self-interest. The commissioner of health noted, "Most of the dealers seem satisfied, believing that by paying from 2 to 5 cents a levy on a can [of milk] they are saving themselves several times that in profits through lack of underselling."[38]

By 1934, as Green prepared to rebuild Teamsters Local 584, previous arrangements among milk dealers temporarily had fallen apart. An indictment by the New York State Attorney General's Office had led to the dissolution of Fay's New York Milk Chain Association.[39] Fay himself was shot and killed in early 1933.[40] Meanwhile, the election of Fiorello La Guardia, a reformer, as mayor in 1933 meant that the Department of Health could not be used to enforce collusive agreements among independent milk dealers. At this point individuals who had worked with Fay apparently turned to the Teamsters Union as another device to use in policing the industry.[41] At about the same time, Green turned in the direction of Fay's old associates for help in his new organizing campaign in Local 584.

We know a great deal about the arrangements made between Green and these people thanks to the testimony of John Patrick Kennedy, who had been hired in 1934 to work as a bodyguard for Green. Later, Kennedy became a cooperating witness in New York District Attorney Thomas Dewey's investigation into racketeering in the milk industry.[42]

When Green first made contact with some of Fay's old group, he brought Kennedy along to the meetings. The leader of the group was Jacob Bernoff, a reclusive gangster from the Lower East Side who allegedly had ties to the leading racketeer of the day, Louis Buchalter. In the meetings that he attended, Kennedy remembered Bernoff making the bargain between his gang and Green explicit: "'Now,' he [Bernoff] said, 'Let's understand this. You're going to go ahead and organize the milk business. We'll give you all the help you need. Nobody is going to bother you. Any trouble comes up, we'll take care of it. We don't want any part of the milk drivers' union. That is yours. That belongs to the union. We don't want any part of the funds. We don't want anything to do with the membership. After the union is organized we are going to form an association. That is where you come in, because by that time you will have the union 100 per cent. You will have everybody in the business organized and you can do what you want with the members and with the bosses. If we have any difficulty then in inducing these people [the employers] to join the association, you will be able to put the muscle on them then." Bernoff and his people planned to make their money by corralling employers into a dues-paying organization and then siphoning off the dues money. According to Kennedy, Green agreed to these terms, stressing that he wanted no interference with the union.[43]

With the help of his new allies, Green's organizing campaign succeeded in greatly strengthening this local affiliate of the Teamsters Union. In about a year, the number of independent dealers that had bargaining contracts with the union went from twenty to 110, and membership rose from around four hundred to 2,600 drivers.[44] Local 584 became an active, forceful union that played an important role in New York's milk industry.

At the same time, Bernoff and his gang had begun to line up employers, periodically turning to Green and the union for help. In 1934 Bernoff's gang started working with a small group of dealers organized under the name Council of Independent Milk Dealers. Eventually, one of Bernoff's associates, Eddie Taylor, became president of the council. In return for a regular assessment, Taylor promised council members, he and his people would guarantee them a fair price for their milk. To enforce the group's price-fixing agreement and pressure reluctant businesses to join, Taylor and Bernoff used Green.[45] Kennedy recalled that sometime in early 1935, "Mr. Bernoff told Charlie [Green] . . . that there was a guy in Harlem, Trinity Dairy, who refused to become a member of the association. It was a real balk, and it was now time for Mr. Green to deliver some of the goods. 'After all,' Mr. Jewey— Mr. Bernoff said, 'We got everybody in the Union for you. Let us see you getting a few of these balks in the association.'" Green asked Bernoff what he wanted done. "Mr. Bernoff said, 'Go down and pull a strike.'" From time to time Bernoff called for similar action against other obstreperous dairies. Even when companies had signed a union contract and abided by its terms, Green would find a pretext for calling a damaging strike.[46] Local 584 thus became a kind of enforcement arm for Bernoff's Council of Independent Milk Dealers.

By 1935 Bernoff's gang built the Council of Independent Milk Dealers into a powerful organization of about two hundred independent dealers. Each member paid dues of one-sixth of a cent per quart of milk sold.[47] In return, the council, under the direction of Bernoff's associate, Taylor, actively policed the marketplace. Storekeepers found it impossible to switch their milk purchases from one dealer to another without first receiving approval from the council. In this way Taylor limited the cut-throat competition that plagued the milk business.[48]

Then, in August 1935, the New York State Attorney General's Office indicted Taylor and three other members of Bernoff's group on charges of operating a combination in restraint of trade. Although no convictions ever resulted from the indictment, it led to the dissolution of the Council of Independent Milk Dealers soon afterward.[49] The end of the council, however, did not curtail Bernoff's activities but rather turned them in a different direction. Kennedy remembered a meeting in 1935, after the indictment and after the council had been disbanded, when other gang members told Bernoff, "Well we can't collect no more money off the milk dealers now. There is no association." Bernoff disagreed. According to Kennedy, he said, "Who was collecting the money when the association was operating [pointing to two of his men]? Murray and Eddie was. So what is the difference now? You will still collect." When asked what would serve as the cover for demanding this money, Bernoff explained, "Well, if the Union goes down and gives them strikes and plenty of trouble, they will run to the same people as they did when the Association was there. They will run to you two, they will pay off."[50] Bernoff easily shifted from collusive organization to what seems to have been simple extortion. It remained a very profitable operation. According to the District Attorney's Office, Bernoff's gang drew in $2½ million from such payments over the next five years.[51]

Yet even after the dissolution of the council, at least some milk dealers continued to value the presence of Bernoff and his gang in the industry. In fact, those who continued to pay Bernoff did so for a variety of reasons. One motive obviously was fear. As small businessmen, the milk dealers wanted to avoid trouble in any form because they could not afford it. As one explained, "If you don't deliver the milk tonight what happens tomorrow? You are out of business aren't you?"[52] Others apparently saw the payments as something like an insurance policy that covered their dealings with the union. As Max Sacks of Eastern Farms explained, "We didn't want any labor difficulties, and it was worth while for me to obtain peace and pay for it so much per week . . . I felt that he [Bernoff's man] had sufficient influence to give me [the] peace of mind that I was looking for, and I continued to pay $75 a week."[53]

To still others, the payments ensured that Bernoff's people would be available to work for them as all-purpose adjusters. When the District Attorney's Office asked Fred Beers, an independent milk dealer in Queens, why he continued making payments, Beers sought to explain: "I don't know whether you would call it protection or what you would call it." He pointed out the precarious nature of the milk industry, in which one milk dealer would steal customers from another and the union represented a new and troublesome feature. Conducting business among a field of hard-driving competitors, Beers needed someone he could call in to straighten things out. "In our line of business there are some boys you can't talk to, and some boys you can. There are people who say, 'You can do your own straightening out,' and a lot of people who won't listen to you, when you get on the telephone they are not there, not at home." When Beers ran into such a difficult situation he turned to Bernoff's lieutenant, Eddie Taylor: "We would call Eddie up and Eddie would get on the job and things would be straightened out." Beers continued to pay Bernoff, at least in part, to take advantage of that kind of informal mediating service.[54]

While businessmen cooperated with Bernoff for a range of reasons that included both fear and self-interest, officials within Teamsters Local 584 viewed Bernoff's gang with a similar mix of emotions. Green cooperated willingly with the gang, but other members of the local's executive board strongly opposed Bernoff's influence. In particular, the local's president, Thomas O'Leary, and its vice president, Neil O'Connell, initially refused to work with the gang. Bernoff had both men assaulted, O'Connell was beaten so badly that he spent two weeks in the hospital.[55]

Bernoff usually combined a use of force with efforts at persuasion. This combination came into play when he sought to reach an agreement with Green's successors in Local 584. In 1937, apparently after his ties to Bernoff's gang became known, Green lost a local election. Two reform candidates, George Blume and John Murphy, assumed the post of business agent. After the two men shrugged off several attempts to arrange a meeting, Bernoff told Kennedy, "You go up there and you tell that Blume and Murphy that we ain't going to stall with them no more; that this is their last opportunity; that either they sit down and talk business with him or we'll knock their brains in."[56]

Blume and Murphy agreed to the meeting. Sometime in early 1938 they went to a bar at 181st Street and St. Nicholas Avenue in the Bronx, where they met Eddie Taylor, the Bernoff lieutenant who seemed to specialize in negotiation. As Kennedy, who was also there, remembered the meeting: "Eddie [Taylor] told Blume, he said, 'Now listen,' he said, 'Charlie Green worked with us for a couple of years. We got along all right. He never got in any trouble. Nobody ever bothered him. And he made himself a pile of jack. We want you to do the same thing.'" Taylor qualified this offer, however, by noting Green's recent defeat in the Local 584 election. "We have learned our lesson," he said. "We wouldn't do with you what we did with Charlie. We put Charlie on the spot too much. And everybody got smart he was working with us. You work with us and nobody will know about it. Do what you got to do. Take care of your barns; take care of working conditions and wages. And from time to time we will ask you to do us favors. What we do don't mean anything to you. You aren't going to meet anybody. You be happy and we will be happy."[57]

Having heard Bernoff's offer as conveyed by Taylor, the two new union officers agreed to "work along with him." According to Kennedy, they wanted it understood that they "wouldn't do anything that was against the rules of the [Teamster] organization." They would cooperate only so long as it was "for the general good and welfare of the men and the people in the industry." Finally, Blume asked what Taylor's interest in the milk business was. Kennedy remembers Bernoff's lieutenant replying, "We just like to see everybody get along." In the end, the two men received $50 a week from Bernoff, and eventually they pulled strikes against companies when he sent them word to do so.[58]

Their cooperation, and the appeal Bernoff used to win it, demonstrates the flexible nature of the ties between organized criminal gangs and union officials. The threat of violence remained an ever-present possibility, but Bernoff, and presumably other gangsters in similar situations, also found more positive inducements useful. They could claim to have no intention of marring the integrity of the union; they would only seek money from employers for managing the industry. They could therefore assure a union official that his cooperation in no way constituted a betrayal of the membership's trust. Union officials such as Blume and Murphy, however, presumably based their decision to cooperate on a fairly complex set of motives. For them, fear mixed with greed, and both combined with an acceptance that this was how things worked. Perhaps Blume and Murphy even believed that Bernoff and his men really did help the industry get along. Clearly, some businessmen did.

The economic environment of small milk dealers offered Bernoff a credible role to play and made it more likely that both union officials and businessmen would cooperate with him. If an industry contained a sizable number of small-scale entrepreneurs who operated on narrow profit margins, then those businesses were vulnerable in a number of ways. New competitors, lost customers, and even a brief disruption in their operations could prove fatal to their enterprise. Anyone offering some measure of security against such dangers, or at least a way to deal with them, provided a much-needed service. Gangsters like Bernoff were, in effect, dependable brokers. In situations where the legal system offered little security, organized crime provided regulatory and mediation services—what some have come to call licensing.[59] Regular payments of protection money thus stemmed in part from the vulnerability of these firms, and businessmen also paid in order to gain access to the services organized crime provided.

Bernoff's brokerage services, although often unwanted, offered union officials advantages as well. As an intermediary, he made it unnecessary for them to meet personally with employers who sought some extra-legal arrangement, and he saved them from having to decide whom to trust. If they took money from him, they could depend on him not to turn them in and to offer them a measure of assistance and protection as well. All of this came in addition to the fact that his relationship to the industry offered a convenient rationalization for working with him and accepting money. Not everyone participated willingly in these arrangements. Force played a constant underlying role but so, too, did a sense of self-interest on the part of businessmen and union officials.

In New York, organized crime played a similar role in sectors of the economy that resembled the world of small milk dealers. Collusion and extortion were endemic in the Garment District; in the city's markets where dealers in fish, poultry, vegetables, and fruit operated; and in restaurants, cafeterias, bakeries, and the ice delivery business as well as among construction subcon-tractors and dry cleaners. By the 1930s those practices usually fell under the control of organized gangs. Like the milk industry, sections of these indus-tries contained networks of comparatively small and vulnerable operations that conducted business in a highly competitive atmosphere where collusion could bring some stability. The same factors that made such businesses wel-come collusion also made it more difficult for them to resist extortion. Unions with jurisdiction in these industries often played a part in stabilizing them, and often a gang leader would coordinate the process and use that same in-fluence to levy protection money. Essentially, such arrangements constitut-ed the heart of what was referred to as "racketeering."

Because of the strategic role of trucking in these enterprises, Teamster locals often provided the most effective leverage with which to regulate or exploit an industry. Thus Teamster locals often figured in the corruption scandals that broke during the 1930s when New York's crusading prosecutor Thomas Dewey attacked the problem of racketeering. Dewey assumed the post of special prosecutor in 1935 and then, drawing on his highly publicized successes, won election to the New York County District Attorney's office in 1937. Investigating rackets in a number of industries, his office came to fo-cus on how gangsters used particular unions to further their schemes. Local affiliates of the Painters, the Hotel and Restaurant Workers, the Amalgam-ated Meat Cutters, and the Retail Clerks all figured in the prosecutions, but local Teamster affiliates predominated. By the early 1940s, Dewey's prosecu-tors had proven that organized crime had used five Teamster locals in New York City—Locals 138, 167, 202, 240, and 584—to further criminal schemes.[60] Although less thoroughly investigated, the Teamsters Union in Chicago ap-parently suffered a similar proportion of involvement in such activities.[61]

Critics then and later noticed the coincidence of racketeering and Team-ster locals often appearing in the same industries and blamed the national union's leadership and its conservative philosophy of business unionism.[62] As one put it, "Uncle Dan [Tobin] fundamentally doesn't care who runs the locals, so long as they take orders and fork over to the International trea-sury."[63] But criticism linking Tobin's conservatism to the infiltration of rack-eteers is unfair. In cases where more progressive unionists faced the same economic environment as Tobin they enjoyed no greater success in keeping out organized crime. Tobin's shortcomings, for instance, might well be mea-sured against those of David Dubinsky, head of the International Ladies Garment Workers' Union (ILGWU). A paragon of progressive industrial unionism, Dubinsky never found a solution to racketeer involvement in New York's Garment Center. Like Tobin, he remained unable or unwilling to clean up the most notorious of local unions. In 1932 the ILGWU chartered its own local union of truckers, Local 102, whose members drove garment pieces to the various shops. By the 1940s, that local had clearly come under the control of organized crime. Dubinsky, however, never actively involved the national union in reforming Local 102. As he explained, his national union stayed out because they were "convinced that any ILGWU official sent in to reform the local would be murdered."[64] It seems unlikely that Dubinsky's reputation would have fared any better than Tobin's had he presided over a national union of many trucking locals caught in the same environment as Local 102.

Sidney Hillman, head of the Amalgamated Clothing Workers of America (ACWA), also had a reputation for progressive, industrial or social unionism, and yet he, too, failed to eliminate organized crime's influence in the New York City locals of his union. Steven Fraser has reviewed allegations that Hillman had reached some sort of working understanding with Louis Buchalter, the notorious Garment Center racketeer. Although Fraser discounts any personal arrangement between the two men, he concludes that Hillman either allowed or chose to overlook Buchalter's use of the ACWA's Cutters' Local to extort payments from garment manufacturers. Throughout the 1930s the ACWA Joint Board in New York also made regular payments to Buchalter's henchmen, money that in all probability made its way eventually to Buchalter. "It seems probable," Fraser concludes, "that Hillman behaved like a great many other trade unionists facing the reality of highly fragmented, decentralized industries like trucking, longshore, and garment manufacturing as well as numerous branches of distribution and retailing."[65] In other words, the progressivism of Hillman, like that of Dubinsky, did not change the difficulties that either man faced in keeping organized crime out of local affiliates in particular settings. Conversely, the conservative attitude of Tobin does not explain the pockets of collusion and corruption that existed in the Teamsters Union during this period.

The Varied Uses and Meanings of Racketeering

Structuralists have been right to offer an economic explanation for the Teamsters' recurring problem with corruption. Understanding the union's notoriety on this issue, however, involves looking beyond the phenomenon of collusive business environments. The sense of crisis that emerged during the 1930s did not stem simply from an increased number of criminal conspiracies. Concerns about the spread of racketeering often reflected a broader sense of anxiety linked to the economic turmoil of the Great Depression. Warnings about racketeering, which proliferated during the era, were also instrumental. In a time of great union growth, a widely drawn definition of racketeering justified efforts to pull back some of the new legal rights won by labor unions.

Although the collusive practices that formed the heart of racketeering occurred only in particular economic settings, warnings about the dangerous spread of racketeering pictured an unstoppable process that threatened to engulf the larger economy. An article in the *Saturday Evening Post* in 1931 asserted that racketeers were "muscling in, finding ways to cut into the profits of every form of legitimate trade."[66] Several writers referred to a coordinated military campaign whose final objective apparently would be the conquest of the national economy.[67] In 1933 Frank Dalton O'Sullivan, in his book *Enemies of Industry,* took the image of a coordinated campaign to perhaps its most hyperbolic length by referring to a nationwide "criminal army" made up of "a million criminals at liberty in the field" who were "scientifically officered," "well disciplined," and under the overall leadership of a "General Big-Shot [who] is in supreme command." The four hundred thousand convicts behind prison walls were, according to O'Sullivan, better understood as "prisoners of war."[68]

The scale, imagery, and language of these warnings share some characteristics of a moral panic.[69] Real changes in organized crime had occurred and crime rates had risen, but the scale of those developments did not measure up to the all-encompassing threat that was frequently pictured. Warnings about racketeering often seemed to reflect a host of insecurities unrelated to specific acts of extortion.[70] Authors described a process of infiltration that had delivered economic power to unseen and largely unknown forces. In an article entitled "Invisible Government: What Racketeering Costs the Home" published in 1931 in the *Ladies Home Journal,* Samuel Crowther asserted, "We now have in every large city in this country a dual system of government." He explained that "hiding behind the ordinary form of government, is a distinct and separate government which promulgates its own laws and levies in the most effective manner a system of taxation that reaches into every pocketbook." As Crowther saw it, "the invisible government" could levy this tax because it exercised "illegal control of almost every variety of business in every large city in the country."[71] The recurrence of the phrase *invisible government* highlighted the fear that unseen powers had assumed control.

Racketeers presented Americans with an insidious threat that furnished an explanation for the lawlessness and disorder of urban America in the 1920s and then later provided a simple rationale for the economic crisis of the Great Depression. An unseen army of racketeers offered a clear, socially acceptable set of villains in a time of frustration and confusion. As villains they often resembled the stock characters of another period of frustration and anxiety, the Red Scare of the 1950s, when many Americans searched for an explanation for cold war reverses. Racketeers and communists were both considered internal threats, and they both allegedly practiced conspiracy and deception. Communists purportedly coordinated a nationwide conspiracy and yet remained unseen, often, it was warned, blending in so well that they could be next door neighbors.[72] For their part, racketeers, it was claimed, had accomplished a similar process of infiltration. In their book *It's a Racket* (1929), Gordon Hostetter and Thomas Beesley explained, "So far as externals go, the successful racket and racketeer are camouflaged into an appearance of complete respectability."[73] As one judge put it, "They appear just like other people."[74] A journalist asserted that a racketeer could "preserve an aura of respectability, which, combined with secret strong arm power can get him places fraternally, or even socially and politically."[75]

By 1931 this covert growth had, according to New York state's attorney general, allowed racketeering to become "the greatest evil in the present American economic structure."[76] If not a cause of the economic depression, racketeering was certainly depicted as a barrier to recovery.[77] Cataclysmic warnings about racketeering, in fact, offered a variety of readings that in different ways addressed a number of broader social anxieties, including recurring fears about moral decline in America.[78]

In a time of great economic turmoil, denunciations of a newly discovered economic criminal provided an easily agreed upon target upon which to vent accumulating frustrations and fears. In this way publicity about racketeers revealed some of the deeper anxieties Americans felt during the Great Depression. Concerns about racketeering grew in a way that was out of proportion to the actual scale and extent of the crime.

From the perspective of the Teamsters Union, that meant the charge of racketeering, often made almost casually in the vituperative world of labor relations, resulted in the virtually irrefutable suggestion of guilt in the public's mind.[79] In 1932, when Frank Hague, the mayor of Jersey City, became embroiled in a dispute with a local Teamster official and labeled him a "racketeer," the union saw no way to repair its reputation. Daniel Tobin wrote to another official, "That word smells so bad to the uninformed mind and the business world that it does not take much for them to decide that perhaps President Tobin knows all about what is going on and is doing little to prevent it."[80]

As that incident illustrates, concerns about racketeering could also be used instrumentally. In fact, they were often harnessed to denunciations of the growing size and power of the labor movement during the 1930s. Aided by legislation, a more sympathetic government at the national (and often state and local levels), and by a strong wave of local militancy, American workers joined unions in huge numbers during that decade. From 1930 to 1940 the percentage of the nonagricultural workforce enrolled in unions increased from 11.6 percent to 26.9 percent.[81] The Teamsters Union itself went from a membership of ninety thousand in 1930 to more than half a million by 1940.[82] The National Labor Relations Act of 1935 (the "Wagner Act") offered legal protection for the right to join unions and bargain collectively, thus ensuring that the increase in union membership would survive the often short-lived episodes of rank-and-file militancy. But the rebirth of organized labor brought with it concerns generally about the power of unions, in particular the misuse of that power by union leaders.[83] A poll taken in the spring of 1941 revealed that 75 percent of Americans believed that "there is too much power in the hands of the leaders of labor unions in this country." By comparison, only 59 percent responded yes to the question, "Do you think there is too much power in the hands of a few rich men and large corporations in the United States?" Fear of the concentration of power in the hands of the federal government lagged even farther behind, with only a third of all respondents voicing such a concern.[84]

Not surprisingly, many who wrote on the subject of labor racketeering expressed deep skepticism about the trustworthiness of union leaders. Sometimes the attitudes of those authors can be traced to a background in conservative politics and anti-union activism. For instance, Gordon Hostetter had served as executive secretary of the Employers' Association of Chicago, a group formed early in the century to combat the growth of labor unions.[85] Westbrook Pegler, who wrote a widely syndicated daily newspaper column and specialized in labor racketeering, had strong connections to the larger conservative alliance against the New Deal.[86] But conservatives held no monopoly over the issue. Critics on the left also expressed distrust of what they viewed as the conservative and irresponsible leadership of the AFL and occasionally chose to do so through exposés of labor racketeering. In *Misleaders of Labor* (1927), William Z. Foster, a member of the Communist Party, profiled instances of labor corruption as part of a denunciation of the AFL's narrow emphasis on business unionism.[87] A decade later Harold Seidman made the same connections in *Labor Czars* as part of an argument in favor of the CIO.[88]

As a politicized word, racketeering could, like corruption, be mobilized for a variety of purposes, one of which was to offer a critique of the expanding role of organized labor. In practice, many who wrote about racketeering tended to blend complaints about organized crime, extortion, and the legal but often burdensome organizing tactics and collective bargaining agreements of organized labor. In *Labor Unions and the Public* (1936), Walter Chambers smoothly shifted from extortion charges made against labor leaders in New York City's poultry and fish markets to complaining about the organizing tactics (involving secondary boycotts, which were job actions against one employer in order to pressure another one) used by the Longshoremen and the Teamsters Union on the city's docks.[89] In *This Labor Union Racket* (1936), Edward Dean Sullivan moved from a review of criminal conspiracy cases to descriptions of union strikes called in order to achieve a closed-shop agreement and then to efforts to have union dues deducted from employees' paychecks. For Sullivan, both of the latter practices amounted to a kind of racketeering. Indeed, he compared the dues check-off system to requiring an employer to make a payoff.[90] In addition to that sort of blending, *It's a Racket* by Hostetter and Beesley also equated labor unionism and racketeering in a more picturesque way through a "Glossary of Hoodlum Language." There, next to "bazoo," "score," and "torpedo," were "B.A.—[union] business agent" and "strike"—as in "the B.A. struck the Laundry Works."[91]

Racketeering had become, for some at least, a word that included legal but unpalatable activities on the part of organized labor. In *Gang Rule in New York* (1940) Craig Thompson and Allen Raymond assert, "The industrial racket, indeed, has to some degree been brought close to the line of legality by continuous refinement, and labor legislation which permits secondary picketing and boycotts. Some rackets have been brought over the line of legality."[92] The expansion of labor's legal rights during the 1930s, according to this view, accounted for the rise of racketeering. Because of the newly passed Wagner Act, one critic observed that "capital lies prostrate at the feet of labor, compelled to pass on to The Public any and all exactions from industry which labor, in its might, feels called upon to levy."[93]

The image of a tyrannical labor movement runs through much of the writing about racketeering. Describing the irresponsible "philosophy of a considerable number of present day labor union leaders," Hostetter and Beesley warned that the unions had become "a vehicle upon which the leader may ride to a tyrannical power which a *Caesar* might envy."[94] Sullivan charged that "labor leaders have been given such a free hand in organizing the employees of industry and are so well protected by legislation, that the irresponsible ones assume power never for an instant intended by law, in an effort to increase the membership and swell the funds of local unions. Where an individual labor leader—and it very often happens that he has a criminal record—is able to tie up completely not one but several industries, he wields a power which obviously should be given only to a man of excellent character." The "racketeer union bosses" whom Sullivan described as running America's labor movement clearly could not be trusted with such power.[95] In this way, the term *racketeering* referred to a form of corruption, and corruption in that sense described not just a betrayal of trust but the irresponsible use of a newly created, tyrannical power.

Given the strategic role of trucking, the Teamsters Union became a prominent target of these warnings. A *Fortune Magazine* article written in 1941 reminded readers that "in most parts of the U.S. the Teamsters' has a stranglehold on all truck-borne commerce"; it was, therefore, "the most powerful labor organization in the United States." The article referred to rumors and accusations of racketeering and also to the union's aggressive picketing tactics, use of secondary boycotts, and sympathy strikes. Citing Tobin's failure to "curb some of the abuses of Teamsters' power," *Fortune* depicted him as an irresponsible monarch "seated on a throne of what amounts to a state within a state . . . he displays little sense of public responsibility, little of the quality of *noblesse oblige* expected nowadays of those occupying positions of great power."[96] Sullivan singled out the Teamsters for their ability to shut down an entire city. "It has been figured out recently in Chicago," he wrote, "that racket leadership of 20,338 men in the janitors, milk drivers, coal teamsters and handlers and garbage haulers—could, under hoodlum domination—completely paralyze that city with its population of 3,475,000."[97] Corruption, in a sense, described the overturning of the accepted order, replaced here by one in which a powerful union apparently unrestrained by law or adequate notions of propriety had the authority to stop the wheels of commerce.

In his attacks on union corruption, the daily columnist Westbrook Pegler exemplified many of these themes. Pegler had begun writing frequently on organized labor in 1937 when he warned against the lawlessness and disorder that stemmed from CIO organizing activities such as the sit-down strikes.[98] By 1939 he denounced unions for rampant corruption, and in 1940 he described the AFL as "a great, arrogant, corrupt, hypocritical, parasitic racket which preys on union men and the public, and persecutes nonmembers and has been getting away with many varieties and all degrees of crime, up to and including murder, for years."[99] He spotlighted cases in which individuals who had ties to organized crime had gained leadership posts in specific unions. But in listing the various aspects of corruption in organized labor Pegler invariably included collective bargaining issues he found objectionable. Thus, for instance, he depicted mandatory dues for union members as a kind of extortion and graft. The four million members of the AFL, he wrote, were "not allowed to work, except if they pay private graft to individual racketeers holding the extortion privilege." Unions that required nonmembers to acquire a work permit for a specific job engaged in "a private racket."[100] Closed-shop agreements reduced "thousands of nominally free Americans to the status of subhuman robots who pay tribute to brigands for the rights to toil."[101] Unions in general, Pegler argued, had assumed the powers of a "supergovernment," but the Teamsters in particular held "the peculiar power . . . to strangle a community."[102] The union's ability to shut off commerce during a strike alarmed Pegler, and he viewed such strike activity as a corruption of the normal and proper order. Commenting on a particular strike, he wrote, "The Teamsters in Pittsburgh, as elsewhere, enjoy a special privilege to slug, burn and deny the use of the public streets and highways to citizens who pay taxes for their maintenance and for the salaries of the cops." Focusing still on the strike in Pittsburgh, Pegler claimed that the public had come to accept "that the Teamsters are a law unto themselves and that their charter, from Mr. Tobin's international headquarters in Indianapolis, amounts to a license to commit crime."[103]

Pegler argued that the problems he described all stemmed from the legal changes wrought by the Wagner Act. He denounced the law in his usual strident manner, writing at one point, "I say the Labor Relations [Wagner] Act was a subtle conspiracy against the right of free American citizens to work at their lawful occupations unmolested by terrorists of the Communistic C.I.O. or extortionists of the A.F. of L. or anyone else."[104] He regularly called for new legislation that would amend the act.[105]

Although his language might seem extreme, Pegler's views carried a great deal of weight. In 1940 his column appeared five times a week in 114 newspapers across the country. A poll of newspaper editors ranked him as the nation's "best adult columnist," and in 1941 he won the Pulitzer Prize for his columns on corruption in organized labor.[106]

Redefining the meaning of the words *racketeering* and *corruption* in this way carried policy implications. Union members and officials not involved in organized crime but engaged in aggressive organizing tactics found themselves legally charged with racketeering. The most important instance of that occurred in New York City, where sixty-two members of Teamster Local 807 were indicted in 1938 under the 1934 federal antiracketeering statute. As the U.S. Attorney's Office saw it, these men had become racketeers by stopping out-of-town trucks and demanding that they use a local union man for in-town deliveries and loading work. Non-union trucking companies were required to sign a collective bargaining agreement with Local 807 or else the union men at freight terminals would refuse to handle their goods. Companies unwilling to use the services of a local union man were still required to pay a day's wage of $9.42 to the man the union supplied. Because such tactics often went hand in hand with physical force or threats of bodily harm, they frequently involved the same kinds of legal violations common among most picket-line disputes. To the Justice Department, however, these demands represented a form of extortion practiced by a union racket. Deploying the term *racketeering* in this way, the department escalated the practice from a run-of-the-mill legal violation to a more serious threat, a case of organized crime.[107]

Local 807's indictment came as part of a broad offensive aimed at using federal antiracketeering statutes and criminal antitrust provisions to curb the power of organized labor. Thurman Arnold, head of the Justice Department's Antitrust Division in the late 1930s, explained that he intended to use federal prosecutions to stop unions from wielding the rights granted by the Wagner Act for "illegitimate purposes." For Arnold, illegitimate and anticompetitive were essentially the same thing. He cited union tactics that harmed "the interests of consumers" and those that opposed "the interests of efficiency." Among the specific practices he described as illegitimate were union efforts to "compel the hiring of useless or unnecessary labor" or attempts to limit the use of "cheaper material, improved equipment, or more efficient methods." He explained that the pursuit of those sorts of goals constituted corruption, and "corruption in unions has become notorious." Then, continuing his thought, he wrote, "The corruption itself was, I think, an incident of allowing a legitimate organization to be used for illegitimate purposes." Combating corruption involved strategically conducting federal prosecutions to prevent "the illegitimate use of organized power."[108] In this way, collective bargaining practices that stood in the way of business efficiency or raised costs to consumers became a form of corruption. Union leaders and members who pursued such goals found themselves labeled racketeers and charged as such.

For their part, Teamster members and officials did not see the issue of racketeering or the related concept of corruption in the same light as Arnold or the union's critics. That does not mean they viewed either word as meaningless or that as a group Teamsters condoned corruption. In general, corruption within the union involved acts that betrayed the interests of the membership. The term *racketeering* referred to conspiracies to turn the union into a profit-making enterprise for outside parties at the expense of members. If pursued for the sake of the membership, practices that the U.S. legal system defined as criminal would not necessarily be adjudged within the union as corrupt, although they might be seen as tactically unwise.

The case of Local 807 highlights the differences in perspective. A federal judge agreed with Arnold's view of corruption in this case, and when a jury found the members of the local guilty of racketeering in 1940 the judge sentenced twenty-six of them to jail.[109] Within the union, however, a very different view held sway. With as many as three thousand Local 807 members either unemployed or working only part time in the mid-1930s, the membership had overwhelmingly endorsed the organizing tactics that had begun in 1936 and later brought a federal prosecution.[110] Members who obtained work thanks to this organizing campaign did not see it as a "racket." James Gaughan, for instance, a rank-and-file member, testified at the trial that in 1937 he had gotten a job with a company based in Millville, New Jersey, thanks to the pressure applied by the union. He certainly seemed to give the company a fair day's work for his pay. On a typical workday, he and a partner took ten to fifteen tons of freight into New York City and made deliveries, starting at 8 in the morning and unloading between two and three truckloads by 5 in the evening. He was on call every day except Sunday but usually worked only three days, earning about $35 a week.[111] As Marie Magan, the wife of another driver put it, "They say it's a racket charge. Well, I sure don't know what they call a racket. If they think that $9.42 a day is a lot of money, they ought to see how many days he gets it."[112] Her husband Manuel and Gaughan were both convicted at the trial.[113]

At the Teamster headquarters, President Tobin took a more ambivalent stand on the case. He expressed understanding for why the local leadership had acted as they did, and he condemned the prosecution for serving the purposes of anti-union employers. As a practical matter he also warned that local unions should obey the law; otherwise they risked tangling with the federal government, a result that could only harm the organization. "Therefore," Tobin said, "we ask our union representatives, no matter how strong the pressure is from the fellow down on the floor who is not working, to observe the laws. Better you lose your prestige within the union than find yourself in the clutches of the Federal Government."[114]

Tobin was equally ambivalent on the issue of collusion between employers and local unions. He acknowledged that employers who cut rates to steal competitors' business constituted a menace to the long-term health of an industry and thus eventually to the conditions won by a local union. But, he warned, efforts to restrain such competition by having the union strike against rate-cutters violated conspiracy and antitrust laws. As he explained, "No local union has the right to enter into any agreement with employers' associations with whom they are doing business that they will not work for an employer in the same business who cuts the price of his manufactured or delivered products." Local officials who went ahead and made such agreements were violating the law, and when they got in trouble they would have only themselves to blame.[115]

Yet the matter had never been that simple. Although he might not personally promote collusive agreements with employers, Tobin had long known that they existed. In practice, such agreements often stabilized an industry and in turn allowed a local union to win better wages and maintain superior working conditions. Passing over the role that collusion played in those gains, Tobin publicized the achievements of such locals and held them up as models of what others could achieve. Thus, for example, he repeatedly praised Local 753, the Milk Drivers of Chicago: "If the men of the Labor Movement today do not realize the benefits of a union, let them look into the conditions of these men."[116] All the while Tobin well knew that Local 753 maintained an agreement with its employers to enforce a standard milk price and bar new competitors.[117]

For their part, local union leaders frequently grasped at collusive agreements as their best hope of overcoming the fierce resistance to union organization that small operators often mounted. Laundry and dry-cleaning businesses, for instance, fought tenaciously against allowing a new local even the smallest of toeholds.[118] To defuse such hostility the leaders of new locals found it worth their while to offer these small businesses some advantage in return for signing with the union. In Milwaukee, efforts to organize laundry drivers had sputtered along unsuccessfully since 1933. Finally, in 1937, after a bitter, two-month-long strike, the organizers of the Laundry and Dry Cleaning Drivers, Local 360, convinced the twenty-five members of the Milwaukee Laundry Association to sign a collective bargaining agreement.

But the local remained on shaky ground. Employers maintained an open shop and favored non-union drivers. Some businesses created their own company unions and began pitting these organizations against Local 360.[119] Casting about for greater support, the local union's leaders instituted a "resolution" that regulated the prices that local members who worked for dry cleaners could charge. The union would control competition among dry cleaners because doing so gave employers a stake in nourishing the new local. Alois Mueller, Local 360's secretary-treasurer, pointed out to the head of the dry cleaners' association, "This resolution is of hardly any benefit to an organization if the industry is not controlled by the whole [i.e., closed-] shop agreement."[120] A collusive agreement gave employers a reason to want a strong union.

To critics, these kinds of arrangements constituted racketeering, but within the union the issue tended to be cloudier. The contrast in perspective at times surfaced quite clearly. When John G. Clay, who led Chicago Laundry Drivers Local 712, was murdered in 1928, the *Chicago Tribune*'s headline read "Slay Racket Boss at Desk." The newspaper's story described him as the "chief figure among the racketeers in the clothes cleaning industry."[121] Union officials objected to the newspaper's characterization. They did not deny that Clay had taken part in a long-term conspiracy to control competition in the city's dry cleaning industry, but, they emphasized, his actions had benefited the local's members and not himself. Tobin described Clay as "one of the best and most loyal men connected with our organization, always faithful and serving his people with loyalty unequaled in the history of our organization." As proof of this honesty and loyalty, Tobin noted the sizable amount of money held in Local 712's treasury. A less-scrupulous leader would have drained the money to enrich himself, and there lay the distinction between Clay and a racketeer.[122] Edward N. Nockels, secretary of the Chicago Federation of Labor, explained, "Racketeers don't leave any money in the treasury of any organization with which they are connected."[123] Clay might have violated the law, but he had not betrayed his membership. For that reason, in the eyes of the union, he was neither a racketeer nor corrupt. From their perspective, a distinction existed between collusion and racketeering.

Conclusion

In spite of their conservative ideology, their commitment to business unionism, Teamsters did not behave with the indifference ascribed to them by many critics. But in confronting the problem of corruption during the 1930s the Teamsters Union faced a number of dilemmas. Its jurisdiction often covered business environments that were conducive to various forms of collusion and extortion. During the late 1920s and early 1930s emerging organized crime groups exacerbated the problem. Drawing on their expertise in violence and their ability to adjudicate extra-legal disputes, gangsters came to place themselves in positions of authority in already troubled business environments. To achieve that status, they combined force as well as persuasion in appealing to vulnerable local union officers. Operating a union in such sectors involved coming to terms with organized crime's role. As structuralists have argued, all unions that sought to operate in those particular sectors of the economy confronted this dilemma, and none achieved a satisfactory solution.

For the Teamsters, however, the problem of racketeering assumed even more troubling proportions during the 1930s because of the heightened nature of public concern about the issue. In some ways the attention focused on racketeering reflected the broad social anxieties engendered by the eco-

nomic turmoil of the Great Depression. In other ways, racketeering provided a rhetorical weapon to be used against the growing power of organized
labor. Given the Teamsters' strategic role in the transportation industry, the
union often became a target of this conservative campaign.

Finally, a distinction existed between what union members and leaders saw
as corrupt and what others in American society labeled as racketeering. As a
more aggressive federal government began prosecuting locals on charges of
racketeering and conspiracy to violate antitrust laws, Tobin urged Teamster
locals to ignore tradition and sentiment and adhere to the letter of the law.
At the local level, however, officials faced the unpalatable task of defying the
membership's wishes and doing without useful organizing strategies. It was
the combination of all of these factors that made corruption both notorious
and intractable in the Teamsters.

6. The Possibilities and Limitations of Union Reform during the 1930s

The public attention focused on the problem of labor racketeering during the 1930s not only created problems for the labor movement but it also afforded real opportunities for reform. The attention spurred action by law enforcement agencies and prompted union officials to adopt remedial measures. Even to the extent that denunciations of racketeering masked anti-union sentiments, union leaders still recognized the need to respond to the legitimate problems being spotlighted. Failure to do so would only validate the critics who pictured all of organized labor as riddled with corruption. Nor can one dismiss all of the era's investigations and prosecutions of racketeering as camouflage for union-busting. At times, reenergized law enforcement agencies hoped to embolden honest union leaders to clean up their organizations and offered practical assistance in that endeavor.

That kind of reform campaign seemed to have the greatest potential for success in New York City. Thomas Dewey became special prosecutor there in 1935 with a mandate to attack organized crime in the shape of municipal corruption and racketeering. Scoring a series of impressive court victories, Dewey won election to the New York County District Attorney's Office in 1937 and continued his vigorous campaign until he left that office at the end of 1941. He prosecuted union leaders for extortion and embezzlement and pursued such organized crime figures as Louis Buchalter who used labor organizations for criminal purposes. A moderate Republican with vast political ambitions, Dewey could not be described as a champion of organized labor. In general, however, he avoided using his office to attack labor unions for the sorts of organizing and collective bargaining practices that—although annoying to many employers—had nothing to do with organized crime. In return, he enjoyed political support from New York's unions.[1] Dewey's concern not to antagonize unions reflected the generally pro-labor atmosphere of New York City during the 1930s. Mayor Fiorello La Guardia, elected as a reformer in 1933, strongly supported the city's labor movement.[2]

Given that political environment, Dewey's antiracketeering campaign offered genuine opportunity for reform. By the early 1940s his staff had won convictions against a number of important criminal figures, men such as Buchalter, Jacob Bernoff, and Joseph ("Socks") Lanza whose threatening presence had cast a pall over the city's labor scene. "The plunderers have been driven from the city," Dewey proclaimed exuberantly in 1937. With their removal, he assumed, the newly free union membership would keep their organizations clean. "Any gangster who tries to get into a labor union in New York City," he asserted, "now will be thrown out by the members before the D.A. has time to act."[3] Dewey's assumption was common to that of most law enforcement efforts in this area. Removal of the threatening presence of organized crime figures would allow union members to police their own organizations through internal democratic procedures. In plain words, they could toss the rascals out.

The Teamsters Union provided a useful test case for this assumption. Organized crime figures had dominated several of its New York affiliates, but important elements within the union, including the national headquarters, had continued to champion the cause of reform. The general president, Daniel Tobin, wore his reputation for honesty like some gaudy sports jacket, frequently proclaiming his unwillingness to accept criminality anywhere within the organization. At the local level a rank-and-file reform movement emerged among the city's locals and sponsored a series of insurgent electoral campaigns aimed at ousting disreputable and dishonest leaders. For these reformers, Dewey's campaign offered assistance. Prosecutors exposed dishonest leaders and put dangerous gangsters in jail. The national leadership could step into the resulting power vacuum and employ remedial measures as local reformers rode into office on the votes of an indignant, newly empowered membership.

Sometimes such a scenario did occur, but in general the results of union reform failed to measure up to Dewey's idyllic pronouncement. National leaders as well as local members worked for reform during the 1930s, but practical constraints hamstrung their efforts. In confronting a corrupt local, national leaders had limited options, none of which could solve the underlying forces that tended to spur recurring collusion and criminality. At the local level, reform movements faced obstacles that stacked the deck against electoral campaigns in particular local unions. These problems did not eliminate all possibility of reform, but they did limit what could be achieved. In the end, those constraints, not lack of personal courage or dedication, limited the union's ability to seize the opportunity for reform during the 1930s.

Fighting Corruption from the National Headquarters

Writing about the ties that emerged during the 1930s between organized crime and labor unions, historian Stephen Fox has indicted the national leadership of the American Federation of Labor (AFL). He lavishes particular scorn on Tobin and Joseph Ryan, head of the International Longshoremen's Association (ILA). "During their entrenched, less than vigorous reigns," Fox maintains, "gangsters moved into most of the important locals of both unions. Meantime Ryan and Tobin were all noise and bluster, puffing up and down on the captain's deck, overtly ignorant of conditions down in steerage."[4]

The image of an indifferent Tobin who apparently had fallen asleep at the switch predominates in most descriptions of the Teamsters during this era. He did very little, these accounts suggest, but talk. In their book on Hoffa, Ralph C. James and Estelle Dinnerstein James assert that "Tobin confined himself to pouring forth paternalistic advice in the International's monthly magazine." In a footnote, they blandly comment, "Actually, Tobin did not try very hard to deal with racketeering in the union."[5] *Fortune Magazine* in 1940 assured readers that although Tobin talked about fighting racketeering, his words amounted to no more than cynical, if long-winded, posturing. The article noted Tobin's active anticommunism and continued, "But he seldom moves against a local with a racketeer reputation unless its leaders have been hauled into courts—and sometimes he fails to act even then."[6]

These criticisms have some merit, but overall they do the union's leadership an injustice. It must be acknowledged that the national leadership's efforts to deal with corruption in the New York locals produced few clear-cut victories. Tobin was something of a blowhard, and the union did wait to move on certain locals until after the courts had exposed corruption in them. Yet for all of that, the national leadership did constitute a force for reform. Across time, Tobin and his colleagues persistently tried to police local unions, at times making tough political decisions in the interest of reform. During the 1930s they opposed racketeering as they understood the term and kept watch on local conditions to guard against the infiltration of organized crime. In doing so they withstood threats and intimidation. Confronted by the intractable presence of a criminal gang based in a particular economic locale and frequently complicit employers, the national leadership wielded what powers it had available to clean up local unions. The fact that it often failed says less about its intentions than about the nature of the problem it faced.

Tobin frequently stressed the importance of having a reputation for honesty. By the 1930s that message constituted a rhetorical staple of his monthly entries in the Teamsters' *Official Magazine*. A typical admonition in 1937 read, "BE A MAN! That means that no matter how poor you are, you can be clean and honest and honorable."[7] For his part, Tobin jealously guarded his personal reputation for honesty. He asked the union's lawyers to investigate filing a libel suit against Harold Seidman, who in *Labor Czars* (1938) had blamed Tobin for the Teamsters' problem with racketeering.[8] When Westbrook Pegler published a scathing column on the Teamsters, Tobin immediately wrote to the columnist in defense of his honor. In careful, patient prose that covered eight pages of single-spaced type, Tobin urged the anti-union journalist to reconsider the charges he had made. He reminded Pegler of the benefits brought by the union to its members and its efforts to address criminal activity within its ranks. Summing up his argument, Tobin wrote, "There is, unfortunately, room for improvement in every vocation in life, and undoubtedly that speaks for the position that I hold. But there is one thing that I cannot be charged with and proven guilty; and that is that I have ever closed my eyes on wrongdoing within the [Teamster] organization."[9]

This was more than just a public relations campaign. The national organization did have a real and historic commitment to reform, one often overlooked. Although he perhaps reminded people too often of that fact, Tobin had been elected in 1907 as part of a reform campaign within the union. The record shows that he took that campaign seriously. In 1915, for instance, eight years after coming to power, he called for continued vigilance. He told delegates to the union's regular convention that he could now describe their union as generally clean and honest, "but, I also have no hesitancy in saying, we have had, and perhaps still have, a few [local officers] who do not feel this responsibility and who have unfortunately misappropriated the funds entrusted to them." The result involved more than just a loss of money. "It is the confidence of the rank and file of the membership that is destroyed. This is what does the damage and this is what brings disgrace upon the union. So, I say to you, watch well your funds, both locally and Internationally, and the watching will not be wasted."[10]

Tobin's private correspondence reflects a similar sensibility. Writing to the Teamster general secretary-treasurer in 1916, he advocated taking a hard line against a Cleveland official about whom rumors of misconduct had emerged. "There are stories of wrong-doing in Cleveland," Tobin wrote, "coming from all quarters. . . . Of course some of this stuff is right, and some of it is exaggerated, but wherever there is smoke there usually is a fire. We all know when a man is right and when he is wrong, and you can give him to understand plainly that he cannot remain in the International unless he is absolutely right."[11]

His charge involved more than just rhetoric. The union's national administration actively policed the financial practices of its local affiliates, and the traveling auditor played the central role in that oversight. The position involved auditing locals' books and records against fraud and making sure that the national office received its fair share of dues. But the auditor held a larger mandate as well. The union's constitution charged him with maintaining broad oversight of local unions above and beyond how they kept their accounts.[12] Indicating the power and importance of the post, the traveling auditor received the same pay as the general president and the general secretary-treasurer, and at union conventions he, too, gave a lengthy and detailed report on his activities.[13]

Held by George W. Briggs until his death in 1927, the auditor's office exerted a strong influence on the general tenor of the union. A doggedly determined man whose sole agenda involved combating misconduct, Briggs tended to force crises that the other general officers might have preferred to evade. In doing so he took personal risks. In 1911 he shook off the advice of other national officers and pried into the conduct of Arthur St. Clair, head of the Teamsters in St. Louis. Shadowed by members of what he called St. Clair's "wrecking crew," Briggs hired bodyguards to protect him while he forced his way into local union offices and pored over the records.[14] In 1918, when a Cleveland local refused him access to its books, he pressured the IBT's General Executive Board into revoking the local's charter.[15] His refusal to be deterred in the case of a Chicago local led its leader, Frank Ray, to pull his organization out of the IBT and join the ranks of the secessionist Chicago Teamsters. The IBT eventually won back the members of the local, but doing so required a tough fight, during which Vice-President Patrick Berrell was shot twice in the back.[16]

As one man set to police roughly six hundred locals, even the indomitable Briggs had his limits. After his death, which was from natural causes, other national leaders moved to have his duties taken up by the union's organizers. The stated hope was that oversight would improve if more people conducted such audits. The results were, however, less impressive. Correspondence from traveling organizers such as Henry Burger indicates that they did indeed audit locals, but they devoted the bulk of their energies to bringing in new members and setting up new locals. They lacked Briggs's single-minded focus on misconduct.[17]

Briggs, however, held no monopoly on reform within the union's national headquarters. At key moments President Tobin and Thomas Hughes, the general secretary-treasurer, moved forcefully against corrupt local officials. In 1920 charges surfaced against George King, the IBT's vice president from Cleveland. Led by Tobin and Hughes, the General Executive Board called King in to explain his actions and allowed him to resign his position. When charges of misconduct continued to swirl about King's union, Local 407, the national headquarters imposed a trusteeship over it.[18] These and similar examples indicate a good-faith effort by the national union to confront corruption at the local level.

The good intentions of the national leadership, however, could not change the practical constraints involved in policing the problem of local union misconduct. These constraints involved both limits on their knowledge of local conditions and their power to change them. For intelligence on local conditions, President Tobin leaned strongly on the judgment and assistance of a corps of regional leaders, officially titled vice presidents, whom he had cultivated and promoted onto the union's General Executive Board.[19] They were his eyes and ears at the local level. His dependence on these men at times hampered the national union's response to local misconduct, but even where the information Tobin received was quite good he still faced significant obstacles. The union's constitution envisioned the locals themselves dealing with misconduct by local officers by means of filing charges that a trial board of fellow local members would consider. That board in turn enforced its ruling by either levying fines or expelling the guilty party. The national organization became involved only when some locals, for a variety of reasons, proved unable to police themselves in that fashion. In such situations, however, the IBT could choose among only three options: refusing to grant a local a charter, throwing a local into trusteeship, and revoking the charter of an offending local.[20]

As the career of Briggs had demonstrated, the national union could use these policies strategically to counter corruption by well-entrenched local officers. But if the elements responsible for the misconduct existed outside the union, for instance in a criminal gang like Jacob Bernoff's, then the policies offered less potential for success. Indeed, in particular economic zones such as the world of small independent milk dealers in New York, organized crime played a persistent, almost natural, role, and nothing the Teamster leadership could do would change that fact. For that reason, national leaders found themselves during the 1930s largely frustrated in efforts to deal with organized crime's growing influence in specific local settings.

Tobin got his information about New York City from Vice President Michael Cashal. Originally a coal wagon driver, Cashal had steadily progressed up the ladder of union positions, beginning in 1906 as an officer of Local 553, the coal wagon drivers' local. He joined the secessionist UTA in 1906 along with most other Teamster leaders in the city who opposed Cornelius Shea. Later, when the UTA returned to the fold, Tobin began to use Cashal in his continuing fight against the fractious element gathered around Shea, who had briefly established residence in New York City. In 1914 Tobin appointed Cashal as an officer of the national union and put him in charge of the New York area, a position he held until his death in 1951.[21]

A compactly built, athletic man who had learned to fend for himself as a young boy on the streets of New York, Cashal displayed toughness and courage.[22] At a time when intra-union contests occasionally involved violence he had plenty of opportunities to exhibit those qualities. In the early 1920s a group of New York Teamster business agents aligned themselves with Robert Brindell, a powerful Carpenters Union official convicted of extortion in 1921. Known as the Board of Business Agents, the group set up a secessionist organization and used a crew of strong-arm men to promote its cause.[23] They ambushed one of Cashal's associates as he left his house in the morning. Cashal described the attack to Tobin: "They stuck a gun to his back and then went to work on him with brass knuckles and knives. He has two big gashes in the head, two black eyes and his face [is] cut up, and six teeth knocked out, and he was lucky on the knife question because they did not get any further than cutting his clothes."[24]

Cashal himself had numerous run-ins with this group in barns and at union halls. On one occasion, as he supervised a local union election the other side entered with a group of men, intending to stuff the ballot box. Cashal intervened. As he described the incident to Tobin, "They came to me and told me that I had to make a living in New York and why did I not be like everybody else and close my eyes and be recognized as a good fellow and that I had a big family that I would be liable to be missing from them and what credit would that be to me or my family." With ten "guerillas" waiting outside for him, Cashal rejected their suggestion. "I told them that I was not worrying about that end of it. I was there to see that the Election was run on the level and that even if I thought they were able to carry out their threats that I would take the same position."[25] Cashal proceeded to conduct the fight against this group in earnest. He took to bringing "friends" with him when he went to meetings, and he asked Tobin for permission to hire someone as special protection at $50 a week.[26] Tobin would later say of Cashal, "Whenever there was trouble, even though the other fellow might be bigger than or apparently tougher than Mike, Mike never backed away."[27]

This was the man who reported to Tobin in the early 1930s that racketeers were attempting to infiltrate the union.[28] Based on his assessment of the motives and background of the individuals involved, he seems to have distinguished between racketeers and legitimate union leaders. Union leaders sought the benefit of the membership, but racketeers used the union solely for personal enrichment. Thus, in 1933 Cashal wrote to Tobin about the "mob" trying to move in on Local 584, the Milk Wagon Drivers Union. Almost certainly he was describing Jacob Bernoff and his associates, although he never mentioned specific names in his correspondence. Referring the leaders of this "mob," Cashal wrote, "They claim that they can organize about five hundred or more [men?] into the Union of small dealers; their real idea is to take full charge of [the] Local Union which has about $7,000.00 in the treasury, and to work in conjunction with the small dealers through force, cut prices, so that the big dealers would have to buy them off."[29] In other words, as he saw it, the collusive arrangement being planned by the mob would benefit only themselves and not the local union whose treasury would be plundered. Because he saw their motives in that way, Cashal viewed their presence as an instance of corruption, and he took a strong stand against it at considerable risk to himself. Threats were made against his life, and gunmen visited his house to look for him.[30]

Because the issue of corruption meant a great deal to Cashal, he differentiated between racketeering and legitimate union activities—a distinction he based on subjective assessments of the individuals involved. Sometimes, even by his own criteria, he proved to be mistaken. In 1935 the New York City commissioner of city markets publicly charged Arthur ("Tootsie") Herbert, head of Teamsters Local 167, with running a racket in the live-poultry industry. Cashal expressed skepticism. "The Market Commissioner wanted me to revoke the charter and prosecute the officers of 167," he wrote to Tobin. "I told him could not do that without having proof and if he knew any one was guilty that we welcomed him to prosecute." According to a news report, Cashal told a meeting of Local 167 members that criticism of Herbert stemmed from a desire by outsiders to destroy the union. "This whole thing is only a smoke screen to tear down your conditions," he advised. "You have a wonderful organization."[31]

Because Herbert had already been convicted of antitrust violations in 1929 and then for contempt of a court order in the same case in 1934, Cashal must have known that Local 167 stood at the center of a collusive arrangement among live-poultry dealers.[32] But the Teamster vice president in this case seems to have concluded that this collusion had been managed for the benefit of the local union and its members. Indeed, under Herbert's leadership Local 167 had won significant wage increases and other benefits in the contracts it negotiated on behalf of its membership.[33] Writing to the national headquarters about the controversy, Cashal concluded, "As you know my position on racketeering or anything along that line I am 100 percent opposed to it. I realize I cannot go into any Local Union without having some proof to remove any set of officers."[34]

As it turned out, Cashal's assessment of the situation was wrong. Herbert was using his union position for personal enrichment at the expense of his members. In 1937 Special Prosecutor Dewey had Herbert and two other top officers in Local 167 arrested and charged with larceny. During the trial that followed, the Prosecutor's Office built its case on the misuse of the union's funds. Herbert had been levying special $50 assessments on members and raising monthly dues at the same time he drained money from union accounts for his personal use. Faced with the evidence in court, Herbert and his co-defendants pled guilty midway through the trial.[35] Presumably, had Cashal audited the local he would have found in the books and records a revealing tangle of missing funds and questionable appropriations. There is, however, no record of Cashal conducting such an audit, and it seems likely that given his assessment of the situation he never chose to do so.

Courageous and honest though he was, Cashal's performance highlights the drawbacks of depending solely on him for information about misconduct in New York. He opposed racketeering, which he understood to be the misuse of union office for private enrichment. Yet his judgment of who constituted a racketeer reflected his personal experience and contacts. The presence of newcomers, in the case of Local 584, triggered his suspicion in a way that the conduct of a veteran Teamster leader like Herbert did not, this in spite of the controversy that swirled around Local 167. Had an independent and powerful Teamster official from outside the New York region been called in on a regular basis to investigate the city's locals, the national union might have received a more unbiased picture of conditions in those locals. No such internal investigations occurred, however, after 1930, when the traveling auditor's position was eliminated. Indeed, the last time an official had been removed from Local 167 occurred in 1920, when an audit by Briggs revealed that the local's secretary-treasurer, Louis Klein, had embezzled $2,218.29 to establish his own poultry business.[36]

Even when the national union received accurate information, it faced limited options in addressing the problem of corruption. Knowing about corruption and being able to do something constructive about it were two different matters. The three main policy options available to the national leadership all carried particular costs and brought limited benefits.

In terms of chronology, the national leadership's first option in dealing with corruption at the local level was to stay out of the situation altogether. In other words, Tobin would refuse to issue a Teamsters' charter to a local union if he believed the local would become corrupt and be run to profit professional criminals. Here he leaned on the advice of Cashal to screen the people involved in newly organized locals. New charters were issued only after Cashal had provided his input.[37]

That policy had obvious drawbacks that can best be seen by considering a particular case. In 1932 and 1933 spontaneous organizing activity took place among New York's taxi drivers. The IBT, which had jurisdiction over cab drivers, came under a great deal of pressure to charter a local for these men. But Tobin, guided by Cashal's judgment, refused. The Teamster president sent a telegram to the AFL to explain his position: "International Union is opposed to issuing charter to taxicab drivers in New York because they are made up mostly of racketeers. . . . If racketeers do not enter at first they get in shortly afterwards through many scheming methods, impossible to keep them out of this craft." Tobin refused to charter cab drivers even though at the time the IBT could have badly used an infusion of new membership; by 1933 the impact of the Great Depression had helped drain twenty thousand members from the union. Tobin informed Cashal, "The International is losing members fast and it would help us to get three or four thousand men in from the outside, but again, I dread taking in any element which might be the means of bringing gunmen into the organization."[38]

Ironies abounded in this policy. To keep racketeers out, Tobin and Cashal denied union charters to workers who happened to be in the wrong kind of industry. As a result, the Teamsters shut out workers who wanted and needed honest union representation of the kind Tobin struggled to preserve. For its part, the IBT limited its growth, and in end the problem of corruption in the industry remained unsolved. Barred from the IBT, the cab drivers formed an independent organization that gangsters associated with Charles ("Lucky") Luciano soon dominated. Still, in spite of those ironies the policy did achieve something. In this case, organized crime had not been able to use a new local union to gain entry into the IBT. When a racketeering case did emerge involving the cab drivers in 1938, the Teamster organization remained untouched.[39]

Denying a charter offered at best a limited solution and provided no relief if an existing local became enmeshed in misconduct. In dealing with an existing local, the national leadership could choose between imposing a trusteeship and taking away the local's charter. Auditor Briggs had vigorously championed both practices during his tenure, but both had serious drawbacks. They proved especially ill-suited to the problem of organized crime infiltration as it occurred during the 1930s.

The Teamster constitution granted Tobin, with the approval the General Executive Board, the authority to impose a trusteeship over a local. The union's constitution called for such action "if the General Executive Board, when in session, receive information which leads them to believe that any of the officers of a Local Union are dishonest or incompetent, or that the organization is not being conducted for the benefit of the entire membership." During the trusteeship, whomever Tobin appointed as trustee enjoyed complete power over the daily affairs of the local, subject to oversight by Tobin. Ideally, the trustee would use those powers to return the local to fiscal soundness while working to remove whatever troublesome element existed. Once problems had been solved, the trustee would oversee a new set of elections in the local and then return it to self-rule.[40]

Where problems in a local stemmed from misconduct of one of its leaders, the trusteeship, perhaps, offered a useful solution. It proved far less effective when a criminal gang had established a presence within a local. At best, the trustee could only interrupt the gang's ability to use intimidation or bribery to influence the local's leaders. Moreover, the trustee himself now became subject to those same attempts at manipulation as long as he remained in office. Such problems were exemplified in the history of New York's Local 138, an organization composed primarily of grocery and furniture truckers. Louis Buchalter and his gang had used the local to set up a racket among flour haulers and bakers. By the late 1930s the local had fallen under the control of a gang of Jewish and Italian American criminals from Brooklyn, commonly referred to as "Murder, Inc."[41] The IBT imposed a trusteeship over the local in the spring of 1940 after the local's entire executive board had been arrested for extortion. Cashal administered the trusteeship himself, and he approached the task with much trepidation. As he wrote to Tobin's assistant, John Gillespie, "This is one of the toughest assignments I think I have ever had, on account of the elements that are involved."[42] Just a year earlier, Morris Diamond, Local 138's business manager, had been murdered on orders of Buchalter's gang.[43] Cashal had no reason to believe himself immune from similar retribution. Reluctantly, he supervised the local for six months. At the end of that time an election was held with police and other neutral observers present, and a new slate of officers was chosen. "This is a rotten mess," Cashal informed Tobin. "One of the worst I have ever handled, and I will be well pleased, after the installation of officers, to get out of the picture, because I haven't much hope for their future."[44] After that he and Tobin cut the local loose and ended the trusteeship.

If imposing a trusteeship offered limited rewards and much risk, revoking a local's charter was hardly better. In December 1940 Cashal brought the case of Local 863 in Newark, New Jersey, to Tobin's attention. The president of the local, Tony Sasso, and the secretary-treasurer, Edward High, both pled no contest to extortion charges. Sasso received a jail sentence, but the paroled High remained in office, apparently immune from electoral defeat within his local. Cashal referred to the case as "another one of these desperate situations." He asserted, "Personally, I think the best thing to do in a case like this would be to revoke the charter."[45] In February 1941 Tobin sent members of Local 863 a flier to warn them that the IBT would revoke the local's charter unless it removed Secretary-Treasurer High from office and expelled him from the union.[46] Within a few days Tobin apparently received a death threat in the mail, one he took quite seriously.[47]

Even before that, however, the Teamster president had viewed the prospect of revoking Local 863's charter with little enthusiasm. It would only, as he explained to Cashal, cause other problems. "If we revoke the charter of this local," Tobin observed, "you fully understand that there are 1500 men who can get a charter from the C.I.O. or who will go independent and create more trouble." They might well go on to sow rebellion in other locals and offer the kind of recurring irritation that the Chicago Teamster organization had exemplified for decades.[48] In the end, and with Cashal's active intervention, High resigned his office, and Local 863 held on to its charter.[49] The outcome, however, offered at best minimal vindication of the IBT's power to intervene in such situations. Tobin demonstrated willingness to pull the charters of other locals controlled by notorious criminals, but he obviously looked upon the tactic as a weapon of last resort—and one likely to backfire on the IBT.[50]

Dewey's antiracketeering offered the national leadership of the Teamsters an opportunity to achieve reform, but the effort to realize that goal proved frustrating. Tobin and Cashal had long remained committed to keeping the union honest, and during the 1930s they resisted the incursions of various organized crime groups. Manning the front lines of this struggle, Cashal amply demonstrated his personal integrity and courage, and yet the results were often disappointing. Over the course of the decade Cashal's judgment proved fallible. As a result, the national union offered assistance to Herbert, a man who later admitted misconduct in union office. Even where Cashal rightly suspected the presence of organized crime, the national organization often could do little of lasting value to ameliorate the situation. The available policy options failed to solve the problems that union leaders faced in a local beset by organized crime. Nor was this dilemma unique to the Teamsters.

Eager for advice, Tobin turned for help to David Dubinsky of the International Ladies Garment Workers Union and Sidney Hillman of the Amalgamated Clothing Workers Union, two progressive leaders known to champion union reform. In 1940 the Teamster leader asked Dubinsky to inform him on the antiracketeering measures included in the constitutions of the two garment workers' unions. Dubinsky's response, although detailed, offered nothing significantly new. Expulsion and trusteeship formed the bulwark, such as it was, of both national unions' efforts to resist corruption.[51] Perhaps for that reason both Hillman and Dubinsky themselves faced the intransigent presence of organized crime in some of their unions' local affiliates.

Reform at the Local Level

While the national office of the Teamsters Union struggled with reform in a number of New York locals, rank-and-file members of those same locals also took up the challenge. Throughout the 1930s individual members dared to take a stand against corruption in their unions. They did so despite the obvious danger involved in such action and with assistance from a regularly published journal, *IBT News,* which apparently had ties to the Communist Party.[52] Groups supported by the journal became active in a number of locals in New York City during the 1930s. The degree of success enjoyed by reformers, however, varied from local to local, and the range of outcomes provides some clues about the dynamics of reform within a local union.

Local 807, a general truckers' local with about nine thousand members, offers one example of locally based reform efforts. In 1936 a reform slate, the Gold Medal Ticket, had won office in the local on promises to better enforce the union's contract and to engage in a vigorous organizing campaign.[53] Within a couple of years, however, the reformers encountered a threat in the form of a waterfront gangster named John Dunn, who moved to take over Local 807. Described by one writer as a "wiry man of slight stature and with steel blue eyes," Dunn ran a gang that dominated the piers along the West Side of Manhattan from Midtown down to the Battery.[54] The gang oversaw a lucrative conspiracy that controlled the business of loading trucks on the city's piers.[55] When he moved to gain control of Local 807, Dunn apparently intended to expand his loading racket from the docks to include over-the-road trucking as well. He needed control over Local 807 in order to create a captive organization of highway truck owners.[56]

During the regular Local 807 election in December 1939, Dunn backed a group within the local. By a narrow margin his group lost out, but they refused to accept the results. For the next year Dunn's group regularly disrupted

Local 807's meetings. Cashal described a visit to Local 807 during this period in a letter to the national office, "In this meeting, there was about four
hundred men (out of a membership of about nine thousand), manhandled
by one hundred of the four hundred. They weren't open to reason or anything."[57]

In spite of the pressure tactics, the reelected officers from the reform slate
maintained their positions. Apparently, Dunn's group eventually decided to
focus its efforts on the union's December 1942 election. Reporting to Tobin
on his concern about the coming election, Thomas Hickey, the secretary-
treasurer of Local 807 and leader of the reform group, wrote, "Please be advised that the real brain behind most of this intrigue, now current in Local
807, is a person by the name of John Dunn. . . . He has notches on his gun
and was present at our meeting on the night of November 18th along with a
large group of followers who are bragging about the results of our election
that might be held in this local union." With good reason Hickey feared for
his safety and worried that Dunn could use intimidation to overthrow the
union's democratic process.[58]

In spite of his concerns, Hickey and his fellow officers hung on and kept
the local free from Dunn's control. In November 1942 they rode out the dis-
ruptive tactics of Dunn's group, running a nominations meeting that lasted
until 5 the next morning but finally allowed competing slates of candidates
to be formally named. To guarantee the fairness of the election they brought
in an outside group, the Honest Ballot Association, to conduct the vote.[59] The
election itself proceeded with no disturbances, and Hickey and most of the
reform slate were returned to office. Dunn's group took two positions, but
it was a far cry from the kind of control to which they had aspired.[60] Having
withstood a daunting challenge to reform, Hickey remained in office long
enough to become Jimmy Hoffa's main opponent in New York during the
1950s.[61]

The history of rank-and-file reform in Local 807 represents the best-case
scenario for democratic reform on the local level. Hickey's group won their
initial electoral victory because of widespread discontent by the membership
over conditions in the local. Once in office, the reformers proceeded to enforce the contracts and to organize the non-union employers. Finally, when
Dunn and his gang threatened the local's independence, Hickey and his supporters displayed courage and determination in maintaining the democratic process. Results in other locals proved less inspiring.

Reformers in Local 202 met with far less success in efforts to clean up that
local. With about five thousand members, Local 202 had jurisdiction over
New York's various markets, from the Fulton Fish Market to the Bronx Ter-

minal market for produce.[62] The local's leadership practiced extortion and took orders from gangsters. Like corrupt Teamster leaders in other sectors of New York's economy, Local 202's officers benefited from the vulnerability of the employers with whom they dealt. The merchants doing business in New York's markets were mostly small operators who worked on a narrow margin and dealt in highly perishable goods. They could not afford to stand up to the extortion commonly practiced by Local 202's officers.[63]

Local 202's officials practiced their extortion with some guidance. The local union belonged to Joseph ("Socks") Lanza, a racketeer who dominated the Fulton Fish Market. When officials from the Retail Clerks' Union wanted the help of Local 202 in organizing fruit and vegetable stores, they found legitimate, straightforward appeals worthless.[64] Only once they had made arrangements with Lanza did Clerks' Union officials receive cooperation from Local 202. Lanza's assistance did not spring from a sense of worker solidarity but rather came at the request of Vito Genovese, alleged leader of the Genovese crime family, with whom the Clerks' Union officials had come to terms.[65]

Opposition to this crooked state of affairs emerged in 1938 when a slate of rank-and-file reformers ran for office in Local 202's regular election. Calling their slate the New Deal, they held an organizing meeting in November 1938, a month before the elections. The 1,200 members present at the meeting voted on a campaign platform that called for more vigorous organizing efforts and full enforcement of the union's contract. The platform also called for regular monthly union meetings and reports from the local's officers on the union's finances.[66] The incumbents in Local 202 now called themselves the Old Deal, and they set up a campaign of their own to counter the New Deal. In one classic electioneering move they issued a fake New Deal flier that promised "we will tax all employed men 10 per cent of their wages to set up a food commissary to feed the unemployed men." The incumbents also hosted beer parties for supporters and reportedly recruited backing among Italian workers by turning to Italian fascist organizations. Finally, they linked their New Deal opponents to the Communist Party.[67]

Despite the heated campaigning, the election took place in December 1938 in an orderly and peaceful manner. Nearly 2,200 members cast their ballots at voting machines provided by the Teamsters Joint Council of New York City as representatives from the Honest Ballot Association, the Joint Council, and the New York Police looked on to make sure nothing occurred to mar the integrity of the occasion. When the results of the vote came in, the incumbents had won by a 4 to 1 margin.[68]

Few of the reelected officers managed to serve out their terms, as one by one over the next couple of years Dewey's investigations began to catch up with them. In the spring of 1939 the district attorney's men arrested the secretary-treasurer, the president, and the business agent of Local 202 for their roles in a variety of extortion schemes.[69] Finally, in January 1941, Dewey announced the arrest of Local 202's newly appointed secretary-treasurer along with Joseph Lanza, the fish market racketeer, and charged them with siphoning off regular payments from Local 202.[70]

As the indictments came down the reformers in Local 202 saw both a vindication and a second chance to win office in a new set of elections.[71] But as time passed it became increasingly clear that no such elections would be held. What was left of the old executive board decided who would be appointed to fill the vacancies created by the arrests, and, not surprisingly, they chose not to appoint any New Dealers. Yet neither did they appoint anyone who had a criminal record or well-known ties to racketeers. Perhaps for that reason, along with some concern for his own safety, Cashal refrained from intervening in Local 202. He never called for a new election. The rank and file of the union watched as bit by bit a new executive board assumed office in their union with no any reference to democratic procedure. As a frustrated member observed in the rank-and-file publication the *IBT News,* "The boys who run the wagons would have really gotten something out of this clean up if a new slate was now in office. We might even be willing to put up with the birds appointed by the Old Deal . . . if we had the say. But the say is what we haven't got."[72]

The International Brotherhood of Teamsters claimed that Local 202 had changed for the better. At a congressional hearing in 1942, the general counsel for the International testified that since Dewey's prosecutions "there has been a very honest administration."[73] A decade later, however, that improvement seemed illusory. When the New York State Crime Commission investigated the local in 1953, they found an estimated $99,680 missing from the union's funds over a ten-year period. The commission also found evidence that the president of the local and a business agent held hidden partnerships in one of the most lucrative trucking firms in the local.[74] When Thomas Hickey looked into the situation for the International in 1953, he discovered that Local 202 did not hold monthly membership meetings, it made no financial reports, and "there is quite a sum of money that has never been accounted for."[75]

Given this long-term high level of corruption, why had rank-and-file reform failed in Local 202? Alternatively, why did reform succeed in Local 807 but fall short in Local 202? Fear played some part in the outcome of the 1938 election. The forces that controlled Local 202 had fearsome reputations. When the American Federation of Labor organizer who had responsibility for New York was asked in the early 1930s to intervene in Local 202, he reportedly said, "What do you want me to do? Find my body in the river?"[76] His concern was not misplaced. Several insurgent candidates who ran in the 1938 election were physically assaulted.[77] It seems unlikely, however, that violent intimidation alone made the difference. Local 807 reformers had suffered threats and beatings. The gangsters there had equally intimidating reputations. But none of that had defeated reform in the case of that local.[78]

Another explanation for the failure of reform in Local 202 involves the charge of communist affiliation that was made against the insurgents.[79] The reformers themselves gave this explanation great credence.[80] As one insurgent explained, the Old Deal had used the charge of communism to frighten both the members of Local 202 and, more important, the merchants who employed them. "In the campaign of 1938, they [the Old Deal union officials] enlisted the aid of most of our employers and they in turn swayed their men by intimidation, threat of dismissal and layoff, into voting for the Old Deal. The main argument used by our bosses was the New Deal is a communist organization. Their ideas are too radical. They will put me out of business and so on and so forth ran the sad tale."[81] Still, this explanation also falls short, because charges of communist affiliation had been made against reformers in Local 807.[82] In the case of Local 807, those charges failed to hamstring reform. Why did Red Scare tactics succeed in Local 202?

For an answer to that question one has to consider the nature of employer-to-worker relations in Local 202. Most bosses in New York's produce markets were small businessmen, many of whom had gone from working in the market to setting up their own small shops. In 1947 Local 202's secretary-treasurer, Joseph Papa, explained the employers with whom he dealt to members of Congress: "They are not industrialists as I said before. They come right from the ranks, some of them did. Some of them drove trucks, pushed hand carts." Putting it even more succinctly, Papa said, "They grew up with us."[83] The lack of class antagonism provided little material on which to build militant unionism, and union leaders had no need to energize the membership into becoming active unionists. Because the small produce commission merchants who made up the bulk of the local's employers could not afford to endure a strike, union leaders could get what they wanted without having to turn to the membership for help.[84]

For their part, members seemed to lack any strong identification with their union. When the staff of the District Attorney's Office asked Local 202 member Hyman Panich about the union, the tenuous nature of his tie to the local quickly became clear. Panich had driven a truck in the market for nearly fifteen years. He loaded fruit onto the vehicle in the early morning hours and then delivered it to various restaurants. Around 1936 he and the other drivers working for a group of fruit merchants had joined the union, but Panich could not identify which Local 202 official had brought them into the organization. "I don't know who organized," he explained. "I don't know because I didn't want to belong." Local 202's officers had used the threat of a boycott to induce the fruit merchants to force their men into the union. Panich had to join, "otherwise they wouldn't let me work." He could not come up with the $25 initiation fee and the first month's dues of $2 so his boss loaned him the money, another example of the ties between boss and worker in this field. Once a member, Panich had only minimal contact with 202. Fellow workers explained how much he would have to pay, and he left his dues money with a salesman for the company, who passed it on to the union. Twice in two years he went to meetings with fellow drivers from this particular group of fruit merchants, but he never went to a meeting of the entire local union. Although he had seen a shop steward on a couple of occasions, it happened so infrequently that Panich remained unsure of the man's name.[85]

This lack of connection between the member and his union had implications for reform. When reformers sought to galvanize Teamsters Union members into action, they always hectored them to reclaim the citizenship rights due them as members of the union. One letter in a rank-and-file publication urged, "We must rid our local of the yoke of racketeering and it can be done cheaply and simply by exercising our right to vote on election day."[86] Another editorial in the same publication stressed the importance of attending union meetings. Referring to an indicted leader who controlled Local 643, the ambulance drivers' local, the writer argued, "Every man that you get to attend his regular monthly meeting makes it that much harder for Cohen, or anybody like him to get away with their tricks."[87] Reformers sought an informed and active membership that would play a responsible role in their local unions.

In Local 202, however, reformers encountered a membership where many seemed to lack that sense of identification. Men like Panich felt no loyalty to Local 202 as an organization. Even had he wanted to become more a part of the local, Panich had few opportunities to form ties with others beyond his immediate circle of fellow drivers. Local 202 seems to have had almost no meetings for the whole membership.[88] Outside of such meetings, members never became involved in any common efforts, such as strikes, that might have drawn them together. When the question of reform came up, therefore, those few members who decided to become involved might well choose to protect what they considered to be the interests of their employers rather than worry about the integrity of an institution to which they felt only the most tenuous of bonds. They might well follow the wishes of the employers and vote against a group of radicals and for the status quo.

Local 807's membership, however, had a far more antagonistic relationship with their employers, and their sense of responsibility to Local 807 led them at times to go so far as to lead their union officers. Part of the difference in attitudes stemmed from the kind of employers for whom Local 807 members worked. The local's jurisdiction included all general freight delivery that occurred within a thirty-mile radius of Columbus Circle. As with other kinds of trucking, general freight delivery had a large proportion of small operators. A newspaper article in 1946 estimated that the average truck owner in Local 807 was a lone proprietor or a partnership that had about ten trucks and twelve employees. The boss probably had begun by driving a truck himself until he acquired start-up capital. On this level, employers in Local 807 seemed to resemble those in Local 202, but important differences existed. Although they made him a small businessman, the ten trucks and twelve employees of the average 807 employer still implied a different scale of business from that of a typical fruit merchant who had two trucks. In addition, Local 807 had its share of much larger employers. The Motor Haulage Company, for example, had 375 men who worked on three hundred trucks, and Local 807 also had contracts with the large retail grocery chains such as A&P and Bohack.[89]

These employers belonged to active and effective employer organizations. Grouped together in this way, bosses in Local 807 would not fold before the threat of a strike. In fact, they at times seemed willing to force one in order to get what they wanted from the union. In September 1938 the truck owner associations balked at following Mayor La Guardia's plan for a wage settlement with Local 807. They were fully prepared to fight it out with the union. Only after the mayor had threatened to use city sanitation trucks to haul freight did the truck owners' united front crumble.[90] Two years later wage negotiations again went to the brink, and in 1946, after the war, a full-fledged strike did break out.[91]

Confronted by employer militancy, Local 807 members came together to face a common threat and fight for shared goals. The officers of the local did what they could to make it an active and inclusive organization. In 1937 the local gave away a thousand Christmas baskets to unemployed members. At the same meeting they discussed a proposal to have members work only five days a week rather than six in order to create more work for unemployed members.[92] Unlike Local 202, 807 held regular monthly meetings for members from every division to attend.[93]

For their part, the members took their relationship to the union seriously enough to conduct wildcat strikes when they felt that officers had not fulfilled their end of a bargain. In September 1938, Local 807 members defied their union's leaders and shut down New York's truck traffic for nearly a week. The drivers sought to force employers to accept their plan to create more jobs for the unemployed by reducing the work week to five days. Although members in other New York Teamster locals seem never to have gone out on unauthorized walkouts, Local 807 members conducted several wildcat strikes.[94] The ability and willingness of members to defy both their union leaders and their bosses reveal something about where the axis of power lay in this local.

A similar unauthorized walkout in Local 202 (although highly unlikely) would have undoubtedly brought the united action of employers and union heads against recalcitrant members. There existed a kind of closed, parochial atmosphere in New York's markets, a sort of small-town community within the larger metropolitan city. When Papa, head of Local 202, said of the employers, "they grew up with us," he referred to a familiarity that defined relations between union officials and employers. Nearly four hundred commission merchants operated within the fifteen square blocks that composed the Washington Market, and their fierce competition effectively was regulated only by the work rules of Local 202.[95] Perhaps employers and union officials did not always like each other, but they always knew each other, and, within that community, arrangements could always be made. Problems were adjusted peacefully. Papa told a congressional committee in 1947, "I don't think we ever had a picket sign of our own on the street."[96] Such ties made the positions of union dissidents extremely tenuous. At a word from a union official a dissident could lose his job, and he would find it very difficult to locate another one.[97]

In smaller IBT locals that kind of parochial familiarity made democratic reform a practical impossibility. In Arthur ("Tootsie") Herbert's Poultry Drivers' Local 167, for example, the five hundred members had very little room in which to maneuver. They worked as casual laborers, and those who did manage to get work averaged about two weeks of employment a month.[98] They received job assignments from the union's leadership, a power that Herbert and the other officers used to build a faction of supporters within the local's ranks and coerce other members into paying for the privilege of working.[99]

Any member who might have tried to get work without the help of the union would find himself an unwanted stranger in a very small town. With thirty commission merchants and a couple hundred slaughterhouse operators, the live-poultry industry was a closed circle. The National Recovery

Administration (NRA) code administrator observed, "Some of the present commission men are the second and third generation. . . . It is very difficult for a new man to come in." In this business, everyone knew everyone else.[100] Unlike the situation in Local 807, bosses in poultry markets did not take a confrontational stance toward the union. Instead, employers and union leaders worked closely with each other. The NRA code administrator explained that no new operator could establish himself in the market "unless the other commission men told the leaders of the union that they would like to have him."[101] In return for the protection the union leader gave them, the bosses hastened to take care of Herbert. The merchants paid his legal fees when the Justice Department indicted him for conspiracy to restrain commerce.[102] On the day-to-day level they would not hire someone if Herbert did not want that man to have a job.

In this incestuous community, no room for dissent existed, and, publicly, none occurred. On the eve of Herbert's trial on charges of embezzling funds from Local 167 the local held a general membership meeting. The five hundred Teamsters present voted unanimously to appear in court the first day of the trial and "to tell the judge, the jury, and Special Prosecutor Thomas Dewey that the union is 100 per cent behind our leaders." Individuals who called themselves rank-and-file leaders took over the meeting at one point and for several hours delivered speeches in support of Herbert and other indicted officers. The *New York Times* correspondent on the scene reported that "not a dissenting note sounded, although every speaker challenged any dissenters to come forward. It was the consensus on the part of the speakers that whatever money the officers may have spent was gladly given to them by the union to use as they saw fit. 'If they embezzled it,' shouted one speaker, 'then we'll raise more money for them to embezzle.'"[103]

This public show of support did not change when, two weeks later, Herbert and the other officers changed their pleas to guilty. In effect, the officers admitted having robbed the union's treasury. When the trial judge announced the sentence he noted that he had received resolutions and petitions for mercy on Herbert's behalf signed by most of the union's membership.[104] Those same members voted to continue making salary payments to their union officers after they had been sent to jail for pilfering union funds.[105]

The absence of open dissent, however, did not mean that members of Local 167 truly accepted the activities of their leadership. The same trial judge who received petitions requesting lenient treatment for Herbert also received letters from union members who denied the validity of those petitions. Addressing the defendants who stood ready to receive their sentences, the judge said that the letters claimed "that the very resolution that has been referred to and which was adopted at this meeting of the union of August 6th last was a hollow pretense, and that persons whose names are affixed to that copy of the resolution sent to the Court, affixed merely their names but not their sentiments or belief in the terms of the resolution." In the letters the men explained that they had been coerced into voting for the resolutions with the threat that otherwise they would be denied work.[106]

The District Attorney's Office stated that it, too, had found evidence of stifled opposition in Local 167. The assistant district attorney in charge of trying the case against Herbert told of having Local 167 members in his office who "say they are afraid to open their mouths for fear that if they open their mouths and express an honest belief, it will mean the loss of their job. They fear they will be assaulted." These members did not like the conditions existing in the union, but by the same token they were unwilling to take a public stance against the leadership. According to the assistant district attorney, "They say to me, in fact, 'If I were forced to take the stand, I would have to refuse to admit those things, because those three persons have our future in their very hands. They have the means of depriving our families of making a living, because they can take away any stead[y] job and they can refuse to issue cards to men who are unemployed.'"[107]

With only five hundred members, Herbert and the other leaders would have little difficulty keeping a general eye on each individual's activities. The degree of control would be proportionately much greater than what Local 202's officers could achieve with their five thousand members. Thus, although neither union provided fertile ground for rank-and-file reform, active, vocal dissent did at least appear in Local 202. A rough sort of correspondence existed in relation to the size of a local, the nature of union-to-employer relations, and the possibility of rank-and-file reform. In the largest local of the city, Local 807, where relations with employers were antagonistic, rank-and-file reform enjoyed great success. The somewhat smaller Local 202, with more pliant employers, still had dissent, but in this case reformers found their efforts stymied. Finally, in the much smaller Local 167, where the union and the employers had a long history of working together, no open dissent occurred.

Evidence exists to show that even the participants in these contests intuitively understood the conditions that would inhibit or encourage reform. In Local 807 there were reports that elements allied to the gangster John Dunn planned to split off a smaller portion of the local union in order to set up a more easily controlled organization.[108] Conversely, in Local 584, the Milk Wagon Drivers Local, it was the reformers who wanted to change the composition of the local union. They sought to bring together, in one unit, drivers for small, independent dealers with employees of the city's two large corporate dairy firms. They hoped in that way to make one larger union that could break the strong ties between independent dealers and officers of Local 584. The reformers aimed to use the progressive influence of the corporate employees to swing the union's elections around.[109]

This evidence regarding the dynamics of reform agrees with some of the work that has been done on racketeering and unionism in the 1930s. Howard Kimeldorf, in *Reds or Rackets? The Making of Radical and Conservative Unions on the Waterfront* (1988), considers why a radical union, the International Longshoreman and Warehousemen's Union (ILWU) could emerge on the West Coast but not on the East Coast. The International Longshoremen's Association (ILA), based in New York City, rivaled the Teamsters as one of the more racketeer-ridden unions. In his attempt to explain the difference between the ILWU and its East Coast counterpart, Kimeldorf gives a great deal of attention to the general social atmosphere in the New York Port, including the ethnic composition of port workers and the types of neighborhoods from which they came. He also notes the prevalence of smaller employers on the East Coast who had set up comfortable, informal ties with the ILA leadership. As one New York stevedoring employer reportedly described collective bargaining with the ILA's leader Joe Ryan, "We call Ryan in once a year or so and say, 'Joe, how much of a raise do you need to keep the boys in line?'" Kimeldorf points out how that situation contrasted sharply with employer-union relations on the West Coast. In San Francisco, the major shipping companies were large corporations that organized into belligerent employer associations.[110]

Rank-and-file reform sponsored by the Communist Party did make some initial headway in the New York ILA locals. By the end of the 1930s, however, that reform movement had completely collapsed. For Kimeldorf, the reason for this failure lies largely in the blundering tactics of the Communist Party, which issued disastrous instructions to its field organizers. Moving in the small, closed world of the average ILA local, organizers received directions that forced them to take an open communist line and support dual unionism. Such tactics did little to build support for reform among the membership. In addition to the poor strategic judgment of the Communist Party, however, Kimeldorf also notes the role of a terror campaign waged against the reformers, as well as the conservative influences of Catholicism and ethnic balkanization among the longshoremen in the New York Port.[111]

Kimeldorf reveals that forces similar to those at work among the Teamsters played a role in stifling reform. New York ILA locals were small, sometimes covering just a few piers, and the men who worked on a pier tended to come from the surrounding neighborhood. The longshoremen had to shape up for work each day, and the supply of labor always outmatched the demand. Thus intimidation could come from physical violence as well as from power over employment. The easy, informal ties between union leaders and water-front employers made control of the membership that much more solid. Conversely, because the union never called a strike, it had no need to mobilize its membership. A member's only tie to the union came from occasional demands for dues payments, nothing more. Members came to think of the union as just another form of taxation to which they had to submit in order to work on the docks.[112]

Conclusion

The history of efforts to combat corruption during the 1930s in New York City illustrates the potential and the limits of reform. Even with the assistance of an active law enforcement campaign, and benefiting from a pro-labor local political environment, reform within the Teamsters remained a problematic endeavor. Organized crime, in the person of John Dunn, could be defeated, but the success of democratic reform efforts largely depended on the circumstances in which the union operated. The courage of reformers would avail nothing if they waged their battle in the wrong union. Similarly, the blunt policy instruments available to national leaders like Tobin and Cashal could do little to combat racketeers in locals that had chronic problems. These organizational constraints doomed most reform efforts to failure. The sad results did not stem, as many critics argued, from indifference toward corruption on the part of members or the national leadership. The history of these overlooked reform efforts—both at the national and the local levels—indicates just the opposite.

PART 3

The Age of Hoffa:
The 1950s and 1960s

A new generation of opportunistic leaders, Dave Beck and then Jimmy Hoffa, transformed the union. They broadened the Teamster jurisdiction and made local union officials into professionals, now more closely overseen by the national headquarters. The union that emerged from those changes achieved substantial organizing victories and won improvements in wages and work conditions, but those changes also decreased the membership's role in their own organization.

In 1956 a major congressional committee investigation began that highlighted corruption in the Teamsters Union. The McClellan Committee exposed Beck's malfeasance and Hoffa's connivance with organized crime. Reflecting the political concerns of its members, the McClellan Committee shaped its investigation to produce revelations that would justify changing labor laws. The results helped transform the political landscape. Even during a period when unions enjoyed popularity and significant gains in membership, the revelations of the McClellan Committee led to passage of a bill, the Landrum-Griffin Act (1959), that hamstrung future organizing efforts.

Although later observers overlooked them, reformers opposed to Hoffa mounted a significant challenge to his leadership. Following a route pioneered in the union's early days, reformers operating at the local union level turned to secession as a way to make their opposition felt and escape possible retaliation if they stayed in the union. Early successes in Chicago and Cincinnati led to the most substantial challenge in 1962–63 when members of the union's fourth-largest trucking local threatened to pull out of the Teamsters. Their defeat marked the decline of reform in this era.

7. "It's a Business with Me": The Teamsters Union in the 1950s under Dave Beck and Jimmy Hoffa

As much as anyone, Dave Beck shaped the Teamsters Union that emerged as the nation's largest labor organization by the 1950s. Looking back on his achievement during an interview in 1978 he explained that he always viewed the union as a business enterprise:

> I have said, as far as I'm personally concerned, it's a business with me. The only thing in the world that these people own is their labor. They don't own laundries or bakeries or fuel companies or department stores or candy stores or anything else. Cut their arms off and they're objects of charity the next morning. The only damn thing in the world they've got to sell is their labor. And they come in here and I join them in our union, take them into affiliation, and I go out in that open marketplace and sell that labor. Just like you're selling steel or glass or diapers, or anything else you want to name. For the price I can get for it in the open market, and I administer an organization to the highest degree of my ability to perfect it.[1]

Beck played a central role in the Teamsters for two decades, and his philosophy of trade unionism remained dominant in the organization after he left the scene. Rising through the ranks on the West Coast, he pioneered organizing techniques and structural changes in the Teamsters that profoundly affected the union. After he became president of the Teamsters in 1952 he forced his innovations on the organization from coast to coast. When James Hoffa replaced Beck as president in 1957, he continued to promote and enforce the policies Beck had begun. Indeed, Hoffa's rhetoric echoed Beck's pragmatic philosophy. "Running a union," he explained at one point, "is just like running a business. We're in the business of selling labor. We're going to get the best price we can."[2]

The attitude of Beck and Hoffa has often been described as conservative, but that term may obscure as much as it reveals about the motives, methods, and goals of the organization these men worked to build. Clearly, they held more conservative views than their counterparts in the labor movement, men like Sidney Hillman, Walter Reuther, and Harry Bridges who viewed their unions as part of a larger process of social change. Each of those three had been involved in left-wing political action centered around either the Socialist or the Communist Party.[3] In contrast, Beck often supported Republican Party candidates, and Hoffa's politics can only be described as opportunistic. Neither man put forward a coherent and consistent larger social vision. But in their dogged devotion to building and defending their labor organization, both pursued goals that put them well outside accepted conservative norms. They built a union that became a byword for aggressive, militant organization, one that functioned as a relentless organizing machine. In doing so, the Teamsters pushed against social conventions regarding race and gender and, when convenient, happily formed alliances with radical unionists that proved quite controversial in the cold war context of the time. For these reasons, business groups and conservatives came to see the Teamsters not as a safe, ideologically acceptable labor organization but rather as a looming threat that had to be stopped.

Within the union itself, this mix of aggressiveness and pragmatism led to an organization that brought the membership real advantages even as its evolving, top-down structure limited their day-to-day role in running the union. Teamster members enjoyed a range of material benefits, shorter hours, better wages, health insurance, and pensions. They also savored other advantages that membership brought, such as job security and protection from the arbitrary whims of employers. It was in this new context that charges of corruption in organized labor came to center on the Teamsters Union in the mid-1950s.

Building an Organizing Machine: The Leadership of Beck and Hoffa

Together, Beck and Hoffa transformed the Teamsters into a tightly knit organization that mobilized its staff on the national and local level to bring in new members. The two leaders pursued this goal in a number of ways. They harnessed the strategic importance of interstate trucking to bring the union into new areas and found ways to integrate local leaders into nationwide organizing campaigns and make those leaders accountable for achieving results in a way that local officials had never been before. Faced with an economy increasingly dominated by national corporations, the Teamsters of the 1950s became a more centralized union, encouraging and enforcing an unprecedented uniformity on local affiliates. Only in that way, Beck argued, could the union confront the challenges it faced in the postwar economy.

The man who engineered these changes grew up poor. Beck's incredible drive to achieve success apparently reflected a determination to escape the life of failure that he ascribed to his father. Born in Stockton, California, in 1894, he moved with his family to Seattle when he was four. For a time his father, Lemuel Beck, ran a small furniture repair shop, with the family living in the back of the store behind a curtain partition. When that business failed, Lemuel became partner in a carpet-cleaning operation, but he never enjoyed much success. Beck recalled, "I never remember all of the years with my father, I don't ever remember him having one hundred dollars at any time."[4] To make ends meet, his mother worked in a laundry, and in the summers she took work at the local canneries. Young Beck had ambitions of going to the university and studying law, but the family's financial condition forced him to leave high school and take a full-time job. He started working in a laundry but soon managed to find a more lucrative job driving a laundry delivery route. Drivers worked on a commission based on their ability to attract and hold customers. Aggressive, enthusiastic, and hard-working, Beck did well and distinguished himself as one of the most successful laundry drivers in the city.[5]

He soon got involved in the union, Local 566 of the International Brotherhood of Teamsters. By 1925, at the age of twenty-nine, he became secretary-treasurer, the chief officer of the local. Most accounts depict him as ambitious and energetic. He avoided alcohol and cigarettes, read biographies of successful people, and took night courses in business. Seeking to make his mark, he began to build up the Teamsters Union in Seattle. He did this in a way similar to many other Teamster leaders, by catering to the needs of the small employers he sought to organize. Beck set up collusive agreements with associations of small businessmen. In the laundry industry, for instance, he encouraged formation of an association of laundry owners, which would limit competition in the areas of price or expansion. Beck agreed to use his Teamsters to police the laundry industry for this association in return for a solid collective bargaining agreement. He worked out the same type of agreement in other industries—garage owners, bakers, milk dealers, and still others. As had been the case with Teamster leaders from Al Young to Charlie Green, this kind of arrangement had a hard edge. Violent incidents involving recalcitrant employers often accompanied Beck's organizing campaigns.

His own exact involvement in the incidents remains unclear. Numerous investigations of these organizing campaigns resulted in indictments of some of his close associates, but he himself remained unscathed.[6]

Although his early success within the union drew on such tried-and-true methods as collusive agreements, Beck's real rise depended on his gift for innovation. More than any Teamster leader who had come before him, Beck saw how the union could operate beyond the local level, how it could wield effective leverage on a multistate, regional basis. Beck helped pioneer changes in the way the union organized workers and who it brought in as members. He convinced a skeptical Daniel Tobin to set up new levels of union government that made such changes possible. Beck laid the groundwork for a new kind of Teamsters Union that negotiated national contracts and took in a variety of workers, from office employees to pilots. He helped create what became the largest labor union in the United States by recognizing the importance of intercity trucking and by pooling the organizing resources of local unions.

Intercity trucking came into its own during the 1930s, beginning a steady growth that continued through the 1950s. The growth had been accompanied initially by ruinous competition, but by 1935 the government had stepped in to provide the regulations necessary to guarantee the industry's health and stability. The Motor Carrier Act (1935) authorized the Interstate Commerce Commission (ICC) to regulate interstate trucking, and the agency did so by licensing firms to haul particular kinds of goods between specific points (e.g., cotton from Galveston to Houston and Tulsa). It put a solid floor on the prices that trucking firms could charge. The stability in rates that followed such ICC controls meant that competition for customers would be conducted by providing better service rather than by discounting prices. The ICC's regulations ensured steady growth in the intercity trucking industry for the next several decades.[7]

The emergence of intercity trucking allowed Beck to use the strength of the Teamsters Union in one city to organize workers at another locale. In the early 1930s he helped build up local unions across the state of Washington by applying pressure against non-unionized trucking operators. Truckers and terminal workers in Seattle would refuse to load or carry merchandise handled by non-union workers in places such as Spokane or the Yakima Valley. In order for their goods to be delivered, companies had to agree to enroll their employees in the union. Beck reshaped the structure of the local Teamster organization to enhance his efforts. As local unions grew in outlying cities he brought them into the Seattle Joint Council so organizing campaigns and strike activities could be coordinated on a statewide basis. In creating the union's first statewide Joint Council, he violated a long tradition of town and city localism that had existed within the IBT. The change, however, allowed him to manage his new intercity campaigns.[8]

In addition, Beck maintained a staff of organizers on the Joint Council's payroll, enabling him to further centralize and direct organizing activity within the union. That, too, represented a break with the past. Traditionally, local unions had done their own organizing with occasional help from the international union. Beck brought officers of those locals together, bolstered and directed by the Joint Council's staff, for aggressive and comprehensive organizing efforts.[9] In seeking to organize over-the-road drivers coming into Seattle, for example, he periodically sent a group of local business agents and secretaries to the weighing station at Snoqualmie Pass on the highway leading into the city from the east. As trucks pulled through, the union staff found out whether drivers were members and took down the license plate numbers of those who were not. A list of license numbers, sent to their contacts in Seattle, yielded a list of drivers' names. Then the real work of organizing began. As Beck recalled, " We'd start checking to see who were close contacts [with the drivers]. What people did we know that knew him personally? Is there any way that we might convince him that if he joined the Teamsters Union and lost his job, maybe there's a better job down the road for him, that we can help him get. That's the kind of detailed organizing the Teamsters were doing."[10]

This full-time staff, new organization, and new tactics allowed Beck to organize most of Washington and then expand his efforts across the West Coast. In early 1930 he launched a sustained campaign in Oregon, moving out from Portland, and by 1935 had set his sights on Los Angeles, long a bastion of anti-unionism. The powerful employers' association of Los Angeles had effectively kept out almost all unions since the early years of the twentieth century. As a result, there was hardly any base of unionism in the city from which to expand. To get the Teamsters Union into Los Angeles, Beck had to leverage his way in, and to do that he had to organize most over-the-road drivers of the West Coast. He convinced Daniel Tobin to allow him to set up a multistate coordinating body, the Highway Drivers Council (HDC). With representatives from all the strong locals on the West Coast from San Francisco to Seattle, Beck used the HDC to conduct a leapfrog kind of organization. Unionized truckers from Seattle and San Francisco would refuse to pull into terminals with non-union workers. When those terminal workers joined the union, they, in turn, refused to deal with merchandise hauled by non-union truckers. And so it went from truck line to terminal to another truck line and on to another terminal.[11]

Trucking companies, which operated on a narrow margin, had little ability to resist such pressure. If they balked at dealing with the union, their customers would go to another firm whose service was not being interrupted. The regulations of the ICC made it impossible for intercity truckers to bypass Beck's roadblocks by delivering freight to another locale. A regulated trucker had authority to haul goods only between specifically defined points. By the late 1930s Beck's new techniques had firmly established the IBT all along the West Coast, even in Los Angeles.[12]

Seeking to consolidate and further increase his organizing accomplishments, in 1937 Beck set up a permanent, multistate organization within the IBT, the Western Conference of Teamsters. Like its predecessor, the statewide Seattle Joint Council, the Western Conference coordinated organizing and strike activities. To take advantage of the new intercity and interstate nature of trucking, Beck had created a new interstate form of Teamsters Union organization.[13]

Within this new regional organization, the ever-aggressive Beck steadily expanded the reach of Teamster jurisdiction. At his behest the union had begun organizing warehouse workers during the 1930s.[14] By 1944 his Western Conference pushed the IBT to obtain jurisdiction over cannery workers, and that same year the union's General Executive Board approved of plans to begin organizing office workers.[15] The split between the AFL and the CIO facilitated this expansion by offering the Teamsters a convenient justification. The IBT claimed to be forestalling the efforts of Harry Bridge's International Longshoremen's and Warehousemen's Union (a CIO affiliate) to spread its form of radical labor organization. The cynical opportunism of such claims, however, became more apparent as the IBT moved in on other CIO unions. When the International Association of Machinists—not known as a radical union—pulled out of the AFL in 1946, the IBT promptly announced that it would now be organizing garage mechanics.[16] The decision of the Brewery Workers Union to go over to the CIO a month later provided Teamsters with another opportunity for jurisdictional raiding. The IBT unleashed efforts to bring entire local unions over from the ranks of the Brewery Workers.[17] AFL unions like the Amalgamated Meat Cutters and the Railway Clerks hardly fared any better as Beck seized on any pretext available for raiding their jurisdictions.[18] Although the national union, still led by Tobin, approved this jurisdictional expansion, Beck's ambition provided the main motivating force. For Beck, notions of craft applied to the union's jurisdiction were but anachronistic impediments. As one union official put it, "Dave will take anybody he can get his hands on, then he'll find some kind of justification for it. A 'teamster' to him is anybody who sleeps on a bed with casters."[19]

Under Beck's successful leadership, the Western Conference of Teamsters grew at an extraordinary pace, and his career advanced accordingly. The entire national membership of the IBT in 1930 numbered a little under ninety thousand; by the early 1950s the Western Conference of Teamsters, under Beck's leadership, had 390,000 members. His region was much better organized than other areas of the country. Although the states covered by the Western Conference accounted for only 13 percent of the nation's population, they made up 25 percent of Teamster membership.[20] Tobin, recognizing Beck's talents, steadily promoted him up the ranks of the union. Appointed as an organizer in 1926, Beck became a vice president of the IBT in 1940. In 1947 Tobin engineered the creation of a new position, the executive vice president, especially for Beck. It recognized his status as the union's main organizational strategist and effectively made him Tobin's heir apparent.[21]

The kinds of changes that Beck pioneered within the union were soon duplicated in the Midwest. A core of Trotskyite socialists in Minneapolis had led a successful strike and organizing campaign in that city beginning in 1934. Out of that group emerged a union strategist whose abilities equaled Beck's: Farrell Dobbs. Dobbs successfully used the same leap-frogging organizing techniques that Beck had developed, and he practiced a similar form of regional consolidation. In 1936 Dobbs set up a statewide organization, the Minnesota Drivers' Council, and a year later he expanded it to a multistate level. As Beck's people moved out from the West Coast, Dobbs's group spread out from Minnesota. By late in the 1930s the two groups met around Omaha, where pressure from East and West forced a group of balky local truckers to finally cave in to IBT demands.[22]

Moving east, Dobbs linked up in Michigan with young Jimmy Hoffa, who had revitalized the Teamster movement in Detroit. Having worked briefly with Dobbs, Hoffa imbibed some of his ideas about the innovations necessary to build and strengthen the union. Soon thereafter Dobbs left the union movement to devote his full attention to socialist politics, and Hoffa then became the most dynamic Teamster leader in the Midwest.[23] Unlike Dobbs, Hoffa's single-minded devotion to his career as a Teamster official meant that he would never be distracted from his efforts to enlarge and defend the union. Those who knew him and worked with him agreed that, for Jimmy Hoffa, the union was an obsession.[24] In 1963, after he became president of the union, Hoffa told an interviewer, "If I couldn't draw a salary tomorrow morning, I would continue to do what I'm doing and remain president of the Teamsters Union. If I had to get a job in the nighttime to carry on, I would do that, too."[25]

Like Beck, Hoffa grew up amid hard times. He was born in 1913, a Hoosier from southern Indiana coal country. His father, who worked in the coal industry, died when Jimmy was seven, leaving his mother with four children to raise on her own. She shifted around various small Indiana towns for a while, and in 1924, looking for better wages, she moved the family to Detroit. Young Jimmy Hoffa attended school on the working-class West Side of Detroit until his early teen years, when he dropped out to work full time.[26]

By the time Hoffa was eighteen he was helping unload the boxcars and trucks that pulled up to the warehouse of a large midwestern grocery chain, Kroger's.[27] It was physically demanding labor that lacked any kind of security or steady hours. In the depths of the depression, however, it was the best Hoffa could do, and he soon took steps to better his condition.[28] In 1931 he led fellow warehouse workers on a strike to protest work conditions and wages. They had timed the job action to coincide with a shipment of strawberries, knowing that the company could not afford to sit the strike out and risk having the strawberries rot in railroad cars. The Kroger's management gave in, and Hoffa began his career as a union leader.[29]

During the 1930s and 1940s Hoffa led a resurgent Teamster movement in Detroit, which followed a pattern previously laid out by Beck. In the two locals where his efforts were concentrated, Local 299 and Local 337, the combined membership rose from two thousand in 1937 to more than twenty thousand by 1950. As with Beck's campaigns in Seattle, charges of violence and intimidation swirled around Hoffa's efforts. Similarly, the Detroit Teamster movement worked with groups of local employers to control competition in return for gaining the closed shop. Whereas Beck had escaped any legal consequences for such practices, Hoffa was not so lucky. In 1940 he pled no contest to charges of violating the Sherman Anti-Trust Act by participating in a collusive arrangement to control competition in Detroit's wastepaper industry. According to the indictment, one of the firms that refused to abide by this collusive agreement had been bombed. Like Beck, Hoffa's desire for more members led him to bring in workers from a range of different occupations, from coat-check girls to undertakers. His willingness to take in different occupational groups apparently knew no bounds, and periodically the national union had to step in to restrain him.[30] In 1942, for example, when Hoffa proclaimed his intention to organize farmers, the national headquarters wrote to his immediate superior, Ray Bennett, "You go over this matter with Jimmy, as you are well aware of the fact that the Teamsters International Union does not want any part in the organizing of farmers."[31] Finally, Hoffa, too, saw the benefits of regional organization and championed it in the Midwest.[32]

By the late 1940s the two men began to achieve real power in the International Union. Beck led the way, moving from the executive vice president's spot to fill Tobin's shoes when he retired from the presidency in 1952. Hoffa had assumed a plethora of local and regional offices by the early 1940s, and in 1947 he was elected to one of the three trustee positions for the national union. In 1952, at the relatively young age of thirty-nine, he became an international vice president and was widely recognized as one of the most influential officers in the union. It was suggested that Hoffa's support had been crucial in allowing Beck to overcome opposition to his candidacy for the presidency. Once firmly in power, Beck used Hoffa as his trouble-shooter and at the same time gave him a free hand in the central region of the country where the Detroit leader had already established predominance. In 1957, when Beck decided not to run for reelection, Hoffa won the right to replace him at the union's convention.[33]

As union leaders, Beck and Hoffa's policies reflected their views on two key issues, the changing nature of the economy and the need for a professional union staff. Both men saw a process of corporate consolidation sweeping across the country, forcing their union to confront a very different kind of challenge. In 1949 Beck warned Tobin about the rise of chain stores and their effect on Teamster jurisdiction.[34] By 1953, now president himself, Beck wrote in the union's official journal, "Processors and distributors of everyday necessities of life are no longer little one-town independents—they are great chains. These chain distributors are in the oil industry, transportation, food, dairy, bakery, laundry—in fact, they are in every phase of our manufacturing and distributive process." As employers, such operations had huge resources with which to resist the union. Beck argued that this economic change required the union to consolidate and centralize its organizing and negotiating apparatus.[35] Hoffa held similar views. As he explained to a reporter in 1957, "The future of labor-management relations is big labor and big business, for there is no room for the small business or the small union."[36]

If they were unified on their understanding of the changing economy, Beck and Hoffa also saw eye to eye on how a union should be conducted: It was a job for professionals rather than amateurs or idealists. For both men, the members were essentially customers who had neither the ability nor the interest to take a responsible role in running the union's affairs. In 1948 Beck reportedly said, "Unions are big business. Why should truck drivers and bottle washers be allowed to make big decisions affecting union policy? Would any corporation allow it?" Hoffa also did not believe that the rank and file could truly comprehend the complex issues involved in negotiations and managing the affairs of the local. Nor did he think that they had much interest in trying to master such details. As he said at one point, "Unfortunately for the would-be modern day reformers, workers do not behave in the manner their hazy theories presume. Most people do not want to participate in the day-to-day operations of their unions—this is the business agent's job." To keep such member-customers satisfied, both Beck and Hoffa believed that union officials needed to become professionals, and that meant a long period of training along with a salary package large enough to attract and hold intelligent and ambitious people. The increase in professionalization they envisioned, however, also involved a loss of autonomy. Like other business executives, union officials who did not produce—whether they failed to organize enough new members or did not adequately service members—were to be weeded out.[37]

As they gained power over the IBT, Beck and Hoffa shaped the union in ways that reflected their views on these matters. They centralized the union. A web of subordinate organizations came to link local union leaders to each other and to their superiors in the union. The process took place gradually as the two men climbed the ranks. Beck's Western Conference of Teamsters, formed in 1937, had been an unofficial organization. The Southern Conference, formed in 1944, enjoyed similar status. But in 1947 the Teamsters Convention amended the union's constitution to formally recognize such structures and to allow the General Executive Board to create them in other districts. When he became president in 1952 Beck promptly ordered the creation of the Central and Eastern Conferences, thus dividing the country into four large districts. Participation by local unions had originally been voluntary, but from 1947 to 1961 it became increasingly mandatory. Within the conferences existed regional trade divisions that covered the range of industries in which Teamsters worked, from local cartage to vending machines. These trade divisions, in turn, also had their own national divisions, which created yet another set of intermediate links between local officers and the national union.[38]

The conferences and trade divisions served a number of different purposes. They helped encourage and sustain organizing campaigns. They also raised money for organizing campaigns, coordinated additional organizing staff, and served as forums in which techniques and victories could be shared. In addition, the regular meetings sponsored by these bodies fostered a sense of professionalism among thousands of local union officials who attended them. Like business executives coming together at a convention, local officials came to develop bonds of familiarity and share a common professional identity. Rules mandating that attendees be paid local union officials rather than elected delegates encouraged the process. These were not meetings for the rank and file but for career officials who worked on salary. Finally, the intermediate bodies provided a means of supervising the conduct and progress of local union officials. Conferences and trade divisions assiduously worked to compile information on the progress of organization in various occupation groups for each local union. Questionnaires were sent out regarding how many shops remained to be organized and what conditions had been achieved for the members already signed up. Much more than ever before, local leaders had someone looking over their shoulders.[39]

Hoffa also pushed the process of centralization along by continually enlarging the size of the bargaining unit. Originally, each local union negotiated its own contracts with the employers in its jurisdiction. Locals involved in intercity trucking had broken away from that practice, however, and Hoffa, ever the innovator, led the way. During the 1930s and 1940s he gradually brought almost all trucking locals in the Southwest, South, and Midwest into one negotiating group that signed a master freight agreement covering employers in the entire region. After he became president of the IBT in 1957, Hoffa worked steadily to bring the remaining areas of the country into one single contract group for trucking. It was a painstaking process, but success finally came in January 1964 when he signed the National Master Freight Agreement (NMFA).[40] The pact covered workers involved in trucking and warehouses, but Hoffa envisioned a similar, if less conclusive, process for other trades covered by the union. In occupations such as the dairy industry, or in food canneries, he hoped to set up areawide bargaining units based on the four conferences.[41]

Many local union leaders resisted that process. Negotiating contracts and administering them had long been the perquisite of local leaders. Areawide bargaining took that away and left locals bound by decisions made in distant locations by their superiors in the union.[42] Moreover, the grievance procedure in such contracts, by which union leaders resolved job disputes and contract violations for members, put them at the mercy of Hoffa and his allies, who dominated conference-level hearing boards. Local leaders known to oppose Hoffa found themselves unable to win grievance hearings for their members.[43] In this way, they watched their autonomy bleeding away as the centralization of bargaining units progressed. By the 1952 Teamsters Convention, where Beck ran for president, some delegates had seen the handwriting on the wall. Peter Hoban from the Chicago Milk Drivers warned, "There is, Mr. Chairman, a very definite fear in the minds of a large number of delegates to this convention regarding the question of arbitrary control over [local] unions and the position of our International Union on the question of trusteeships and local autonomy."[44]

In fact, neither Beck nor Hoffa had much use for local autonomy. Donald Garnel, who has written the best study by far on Beck's early career, asserts,

"Had his authority been unfettered, Beck most likely would have placed all locals under trusteeship in order to weld them into an effective organizing machine."[45] Hoffa, too, willingly intervened in local affairs whenever he felt a local and its leadership had failed to measure up to his standards. As he explained, "I just don't go in front of the membership and say please what do you want. I bring out the demands. I tell them what I think they're entitled to, what I think I can get, and then I fight to get them to accept my idea." If a local proved resistant, Hoffa stepped in and took over. "If we have a strike, where they won't listen, then we put the local in trusteeship."[46]

Both men used trusteeships to promote the professionalization of local union leadership. For Beck, trusteeships provided a useful tool for developing and overseeing a union official's career. As new local unions were organized in the Western Conference of Teamsters, Beck kept a sharp eye on the local leaders who emerged. Usually the first officer was someone popular among the rank and file, probably a good speaker. As time went by, Beck would monitor the local's membership size. If no increases occurred, if some of the membership fell away, or if the union failed to organize its local industry, he would meet with the local leader. He would also inquire about the difficulties being encountered and issue a warning. If things did not improve in the next three to four months, Beck would admonish, the local would go into trusteeship. "We were setting up these organizations and we were getting people elected into office, and after a period of six, seven months, a year, year and a half, [the locals] were standing still or going backward. They were developing no qualities of leadership." In such cases Beck placed the local into trusteeship and appointed the new leader based on his own assessment of the potential pool of candidates. Often enough he chose one of the organizers who worked on his staff at the Western Conference. The new man faced the same pressure to perform and suffered the same fate when he failed.[47]

When Beck became president of the national union, local leaders all across the country came under the same pressure to succeed. According to one account, in a speech before the Ohio Conference of Teamsters in early 1953 Hoffa told assembled local officials that they had better get busy and organize. If they did not, he warned, Beck now had the authority to throw their locals into trusteeship, and, Hoffa assured them, that is precisely what he would do.[48] The trend continued after Hoffa became president in 1957. In 1958 he told Eastern Conference delegates that he would hold local leaders to standards of productivity. "It is going to be necessary," he said, "to review individual [local union] charters and see whether they are organizing their jurisdiction, or whether they are taking the position that they have a little kingdom all their own." The days of such autonomy, he announced, were over.[49]

Under this regime the Teamsters became very aggressive organizers. When Beck became executive vice president in 1947 he launched a series of organizing campaigns that helped increase membership from 890,000 to 1,120,000 by 1952. On assuming the presidency, he redoubled those efforts. Money spent on organizing grew ninefold during Beck's administration. Membership went from 1,075,508 in 1951 to 1,368,082 in 1956. During Hoffa's first term in office he further increased spending on organizing, and even amid a wave of hostile publicity the union continued to grow.[50] In this onslaught, staunchly anti-union corporations gave up their resistance. The old nemesis, Montgomery Ward and Company, long a bastion of defiance to union organizers, signed a national agreement with the Teamsters in 1955, bringing fifteen thousand workers under contract.[51]

Such was the union's reputation that dissatisfied leaders from CIO unions brought their locals into the IBT to benefit from its organizing elan. In 1948 in St. Louis, Harold Gibbons pulled his warehouse workers union out of a CIO affiliate and into the Teamsters, explaining to his members, "We picked the most aggressive union in America to become part of."[52] At the local level, union representatives bragged to employers that the Teamsters would organize absolutely everyone within their sprawling jurisdiction. A small employer in rural Nebraska recalled being told in 1955, "It was the intention of the Teamsters Union, through these tactics, to organize everybody in the State of Nebraska, clear on down to what he [the Teamster official] called the prune peddler, referring to grocery store clerks. 'First we will get you and all the rest of the truckers. Then we will get the warehousemen, and then we will get every grocery store and hardware store in the State of Nebraska through the same methods.'"[53] The representatives sounded both assured and relentless.[54]

The Achievements and Shortcomings of an Opportunistic Union

The union's growth served no overriding ideological purpose. Seen by its leaders as a kind of expanding service enterprise, the IBT made no claims beyond seeking to meet the needs and desires of the membership. Neither Beck nor Hoffa sought to challenge or reform the capitalistic economic system, and given their narrow field of focus they seemed unlikely to become agents of social change. And yet, precisely because of their single-minded devotion to building the size and strength of the union, both men practiced union policies that occasionally pushed against the accepted conventions of the day. Ideologically crass, they occasionally formed alliances with radicals who, at the height of the cold war, the rest of the labor movement had declared persona non grata. Their desire to strengthen the union in the South led them to challenge racial conventions and made the Teamsters a target of criticism by white supremacists. This union of very traditional-minded men even found itself defending the equal workplace rights of women—once women became members. These developments should not be overstated. Because such policies stemmed from opportunism, they had at best a limited effect; racism and sexism remained very real problems within the union and the workplaces it covered. But the business unionism practiced within the Teamsters did bring real benefits, both tangible and intangible, to the mass of workers who belonged. That was true across the boundaries of ethnicity, race, and gender. Even though the union set limited goals, it still must be admitted that it brought its membership very real benefits.

Both Beck and Hoffa frequently talked about politics, but neither had an emotional commitment to any particular party, agenda, or ideology. Rhetorically, Beck plied a very conservative, laissez-faire, pro-business line. As the journalist A. H. Raskin put it, "His tributes to free enterprise would make Babbitt blush."[55] All of that talk, and by all accounts there was a lot of it, had little connection to Beck's actual policies and agendas. He backed political candidates based on whether he believed they would win and would support his union, paying little attention to political party. Thus, at the same time he supported a New Deal Democrat for governor in one state and a Republican in another. Often he would put union money into the campaigns of both candidates for an office, hoping to buy the gratitude of whomever won. He read off speeches praising free enterprise, but in practice he used the union to engineer collusive agreements that strictly regulated competition in organized industries. He denounced the threat of communism loudly. But when union leaders who had alleged communist ties sought to take their locals out of the Brewery Workers Union, Beck welcomed them into the IBT, blithely weathering the criticism he received as a result. When he was president, his Western Conference of Teamsters signed a mutual aid pact with the International Union of Mine, Mill, and Smelter Workers, an organization expelled from the CIO because of its alleged communist affiliations. Beck tacitly approved the deal. The point is not that he had secret leftist sympathies but that he had little real commitment to any ideology and simply sought to better the position of his union. Until the rise of the CIO, Beck often had been castigated as a radical threat, and in response he apparently had seen the practical benefits of publicly identifying himself as pro-business. It made the union's accumulation of power seem less threatening, and it lessened the resistance of the business community. Asked about Beck's proclivity for conservative rhetoric, a union official who had worked closely with him explained, "He talks about free enterprise with tongue in cheek, I think. He thinks it will enable him to organize big groups of workers."[56]

Except for the fact that he engaged in no pretense on the matter, Hoffa's political orientation followed the same pragmatic bent as Beck's. As one journalist who profiled him wrote, "Ideas don't interest Hoffa. Neither do political issues that don't directly affect labor."[57] He identified strongly with neither party, and he backed political candidates on both sides when doing so served his purposes.[58] With no strong ideological moorings, his actions occasionally defied expectations. Thus, although most observers saw him as a conservative unionist, Hoffa flaunted his indifference to the anticommunist strictures of the times. During the late 1950s he reached out to the head of International Longshoremen's and Warehousemen's Union, Harry Bridges, whose ties to the Communist Party had led the CIO to expel his organization. The Teamsters, Hoffa asserted, "are not interested in Bridges's politics— we are interested in avoiding jurisdictional conflict as automation takes over the docks." Seeing a similar need, Hoffa established a mutual aid pact with the radical Mine, Mill, and Smelter Workers Union.[59] Outraged conservatives in Congress held hearings on the matter, but Hoffa refused to respond to their concerns.[60] His opportunism led him to work with unions whose radical affiliations made them pariahs to the rest of the labor movement.

Because they were ideologically crass and narrow-minded, examples of Beck and Hoffa's openness to the left-wing element in the union movement can easily be counterpoised against innumerable instances of red-baiting. When it served their purposes both men raised the issue of communism to denounce opponents and rivals. Thus Beck, in the 1940s, worked to destroy the Food, Tobacco, Agricultural, and Allied Workers of America (FTA) because it stood in the way of the Teamster drive in California canneries. A progressive union whose leadership had connections to the Communist Party, the FTA had been the first labor organization to seriously address the needs of the cannery workforce. The FTA offered a model of democratic openness, welcoming immigrants, minorities, and women into its leadership ranks. More than that, it pioneered a workplace feminism that empowered women and used the union contract to meet their specific needs. FTA contracts, for instance, called for maternity leave without loss of seniority. The union advocated a broad agenda of social justice that involved not just workplace issues but the rights of women, minorities, and the poor in society.

Making the charge of communism a mainstay of his campaign, Beck directed a successful effort to supplant the FTA in the northern and central California agricultural regions. By the 1950s it had faded from existence.[61] For his
part, Hoffa played an important role suppressing a Trotskyite Teamster local Minneapolis in the 1940s because Tobin had made it clear that doing so
would help his career.[62] Teamsters under Beck and Hoffa, therefore, may have
defiantly ignored convention, but they did little to advance the overall cause
of progressive unionism.

The union's attitude toward African American civil rights grew out of a
similar spirit of opportunism, but here the Teamsters made more substantial claims for themselves. A publicity document put out by the organization
in 1964 asserted, "Without headlines, through consistent application of the
union's doctrine of uniformity for all, the Teamsters probably have done
more constructive and successful work for civil rights than any other single
organization." They boasted of having two hundred thousand African American members, accounting for about 20 percent of all blacks enrolled in
American labor unions. As members, African Americans were guaranteed fair
treatment, it was argued, because the IBT maintained a formal clause in its
constitution against racial discrimination. As the brochure put it, this was
"civil rights—WITHOUT HOOPLA."[63]

In fact, the union had taken some relatively progressive steps in the area
of race relations. When the Teamsters had begun vigorous organization in
the South during the 1940s they had to confront conventions of white supremacy that challenged collective action by black workers and were particularly hostile to any kind of collective action that blurred racial lines. In contrast to other AFL affiliates, the Teamsters pushed for a more inclusive labor
movement in the South. In Memphis, for instance, they sought to distance
themselves from the AFL. As one organizer wrote to the national office, "The
population of this city is comprised of about 48 percent Negroes. It is a known
fact that the Negroes who go to the [AFL] Labor Temple are not welcome
there by the powers to be, and on several occasions they have been thrown
out of the Labor Temple individually. This kind of treatment is certainly
organizing, or playing into the hands of the CIO."[64] Working outside the
AFL's structure, Teamster organizers in that city focused on organizing black
workers.[65]

At the same time, the IBT's policies regarding segregation in the South
remained ambiguous. Memphis's Local 667 was integrated, but separate all-
black locals continued to exist elsewhere.[66] Throughout the 1940s and early
1950s the IBT made no formal pronouncement on the rationale for allowing such locals to continue, but neither did it see them as undercutting the

union's claims of equal treatment. In 1954 a report on Joint Council 58 in South Texas asserted, "Local unions are breaking down racial barriers and giving the Negro population and those of Mexican descent equal opportunity to earn a livelihood. They not only give strong support to all-colored locals in their disputes, but their mixed locals are going out of their way to avoid discrimination in job placement."[67] Only after Hoffa became president in 1958 did the union move with determination to end segregated locals in the South.[68]

After World War II the union publicly staked out a progressive position on race relations. During the war, Beck had led the way in denouncing Japanese Americans and demanding their removal from the West Coast. By the war's end, however, he abandoned such rhetoric and over time came to speak out against discrimination.[69] In 1955, the year after the Supreme Court's decision in *Brown v. Topeka Board of Education,* Beck announced in the union's journal:

> I repeat that our union does not recognize a color line. I care not whether this is popular or unpopular. I know it is right and you know that it is right. Everyone who searches his conscience knows that it is right. That is the basis upon which we are building this International Union. The Teamsters Union does not care what a man's religion is, or what his race or his color or his creed is. All of us have the same hopes and the same desires. We all have a wish that our children shall have it a little better than we did. These are the things your union will fight for in the South.[70]

By way of comparison, Dwight Eisenhower, whom Beck had supported for president in 1952, opposed desegregation of the Armed Forces and refused to endorse the Supreme Court's decision in the *Brown* case.[71] For his part, in 1965 Hoffa directed the IBT to donate $25,000 to Martin Luther King's Southern Christian Leadership Conference.[72]

Defenders of white supremacy in the South came to look upon the Teamsters with hostility. For example, the *White Sentinel,* whose masthead bore the slogan "Racial Integrity—Not Amalgamation," devoted several pages of its April 1959 issue to criticizing the Teamsters under Hoffa. A picture on the front page showed Hoffa shaking hands with an African American Teamster official. The paper blamed the union for forcing southern employers to integrate their workforces by installing antidiscrimination clauses in Teamster contracts.[73]

Although the union's policies raised the ire of southern white supremacists, it did not consistently champion civil rights for black workers. At the local level, in the South and the North, various kinds of discriminatory practices blocked African American members from achieving real equality. For instance, separate seniority lists for local delivery and dock labor kept blacks from gaining their share of the more lucrative long-haul trucking assignments. Although they might have been members for more than a decade, their seniority did not apply to any bid they might put in for over-the-road jobs at their companies. For all of its talk about fairness, the IBT did not mobilize to end such practices.[74]

Not being ideologically committed to civil rights, Beck and Hoffa were willing to go only so far in the name of fairness. They balanced the gains the union might make in recruiting black members against the dissension that a real civil rights campaign might generate among conservative white members.[75] A strong union, not the vision of racially egalitarian society, motivated them, and they acted accordingly.

In weighing the shortcomings of the IBT in this area, however, it is worth considering the conduct of other unions during the same period. Kevin Boyle has described the racial policies and practices of the United Auto Workers (UAW) during the 1950s. African Americans constituted about the same proportion of membership in both unions. The top leadership of the UAW took a much more progressive political stance than Beck and Hoffa, but, Boyle notes, the UAW was troubled by many of the same discriminatory practices. Although the union rhetorically championed civil rights, Boyle concludes that African American members achieved only a measured victory in the UAW. On the one hand, they benefited from the seniority and grievance provisions of union contracts as well as the substantial wage gains won by the union. On the other hand, however, they were denied equal access to the full range of jobs in the UAW jurisdiction.[76] In the IBT the prevalence of local discrimination, balanced against the benefits brought by membership, offered a similar measured victory to black Teamsters.

The same kind of qualifications apply to generalizations about the IBT's treatment of female members during this period. In the early 1960s about eighty thousand women belonged to the union, which by then claimed 1.7 million members in total.[77] Typically, the women worked assembly-line jobs in the dairy and canning industry, although many also were employed in warehouse operations. As it had done in the case of its African American membership, the IBT made proud claims of equal treatment for female Teamsters, motivated once again by a desire to build the union's strength. Promoting this vision of equality in 1955, the *International Teamster* profiled Mrs. Helen Foley Gavin as a typical member. She was described as a dutiful shop steward who appreciated the wage gains won for her by the union. The article concluded, "She and her sister workers have learned that their union is not 'a man's union' which will 'sell the women down the river' when the going gets tough."[78] Officially, the union championed the goal of workplace equality between the sexes. The Teamster leadership asserted that "equal wages would be paid to all men and women doing the same work."[79] Yet one need not dig too deeply for evidence of discrimination at the local level. Officers connived with the male-dominated membership to keep women out of particular occupations, such as cabdriving.[80]

Still, membership for women, even under such conditions, had its benefits. A Teamsters Union contract offered higher wages and a form of protection for working women, and they could use the union's grievance process as a venue for complaints about gender discrimination. Women dairy workers in Wisconsin during the early 1950s, for instance, drew on the language in their contract to pressure their local union leadership to take steps to stop management from reassigning their jobs to men.[81] In this way, women Teamsters formed part of a larger process of change that has received growing attention from women's historians. Although they might not have identified themselves as feminists, and although they pre-date the rise of second-wave feminism, women union members during the 1950s used their labor organizations to struggle against gender-based discrimination. Their efforts constitute another side of the women's movement, one centered on the needs of working-class women. As Dorothy Sue Cobble summarizes this argument, "In the 1940s and 1950s, labor organizations may have spurred feminism among wage-earning women much as civil rights and New Left organizations did for a very different group of women in the 1960s and 1970s."[82] Women in the Teamsters who used their union contract to demand fairer allocation of work were taking part in that larger process of change.

Under the leadership of Beck and Hoffa, the Teamsters conducted a sprawling expansion that brought the union into a range of different industries and increased its presence in the South and West. In the process, the union welcomed into its ranks women and minorities and offered them higher wages and workplace protection. The Teamsters remained, however, a union led by white men interested in building an organization rather than achieving social justice. Beck and Hoffa willingly flaunted social convention if doing so served their interests, but they scorned the progressive visions of their counterparts in the labor movement. Given their limited goals, the union's complacent attitude toward discrimination within its ranks is unsurprising. The way in which this ideologically crass leadership did, in the end, aid the forces of social change, however, make it wrong to merely label it conservative.

Delivering the Goods: What the Members Received

Although they did not aspire to change society, Beck and Hoffa did promise to give the membership real benefits in return for their union dues. These benefits came in the form of better wages and working conditions and also involved more emotionally laden issues such as status and security. Measuring how well the leadership made good on those promises raises some methodological issues. What exactly members received varied according to their occupation and the contracts negotiated for them. The Teamsters Union of the 1950s covered such a broad range of workers that identifying a typical member in order to describe his or her benefits is a quixotic endeavor. Officially the union's jurisdiction included "drivers, gas station attendants, warehousemen, dairy employees, ice cream plant employees, cannery workers, all truck terminal employees, including office workers, and brewery workers." A catch-all provision expanded this jurisdiction even further by including any "other workers where the security and the bargaining positions of the above classifications requires the organization of such workers."[83] Numerically, warehouse workers, who made up 25 percent of the membership, may have been the most sizable block. In many ways, however, truckers, especially over-the-road drivers, formed the heart and soul of the union.

With about a million members in 1950, the IBT estimated that two hundred thousand of them worked for interstate trucking firms.[84] Hoffa, who had entered the union as a warehouse worker, came to identify closely with these drivers. Indeed, he took time off at the peak of his career in 1961 to learn to drive a tractor-trailer.[85] It was not simply a romantic gesture. Hoffa understood that the IBT had grown and prospered because of the strategic power of long-haul truckers. During his career the most famous of Teamster presidents always paid special attention to that segment of the union.[86]

As a union constituency, the over-the-road drivers had a particular set of attitudes and concerns. Although they were a relatively recent creation, in many ways the drivers resembled the teamsters from the turn of the century. Like that earlier generation, long-haul truckers worked at a job that many considered low skill and one that seemed to carry no prestige. As with their predecessors, that low-skill image was deceptive. To drive a fully loaded big rig demanded a great deal of skill and endurance—and often a hefty amount of nerve. M. Murphy, a writer for the *New Yorker,* hitched a ride with a long-haul driver in 1949 from Terre Haute, Indiana, to New York City. Murphy noted that "the standard portrayal" of a trucker was "as a stupid fellow, a roughneck, or a homely philosopher." A short stint onboard a truck, however, convinced Murphy that the over-the-road drivers were "by and large, as competent and intelligent a group of skilled workers as one could find anywhere." The job demanded concentration. Good drivers paid constant attention to their engines and to the road. Murphy observed, "The truck felt, as sensitively as a carpenter's level, every deviation from dead horizontal." The driver in turn shifted to accommodate each minute change in the road's grade, sometimes shifting as often as every few seconds. The goal was to get as much out of the engine as possible "without straining it by staying an instant too long in a gear higher than the truck's speed and the grade of the road warranted."[87]

Traffic also required the driver's attention. The open road had its share of other cars and trucks, but in the 1940s and 1950s, before the creation of the interstate system, an over-the-road driver's route almost always went through the heart of several cities and towns. Murphy's companion in 1949 made his way steadily through downtown Indianapolis and a string of smaller towns from Ohio to New Jersey and into the West Side of Manhattan.[88] Another trucker who began hauling steel in those same years recalled the tortuous route from the steel mills of Gary, Indiana, to his destination in Milwaukee, Wisconsin. It took him two hours of hard driving to get to the North Side of Chicago. On the way, he encountered seventy-six traffic lights. "Every one of them had to be individually timed and played differently. If you have to stop that truck and start it, it's not only aggravating and tiring, but you'd wear out the truck twice as fast as you would if you made those lights. It was a constant thing of playing these lights almost by instinct."[89]

Driving was only part of the battle. Truckers also had to pay attention to how their freight was loaded. Each commodity presented a different set of problems in terms of weight, balance, and distribution. J. W. Dildine, who began driving in 1954, recalled the "peculiarities" of delivering new cars to auto dealerships—what he termed the "car haul craft." Dildine described how drivers who did such work needed special training and abilities "to learn how to load and properly tie down the units, keep them free from damage, as well as unload them. Some people can't do it because they are fearful of heights. They have to climb up and down and sometimes work with both hands and have a leg wrapped around a stanchion or something to keep balance." The work presented a range of risks. Dildine described men losing legs, suffering other serious injuries, and even being killed in accidents that occurred as they sought to load or unload cars. Looking back on his years driving car haul, he concluded, "It takes a special kind of guy that can really do this job."[90]

For all of their expertise, truckers often felt ill-treated by much of the rest of the working world. In this way, too, they echoed the Teamsters of an earlier generation. Al Young, who had helped to found the Teamsters Union in Chicago, declared in 1903, "We have to stand more abuse than any other craft in existence. We have to stand the abuse of every shipping clerk, in every office, as well as the abuse of everyone who has charge of the freight we handle."[91] Seventy years later, when journalist Studs Terkel interviewed an over-the-road trucker about his career, he heard a complaint that closely resembled Young's charge: "In the steel mill, the truckdriver is at the absolute bottom of the barrel." Terkel's interviewee felt that the lower echelons in steel mills tried to heighten their status by hassling truckers. That attitude, the driver argued, ran throughout plants and included the men who set loads for trucks. "He wants to feel that he's better than somebody. He figures I'm better than this steel hauler. So you get constant animosity because he feels that the corporation looks down on this steel hauler, and he knows he can order him around, abuse him, make him wait. It's a status thing. There's tremendous feeling."[92]

To the drivers, American society in general seemed to offer only more of the same dismissive attitude, and that rankled them. Earl Quigley, a local union official in Cincinnati, reviewed a half-dozen examples that highlighted the lowly status of truckers in popular culture. In a film, he asserted, a woman had expressed indifference to a potential suitor by saying, "I'd rather marry a truck driver." A cartoon pictured a boy swearing. When rebuked by his father he replied, "But, Dad, if I'm going to be a truck driver I have to learn to swear." Quigley did not find such references humorous. "Why," he asked, "should the truck driver be singled out as the lowest and most degraded form of humanity? Why should truck drivers be treated as though it were impossible for them to achieve anything requiring intelligence beyond the mental age of three?"[93] Derided and abused, drivers felt that their dignity as workers, and as adults, was under assault.

The union offered protection in both wages and hours and in terms of self-respect. Apparently, separate statistics do not exist for long-haul truckers, but union truck drivers in general saw their wage rates increase by 88 percent between 1939 and 1949. Truckers in Beck's West Coast region led the way with the highest average wages among truckers across the country. In the same period, the hours of work decreased.[94] According to survey information from the Department of Labor, the average driver worked 12 percent fewer hours in 1956 than in 1936.[95] The U.S. Census reported that truckers in 1950 had an annual median income of $2,030; workers in manufacturing, by way of contrast, had a median income of $1,783; and those in construction earned $2,024.[96]

Along with wage increases came an attractive set of fringe benefits. A 1956 survey by the Department of Labor found that 85 percent of all local truck drivers and their helpers were covered by a welfare plan, and 50 percent had pension coverage. For 90 percent of those workers such coverage came at no personal cost but were funded by contributions from employers. Pension benefits tended to be relatively generous. In 1961 a member of Hoffa's Central States bargaining group could retire at age sixty-five, after twenty-five years of service, and receive a monthly pension of $200 for the first five years. By way of comparison, a member of the United Mine Workers Union who retired at sixty-five would receive a monthly payment of $75; in the United Auto Workers, an employee of General Motors could collect $70.[97] In addition, drivers received regular paid vacations every year: one week after the first year of employment, two weeks after three years on the job, three weeks after twelve years of seniority, and, finally, four weeks after working for twenty years.[98]

Every union trucker had only to look at a non-union, independent contractor counterpart to regain appreciation for what the union had accomplished. "Gypsy truckers" contracted on an individual basis for every load they carried. They often lived in a kind of debt peonage, working long hours to try to make the mortgage payments on their trucks. These were the drivers who popped amphetamines to make back-to-back, seventy-two-hour hauls across the mountains. They would grab sleep in their truck cabs and push the limits of endurance, sometimes too far. With no protection, these drivers had to take whatever was handed to them.[99] It was conditions as much as money that changed when the union organized the trucking industry; the IBT offered security and a measure of dignity. As one driver told a reporter for the *New Republic* in 1947, "Now you can be a human being when you work, not a goddamn slave. It's all in the contract."[100]

Teamster contracts, in fact, offered members a range of provisions that went beyond wages and fringe benefits to guard the security of members on the job against a variety of threats. The union worked to protect them from the often casual nature of employment in the industry. Most contracts specified that once a member had been called in to work, he was guaranteed a certain specified number of hours; by 1955 more than a half-million members worked under contracts that guaranteed them a forty-hour work week.[101] Such provisions provided the basic stability that came with a steady paycheck. Another kind of stability came from contract language that required regular delivery routes to be assigned a year at a time, with drivers allowed to bid for them based on seniority. In addition, the basic terms of the contract blocked an employer, or the employer's supervisor, from tyrannizing the workforce. Any firing over a disciplinary matter had to first be preceded by a formal written warning, with a copy sent to both the member and the local union. Only in cases of dishonesty, drunkenness, and reckless driving that led to a serious accident could an employee be fired on the spot. Even then, they had the right to have the decision reviewed. These provisions did not make members invulnerable, but they did provide security against the unjust whims of hostile supervisors.[102]

The union, in the form of a local officer and shop steward, served as an advocate for fairness and justice in the workplace. Local 695, based in Waukesha, Wisconsin, sent its shop stewards a short guidebook on their jobs that explained, "When given a complaint, a Steward, Shop Chairman or Committee Member should ask himself these questions: Has the contract been violated or has the employee been treated unfairly by some action of the company? A 'yes' to either of the questions indicates a grievance." Stewards were admonished, "Your job is not just to go along on a grievance. Your job is to get a settlement consistent with the justice of the case."[103] Local 695's paid officers, business agents, followed the same philosophy. On a regular basis they intervened in workplace disputes where drivers felt themselves unfairly treated in ways as mundane as being made to work through lunch breaks or being asked to come in on their days off to wash the trucks.[104] In and of themselves these were small incidents, but they exemplified an important role for the union. Faced with an intimidating supervisor, local officers gave voice not just to contractual issues but to vaguer concerns about members' workplace environments.

That such nonpecuniary benefits mattered was demonstrated by an extensive opinion survey of Teamster members in a St. Louis local during the early 1950s. The sociologist who oversaw the study noted, "Getting higher wages (or the equivalent) stands out in most workers' minds as the most important purpose of a union, of course, but substantial proportions spontaneously mentioned getting job security, gaining rights, and getting benefits off the job (such as opportunities for recreation, medical care, and legal advice)."[105]

In the end, wages, hours, benefits, and security provisions all made up a package of benefits provided by the Teamsters, and they were often lumped together when workers described what their membership brought them. The total package provided a chance to establish a dignified and decent lifestyle. In turn, for the overwhelmingly male membership, that dignity involved fulfilling the patriarchal role of father and domestic provider. The profile of a union cabdriver in the *International Teamster* in 1956 began, "Things were tough for Martin O'Donnell of Philadelphia until 'the union' came, bringing job security, dignity, contentment." The accompanying text and pictures, emphasized how the union had allowed O'Donnell to fulfill his patriarchal role. Union wages had allowed him to buy a "handsome two-story house," and the regular schedule enforced by the contract allowed him to be an active father to his five children. "Evening is a family affair at the O'Donnell home," the article explained, "where all present gather in the living room to await the favorite TV program." Twenty years earlier, the O'Donnells had to get married on the Fourth of July "so that he wouldn't lose a day's work and a day's pay." Because of the union, however, O'Donnell could take three days off to bring his sons to a basketball tournament in New York City.[106] The union ensured a man's financial ability to fulfill this paternal role. A local Teamster leader in Cincinnati wrote to the columnist Westbrook Pegler in 1947, "The average truck driver is a family man, earning a living wage (thanks to the union), who takes pride in his home and his job."[107]

Conclusion

From the perspective of what the Teamsters Union might have done, the IBT has appeared to many current observers as largely a disappointment. Led by quintessential business unionists, the IBT focused on the narrow goals of better wages and hours. Meanwhile, the union's officers enmeshed the rank and file into a web of contractual obligations that offered members security and good wages in return for obedient compliance. At the local level, the organization often abetted discrimination against minorities and women. Meanwhile, a corps of salaried officials turned an organization that might have been a force for social change into something much more like a profitable service industry. For these observers, the fate of the nation's largest union highlighted the generally disappointing outcome of American organized labor after World War II.[108]

Seen from the perspective of the times, however, that conclusion is more problematic. Conservatives, business groups, and the media viewed the Teamsters not as a safe vehicle for controlling the unruly working class but as a dangerous organizing machine. It led the way in what to the 1950s seemed a very aggressive labor movement. When *Fortune* profiled the IBT in 1953, the magazine asserted, "Dave Beck's Teamsters are the 'hottest' thing in the labor movement since the formation of the C.I.O." In the IBT's relentless quest for more members and a stronger union, the organization brushed aside many conventions of the day. In the process, it offered tangible benefits to minorities and women. Wages, hours, and contractually determined work rules all formed part of a package that helped its general membership fulfill broader expectations. To the typical truck driver, the union offered a chance to achieve dignity. Only when that chance was betrayed would members see their organization as a disappointment.

8. The Revelations of the McClellan
   Committee: Corruption in the Teamsters
   during the 1950s

From 1957 to 1959 the U.S. Senate's Select Committee on Improper Practices
in the Fields of Labor or Management, better known as the McClellan Committee, held hearings on the problem of union corruption. The single largest investigation into labor corruption in American history, the McClellan
Committee mobilized impressive resources. The hearings lasted for two and
a half years, and in that time 1,525 witnesses testified, their testimony filling
more than fifty bound volumes. All told, the massive record compiled by the
committee ran to more than fourteen million words. The committee's staff
of over one hundred, including thirty-five investigators and forty-five investigative accountants, was the largest yet assembled for a congressional committee. Robert F. Kennedy served as chief counsel to the committee, exhibit-
ing a flair for recruiting and motivating a talented staff of investigators.[1] As
a result of their hard work, the problem of labor corruption received enormous public attention and became a cause of great concern. By 1959 Americans polled listed "labor union problems" among the top eight problems
facing the country, equal with the problems of national defense, the space
race, and education.[2]

   The McClellan Committee investigated a number of different unions, including the United Auto Workers, the Carpenters, and the Operating Engineers, but it directed the bulk of its attention to the International Brotherhood
of Teamsters (IBT).[3] In a series of hearings and reports the committee publicized the misconduct of numerous Teamster leaders and made the Teamsters
the most widely known example of the problem of union corruption.

   The findings of the committee offer a window into the problem of corruption in the Teamsters during the 1950s. They demonstrate that both Dave

Beck and Jimmy Hoffa engaged in activities that violated the trust of their membership. For his part, Hoffa also abetted the growing influence of organized crime within the Teamsters, and his career affords an example of the problem of union officials with mob ties. Moreover, during Hoffa's leadership of the union a new and lucrative source of corruption emerged as he facilitated efforts by organized crime to tap into the union's benefit funds. As in previous periods, the source of the corruption cannot simply be explained by reference to individual immorality or to a particular official's ideological leanings. The opportunistic business unionist and the progressive union crusader found themselves facing the same difficult choices. The actual decision made depended more upon the resources available than the ideological predisposition of the official involved. Finally, the scale and nature of the corruption that occurred corresponded to long-term trends in the Teamsters Union, and those trends reflected the economic environment in which the union operated.

Acts of Betrayal

The McClellan Committee drew on the previous work of investigative journalists, other congressional committees, local investigations, and its own sizable staff of investigators to lay bare recurring patterns of misconduct within the Teamsters Union.[4] Dave Beck, president from 1952 to 1957, engaged in various kinds of financial practices that at their worst constituted embezzlement and at best were a breach of fiduciary duty. For his part, Hoffa, who became president in 1957, took part in business ventures with employers that created a conflict of interest with his union position. Given his attempts to disguise these ventures, it seems probable that they served as a way for him to receive gratuities. More than that, however, the McClellan Committee profiled Hoffa's apparent willingness to support and encourage the presence of well-known gangsters within the union. He seemed to function as a conduit for the influence of organized crime in the Teamsters. Taken together, these actions amounted to a betrayal of the memberships' interests, thus fitting the narrowest definition of the term *corruption*.

The McClellan Committee's earliest revelations centered on the financial activities of Beck. Always eager to tout his success, in the early 1950s he let it be spread about that he had become a millionaire. His wealth, he claimed, came from successful real estate and securities speculation. The $50,000 a year he received from the Teamsters Union, he said, went almost entirely to pay the taxes on his private income.[5] News stories about his wealth attracted the attention of a Seattle agent for the Internal Revenue Service (IRS), who began to dig into Beck's tax records. He soon found a problem. Beck's net worth had gone from $63,000 in 1943 to more than $1 million in 1954, but the means of that ascent were unclear. Beck could not account for where a big chunk of his wealth had come from. As it turned out, he could not do so because a significant portion had come from the union's treasury. Between 1949 and 1954 he took about $370,000 out of union funds for his personal benefit, mainly to reconstruct his house and pay personal bills.

Responding to the scrutiny of the IRS, Beck now referred to this money as a series of interest-free loans, and he set about finding a way to pay it back. In the short term, he arranged to get a $200,000 loan from a large trucking company. But when that company wanted its money back, Beck went to the IBT and asked the union to buy his house from him. Here he followed a precedent begun under Tobin, who had lived in a residence owned by the union. The difference in this case was that Beck had already used $196,000 from union funds to pay construction costs for the house. He was double-billing the union. The vice presidents on the General Executive Board expressed some objections, but eventually they gave Beck $163,000 for the house he had rebuilt with union funds. Beck, in turn, used that money to pay his debts.[6]

As he was in the process of trying to resolve his tax problems through these transactions, Senate investigators began looking into his affairs. In a series of hearings held in the early part of 1957, the McClellan Committee placed Beck's financial practices before the public. The hearings reviewed the troubling history behind the union's purchase of his house. They also profiled a number of other deals in which Beck had engaged that seemed to cross the line of propriety if not legality. Over the course of several years, Beck had received $85,000 worth of personal items paid for out of union funds. The items had been bought at Beck's request by a labor relations consultant named Nathan Shefferman. In turn, Beck had the union reimburse Shefferman for these purchases by paying out union funds to the consultant for nonexistent work. To highlight the fact that these purchases went directly toward subsidizing Beck's lifestyle, the committee had Shefferman read out a list of the items for which Beck had sent him bills requesting payment. The list was long, and Shefferman kept up a running commentary, "Shirts, he wears pretty good shirts . . . golf balls, I don't think he played golf, but he was very generous." Other testimony indicated that Beck had manipulated the trust fund of one his closest friends after the man's death in order to earn a profit at the widow's expense. He apparently schemed to make money on the purchase of land for the national union's new headquarters. And at one point he even used his office as president of the union to force local officials to buy little toy trucks from a company run by Dave Beck Junior. In sum, the hearings put forward a portrait of Beck as grasping and unprincipled.[7]

These revelations helped end Beck's career as a union leader. In 1956 the AFL-CIO Executive Board had approved a code of ethics that forbade a union officer from invoking Fifth Amendment privileges against self-incrimination "for his personal protection to avoid scrutiny by proper legislative committees." When Beck invoked the Fifth before the McClellan Committee, the AFL-CIO Executive Board met and voted to suspend him as a member of that board.[8] At the same time his support within the IBT evaporated, and by May 1957 Beck announced that he would not run for reelection in September.[9]

With Beck out of the picture, Hoffa eventually became the front-runner to replace him. Indeed, some evidence suggests that Hoffa fed the McClellan Committee investigators early leads about Beck's activities hoping for just such a result.[10] If that had been Hoffa's plan, however, his hopes seemed fairly bleak. By May he faced serious legal problems of his own. In February 1957 Hoffa had offered to pay an attorney, John Cye Cheasty, to spy on the Mc-Clellan Committee for him. Cheasty was to get a job on the committee's staff and then supply Hoffa with inside information about its investigations. Unfortunately for Hoffa, Cheasty reported the offer to Robert Kennedy, the chief counsel for the committee. Kennedy then arranged with the FBI to have Cheasty play along with Hoffa in the hope of catching him in the act of bribing a government official. The committee hired Cheasty, and Hoffa, under the watchful eye of the FBI, met with him to receive information. After the second rendezvous, the FBI stepped in and arrested Hoffa, who had in his possession committee documents for which he had just paid Cheasty. The case seemed air-tight. Robert Kennedy even jokingly offered to jump off the Capital dome if Hoffa escaped a guilty verdict.[11]

Sure that Hoffa had already been dealt with, Kennedy and the McClellan Committee moved on to other targets in the Teamsters and in other unions. Then, in July, a Washington, D.C., jury acquitted Hoffa on all charges. The jury had been swayed by Hoffa's forceful testimony in his own behalf. Overnight he went from an apparent lost cause to the leading candidate in the coming Teamster election. McClellan Committee investigators scrambled to gather enough material to hold hearings on Hoffa before the election. They hoped to produce the same kinds of damaging revelations on Hoffa that they had on Beck, and they assumed the result would be the end of Hoffa's career.[12]

But Hoffa proved to be a much more difficult target. By his own account he had faced almost a lifetime of hostile scrutiny. He told a reporter, "Since

1932 I been investigated almost on a continuous basis. By anybody and everybody. Private investigators hired by employers. Two congressional committees. Now the Senate Committee. Several grand juries. My wife and I been twenty-two years in this damn foot race. Twenty-two years of it." As a result, he took precautions. Hoffa never paid by check; he maintained no bank account; and he conducted important conversations either in person or over a pay telephone, keeping a supply of quarters ready for that express purpose. He also had his local union's records destroyed at regular intervals.[13]

His modest lifestyle belied charges of financial misconduct because it was hard to see what he was doing with illicit wealth. In contrast to Beck, Hoffa never developed a taste for ostentation. The Detroit Teamster leader continued to live in the same modest house into which he and his wife had first moved after they married. The family had acquired a summer cottage on a Michigan lake, but in this case the term *cottage* proved apt. It was a modest, almost Spartan place. Beck had used misappropriated Teamster funds to outfit himself in expensive new clothes, stylish suits, and Sulka ties, even one time spending $90 for socks from Saks Fifth Avenue. Hoffa's taste in clothing remained that of a working-class guy whose new job forced him to dress up occasionally. He refused to stop wearing plain white socks. One could see them poking out below the pants legs of his ill-fitting suit, even when he testified before Congress. Dark socks, he explained, made his feet sweaty.[14]

Finally, he was cagey. Hoffa never claimed complete innocence but was always willing to engage in verbal fencing with his interlocutors. He told a reporter that he prepared for the hearings by writing down everything he could think of that the committee might ask him. It amounted to several sheets of paper. As he explained it, "Then I got with the lawyers and went over each item. We'd rehearse what Kennedy would do. He isn't the brightest fella in the world. And he's got to investigate for weeks and weeks to find out what we already know . . . I know what I done wrong and what I didn't. I know what they'll uncover and what they won't. And that's two thirds of the worrying. All my life I been under investigation." On the stand, he carefully hedged his answers, qualifying them with "to the best of my recollection" and fiercely debating the implications of any line of questioning.[15]

In spite of Hoffa's preparations, the committee's hearings did present damaging information about his leadership of the union. He had profited from a truck-leasing business set up in the name of his wife and the wife of another union official. Both women had used their maiden names on the certificate of incorporation. The business papers had all been drawn up by a lawyer who had connections to a prominent trucking firm. That same firm had granted the women a very lucrative contract that in seven years yielded them a profit of $125,000 on an initial investment of $4,000. And, perhaps not coincidentally, that same trucking firm had previously been involved in a wildcat strike with its Teamster drivers. Hoffa explained that he had intervened to enforce the contract and sent the drivers back to work. The committee argued that Hoffa's leasing agreement was not a straightforward business deal but rather a way to reward a cooperative union official.[16] Hoffa vehemently denied this, but his decision to have the transaction conducted in his wife's maiden name suggested that he, too, had viewed it as improper and thus judged it best kept a secret.

The committee also raised the subject of a Florida land deal in which Hoffa had involved the union. A sometime real estate speculator had set up a retirement housing development while on the Teamster payroll, ostensibly working as a business agent in Hoffa's Detroit local. Hoffa arranged for the union to transfer $500,000 to a Florida bank in return for the bank advancing a like amount of credit to the speculator for his development. Teamster members were solicited to buy lots in this development for their old age. All the while Hoffa had a secret option to obtain a 45 percent interest in the project if it went anywhere.[17]

More than anything else, the committee questioned Hoffa about his role in bringing undesirable elements into the union or in sheltering the undesirable elements who were already there. They asked him, for instance, about two officers of a local union in Pontiac, Michigan. When rank-and-file members of the local had complained to Hoffa that their chief officers, Dan Keating and Louis Linteau, were taking payoffs from employers in return for not enforcing the union's contract, he sided with the officers. Later the two men were indicted by a Michigan grand jury on similar charges. Beck, then still president of the national union, removed them from office and appointed Hoffa trustee of the local. Hoffa turned around and installed Linteau and Keating to run the union for him. Eventually, both men were convicted and sent to jail on criminal charges that paralleled the initial complaints of the local's membership. Hoffa saw to it, however, that the officers' salaries were continued, and when the men got out of jail they received a union pension.[18]

Hoffa had explanations ready for all of these charges. Because the AFL-CIO had recently issued a code of ethical practices that forbade union officials from doing business with employers, he would have his wife sell her interest in the truck leasing firm. He still did not think involvement in such business deals was wrong, because, he claimed, they gave a union leader helpful insights about the employers with whom he dealt.[19] In regard to the real estate development, Hoffa asserted that the lots originally had been offered to Teamster members at $150 each and now were worth between $800 and $1,000. He did not tell the members or other union officials about his option on the deal "because nobody thought to inquire and I didn't think to tell them." And he stuck by people like Linteau and Keating because an indictment did not necessarily mean a conviction.[20]

All of his explanations, however, could not disguise the fact that he allowed certain individuals to use their union offices as a cover for criminal activity. Perhaps the McClellan Committee's most damaging revelations in this regard centered on the ties between Hoffa and John Dioguardia, sometimes known as "Johnny Dio." Reputedly a capo, or mid-level official, in the Lucchese crime family, Dioguardia was a well-known figure in New York's Garment District. Dress manufacturers who wanted to avoid being bothered by the union would go to him for help.[21] He maneuvered his way into a union position in 1950 with a charter from the United Auto Workers–AFL (UAW-AFL), a small labor organization that had broken with the more well-known United Auto Workers Union of the CIO. Eventually, the UAW-AFL issued Dioguardia a series of charters, and he made himself the union's district organizer in New York. These locals served as a pretense for milking money from small employers. The union's officers, mostly ex-convicts and career criminals, focused their activities on small manufacturing shops around New York. The owners of such shops would be approached by one of Dioguardia's associates with the proposition that the union, for a price, would grant them a very lenient contract. The contracts granted workers nothing more than minimum wage. By agreeing to such a contract and contributing the requisite dues, employers purchased protection from any other union that might come along to organize their workers. As usual, the line between bribery and extortion remained fuzzy. Some employers made payments out of fear, often as a result of threatened labor violence by Dioguardia's organizers. Others viewed the payments as a kind of insurance that protected them from Dioguardia but also from other bona fide unions. The only clear-cut victims were the workers trapped in a union that did nothing but extract dues payments.[22]

When a reform faction in the UAW-AFL moved to push out Dioguardia, Hoffa worked to bring him into the Teamsters. Apparently, Hoffa hoped to use the votes of Dioguardia's locals to swing a critical election in the New York Teamsters Joint Council toward his ally, John O'Rourke.[23] Hoffa's ties to Dioguardia, whom he described as a personal friend, drew much attention because in 1956 Dioguardia had been implicated in an acid attack that had blinded the labor journalist Victor Riesel.[24]

In the case of the former UAW-AFL locals, Hoffa ceded all control to men he knew were professional criminals. At best he made only a pretense of supervising what occurred in these locals. The McClellan Committee, for instance, had profiled the case of Teamsters Local 239, one of whose officers was Anthony ("Tony Ducks") Corallo, reportedly a powerful gangster and later to be listed as the head of the Lucchese crime family. During July and August 1957 the committee held hearings on Corallo's extensive arrest record and those of his fellow Local 239 officers. One of these other officers, Samuel Goldstein, had just been convicted of bribery in July 1957. In response to these revelations, Hoffa promised the committee that he would take action to clean up the local. In the fall of 1957 he vowed, "Those characters I am going to deal with, if it means I have got to have an argument with some people that I know and maybe get pretty serious. It will have to get serious and I will have the argument and we will straighten it out." A year later, when the committee looked at those locals again, Corallo was still an officer and so was Goldstein. The only change in the interval had been Goldstein's guilty plea to an extortion charge in March 1958, his second criminal conviction while serving as officer of Local 239. When the committee came back to the local again in June 1959, Corallo had resigned but Goldstein, although now in jail, continued as president of the local union.[25]

Hoffa's actual attitude toward all of this became apparent after the New York County District Attorney's Office released a transcript made from a listening device hidden in Corallo's apartment. The bug recorded a conversation on June 30, 1959, between Corallo and one of his associates who recently had returned from a visit with Hoffa. The Teamster president had just finished testifying at a McClellan Committee hearing on continued corruption in places like Local 239. According to Corallo's associate, Hoffa wanted the now-twice-convicted president of Corallo's Local 239, Goldstein, temporarily to step down from his office. Hoffa made it clear, however, that this would be only a short-term inconvenience until the McClellan Committee adjourned its hearings in a few months. The associate of Corallo explained, "Tony, the guy told me straight out, and I ain't making like my own words. I'm saying his words: I don't care if you want to—you want to steal, you want to rob, go ahead, he says—don't get caught, don't get caught***. [Asterisks served as ellipsis for New York Police wiretap transcribers.] He says, and he says, listen you're worried about money. I don't care how you take the money. I don't care how you take it—get it under the table—get it any way you want."[26]

By allowing professional criminals to use local unions as moneymaking ventures, Hoffa betrayed the interests of the members trapped in them. It was not just that he failed to take action in such cases but that frequently he intervened to protect and promote the offending leadership. In Chicago, Joseph Glimco led Taxidrivers Local 777 after using threats to force the union's previous leadership to give up their posts.[27] A notorious gangster, Glimco would later be identified as one of the top twenty-six leaders of organized crime in Chicago.[28] One Teamster leader in Chicago said of Glimco in 1954, "He is the mob. When he opens his mouth, it's the syndicate talking."[29] Critics charged that Glimco focused his energies on collecting protection payments from businessmen for his criminal associates, and Local 777 did little for members but process their dues payments.[30] The McClellan Committee found evidence that Glimco had siphoned funds from the local to pay for his personal expenses.[31] In 1959 members of the local, tired of the poor service provided by their union, rebelled against his leadership. Hoffa reacted by stepping in to offer Glimco complete support. He campaigned personally for Glimco in the local election contest, bringing with him a team of organizers from the national union.[32] He also appointed Glimco to a prestigious committee assignment during the IBT's 1961 convention.[33] In short, he sided with a known gangster against what turned out to be the majority of the local's membership who had proclaimed their desire for honest and responsible leadership.

In their investigation of Beck and Hoffa's leadership of the IBT, the McClellan Committee uncovered misconduct that fits within a simple and direct definition of corruption. Beck abused the trust placed in him and his office by mishandling the finances of the union in order to enrich himself. Hoffa accepted a secret gratuity from an employer in the form of a lucrative truck-leasing contract. Unlike a bribe, which would have been a payment for him to violate his duty, the gratuity simply rewarded him for stepping in to enforce the union's contract against a wildcat strike. Still, it represented an attempt to influence him and shape how he conducted his office. The fact that he took pains to keep the payment secret, using his wife's maiden name to cover the transaction, indicates that he saw it as improper and that he believed the members would view it the same way. In neither Beck nor Hoffa's case, however, did the committee find clear-cut evidence of a bribe paid to them by an employer in return for granting exemptions from the contract or for signing an inferior contract. The committee did find plentiful evidence that Hoffa had betrayed the interests of members trapped in local unions that he knew to be misused by professional criminals. If he never took bribes himself, Hoffa seemed to condone such behavior in other officers.

His actions in those cases probably were determined by a number of factors. Like Tobin before him, Hoffa faced several practical constraints. Moving against the interests of someone like Corallo would likely incur violent retaliation. Moreover, union politics had to be taken into account. Hoffa had received political support from some of these leaders, and if he abandoned them it might undercut his credibility as an ally. More than that, he seems to have identified with these figures, forming a personal connection to them that shaped his policies. For a man who had always cultivated an image of toughness, associating with gangsters, the ultimate tough guys, had a certain appeal. And in an odd way he saw them as people whom he could really trust. Ralph James and Estelle James, labor economists who spent nearly a year traveling around with Hoffa during the early 1960s, emphasized the issue of trust when they addressed Hoffa's choice of associates. They cited his continued ties to Frank Matula, a Los Angeles Teamster leader convicted of perjury, and Abe Gordon, a New York leader closely associated with Dioguardia. "One thing is for sure," Hoffa told the Jameses, "Gordon and Matula are not working for Bobby Kennedy. They are probably toward the top of Kennedy's 'drop dead list.'" Such people, he seemed to conclude, would never betray him to law enforcement.[34]

Mob Ties

In addition to these considerations, however, Hoffa's leadership also reflected the arrangements he had made with criminal gangs. The McClellan Committee hearings gave a great deal of publicity to those organized crime connections, and the revelations shaped the public's perception of Hoffa and the Teamsters. In 1959 the labor journalist Paul Jacobs summed up the source of Hoffa's notoriety: "Other union leaders grow angry when crossed; others are avaricious for power; others use violence. It is Hoffa's attitude to the underworld that sets him apart."[35]

To move beyond the charges of the McClellan Committee and get at the actual details of Hoffa's arrangements with criminal gangs presents a number of difficulties. Although sensationalized accounts have proliferated, almost nothing of a firsthand nature exists to record the history of Hoffa's actions in this area, much less to reveal his motivations. Secondhand accounts, some of them from anonymous journalistic sources, some anecdotal, and most provided decades after the events took place, provide the bulk of our information. One way to compensate for these limitations is to approach the subject from several different angles. What is known of Hoffa's history in this area can be presented by balancing secondhand accounts against documentary material. In addition, his story can be fit within the context of other Teamster leaders who made similar accommodations at roughly the same time. The results of these approaches should yield a more complete account of Hoffa's relationship with criminal gangs.

These criminal gangs usually get lumped together under the rubric *Mafia*. Often invoked loosely to mean any criminal group, in this case the term refers to a kind of entrepreneurial gang with roots stretching back to the secret societies of rural Sicily during the nineteenth century. In the United States, Italian American criminals adapted the traditions of the Sicilian Mafia, involving codes of manliness, respect, and secrecy, to the needs of organized criminal activity. That adaptation followed no uniform centralized plan but apparently occurred in a haphazard way in differing fashions from city to city. By the 1940s and 1950s a rough set of common rules and rituals had emerged that extended to Mafia organizations, referred to as "families," from New York to Los Angeles. Formal membership was limited to those of Italian descent, although non-Italians played important, even leadership, roles in a number of locales. A secret initiation ritual marked the passage into formal membership, making one an "amico nostra" (a friend of ours) and thus a member of "La Cosa Nostra" (our thing).[36]

Looking beyond the ritualist trimmings, the rhetoric and rules of the Italian American Mafia offered criminal gangs a convenient structure and the possibility for entrepreneurial contacts that would extend beyond the confines of one city. Common terminology set up a fairly well-defined hierarchy and created a protocol for resolving disputes among members. Although this structure is often depicted in language laden with corporate metaphors, the average member, or soldier, functioned more as an entrepreneur than as some disciplined cog in a larger bureaucratic structure. Members of the Mafia and their associates were men on the make, looking for any opportunity to acquire money and using the Mafia organization as an all-purpose resource. The organization provided a member with access to violent force, but more often it provided connections. Sophisticated illegal deals required an element of trust, someone who could vouch for all of the parties involved and resolve disputes that invariably arose. In each city the Mafia fulfilled that function. In return, members and associates passed on a share of all earnings to their superiors, the capos (captains); they, in turn, passed money up to the head of the family, the boss or godfather.[37]

A set of loose ties allowed a similar process of deal-making to occur among members of different families. Five separate families coexisted in New York City, but in other cities a single family prevailed. The separate families operated as independent organizations, but mechanisms were created to encourage and monitor cooperation. The heads of the five families of New York sat on a commission that met on an irregular basis as needed. Crime families in cities from Cleveland to the East Coast referred to the commission for advice or the resolution of disputes between families. Families from Detroit to the West Coast looked to leaders of the Chicago family, known as "the Outfit," for the same service. Deals struck among members of different families drew on the same guaranteed network of connections that would occur within one family and followed a similar protocol in dividing profits with the leadership. To facilitate that kind of loose coordination, the leaders of various families occasionally held national conferences. Just such a meeting was in the process of beginning on the estate of Joseph Barbara in Apalachin, New York, on November 14, 1957, when the New York State Police came in to investigate.[38] It was the conference at Apalachin that created widespread publicity for the term *Mafia* at just the time the McClellan Committee focused its efforts on Hoffa.

Most accounts suggest that Hoffa first went to the Detroit Mafia in the early 1940s. The Teamsters had become involved in a violent feud with the United Mine Workers' District 50, an organizing arm of the Congress of Industrial Unions (CIO) led by Denny Lewis, the brother of John L. Lewis, the head of the CIO. Denny Lewis and a group of organizers sought to bring into their organization the truckers who hauled automobiles made in Detroit. Those same drivers were an essential part of Hoffa's home Local 299 of the IBT, and he resisted the organizing drive fiercely. In the violent contest that ensued, according to these accounts, the CIO organizers overwhelmed Hoffa's Teamster officials.[39] Dave Johnson, a Local 299 official who was with Hoffa at the time, recalled, "We weren't enough. The CIO had tougher guys than any of us expected. So Jimmy went to see Santo Perrone."[40] A reputed gangster who later was listed as one of the leaders of the Detroit Mafia, Perrone had previously been hired by various manufacturing firms to help keep out the United Auto Workers Union (UAW). Some evidence links him to the 1948 assassination attempt on Walter Reuther, president of the UAW, and a later attack on his brother, Victor Reuther.[41] Whether Hoffa in fact employed Perrone or not, a shift in the balance of forces between the Teamsters and the CIO did become apparent. Denny Lewis told the *Detroit Free Press* in 1941 that "professional hoodlums and gangsters" were at work, forcing drivers into "joining the AFL Teamsters Union."[42] Eventually, the CIO gave up the fight, but according to these accounts Hoffa's ties with the Detroit Mafia continued.

Although the accuracy of those accounts remains open to question, by the early 1960s Hoffa did have a firm tie with individuals who belonged to the Detroit Mafia. His main contact was with Anthony ("Tony Jack") Giacalone, whom a Detroit newspaper described in 1969 as a "sun-tanned, middle-aged, Beau Brummel with shined shoe soles and a hard look in his eye." Giacalone allegedly managed several gambling operations and engaged in loan sharking on the side.[43] To protect those operations he oversaw regular payoffs to a large number of Detroit-area police.[44] An illegal FBI wiretap of Giacalone's offices that ran for several years during the early 1960s indicated that he had almost daily contact with Hoffa.[45] Referring to Hoffa, Giacalone was reported to have told other Mafia members, "This is our connection."[46]

Transcripts made from that illegal bug suggest a complex relationship between Hoffa and Giacalone. In some ways it seemed a familial bond. The main go-betweens were Sylvia Paris and her son, Charles ("Chuckie") O'Brien. Paris, born Sylvia Pagano in Kansas City, had originally been married to a gangster there named Bing O'Brien. After his death, she married John Paris, an officer in a Detroit local of the International Laundry Workers Union and a friend of Hoffa's. When John Paris died in 1957, Sylvia and her son moved in with the Hoffas, and they lived together as a kind of extended family unit. She became a close friend of Josephine Hoffa, Jimmy's wife, keeping her company during Jimmy's many absences. Shortly after John Paris died, Sylvia began a long-term affair with Giacalone. In the transcripts, it is Chuckie O'Brien and Sylvia Paris who carry word back and forth from Giacalone to Hoffa. And Sylvia Paris, with emotional ties that extended to everyone involved, became the glue holding the whole arrangement together. According to Giacalone, "Sylvia is the only person . . . that can handle Jimmy Hoffa."[47]

It was also a business relationship based on mutual need. The transcripts show Hoffa at one point asking Giacalone to do him a favor and talk to a potential witness against him in an upcoming criminal trial. The exchange implies that Giacalone should intimidate the man in order to make sure he provides no damaging testimony. In turn, Giacalone went to Hoffa for several favors. Facing trial on a police bribery case, Giacalone asked Hoffa to intercede with the judge and negotiate a payoff. According to Giacalone, a responsive Hoffa immediately rushed to fulfill this request, advancing the $10,000 bribe out of his own pocket. Giacalone also described how Hoffa directed union pension fund loans to benefit the Detroit Mafia. At one point, Giacalone quoted another top Mafia leader as saying, "We need this guy [Hoffa], for instance say we get something that looks good and we present it to him. He said this guy is in a position to loan us money on what we want." The tapes reveal Hoffa dealing with Giacalone and his Mafia superiors over a loan from the pension fund to Jay Sarno, an entrepreneur who built the Circus-Circus casino in Las Vegas. One possible implication was that Sarno either had to kick back money to the Detroit Mafia or give them an ownership interest in his casino in return for their influence with Hoffa. These were not one-sided business deals; Hoffa also made money in them. The transcripts refer to one $60,000 kickback on a union insurance deal in which Hoffa's share amounted to $30,000 and Giacalone was left with $15,000 to be split among his Mafia associates.[48]

Giacalone, of course, was no ordinary business associate, and beneath the give-and-take lay a darker, more exploitative side to the relationship. His superiors in the Mafia wondered if they could not do more to exploit their relationship with Hoffa. Giacalone described one conversation in which another Detroit Mafia member complained, "They're using us and we're not making no (expletive) money." In the fall of 1963 Giacalone reported that Anthony Zerelli, apparently his superior in the Detroit Mafia, "made the remark that they should 'grab that Jimmy Hoffa.'" Giacalone dissuaded him, but other recorded conversations indicate that he and Paris planned to break into a safe belonging to Hoffa and rob him of the cash that he stored there. Even the familial ties could be twisted. The Detroit gangster and Paris played on the weaknesses of Josephine Hoffa, depicted in transcripts as suffering from a problem with alcoholism.[49] Finally, the possibility of violence was always present. The day Hoffa that disappeared, July 30, 1975, he had apparently been going to a meeting with Giacalone. The FBI strongly suspected that he was murdered that day after he got into the back seat of Chuckie O'Brien's car.[50]

If exploitation was the true foundation of this relationship, Hoffa cannot be consigned to the role of the exploited victim. In the early 1960s Giacalone apparently believed that it was Hoffa who got the most out of the relationship. He described the Detroit Teamster leader as "the type of guy you can't bulldog." Working with him meant proceeding cautiously and not pushing too hard. "With Jimmy Hoffa," Giacalone told his superior, "we'll take one step at a time." As a result, Hoffa looked less like the victim and more like an equal partner, if not the one doing the exploiting. According to the transcripts, Giacalone at one point ruefully admitted, "Listen, they ain't nobody sharp enough for Jimmy Hoffa. In this town or any other town. He's going to use everybody, every SOB in the world."[51]

What these transcripts do not reveal is how the relationship between Hoffa and Giacalone began and why the Teamster leader chose to involve himself in such a dangerous arrangement. Indeed, given the fact that Perrone and Giacalone came from opposing factions within the Detroit Mafia, it seems unlikely that Hoffa's battles with the CIO proved to be the origin of this relationship. Another way to approach the puzzle is to consider the case of other Teamster officials involved in the same scenario.

One such official was Roy Williams, who came to lead the Kansas City Teamsters in the late 1940s. Unlike Hoffa, Williams lived to give a firsthand account of how his relationship to the Mafia developed. The seventh of twelve children raised on a struggling farm in the Ozark Mountains, Williams had turned to truck driving in the late 1930s. When he came back from military service in World War II, he eventually drifted into a career as a union official, moving up through the ranks of Kansas City's Local 41.[52] Through his work with the city's Democratic Party machinery, Williams became friendly with Nick Civella, the head of a Democratic Club on the North Side of Kansas City. As Williams remembered it, his first clue that Civella had connections extending beyond the local Democratic Party came in the wake of newspaper stories about the arrests at Apalachin. When Williams asked Civella about that meeting, the Kansas City Teamster recalled, "Civella told me that, among other things, territory and cooperation were discussed." It turned out that Civella led the Kansas City Mafia. Williams remembered, "Civella said that he had Kansas City as his territory. He had working relations with other areas. He had friends in Wisconsin, he had friends in Chicago, he had friends in Cleveland, and he had friends in New Orleans." The people with whom he had met at Apalachin, Civella explained, were "his friends." Civella told Williams that if he ever needed help in another city "to get ahold of him and he would get ahold of his friends." The Teamster official took advantage of the offer on a couple of occasions when he expected trouble at a meeting in another part of the country.[53]

This assistance, Williams discovered, came at a price. The union had established a benefits fund in 1955, and by 1957 they had accumulated enough money to start making investments. Civella now began to pressure Williams to make certain loans with the pension fund money and set up a particular health plan. Williams shrugged off the suggestions. Then one night after he left a union meeting two men kidnapped him, blindfolded him, and took him to a darkened room somewhere. They sat him down on a chair and took off the blindfold. "There was a great big light over my head that showed around about ten feet of my stool that I was sitting on," Williams recalled. "They told me that I was brought there for a reason. That I was going to have to cooperate closer with Nick Civella. I didn't recognize any of them." The men told Williams that if he did not cooperate they would kill his two daughters, one twelve and one six. They would kill his wife. "And you will be the last to go." Williams was taken back to his car and allowed to go free, but now he was afraid.[54]

He went to someone higher up in the Teamster hierarchy, and that man sent him to Hoffa, who advised Williams to go along with Civella. According to Williams, "He said, 'Roy, it's a bad situation.' He said, 'You can run, but you can't hide. You could quit. You still can't hide. My advice to you is to cooperate or get your family killed.'" Hoffa told Williams that people like Civella were "bad people. And they were here a long time before you and I come, and they'll be here a long time after we're gone." They had infiltrated a number of locals in the Teamsters Union, Hoffa explained. They existed in other AFL-CIO unions, too. "They're bad and certainly that I think you should go cooperate with them." In his own case, Hoffa admitted, "I'm tied as tight as I can be."[55]

Fear thus played a part in Williams's relationship with Civella, but the arrangement, like Hoffa's ties to Giacalone, amounted to something more complex than simple extortion. Asked to explain his feelings toward Civella in the 1980s, at the end of a relationship that had spanned more than two decades, Williams offered contradictory assessments. He praised Civella's intelligence and wisdom and referred to him as a "very close" and "very personal friend."[56] Williams said that he often turned to the Mafioso for advice and guidance. He knew Civella met occasionally with Hoffa, and he believed that Civella had helped promote his advancement up the union ranks. Moreover, the crime leader offered Williams a kind of protection. From time to time other people approached him with requests to become involved in illegal deals, they might even invoke the name of a gang leader from another city to exert pressure on him to participate, but Williams would refer them all to Civella. And Civella admonished him to take money from no one else but him.[57] In this way Williams's exposure to illegal activity and the consequent danger from law enforcement was minimized. Civella himself described this side of his role by saying at one point to another Mafia figure, "I want to protect Roy. He's a friend of mine. When you consider where he came from, how he got to where he is now, you have to be a little afraid."[58] Still, behind all of this language of friendship, Williams's tie to Civella continued to rest, at least in part, on a foundation of fear. As Williams put it, "Well to be right frank about it, if I didn't want to get killed, I was his boy."[59]

Considering the careers of Hoffa and Williams, one might conclude that involvement with the Mafia constituted a kind of Faustian bargain. Ambitious men, careerists in union office, and unrestrained by any zealous commitment to the larger social goals of organized labor as a working-class movement, it could be argued that they felt little compunction in forming an alliance with criminal gangs. Ideology—or in this case the lack of one—might seem, therefore, to explain the arrangements that emerged. However, a third example, the case of Harold Gibbons, casts doubt on such an explanation.

A dedicated, progressive unionist, Gibbons had come to St. Louis in 1941 as an organizer for the CIO's United Retail, Wholesale, and Department Store

Employees Union (URWDSE). He reorganized a group of struggling local unions made up of warehouse workers and led them on an aggressive organizing campaign. Frustrated with the top leadership of the URWDSE, Gibbons pulled his St. Louis locals out of that national union and in 1949 brought them into the IBT, where they merged with Teamsters Local 688. In the Teamsters, Gibbons continued active organizing and won impressive wage gains for his growing membership. But he always believed unions also should be a force for broader social change. He himself was a charter member of a liberal group, Americans for Democratic Action, and the research director in Local 688 led the St. Louis chapter of the NAACP. Together they put Local 688 at the forefront of a number of progressive causes. In the early 1950s, for example, Gibbons headed a campaign to desegregate the city's schools.[60]

And yet in 1952 Gibbons faced a dilemma quite similar to the one that had confronted Williams. As he told the story to the journalist Steven Brill, "In those days it was common knowledge that the guys running the [St. Louis Teamsters] joint council were hoodlums. One day one of my guys was grabbed in a bar by one of these hoodlums and told that either we put some of their people on the payroll of [Local] 688 or he was going to kill me."[61] The man behind these threats was Frank ("Buster") Wortman, who led a gang located in East St. Louis, Illinois. The St. Louis Police characterized Wortman as one of that city's two main mob bosses. He allegedly ran a number of gambling operations, handbooks, and casinos and also maintained interests in trucking and construction. He had gained influence in several St. Louis unions, especially the Steamfitters and the Teamsters, by forcing the locals to put his gunmen on the union payrolls. By all accounts he was a very frightening man.[62] When he threatened the regional manager of the Wurlitzer Corporation over a jukebox dispute, for example, the man refused to leave his hotel room again until the company's president flew in to make peace with Wortman.[63]

Justifiably frightened, Gibbons went to the police for help, but got little satisfaction. The force had a reputation for corruption, and, as Gibbons himself remarked, the police "had never been good at protecting the enemies of [Wortman's] Steamfitters." Moreover, local police long had been hostile to Gibbons's aggressive efforts to organize warehouse and department store businesses; members of the force had roughed up Local 688 officials during picket-line disputes.[64]

Police records show that Gibbons first came to them in January 1952, soon after the initial threat, and applied for a pistol permit. The police put him off, telling him he would need to have a number of forms filled out, including one from his employer. In March he came back, reporting that he was getting death threats over the telephone and wanted police protection. The response was less than encouraging. Police Captain Thomas L. Moran later testified, "So we did the usual police procedure. We did alert the men patrolling the area where the union building was located and also the men riding in the scout cars." But they made no special assignments and posted no guards. By this time Gibbons had every reason to feel vulnerable. On March 14, 1952, the same month he reported getting threatening calls, an official in the Laborers Union was murdered as part of an effort to take over that local. A few months later, in August, a second official in the same local was killed. The police never arrested anyone for either killing.[65]

Getting little help from the authorities, Gibbons made what preparations he could. He sent his wife and children into hiding. He had the local buy shoulder holsters and perhaps some guns to arm the staff. But it seemed a hopeless situation. Aware of what was going on, the business editor at the *St. Louis Globe Democrat* predicted that Gibbons would not survive the year.[66]

Finally, someone suggested that he go see Hoffa. The Detroit Teamster encouraged Gibbons to continue to resist Wortman and arranged to help him do so. Unfortunately, the help Hoffa provided, seemingly the only help available, came with strings attached. As Gibbons recalled, "Jimmy offered to help. He came in to town with his boys. You see he had the ok of the Chicago mob and the Detroit mob to get rid of the Workman [*sic*] gang. And he told them [the Wortman gang] that whatever they tried to do to us, he'd do double to them."[67] By the spring of 1953, Gibbons was accompanied by armed bodyguards chosen by Hoffa and paid for by the IBT Central Conference. These bodyguards included men like Robert Baker, who had belonged to John Dunn's gang on the New York waterfront in the 1930s.

Once in St. Louis, Baker established close ties to John Vitale, thought to be a leader of the St. Louis Mafia. At Hoffa's behest the national union threw the St. Louis Joint Council into a trusteeship in the spring of 1953, and it backed Gibbons's efforts to clean out officials with ties to Wortman. But in their place Gibbons often allowed men like Baker to filter onto the union's payroll.[68] In the years that followed, Gibbons became Hoffa's biggest supporter, and in the process his leadership began to be a lot like Hoffa's. He had saved the St. Louis Teamsters from Wortman's gang, but in exchange he allowed the local Mafia to wield influence over the organization. By the late 1970s the leading candidate to succeed Vitale as head of the St. Louis Mafia was reportedly Nino Parrino, a long-time officer of Teamsters Local 682.[69] And in 1977 an FBI informant alleged that Gibbons was among a group of the top officers of the IBT who were loyal to the Chicago Outfit.[70]

Far from being a crass business unionist, Gibbons's limited options, not his ideology, determined his actions. Examples of other union officials who made decisions quite different from his reinforce that point. In Chicago, William Lee, head of the Chicago Teamsters Joint Council reported to newspapers that he had been approached by members of the Chicago Outfit in September 1950. They wanted to have a say in his management of the unions, and he turned them down. For years afterward he was accompanied constantly by Chicago Police bodyguards.[71] In Detroit, Walter Reuther survived two assassination attempts and continued to exercise his offices in the UAW without regard to the interests of the Detroit Mafia.

In both cases, however, the decision to avoid coming to terms with the Mafia had as much to do with the leaders' circumstances as it did with ideology. In contrast to Gibbons, Lee was dedicated to the ideals of business unionism. He was also an old friend of Chicago's mayor, Richard J. Daley, who had belonged to Lee's local union before embarking on his career in politics. Lee served as Daley's first civil service commissioner, and as a result, unlike Gibbons, he could count on a sympathetic and responsive police force.[72] In Reuther's case, by the time the attacks occurred he had climbed the ranks of the UAW to hold the presidency of the organization. Efforts to protect him thus drew on resources far more significant than what Gibbons's Local 688 could mobilize. The UAW built a secluded and well-guarded compound for Reuther and his family. National union funds paid for a staff of bodyguards, and Reuther never had to turn for help to Hoffa or his equivalent.[73]

Thus, in explaining the decisions made by Teamster leaders like Williams and Gibbons, ideology—or the lack of it—is not sufficient. The same holds true for Hoffa, who would have been faced with the same practical considerations when he was coming up in the union and leading Local 299 in Detroit. A number of forces were at work when these Teamster leaders formed working relationships with the Mafia. Fear played a part, as did realization that little protection could be expected from the police. But union leaders acted out of ambition and self-interest, too. Williams, for instance, firmly believed that his alliance with Civella advanced his career. An informal sense of history also affected their decisions. In the union movement these men knew, local officials had been forced to make such accommodations for decades. When Williams and Gibbons sought advice on what to do, Hoffa explained the way such things worked. It seems likely that when he faced the same decision in his career someone had offered similar advice. Finally, a union leader could make this kind of arrangement and still believe that he had not betrayed the interests of his members. Although Williams described himself as Civella's "boy," he adamantly denied that the Kansas City Mafia leader ever told him how to negotiate a union contract or asked him to allow an employer to violate that contract.[74] Gibbons always maintained a reputation for impeccable honesty.[75] And although Hoffa faced relentless scrutiny of his conduct, no one ever proved that he took a bribe in return for negotiating a weaker contract or failing to enforce a contract.

Of course, if Hoffa, Williams, and Gibbons personally avoided taking bribes, others in the Teamster chain of command did not. Lower-level officials, protected and sponsored by Mafia members like Civella, Giacalone, and Dioguardia, sold out the membership. Brokering such arrangements provided money-making opportunities for Mafia members. When Hoffa, Williams, and Gibbons appointed crooked officials and sheltered their misdeeds, they helped the Mafia make money at the membership's expense. Indeed, had the relationship between Williams and Civella been as blameless as the Teamster leader liked to portray it, the Kansas City Mafia leader would have gained little because he would have had little to broker. Williams refused to acknowledge it, but the distinction between actual participation in corruption and this kind of accommodation was more apparent than real.

The Benefit Funds

If Hoffa played a largely passive, accommodating role in much of the corrupt activity that occurred, he took a more commanding part in the lucrative manipulation of the union's benefit funds. He used these funds to firm up his relationships with various members of organized crime. He also may have milked them himself through illicit deals that involved a conflict of interest with his duty to his membership.

One of the earliest benefit funds under Hoffa's management was the Health and Welfare Fund of the huge Central States bargaining unit. The Central States contract first included employer contributions to create those funds in 1949. Soon thereafter, Hoffa used the management of these funds to help develop his relationship with key members of the Chicago Mafia or "Outfit." The central figure in the arrangement was Paul ("Red") Dorfman, president of the Chicago Waste Handlers Union. Sometime during the late 1940s Hoffa had become friends with Dorfman, a former boxer who had assumed the presidency of the Waste Handlers soon after its former leader was murdered. He was reportedly a close associate of Anthony Accardo, one of the successors to Al Capone in the Outfit. The McClellan Committee charged that Paul Dorfman was "the contact man between dishonest union leaders and members of the Chicago underworld." Sources who knew Hoffa at the time said that Dorfman provided him with his first important links to the Chicago Mafia.[76]

The McClellan Committee discovered evidence that during 1948 and 1949, soon after they met, Hoffa and Dorfman worked together to make sure that Dorfman's son, Allen, won the contract to handle the Central States Health and Welfare Fund's insurance business.[77] Eventually, Allen Dorfman used the lucrative business he did with the Central States to build a large and prosperous insurance enterprise, but before 1948 his only professional experience involved working as a gym teacher.[78] For Hoffa, Allen Dorfman's professional qualifications apparently mattered less than his connection to the Chicago Mafia. An FBI wiretap from 1979 makes it clear that in dealing with Dorfman, Hoffa in fact was conducting business with an associate of the Chicago Mafia. The government had been investigating Dorfman's connection to a reputed capo in the Chicago Mafia, Joey ("the Clown") Lombardo. On one occasion the FBI recorded Lombardo interceding for Dorfman in a money dispute with a third party. Referring to the local Mafia, Lombardo explained, "Allen belongs to Chicago." The arrangement, as Lombardo described it, amounted to a partnership. "Whatever he's got coming," Lombardo said, "half comes to the people here." In return the Mafia protected and fostered Dorfman's financial interests. "Well, well, we got a piece of, they got a piece of Allen," Lombardo observed. "If Allen can't get it, they'll reach out and get it for him."[79] Placing the Health and Welfare Funds business in the hands of Dorfman did not, the McClellan Committee contended, provide the membership with the most cost-efficient insurance. It did, however, allow Hoffa to do a favor for the Chicago Mafia.

Hoffa used the pension funds for similar purposes, once more putting such considerations ahead of the interests of the members. By the 1950s, numerous Teamster pension funds existed in varying degrees of conglomeration scattered across the country, but the Central States Pension Fund was one of the largest. It came into existence in 1955 when Hoffa negotiated weekly contributions from employers in this bargaining group. By law, such contributory funds were to be jointly managed by representatives of the union and the employers. In practice, however, Hoffa made sure that union representatives dominated the decision making process. And he, in turn, dominated the union representatives. Other bargaining groups within the union, such as Beck's Western Conference, used professional investment firms to manage their pension funds, but not the Central States. Hoffa made most of the decisions about how to invest the money himself, and he seemed to have a preference for speculative real estate loans, land development, or new building projects.[80]

These sorts of investments put members' funds at greater risk than a conventional strategy, but once again they allowed Hoffa to do favors for different criminal groups. For example, Moe Dalitz became one of the largest recipients of loans from the Central States Pension Fund. He used the money to fund a series of casinos in Las Vegas. According to former FBI agent William Roemer, an illegal listening device planted by the agency during the early 1960s revealed that the Chicago and New York Mafia secretly controlled a share of Dalitz's casinos. The secret ownership represented a form of compensation for the Mafia's influence in having the Teamsters grant these loans. Allegedly, several other casinos in Las Vegas, funded with loans from the Teamster pension fund, were involved in similar hidden agreements with other Mafia families from New England to Kansas City.[81] At Hoffa's behest the membership's money was being used to bankroll the fortunes of professional criminals.

Evidence indicates that Hoffa manipulated the fund's loan process for his personal profit as well. Loan applicants frequently reported being asked to pay a "finders' fee"—in fact, a kickback—in order to receive a loan from the fund. Usually this kickback amounted to 10 percent of the total loan amount, and applicants who complained were told to increase the size of the loan to help pay the fee. The kickback went to middlemen, individuals familiar with Hoffa and the workings of the fund, and they told loan recipients that the money eventually went to Hoffa. Testimony about the kickbacks led to Hoffa's conviction on mail fraud charges in 1964.[82] Several years later, the fund's accountant, David Wenger, was convicted for a similar scheme. A government witness at Wenger's trial in 1970 testified that Wenger had told him that Hoffa, then in jail, still received a payoff for the fund's loan decisions.[83]

In addition to these finders' fees, some evidence suggests that Hoffa used the pension fund to support his own investments. In the mid-1950s he held a secret 22.5 percent share in Sun Valley Inc., a real estate development initially supported by manipulation of various Michigan Teamster funds. When that project began to fail, Hoffa pressured various pension fund loan applicants to take it over as part of the price for receiving a loan. Those machinations also played a part in his fraud conviction in 1964.[84] There is other, more circumstantial, evidence that he used the pension fund to enrich himself. By the 1970s the single largest recipient of Teamster Pension Fund loans was Morris Shenker, a prominent attorney from St. Louis who was also Hoffa's personal attorney. Shenker used the money in a series of real estate investments, in one case buying the Dunes Hotel, a casino in Las Vegas.[85]

An FBI wiretap in 1979 caught Shenker discussing some of these investments with Allen Dorfman and Joey Lombardo. Trying to resolve the division of money from a series of Dorfman's hidden investments, made through Shenker, the two men alluded to deals in which Shenker had held similar hidden interests for Hoffa. In the case of one particular hidden investment, Shenker noted that Dorfman's share had come through Hoffa, who had turned over part of his own share to Dorfman. Shenker explained, "I did business with Hoffa, and Hoffa said you [Dorfman] went in on it, that's it." The conversation suggests that Hoffa regularly held a hidden interest in Shenker's investments, which were made with pension fund money loaned at Hoffa's behest.[86] If true, it means Hoffa used the fund to bankroll his own speculative investments. He apparently had become quite wealthy by the 1970s, and he took great satisfaction from that fact. By 1975, shortly before his disappearance, Hoffa bragged, "How many men can come up with two million cash immediately?"[87] Whether that money came from dealings with Shenker remains uncertain. What is known is that after he died in 1995 at the age of eighty-two Shenker left some seventy thousand files that took up the equivalent of nine single-car garages in space. All of his records pertaining to Hoffa, however, were missing.[88]

Conclusion

In considering all of these activities, questions of scale, proportion, and significance need to be weighed. That corruption occurred cannot be denied, but its effect on the union remains subject to debate.

In a speech before the University of Virginia Law School in 1958, Robert F. Kennedy reportedly charged, "In every major industrial area in the nation, the Teamsters Union is controlled and operated by men with criminal records, ranging from armed robbery to extortion."[89] In his book on the Mc-Clellan hearings, *The Enemy Within* (1960), the committee's chief counsel took a slightly more guarded stance but still offered a scathing condemnation. He focused on the charge that the union's top leadership under Hoffa had degenerated into a collection of professional criminals. "The inner sanctum of the Teamsters' hierarchy," Kennedy wrote, "has no counterpart in the United States today." He detailed the scandals of twenty Teamster officials but went on to assert that the committee "had derogatory information on over 150 Teamster officials, more than one hundred of whom appeared before the Committee and took the Fifth Amendment." With these men in charge, Kennedy warned, the finances of the entire Teamsters Union stood in jeopardy. "The vast millions of dollars assigned to the various treasuries and funds of the International Brotherhood of Teamsters . . . are under the complete and absolute control of Mr. Hoffa, and are available to himself and his friends and cronies. He has to account to no one else. And he accounts to no one else."[90]

In considering the state of corruption in the Teamsters, however, Kennedy's generalizations should not be taken at face value. The union's top leadership, elected as part of Hoffa's slate in 1957, included eighteen national officers: thirteen vice presidents and three trustees in addition to the general president and the general secretary-treasurer. By 1959, the last year of the hearings, only four of those officers had become subjects of investigation by the McClellan Committee. In a twist of fate, one of those four, John O'Rourke, would later become an opponent of Hoffa and a valued political supporter of Robert Kennedy.[91] Intensive scrutiny by the committee had made it clear that John F. English, the general secretary-treasurer of the union and the man in charge of handling its funds, performed his office with deliberation and probity. In contrast to Kennedy's assertions that an irresponsible Hoffa controlled all of the union's money, in fact no money could be spent by the International without formal approval from English. Indeed, the union's good organizational health belied charges of rampant criminality and corruption. The Teamsters continued to gain new members while existing members generally earned wages and benefits that set the standard for industrial America.[92]

The figure of 150 officers about whom, Kennedy asserted, the committee had derogatory information needs to be examined more carefully as well. Kennedy's interpretation of "derogatory" did not necessarily constitute corruption, at least not in the sense of violating the membership's trust. Violence along the picket line, or as part of an organizing campaign, might well be criminal, but in the face of equally ruthless employer opposition, members would not necessarily see it as a betrayal of their interests. Thus several cases of criminal behavior, cited by Kennedy, did not actually involve corruption.[93] In other cases the derogatory allegations of the committee fell flat when tried as actual criminal charges.[94] Finally, the remaining number of officers involved in actual corruption, even if it remained above one hundred, needs to be set against the total number of officers and local unions in the IBT. With more than eight hundred locals in existence at any one time, the Teamsters had at least 5,600 elected local officers in the union; if nonelected business agents and national organizers were included, the number topped six thousand.[95] Thus Kennedy's number of corrupt officers made up, at best, 2.5 percent—perhaps as few as 1.5 percent—of the total. For the Teamsters, it was still nothing to brag about, but it does throw into question such adjectives as "racket-ridden."[96]

If Kennedy's hyperbolic assertions must be viewed with caution, it remains true, however, that corruption presented the Teamsters with a significant problem during the 1950s. Both Beck and Hoffa had engaged in activities that violated their trust to the membership. Hoffa had developed a network of ties with members of organized crime, and those ties directly affected his administration of the union. They shaped the way he reacted to criminality at the level of the local union, and they affected his management of the benefit funds under his control. Below Hoffa, other Teamster officials, like Gibbons and Williams, had developed similar relationships with members of the Mafia, and thus a pattern of passive accommodation to corruption was repeated in several areas across the country.

On a day-to-day level, illicit arrangements among union officials, employers, and organized crime had changed little from the 1930s. The bulk of the McClellan Committee's revelations centered on local unions with jurisdictions that resembled those of Teamsters Local 584 in the days of Jacob Bernoff and Charles Green. The small employers in these jurisdictions operated on narrow margins in tightly competitive business environments, and recurring efforts at collusion had come to involve union leaders and organized crime. The resulting arrangements blurred the distinctions among extortion, bribery, and conspiracy to violate antitrust laws. Unions involved in construction, laundry services, garbage hauling, vending machine distribution, and various other kinds of local trucking all fit within this pattern, and the McClellan Committee's most successful hearings focused on such areas. This was the world Dioguardia and Wortman inhabited. Union officials like Gibbons, who sought to enter such areas and lacked significant resources to protect themselves, found it necessary to make accommodations with such figures. Acts of bribery and extortion did on occasion take place outside such collusive economic environments, but endemic corruption remained rooted there.[97]

The most significant change during the 1950s centered on Hoffa and the benefit funds. Although Beck had breached his fiduciary duty, no evidence has ever emerged that he maintained a relationship with organized crime. Thus, while both Beck and Hoffa's leadership policies reflected opportunism, Hoffa's also stemmed from a desire to cultivate ties with people like Glimco and Accardo. In addition, the emergence of sizable benefit funds created a new dynamic. For professional criminals, the funds represented a new source of wealth to be tapped and a new reason to cultivate relationships with union officials who could grant access to those funds. Still, the corruption of these funds should not be overgeneralized. Scattered across the union were some two hundred separate funds, most of them professionally managed and fiscally sound. The Western States Pension Fund, for instance, held the largest assets of any Teamster pension fund and remained free of scandal. From the time Hoffa became president until the mid-1970s, however, the large Central States Pension Fund increasingly came under the control of several Mafia families. As a result, the success of loan applicants had more to do with their willingness to make an illicit deal than with their financial merit. By the mid-1970s the fund's mismanagement had reached dangerous proportions.[98] The corruption of the 1950s, therefore, was both real and significant in its effects on the membership of the union.

9. Raising the Specter of Hoffa: How the McClellan Committee Shaped Perceptions of Union Corruption

The McClellan Committee's investigation provided much information about the activities of certain Teamsters Union officials during the 1950s. It revealed numerous acts of betrayal by union leaders, and it raised the subject of their connections with organized crime figures. But the McClellan hearings cannot be understood simply as a disinterested search for the truth. Rather, the hearings played a part in a political struggle over the place of organized labor in American society. The McClellan Committee used the hearings, and the scandals involving the Teamsters, to reshape public understanding of union corruption.

To say that the McClellan Committee used the issue of union corruption, however, does not negate the fact that real problems existed within the Teamsters and several other labor organizations, including the Hotel Workers and the Operating Engineers. All suffered from the misconduct of officers who betrayed the interests of their membership. Indeed, criticism of such activities came from within the labor movement itself. The Congress of Industrial Organizations (CIO), beginning in the 1930s, had criticized the corruption that existed within its rival, the American Federation of Labor (AFL).[1] For its part, the AFL acknowledged the importance of the issue in 1953 when it responded to revelations about corruption on New York's waterfront by expelling the International Longshoremen's Association.[2] After the two labor federations merged in 1955 they institutionalized a set of standards for appropriate union conduct and set up a process for dealing with recalcitrant cases. When the McClellan Committee began in its investigation in 1957, the AFL-CIO announced its support.[3]

But the McClellan Committee depicted the problem of union corruption as intrinsically bound up in the phenomenon of union power, and it pursued a political agenda intended to win new restraints on that power. The committee's efforts benefited from a cooperative relationship with members of the media that allowed it to carefully shape the message the public would receive from the hearings. Although the committee's title referred to "improper practices in the fields of management and labor," the formal agenda of the investigation centered on union abuses. The committee depicted the illegal activities of employers as the result of aggressive union demands, consistently depicting the employers as victims rather than participants in corruption. More important, the committee worked to popularize a political understanding of corruption as legal activities that involved the exercise of aggressive union power became examples of corruption. The committee argued that all of this presented an even greater threat to the nation because of the involvement of organized crime, which the hearings portrayed as a tightly controlled conspiracy aimed at total control of the nation's economy.

By presenting the issue of corruption in this way, the committee transformed Hoffa and the Teamsters into a threat to the nation's well-being. The resulting public concern helped undercut the political, and eventually the legal, position of organized labor. Although trade unions enjoyed both strong membership numbers and apparent political strength during the late 1950s, the McClellan hearings offered opponents of organized labor a potent strategy for a counterattack. The political interpretation of corruption allowed conservatives to pass anti-union legislation in 1959, when labor's position had seemed more secure than at any other time since 1937.

Shaping Public Opinion

The McClellan Committee raised public concern about the problem of union corruption and adeptly promoted a particular version of what constituted such corruption. In doing so, the committee, like many congressional bodies before and since, benefited from a symbiotic relationship existing among sympathetic journalists and members of Congress and committee staffs. Ongoing exchanges of tips, leads, leaks, and favorable publicity offered advantages to both the journalists and the investigating committee. The relationship also allowed the revelations of the McClellan Committee to be orchestrated and packaged in order to advance a conservative anti-union agenda. Thus, although the outward trappings of congressional hearings mimicked a criminal trial and purported to uncover hidden truths, the reality of the proceedings more closely resembled a carefully managed media event.

The McClellan Committee developed strong and mutually beneficial ties with members of the news media. Journalists involved in an ongoing relationship with the McClellan Committee enjoyed a number of advantages. Working with committee investigators allowed them to pursue leads much farther than ordinary journalistic methods would permit. Investigators wielding subpoenas could dig into financial records and gain access to privileged law enforcement materials, uncovering facts a journalist might only suspect. Moreover, by encouraging the committee to pursue a particular story, a reporter could transform what might amount to no more than a collection of suspicions and innuendo into a bona-fide news item. In this way, journalists benefited from the fact that all congressional testimony enjoyed immunity from libel suits. Unsupported allegations, if first made public at a hearing, no longer constituted libel or slander.[4] Edwin Guthman, a reporter for the conservative *Seattle Times*, weighed these considerations in late 1956 and decided to form a working partnership with Robert Kennedy's investigators. He joined a circle of journalists, including reporters for some of the country's top newspapers, who enjoyed a similar relationship.[5]

As a result of this network the committee could shape the news coverage it received. The inside group of journalists received detailed briefings the night before key hearings. At these briefings Kennedy reviewed the evidence that would be presented and the questions to be asked, and he would explain the significance of the answers the committee expected to get.[6] There were to be no surprises. Witnesses had already been questioned in executive sessions, and Kennedy himself explained at one point that he never asked a question for which he did not already have the answer.[7]

The care with which all of this was staged became apparent only on occasions when something went wrong. In one case in 1957, Clark Mollenhoff, a prominent journalist with close ties to the committee, complained to his boss at Cowles Publications, a newspaper chain, that their editors had changed the lead in one of his stories. Confused by the various numbers surfacing during the hearings on Dave Beck, the editors had dropped Mollenhoff's focus on the charge that Beck had misappropriated $270,000. Instead, they went with a larger number, $709,000, that had come up during the day's testimony. An exasperated Mollenhoff explained, "This was not a case of me feeling that everyone else was wrong. I had gone over the evidence with Bob Kennedy before it was presented and knew that the $270,000 traced to Beck through construction and public relations was the big bomb for the Friday hearing. When the *Star* story came out with the $709,000 in the lead Kennedy was amazed and so was McClellan."[8]

In addition to cultivating helpful relationships with the journalists covering the hearings, the McClellan Committee also enjoyed a more direct way of shaping the coverage it received. In several cases national magazines invited the committee's chair or chief counsel to take part in writing articles on their work. John L. McClellan's two-part "What We Learned about Labor Gangsters" appeared in the *Saturday Evening Post* in May 1958, followed a few months later by Robert Kennedy's piece entitled, "Hoffa's Unholy Alliance" published by *Life* magazine.[9]

Articles not formally credited to committee members still occasionally reflected a cooperative effort. John Dos Passos drew on material selected and provided to him by the committee when he wrote "What Union Members Have Been Writing Senator McClellan," which appeared in the *Reader's Digest* in September 1958. Dos Passos cited hundreds of letters from rank-and-file members complaining about their union's leadership, but—perhaps because he was unaware of them—he failed to mention the existence of numerous other letters from union members who criticized the committee as biased and antilabor.[10] A year later when *Reader's Digest* planned another article on the hearings, the magazine's editor wrote to McClellan to invite his participation. "I am sure you realize," the editor wrote, "that our attempt here is to present an entirely sympathetic and favorable account of your magnificent work on the committee." Following the magazine's instructions, the article's author sent McClellan a rough draft to edit, which the senator quite readily did.[11]

The Fear of Union Power

The committee's interest in shaping the media coverage reflected the fact that Congress considered the hearings as a chance to raise a particular set of issues. The majority of the McClellan Committee's eight members viewed the aggregation of union power with foreboding and saw an investigation into corruption as a way to mobilize opinion against a broad range of organized labor's activities. John L. McClellan, the conservative Southern Democrat who chaired the committee, certainly held such views. Defending himself from charges that he was antilabor, he explained at one point, "My criticism of labor leaders is directed only at those who drive for national power at the expense of the rest of our society."[12] On another occasion, he raised the issue of "the tremendous powers of labor unions under law" and asserted, "It is the possession and the present lack of regulation of these powers which invites corruption."[13] Taking a similar tack, Sen. Barry Goldwater, another member of the committee, asserted, "Unionism in its proper sphere, accomplishes good for the country. . . . But the pendulum has now swung too far in the opposite direction and we are faced, as a people, with the stern obligation to halt a menacing misappropriation of power." Goldwater quoted the conservative thinker F. A. Hayek, who had written, "The whole basis of our free society is gravely threatened by the powers arrogated by the unions."[14]

Other members of the McClellan Committee shared these concerns and viewed the investigation as a tool for developing remedial legislation to curtail the excessive power wielded by unions. Sen. Carl T. Curtis, a midwestern conservative, put his concerns bluntly. "I believe that unions pose a serious economic threat because they are large and wealthy organizations."[15] The committee's investigations, Curtis expected, would help him push through new restrictive legislation. "I feel that we are, in the McClellan Committee hearings, giving the Congress an opportunity to make some long-needed corrections in labor practices. I believe that public attention to the unfairness of certain unions is about the best support I can get for the enactment of my legislation to prohibit secondary boycotts, as well as passage next year of legislation to outlaw compulsory union membership and to bring organized labor under the Anti-Trust laws."[16]

The similarity of views should not be overstated. The eight members of the McClellan Committee represented no monolithic opinion. Partisan divisions separated Republican conservatives—Carl Curtis, Karl Mundt, and Barry Goldwater—from Southern Democrat conservatives Sam Ervin and John McClellan. John F. Kennedy and Irving M. Ives held moderate views on unions, and Pat McNamara represented a distinctly pro-union position until he resigned from the committee after its first year of hearings. Political infighting among committee members remained a continual problem. Throughout the course of the investigation Chief Counsel Robert Kennedy and McClellan wrangled with Republican conservatives who sought to enlarge the committee's investigation of Walter Reuther, the liberal president of the UAW and a potential supporter for John F. Kennedy's presidential bid in 1960.[17]

Still, the majority of the committee members and their chief counsel shared a concern about the growth of irresponsible union power. Moreover, they saw Hoffa as the embodiment of that power. That was true even for the Kennedy brothers, who sought to hold a moderate position regarding organized labor. Robert Kennedy asserted on Jack Paar's television show in 1959 that both he and his brother the senator viewed the present balance of power in American labor relations with great alarm. Referring to the Teamster leadership, he said, "I think that they feel that they are above the law and the government of the United States, he [Hoffa] and his colleagues." Such an assumption, Kennedy asserted, threatened the safety of the nation. "I don't think there's any question," he said. "This country just can't survive if you have some one like that operating and this country is going to survive. . . . He feels that he's bigger than the country." For that reason Kennedy urged the passage of new restrictive legislation.[18]

The concerns of the McClellan Committee members helped to shape the way they approached the problem of union corruption in several ways. The committee came to view the problem of corruption in labor relations as essentially a problem with unions. In its investigative agenda it focused on labor organizations, not their business counterparts. Employers involved in corrupt acts became nothing more than victims, culpable usually only because they failed to resist vigorously enough. Moreover, the committee came to define corruption in ways that included more than acts of embezzlement and extortion. The broader, political interpretation of corruption put forward by the committee included acts of labor violence, exercise of political influence, aggressive organizing tactics, and purported power over public roadways.

Culpable Unions, Victimized Employers

Formally, the McClellan Committee aimed to investigate the improper activities of both management and labor in the field of labor relations, and it did make some gestures toward impartiality. McClellan professed himself to be in favor of unions, although he carefully qualified his endorsement: "Labor unions properly and efficiently managed by able and sincere leaders of good faith, constitute a major and stabilizing force in our democracy and in our economy." On occasion, he put corrupt businessmen in the same category with corrupt labor leaders. "A corporation or the proprietor of a business, who conspires with corrupt labor leaders to their mutual benefit and advantage and to the harm and detriment of working men bring disrepute upon management, and are equally guilty and should be treated, and punished accordingly."[19] In one of its early set of hearings the committee focused on the activities of a labor relations consulting firm that regularly practiced bribery and intimidation to help clients deal with unions. The committee roundly condemned such activities.[20]

Fairly early on, however, it became clear that the committee would focus on the misdeeds of organized labor rather than those of the business community. That decision became formalized during a set of executive sessions held after the first six months of hearings, when committee members hammered out a chain of organization as well as an agenda for future hearings.[21] By August 1957 McClellan had produced a set of eleven priorities for the investigators. Nine of the eleven had to do solely with union misdeeds: lack of democracy, misuses of funds, gangster influence, secondary boycotts, extortion, organizational picketing, violence and damage during strikes, bogus locals, and political activity. One of the remaining two priorities had to do with "improper activities by management to prevent organization," but it seemed to be an afterthought.[22] That priority came last on the organizational chart created by the committee staff, and, unlike secondary boycotts, it merited no specific staff assignment.[23] Indeed, after the one set of hearings on the problem it never again became the subject of any hearings.

The remaining investigative priority covered both labor and management and was labeled "labor and management collusion."[24] By "collusion," the committee meant illicit arrangements reached between management and union officials that affected the nature of the collective bargaining agreement. Typically, such arrangements took the form of either bribery or extortion, the difference being that payments made in response to a threat constituted extortion. In practice, however, the committee came to depict almost every act of collusion as a case of extortion, making the union the aggressor and the employer the perennial victim.

A good example of this pattern can be found in a set of hearings that took place in August 1958. In those hearings, the committee heard testimony about a set of collusive payments made in 1949 by laundry operators in Detroit to Joseph Holtzman, a labor relations consultant with close ties to Hoffa. Robert Kennedy believed that part of the $17,500 that Holtzman received had been passed on to Hoffa in return for his intervention into the contract negotiations then going on between the laundry operators and Teamsters Local 285.

As evidence of Hoffa's corruption the case never really came together. Several laundry operators testified to paying Holtzman, and to varying degrees they admitted that they believed he had wielded influence with Hoffa. But none of them knew whether Hoffa had actually received any money. Holtzman was long since dead by the time of the hearings, and the committee's investigators found no tangible evidence of how the $17,500 might have been passed on to Hoffa. The attorney for the laundry operators, who had conducted negotiations with Local 285, knew nothing about the payment. As he recalled the contract negotiations in 1949, they had been stubbornly argued over and eventually resolved in a series of twenty-two meetings with the local's president, Isaac Litwak. Everyone agreed that Litwak would never have taken money from an employer. For his part, Hoffa had played no significant role in the collective bargaining process. Far from being a sell-out, the contract that emerged seemed exceptionally tough to the employers, who complained loudly to the committee about its onerous provisions.[25]

If this case failed to score the knockout punch against Hoffa for which Robert Kennedy had hoped, it still offered a clear-cut instance of attempted collusion.[26] The committee, however, refused to place any of the blame on employers. In spite of overwhelming evidence to the contrary, in presenting the case it doggedly sought to portray the attempted collusion as an example of extortion by the union.

The employers who testified all agreed that they had initiated the idea of making a payment. As negotiations became sticky and the union began to prepare for a strike, one recalled, "I suggested that perhaps we should go to someone higher up in the Teamsters and attempt to reach a settlement." As a group they approached Moe Dalitz, a notorious organized crime figure, and he put them in contact with Holtzman. A committee of the laundry operators met with Holtzman and agreed to pay him $17,500 on the understanding that he would use it to get them the contract they desired. The president of the laundry employers' association, William H. Balkwill, referred to the money as "a payoff."[27]

Senators Ives and Church both sought to highlight the employers' culpability in this episode, but the committee's chair, McClellan, kept portraying the men as victims of extortion. Questioning one of the employers about the money he had paid, McClellan pointedly asked, "You regard it as a form of extortion, do you not?"[28] To another witness he asserted, "Do you know any other name for this except extortion?"[29]

The claim of extortion stemmed from the laundry operators' explanation that had they not made the payment they feared the stalled negotiations would lead to a strike. The threat behind this case of extortion thus amounted to the union's plan to stage a strike if and when negotiations broke down. The key issue at stake in those troubled negotiations in 1949 was the length of the work week. Litwak and Local 285 sought to reduce the standard work week from six days to five. Unwilling to accept that demand, the employers paid Holtzman $17,500 to get a contract that maintained a six-day week. Rather than a case of extortion, the payment to Holtzman seemed more an attempt at a bribe, a crime that would make the employers, not the union, culpable.[30]

The news coverage, however, ignored such considerations and followed McClellan's lead in absolving the employers of any guilt. The lead of the *New York Times*'s front-page story referred to the "$17,500 extortion" that had occurred.[31] The *Chicago Tribune*'s headline read "Witnesses Name Hoffa in Union Shakedown." In the story's text, the employers were referred to as "victims" who had been forced to pay Holtzman in order to find relief from the unreasonable demands of Local 285.[32] The Associated Press followed a similar tack in its story, asserting that $17,500 "had been demanded by Hoffa as a payoff." No mention was made of the employers' initiative or their motives in the affair, and the assertions about Hoffa's role flew in the face of the actual testimony.[33]

If these laundry operators could be depicted as victims of extortion it would be hard to hold any employers responsible for the acts of collusion that took place. All bribes paid in order to get more lenient contracts became cases of extortion. That reflected the predisposition of the committee's chair. Collusion, as McClellan saw it, resulted from the greed of labor leaders, and at most employers could be blamed for not resisting as energetically as they might. Interviewed in June 1957, McClellan responded to the question of who was to blame for the corruption his committee had uncovered: "This responsibility in labor, I think, lies with unscrupulous labor leaders who let personal interest, greed, and avarice dominate them." Turning to employers, he said, "I think management people should reject and resist any pressures that are applied to compel them to yield in those instances. When they do yield, I think it is most improper and unfortunate."[34] In this way the McClellan Committee promoted the idea that labor corruption in the form of collusion occurred because union leaders held great power and lacked scruples. Businessmen, even when they took the initiative in offering payments, could be blamed only as victims whose resistance lacked appropriate vigor. The root of the problem lay in the unions.

A Political Interpretation of Corruption

Besides assigning blame for the acts of criminal collusion that occurred, the McClellan Committee hearings also provided an opportunity to popularize a broader conception of what constituted corruption. The majority of committee members used the term to refer to a range of union activities, and in general they applied the word to the phenomenon of union power. The hearings offered them a chance to highlight the dangers presented to American society by union leaders like Hoffa, who held great power over the nation's economy and yet seemed answerable to no one. To committee members, that situation represented a corruption of society's normal order. The committee's broad understanding of the term came through in the concerns they expressed, the issues they investigated, and the conclusions they drew from those investigations. Popular accounts of the hearings helped spread this political interpretation of corruption.

Members of the McClellan Committee worried about the criminal activity they uncovered, but they also saw extortion and embezzlement as mere distractions compared to the larger problems they sought to expose. Writing to Raymond Moley, the contributing editor at *Newsweek,* Senator Mundt asserted, "In my book, the most important 'racket' we can expose is the relationship of union power and union money to our body politic."[35] For his part, Senator Goldwater believed that "graft and corruption are symptoms of the illness that besets the labor movement, not the cause of it. The cause is the enormous economic and political power now concentrated in the hands of union leaders."[36] The committee's chief counsel, Robert Kennedy, put forward a similar view when Jack Paar asked him to compare the faults of Beck and Hoffa. "Oh, there's no comparison between them, Hoffa and Mr. Beck," Kennedy exclaimed. "Mr. Beck was just a thief . . . Mr. Hoffa is a far more serious threat than a Mr. Dave Beck." What made Hoffa so much worse was his willingness to build up the union's power, to use it, and to defy the government. "The Teamsters Union," Kennedy said, "as it is operated now by Mr. Hoffa, because of its control over transportation, is probably the most powerful institution in the United States next to the government."[37]

Thus, in studying improper activities the McClellan Committee spent a significant amount of time on issues that fell well outside a narrow definition of corruption. In some cases, such as the use of violence in labor disputes, these matters still involved clear-cut criminal violations, but in other cases the committee condemned legal activities that raised the specter of union power. Whether legal or illegal, however, the acts did not involve any betrayal by union officers of their duty to members. Instead, the actions stemmed from a ruthless pursuit of the members' interests.

Secondary boycotts provided the best example of this kind of activity. These job actions, in which a labor organization forced one employer to no longer do business with another employer, provided unions like the Teamsters with a way to cripple businesses that resisted organizing campaigns. Technically outlawed by the Taft-Hartley Act (1947), the Teamsters had continued to use the tactic thanks to a legal loophole left in the law. The continuation of secondary boycotts had drawn such ire from employers that the U.S. Chamber of Commerce had created the Secondary Boycott Committee to direct a legislative campaign against them. Senator Curtis regularly submitted legislation drafted by the committee to Congress, and, although none of the bills had yet passed, he clearly hoped the McClellan Committee hearings would help his efforts.[38]

In its investigation of secondary boycotts the McClellan Committee focused upon a Teamster organizing campaign during the mid-1950s in Nebraska, Curtis's home state. In particular, the committee publicized the story of a small trucking firm, the Coffey Transfer Company, driven out of business by a secondary boycott when it resisted Teamster organizing efforts. Thanks to a lengthy memo sent by committee investigators to Curtis, more is known about what occurred during the organizing campaign than what was presented to the public during the hearings. Once again, the committee's depiction of the employers as victims and the union as aggressor does not match the more complicated facts of the case.

That investigative memo and the testimony presented at the hearings described a bitterly fought organizing campaign. Although the major trucking companies of the Midwest had long been organized by the Teamsters, a number of smaller firms that hauled goods to rural areas had maintained their non-union status into the 1950s. In Nebraska these non-union drivers often earned half of what their unionized counterparts made and worked an average of fifty-five hours a week compared to the standard forty-hour week won by the IBT. At Beck's aggressive urging, local union leaders in Nebraska began to organize the small firms in the mid-1950s. In Omaha, Teamsters Local 554, led by Albert Parker, began to work on Coffey Transfer Company's employees in 1955. The union's organizers convinced four of the seven workers at the company's Omaha terminal into signing cards to authorize the Teamsters to serve as their collective bargaining agent. Parker wrote to the company's owner, Thomas Coffey, to inform him that the majority of his local employees had joined the Teamsters. At a subsequent meeting, Coffey resisted Albert's request to sign a union contract and argued that the appropriate bargaining unit should include all of the company's twenty-two employees, including those who worked at terminals in Lincoln and Alma. Coffey's argument deftly placed an almost insurmountable logistical barrier in the way of the union's organizing efforts. Alma is located more than two hundred miles from Omaha, half-way across the state of Nebraska. Faced with Coffey's opposition, Local 554 began a strike against Coffey, and four of his employees in Omaha picketed his terminal there. Coffey promptly fired all four employees and hired permanent replacements. At this point, lengthy legal proceedings involving the National Labor Relations Board (NLRB) began. The NLRB sought to hold an election of Coffey's employees to see if they wanted to join the Teamsters. Before the results of that election could be decided, however, the board had to determine what was the appropriate bargaining unit in this case and decide whether the striking, and now fired, employees would be allowed to vote.[39] These were crucial issues. If Coffey could get the NLRB to exclude the striking workers, or, alternatively, include all the company's far-flung employees in the bargaining unit, he would have defeated the organizing campaign.

Meanwhile, the Teamsters mounted a secondary boycott against Coffey in order to pressure him to give way. The Taft-Hartley Act had made secondary boycotts technically illegal, but the Teamsters and other unions had found ways to circumvent those restrictions. Their practices had been formally approved by the Supreme Court in a series of cases heard during the 1950s.[40] Thus the contest between Local 554 and Coffey Transfer came to revolve around the company's ability to win the rulings it wanted from the NLRB and meanwhile survive the crushing economic effects of a union boycott. Coffey put up a good fight, but he did not quite make it. In early 1956 the NLRB held the election, limiting the bargaining unit to Coffey's Omaha terminal but not allowing the striking former employees to vote. As a result, Coffey won the balloting. Still, in a final twist, the union's legal protest of the decision delayed the final NLRB ruling for several months. In the meantime, the financially exhausted Coffey gave up and sold his business.[41]

In its hearings, the McClellan Committee depicted Coffey as the tragic victim of a ruthless Teamsters Union. Called to the stand, he answered questions from sympathetic members of Congress and Chief Counsel Kennedy. Neatly ignoring the issue of the Coffey employees who had been fired for going on strike, Kennedy asked, "And during this whole period of time, as I understand it, the Teamsters refused to permit an election of your employees, or refused to voluntarily submit to an election?" When Coffey agreed, Kennedy continued, "Then when they were forced to submit to an election, they wanted an election just in a limited area?"[42] In this way, all of the union's concerns about the election became nothing more than stalling tactics. No one challenged Coffey's assertion that his employees had never wanted a union or his claim that the union had engaged in top-down organizing. Although several other employers were called to testify, as was Coffey's terminal manager, the committee never heard from the actual workers involved.

The union's side of the story remained untold. By 1958, Local 554's leader, Albert Parker faced a contempt of court charge for his alleged continued use of the secondary boycott in the face of a judicial injunction. Called to testify before the McClellan Committee, he followed his attorney's advice and claimed his Fifth Amendment privilege against self-incrimination rather than answer questions from a hostile committee, answers that might later be used by prosecutors. Court rulings on the use of the Fifth Amendment before congressional committees meant that witnesses had to choose either to answer all questions asked or none at all. Having once claimed the Fifth, a witness could respond in no other way to any subsequent question except to read out the formulaic response "I respectfully decline to answer, because I honestly believe that my answer might tend to incriminate me." Otherwise, they faced contempt charges.[43]

Aware of that fact, committee members took advantage of Parker's circumstances to reinforce the story they wanted to tell. Unable to deny any allegations against him, Parker was charged with taking part in violence and threats during the strike against Coffey Transfer. Knowing that he could only take the Fifth, the committee asked if he was married or had children and then expressed amazement that a man could be so debased as to refuse to answer such questions. Finally, Senator Ervin, who chaired this particular session, asked, "I wish you would tell the committee whether you would take more pride in the Teamsters if their officers had handled themselves in such a way that they could come before a committee and make an honest disclosure of what they knew."[44]

When McClellan summarized the results of the hearings on the secondary boycott he pointed to the case of Coffey Transfer and concluded, "There is something wrong with our laws when the Teamsters Union can by these methods completely destroy a small business enterprise. It is a tactic that is reprehensible." McClellan called for "the enactment of laws that will protect innocent business people and their employees, and communities from this sort of abortion."[45]

For McClellan, secondary boycotts and other examples of the Teamsters' power, even when technically legal, constituted a kind of corruption. Thus, when he explained the meaning of his committee's findings in 1958, he told *U.S. News and World Report* that many of the abuses stemmed from "compulsory unionism," by which he meant both closed-shop and union-shop agreements. In the same interview, he described organizational picketing and secondary boycotts as equivalent to racketeering. In cases where these tactics had pressured an employer into forgoing an NLRB election and signing a union agreement, McClellan asserted, "That I regard as a form of extortion."[46] By labeling such practices extortionate, he decried the power that they granted to union leaders and placed them within his broad understanding of labor corruption.

Indeed, McClellan's conception of corruption was broad enough to include not just specific acts but the very existence of what he saw as excessive Teamster Union power. In his book *Crime without Punishment* (1962), Mc

Clellan spelled out this broad construction of corruption. Drawing on the title of his book, he explained that, for him, criminality involved more than just the violation of particular laws; it also resulted from a corruption of the appropriate social order. He wrote, "Crime, however, travels in countless guises, sometimes wearing various cloaks of benevolence, humanism, and welfare. Activities of this kind are carried on in the plain light of day, in full view of anyone who cares to observe." These activities were criminal in spite of the fact that they were "within the law as the statutes have established it." Such a crime occurred, McClellan asserted, when the power of the Teamsters Union posed "a threat to the transportation lifelines of the nation."[47] Thus he identified the dangerous accumulation of union power as a kind of crime because it corrupted the social order.

Drawing on the hearings, critics of the union movement worked to popularize this broad political understanding of corruption. One popularizer was Sylvester Petro, who wrote *Power Unlimited: The Corruption of Union Leadership* (1959) to present the findings of the McClellan Committee to the public at large. As his title indicates, Petro followed McClellan's reasoning in seeing the connections between union power and corruption. "The lust for power," he observed, "served through the virtual privilege to engage in violence and monopolistic coercion of the picketing and boycotting variety, lies at the bottom of all the McClellan Committee disclosures." For Petro, the lust for power on the part of union officials, and the way they managed to satisfy it, formed the heart of the phenomenon of corruption. Like McClellan, Petro labeled militant strike activity as a kind of extortion, thus making all unions guilty of that kind of corruption. "When a traditional union gets higher wages by violently preventing employers from operating with workers who are willing to take less money, the public as a whole is the victim of unlawful extortion." This view of corruption led Petro to dismiss the distinctions between criminals who had infiltrated the union movement and the traditional leaders who had worked their way up through the ranks. "The harm done by criminals masquerading as union officials is enormous and filled with ominous signs for the future of society. But it is still less than that produced by the power of traditional unions. They daily coerce and brutally attack workers who decline to join or refuse to participate in strikes." Following the lead of the committee, he focused much of his criticism on the Teamsters. Other unions exercised great power but, according to Petro, "that union [the Teamsters] is undoubtedly the most powerful." Based on this understanding of corruption, Petro called for broad reforms that would circumscribe the power available to unions and their leaders. "Out of unlimited power," he warned, "unlimited corruption is breeding."[48]

Clark Mollenhoff's popular account of the hearings, *Tentacles of Power: The Story of Jimmy Hoffa* (1965), emphasized similar themes. Writing in the wake of Hoffa's criminal convictions in the early 1960s, Mollenhoff offered a fast-paced narrative of the McClellan Committee's investigations. Like McClellan and Petros, Mollenhoff argued that actual criminal violations made up only part of the story of corruption. According to Mollenhoff, the real source of the corruption "was the total power which flowed from the so-called 'legal immunities of labor unions.'" Mollenhoff maintained that because the roots of union corruption lay in these special legal immunities, corruption could never really be ended until the power of unions was curbed.[49]

Not all media accounts of the McClellan Committee hearings fully articulated this broad, political view of corruption. Most of them, however, did describe the power of the Teamsters as a very serious problem that required new legal restrictions on organized labor. Indeed, the committee did a very successful job of making the danger of union power a popular issue in newspapers and magazines. The sense of threat in these news accounts was always tangible and often somewhat hysterical. According to a headline in the *Chicago Daily News* from July 1958, "Hoffa's Dream of Empire Cause for National Alarm: Control of Transportation His Aim."[50] The *Cincinnati Enquirer,* in an editorial entitled "Labor's New Little Caesar," asserted, "A nation at the mercy of James R. Hoffa is frightening to contemplate, yet in recent weeks we have seen clear indications that the 'crown prince' of the Teamsters Union is aiming at just that."[51] In a 1959 profile of Hoffa and the Teamsters, *Life* magazine opened by asserting, "In this issue, *LIFE* begins a three-part series on the nation's biggest union, the International Brotherhood of Teamsters, which has become a national menace."[52]

The press warned of the danger of union power, and, following the McClellan Committee's lead, they urged legislative action to correct the problem. When legislation growing out of the McClellan hearings appeared to stall in Congress, *Life* urged the public to mobilize in support of action against union leaders, to whom it referred as "malefactors of great power."[53] The *New York Times* made a similar point. In an editorial that followed Hoffa's reelection as president of the Teamsters, it asserted, "It is both possible and necessary, however, to arm the government with additional legal weapons to protect the public against the misuse of the concentrated economic power that Mr. Hoffa, a man with no discernible sense of social responsibility, now is in a position to wield over the nation's transportation."[54] The pictorial representation of this legal imbalance, and the need to correct it, was a common motif in political cartoons. These cartoons pictured Hoffa literally holding a whip hand over Uncle Sam, thus graphically portraying the danger created by the fact that his power had exceeded that of the elected government.[55]

In this way the political interpretation of corruption achieved popular currency. McClellan Committee members had argued from the beginning that the problems that truly mattered had less to do with actual criminal behavior than with the phenomenon of excessive union power. The committee used the hearings to present negative examples of that power, such as the Teamsters' use of the secondary boycott to crush Coffey Transport. In summarizing the findings of his committee, McClellan labeled such boycotts and other legal union tactics as corrupt. Indeed, he identified the very existence of great union power as a form of corruption.

Although few Americans would ever read the voluminous record compiled by the committee, popular accounts of those hearings made many of the same arguments as those put forward by McClellan. Magazines and newspapers warned that dire consequences were possible unless union power was restrained. By focusing not just on the criminal actions of Hoffa but on the power he wielded, the McClellan Committee offered a compelling reason to see the legal rights of unions as problems in need of reform. The *Wall Street Journal* explained that point in a perceptive editorial in 1959, "The Virtue of Mr. Hoffa": "The difficulty in curbing labor union power thus far, has been that the people have not clearly seen, or believed the danger." After the McClellan hearings that was no longer the case. Everyone saw it personified in the president of the Teamsters Union.[56]

The Enemy Within

The McClellan Committee's success in raising so much concern stemmed in part from its ability to connect the abuses of some union leaders, like Hoffa, to a dangerous internal conspiracy. Drawing connections between this internal conspiracy and the better-known threat posed by America's communist rivals, the committee depicted an ongoing process of internal subversion whose scope had only recently become apparent. The villain responsible for the threat was the newly rediscovered Mafia. The McClellan hearings depicted the Mafia as a tightly knit, national conspiracy that sought to achieve total dominance over the country. In this light, Hoffa's associations with various gangsters assumed a new appearance. No longer the pragmatic moves of an unscrupulous labor leader, they became part of a dangerous scheme to use a captive labor movement against American society. Such a depiction made new legislative curbs on labor unions all the more imperative. America's national security, not just the interests of a few businessmen and union members, was at stake.

The McClellan Committee raised the issue of organized crime at an early stage in its hearings, but the committee began to emphasize the problem in 1958, the second year of hearings. In November 1957 the New York State Police had stumbled upon a meeting of Mafia members from across the country gathered together at the estate of Joseph Barbara in Apalachin, New York.[57] For committee members and Chief Counsel Robert Kennedy, the meaning of Apalachin seemed apparent. It proved the existence of a criminal conspiracy known as the Mafia, and it indicated the national scope of that organization.[58] An explanation now arose for the recurring presence of gangsters in the affairs of the various businesses and unions studied by the committee. A national criminal conspiracy, the Mafia, had embarked upon a campaign of infiltration aimed at controlling the entire economy.

The committee sought to publicize and explain this conclusion through a series of hearings that began in July 1958. The hearings commenced with one entitled "Mafia" in which the committee explored the lessons to be learned from Apalachin. Opening the hearings, Senator McClellan explained that they would prove the existence of a "criminal conspiracy" that had "operated for many years in America . . . beneath the mainstream of American life." He emphasized the seriousness of the issue: "Because we are dealing with a clandestine group, because they are highly organized and disciplined, they present a formidable problem." The threat was twofold. This criminal syndicate had managed to keep its existence largely hidden from sight, with many of its members achieving apparent respectability. Second, its tight national level of coordination heightened the effectiveness of its schemes. The main scheme at present involved a campaign of economic conquest through a process of economic infiltration. Summing up the Apalachin hearings, McClellan asserted, "The testimony we have heard can leave no doubt that there has been a concerted effort by members of the American criminal syndicate to achieve legitimacy through association and control of labor unions and business firms. The extent of this infiltration poses a serious threat to the very economy of our country."[59]

To prove the existence of this process of infiltration, the McClellan Committee spent a great deal of time studying the presence of organized crime in a few industries, namely garbage removal, commercial linen supply, and jukeboxes. These industries became the committee's chief examples of the process of infiltration at work. The committee ignored the fact that collusive practices between businessmen and unions in these industries antedated the presence of Italian American organized crime figures. Rather than corrupting particular business environments, the Mafia was drawn to industries where patterns of impropriety had long existed.

Jukebox operators in Detroit, for instance, had been conspiring together to control competition since the 1930s. Their efforts included forming captive unions that would take action against operators who violated their collusive agreements and also keep out new competition. Such arrangements made jukebox distribution in Detroit a highly profitable enterprise, but most people had to resist such an inviting business prospect out of fear of physical retaliation from the operators. Investors who had connections to the Detroit Mafia, however, could defy such intimidation. As a result, a small group of Mafia-connected jukebox operators entered the industry during the 1940s and eventually came to control about one-quarter of the locations in the city. At this point the rest of the jukebox operators decided, as one put it, "to get together with the Italian syndicate and go back into this new union and try to get along with them." The new collusive arrangement, reached in 1946, used Teamsters Local 985 as an enforcement mechanism and included both the older businesses and the Mafia-connected ones. The presence of organized crime stemmed from a particular economic environment that made collusion both possible and profitable. Businessmen had not needed the Mafia to engage in such collusion, but neither could they keep Mafia members from profiting on the illegal arrangement.[60]

To the committee, however, the presence of Mafia figures and their family members in the industry illustrated a larger campaign of infiltration. The long history of collusive arrangements in the industry was deemphasized, and the businessmen were fit once again into the convenient category of victim. Summarizing the gist of the committee's questions and allegations, a United Press International account described how "a gangster-backed group" had "infiltrated the juke box business."[61] Looking at the jukebox industry nationally, the committee's *Final Report* asserted, "In many metropolitan areas, reputable businessmen who have been in the industry for many, many years are just throwing up their hands and getting out, because they cannot do business on the terms they have to compete with people who have hoodlum connections."[62] The subversion of the jukebox industry, McClellan explained, provided just one example of an ongoing process. "Juke boxes happen to be just one of the many, many legitimate businesses in which racketeers and underworld characters have become entrenched, and to the extent that they are in the process of becoming a dominant force in our economy. This situation creates a serious menace."[63]

In depicting a national crime conspiracy, the committee drew similarly broad conclusions from the unwillingness of many alleged members of organized crime to answer questions under oath. Knowing that by agreeing to answer a single question they would be required to answer all other questions, individuals with organized crime connections chose to claim their Fifth Amendment privileges. As a result, the hearings often consisted of long, one-sided exchanges. Chief Counsel Kennedy would ask questions, and witnesses would respond again and again, "I must decline to answer. . . ." When a student wrote to ask McClellan if he did not find such refusals to testify an obstacle in achieving the committee's goal, the chair offered an intriguing reply. "The invoking of the Fifth Amendment by so many witnesses (343 out of 1525)," McClellan wrote, "was possibly more revealing of the true state of affairs than if they had answered the questions and given the Committee the facts within their knowledge."[64]

Their silence allowed the committee to draw and promote its own conclusions. At one point during the Mafia hearings, McClellan interjected, "We interrogate these witnesses and they resort to the Fifth Amendment and take the position they can't talk about their business, or state what business they are in, what profession they follow, or give any account whatsoever of their activities, it is becoming clearer all the time that there is a challenge from organized crime in this country to the free enterprise system and then to legitimate business and also legitimate labor organizations."[65]

Such conclusions became part of the press coverage of the hearings. The media offered McClellan's assertions as uncontroverted, hard news. Thus an Associated Press story on the Mafia hearings stated, "In a statement at the close, Senator McClellan said the testimony and the alleged racketeers' refusal to answer showed that a conspiracy existed and that the Black Hand, known as the Mafia, was responsible. He said that what was disclosed amounted to 'an arrogant challenge to the government and to the decent people of this country.'" Indeed, as a kind of staged theatrical event the act of watching a notorious gangster repeatedly refuse to explain his actions generated a sense of outrage. That outrage is evident in reactions to hearing coverage. Referring to the testimony of the alleged organized crime figure John Dioguardia, a *Philadelphia Inquirer* editorial rhetorically asked whether it was worthwhile to hear a witness claim his Fifth Amendment privilege 140 times. It was, the editorial maintained, because "it is doubtful whether a more disgusting exhibition of contempt, arrogance and indifference to common decency has been put on in the whole Senate Labor inquiry. It was an exhibition which demonstrated beyond any remaining doubt the need for new and drastic laws to wipe out labor racketeering and strengthen the hands of our authorities in dealing with lawlessness generally." Their silence made criminals seem all the more defiant and suggested that they were indeed a part of a national conspiracy whose power left them free to defy the government.[66]

As the McClellan hearings depicted them, the conspirators of the Mafia had a lot in common with their counterparts in the Communist Party. Indeed, Senator Mundt responded to the expert testimony of one law enforcement witness by saying, "Everything you have said about the Mafia is equally true of the Communist cells of this country."[67] Both allegedly maintained tight discipline over members, exacted ruthless sanctions for dissent, and engaged in an amoral pursuit of power. Both also fed on the complacency of the public and governmental agencies meant to police them.[68] Individuals who hid their membership in each organization had achieved positions of respectability and power in American society. No one of quite the level of Alger Hiss had been uncovered in the Mafia. But, as McClellan pointed out, until John Charles Montana was arrested at Apalachin he had been viewed as one of Buffalo's more successful and civic-minded businessmen.[69]

The main distinction, it appeared, between the communists and the Mafia was that Americans had become aware of and mobilized against the communist threat. The FBI had successfully penetrated the cells of the Communist Party with undercover agents and informants. The McClellan Committee complained that no such effort had been made against the Mafia.[70] Seeking to raise an alarm, the committee succeeded, at least in some quarters. The very fact that Apalachin had been discovered by accident, *Life* noted, "revealed that a conspiracy, as secret as the Communist underground and certainly as dangerous, was operating without any of the surveillance and penetration which has all but destroyed the latter."[71]

Like the communists, the Mafia sought to systematically infiltrate the union movement in order to aid its larger conspiracy. Just as various dupes and fellow travelers had, for a variety of reasons, aided the efforts of communists, so, too, were certain union leaders aiding the endeavors of the Mafia. Here Hoffa's role achieved its sinister significance. The problem had reached such an extent that new legislative intervention had become necessary. Although anticommunist provisions of the Taft-Hartley Act had largely rid the unions of communists, Senator Mundt explained, the threat of organized crime continued to grow.[72]

The need for dramatic action was heightened by the cold war context in which the country could not afford to leave itself unguarded against an internal enemy while facing the danger of imminent conflict with enemies abroad. The McClellan Committee's *Second Interim Report* (1959) warned, "The committee is convinced that if Hoffa remains unchecked, he will successfully destroy the decent labor movement in the United States. Further than that, because of the tremendous economic power of the Teamsters, it will place the underworld in a position to dominate American economic life in a period when the vitality of the American economy is necessary to this country's preservation in an era of world crisis. This Hoffa cannot be allowed to do."[73]

Committee members even raised the possibility of an alliance between America's two enemies. McClellan suggested, "Hoffa and his satellite unions—satellites at least for a time—if they had the power to exercise a paralyzing influence over the entire system of free enterprise in this country, could then, upon their own iniative, or in cooperation with criminals or Communists, compel the nation to submit to whatever arbitrary terms, unfair conditions, and unreasonable demands they might choose to make."[74] Senator Mundt argued, "Russian Communists would be willing to pay the rich rewards which criminals seek to secure from their control of labor in order to place their own foreign agents in the controlling positions which crooks and criminals might thus be able to sell to foreign agents."[75]

Press reports and letters sent to the committee by citizens suggest that the hearings generated much concern about the newly uncovered conspiracy. The *New York Herald Tribune* pointed to the hearings as evidence of an "invisible government" at work in America, committing crimes and wielding hidden influence over the government and the economy.[76] "Who's running this country anyway?" *Life* asked. "Is it the legal government elected by the citizens, or is it an invisible government of hoods, thugs, gangsters, terrorists and murderers?"[77]

The letters that concerned citizens sent to McClellan demonstrate how well some had absorbed the intended message. After watching the committee's televised hearings on the connections between organized crime and labor racketeering in Chicago, Irving Bauer wrote to thank McClellan for his efforts. "It is the only way in which we plain and ordinary everyday citizens can be made aware of the great danger confronting our country, not only from COMMUNISM, but from the ruthless and cruel defiant gangsters which have certainly proved their power, even to defying the United States Senate." Frances C. Wells disclosed feeling more and more "disillusioned." "America," she observed, "seems truly in the grip of a small but terribly powerful clique of gangsters and thugs."[78]

The fact that the illicit arrangements between a few assorted small businessmen, union leaders, and professional criminals could raise such a sense of disproportionate threat suggests the existence of a moral panic. Indeed, amid the discussions of how this corruption menaced the liberty of the country lay references to an underlying sense of vulnerability. Outside stood an enemy waiting to strike at any sign of vulnerability, and among many there existed a gnawing fear that the spiritual vitality and moral fiber necessary to hold the foe at bay had begun to dissipate.[79] Evidence of growing corruption, as supplied by the hearings, thus assumed great significance

As much as anyone Robert Kennedy put that connection into words. In a speech given in October 1959, he placed the findings of the McClellan Committee alongside other "evidences of [America's] moral and physical unfitness" such as the quiz show scandals and a recent study that revealed how many American school children were out of shape. Lumping these phenomena together, he warned, "Dangerous changes in American life are indicated by what is going on in America today. Disaster is our destiny unless we reinstall the toughness, the moral idealism which has guided this nation during its history."[80] In a speech given two years later, after he had become attorney general, Kennedy asserted, "It is not the gangster himself who is of concern. It is what he is doing to our cities, our communities, our moral fiber."[81] Kennedy's book on the McClellan Committee hearings, *The Enemy Within* (1960), closed with a section devoted to those concerns. There he ruminated on the possibility that America's economic prosperity "had so undermined our strength of character that we are now unprepared to deal with the problems that face us." Indeed, he described "the revelations of the McClellan Committee . . . as merely the symptom of a more serious moral illness." It was that illness to which Kennedy referred in the closing admonition, when he wrote that in order "to meet the challenges of our times . . . we must first defeat the enemy within."[82]

Organized crime thus constituted a threat to the country's national security and its moral fiber at the same time. By linking this dangerous conspiracy to the problem of union corruption, the McClellan Committee made an even more forceful case for the passage of remedial legislation. The stakes were much higher than the misuse of union office by a few union leaders. When he appeared on the *Jack Paar Show* in 1959, Robert Kennedy urged new legislation. "Unless something is done about it," he warned, "this country is not going to be controlled by people such as yourself or people such as are here, but it's going to be controlled by Johnny Dioguardia, and Jimmy Hoffa, Tony 'Ducks' Corallo, these people who are gangsters and hoodlums. This is a question really of survival, because it is a question of who is going to control."[83]

A Law to Get Jimmy Hoffa: The Landrum-Griffin Act (1959)

The revelations of the McClellan Committee offered much support to efforts to amend the National Labor Relations Act of 1935 (the Wagner Act). Business and conservative groups had long sought a package of reforms that they believed would inhibit both organized labor's political influence and its organizing strength. These groups deftly moved to harness the findings of the McClellan Committee to their political efforts. The members of the committee, however, had their own ideas about how to amend the Wagner Act, and those differed in important respects from those of the business community. Under Senator McClellan's guidance the committee emphasized the need to protect and enhance union democracy. Once the legislative process had gotten underway, numerous other groups, including various elements of organized labor, took part in a chaotic scramble to shape the legislation that would emerge. Still, looming over all of this political maneuvering, a kind of ominous shadow, stood the figure of Hoffa as the committee had constructed him. He was not just an ambitious and unscrupulous labor leader but a threat to the nation and symbol of the dangers of irresponsible union power. Invoking his name offered a powerful justification for any particular legislative proposal. Thus, in introducing legislation in 1959 Sen. John F. Kennedy assured Congress that "it will stop those practices [upon] which, based upon the testimony before our committee, it would appear Mr. Hoffa's career and power are based—and it will in short, virtually put Mr. Hoffa and his associates out of business."[84] The law that finally resulted from this process, the Landrum-Griffin Act, reflected the complex ways that Hoffa and Teamster corruption had been presented to the American public.

Members of the business community regarded organized labor in the 1950s with increasing concern. They saw it growing in numbers and apparently gaining in political influence as well. Union growth had flattened out immediately after World War II but picked up again during the 1950s. There had been about 14.8 million union members in 1945, by 1951 that number increased to around 16.7 million, and in 1956 it peaked at 18.4 million. By 1955 one-third of all non-agricultural workers in the United States belonged to unions.[85] A group of huge new super unions emerged, including the United Auto Workers with 1.2 million members in 1957, the United Steelworkers with one million, the Carpenters and Machinists with eight hundred thousand each, and the Teamsters with 1.4 million.[86]

When the AFL and the CIO merged in 1955, many observers feared that the already substantial power of organized labor would increase precipitously. Critics worried that organized labor's political influence, newly unified under one organization, might dominate the government.[87] In January 1956 an internal document from the National Association of Manufacturers (NAM) warned, "One of the gravest threats to management's right to manage is the vastly increased size and power of organized labor, now that the AFL and CIO have merged into one giant organization. 1956 will be a pivotal year in the field of labor-management relations, not only because of the greatly intensified activities of the new-born giant but also because of the political implications deriving therefrom."[88]

At the same time, business attitudes toward collective bargaining began to stiffen, and efforts at accommodation increasingly gave way to a steady and determined resistance. An economic downturn that began in 1957 fueled the new attitude, as did the emergence of serious foreign competition in the manufacturing sectors. At bargaining sessions, management took a "tougher line," fighting against restrictive work rules and for greater wage flexibility. Resistance to union organization increased, and in such contests employers showed greater willingness to take off the gloves and fight dirty. The number of unfair labor practices cases at the NLRB doubled during the late 1950s.[89]

In this atmosphere conservative business groups mounted campaigns to legislate new restrictions on organized labor. The National Right-to-Work Committee, formed in 1955, drew on the anti-union hostility of the small businessmen and commercial farmers who made up its core group of activists. Working through state-level Right-to-Work Committees, the group sponsored state laws to abolish union-shop contracts (which required all employees in a workplace to belong to the union).[90] Other business groups such as the U.S. Chamber of Commerce and the NAM campaigned for new restrictions on secondary boycotts and organizational picketing as well as tighter limits on the unions' ability to make political contributions. Complaining loudly about "labor monopoly," they sought an end to the exemption granted to unions from antitrust regulations.[91]

The Republican Party offered the business community assistance in these efforts. President Dwight Eisenhower had begun his administration in 1953 by reaching out to the moderate wing of organized labor in the AFL. By the middle of the decade, however, that policy had given way to one that placed hostility to unions at the center of the partisan agenda. In 1956 the Republican Party's policy committee put out a pamphlet entitled *The Labor Bosses: America's Third Party,* which tagged the Democrats as an organization held captive by dictatorial union leaders. Up-and-coming stars in the Republican Party—for example, Barry Goldwater—took the lead in attacking unions in Congress. And when the revelations of the McClellan Committee led to legislative proposals, Eisenhower's White House actively oversaw efforts to turn back moderate changes in favor of the more restrictive language sought by the business community.[92]

The McClellan Committee hearings provided these groups with a great opportunity, and they quickly moved to take advantage of it. At the U.S. Chamber of Commerce, the group's Secondary Boycott Committee found its calls for remedial action against the boycotts at last receiving more attention in the press and Congress. As one member of the Chamber's Boycott Committee happily explained, "The McClellan hearings gave us the train to ride on; they were the bulldozer clearing the path."[93]

These business groups, however, held no monopoly on the legislative process, and the proposals that appeared in Congress in response to the McClellan hearings originated from several sources. An early proposal by the moderate Senators Kennedy and Ives sought to address concerns raised by the hearings without including any provisions that would weaken the position of organized labor. Indeed, at the behest of the unions the Kennedy-Ives bill included changes in the Taft-Hartley Act that offered advantages to unions. That act passed the Senate in 1958 but stalled in the House of Representatives. Kennedy offered it again in 1959, but this time Senator McClellan led efforts to amend the bill in significant ways.[94]

McClellan held far more conservative views than Kennedy regarding organized labor, and the Arkansas senator agreed with many of the business community's concerns about the power of organized labor. Still, his opinion on what reforms were needed also differed significantly from that of the business groups. The differences centered on the issue of union democracy. McClellan had come to the conclusion that the most effective cure for the problem of union corruption lay in guaranteeing the democratic rights of members. Without such protections, he asserted, other remedies might achieve little in the way of results. He told the Senate, "I do not believe that racketeering, corruption, abuse of power, and other improper practices can be, or will ever be, prevented until and unless the Congress of the United States has the wisdom and the courage to enact laws prescribing minimum standards of democratic process and conduct for the administration of internal union affairs. . . . Without such protections, other provisions of law may be of little benefit and meaningless."[95]

McClellan and other congressional conservatives put great faith in the democratic empowerment of union members for a number of reasons. They saw the membership as the muzzled conscience of the union movement. Thousands of letters sent to the committee repeated a similar refrain from members who objected to officers involved in misconduct, embezzlement, and conflict of interest but complained that they had no voice in their union's affairs. Empowered members would be able to drive crooks and thieves from their unions. For a conservative like McClellan, this essentially voluntarist method achieved reform while limiting the expansion of the state.[96]

McClellan and others also saw union democracy as a way to check the efforts of union leaders to acquire more power over the nation's economy. McClellan imagined that democratic norms would discourage the most power-hungry of men from even bothering to pursue union office. Here McClellan distinguished between two archetypal union leaders, "the decent traditional leaders" who presented no threat to society and "the boss type" who sought "unrestrained power and personal riches." Referring to "the boss type," he asked, "There is something there [in the unions] which is attractive to them. What is it?" The answer was, he asserted, "It is power." This kind of union leadership could be weeded out by making the union leader's job less attractive to them. "I believe it reasonable to expect," McClellan explained, "that removal of temptation, the ending of autocratic rule by placing the ultimate power in the hands of the members where it rightfully belongs, so that they may be ruled by their free consent, may bring about a regeneration of union leadership." But he also suggested that the scale of collective organization might be restrained by strengthening the individual rights of union members. Thus, he warned the Senate, unless his proposals to guard the union members' democratic rights became law, "The next step that will have to be taken in order to control the Hoffas" would be antitrust legislation. "We shall have to put the transportation unions of the country under the anti-trust law; that is the only power we have left to control them."[97]

Conservative business groups, however, had no desire to promote the cause of union democracy. Unlike members of Congress, they expressed none of the roseate opinions about the inherent virtue of the average union member, and they may well have viewed the memberships' actual empowerment with some trepidation. A democratic union could be a very militant union. The legislative wish-lists put together by both the Chamber of Commerce and the NAM offered no support for efforts to regulate internal union governance or to protect the democratic rights of the rank and file. The NAM's Subcommittee on Labor Disputes and Collective Bargaining explained why the group should avoid taking a position on the issue. "NAM's basic position is 'against more government regulation' and, further, than [that] any specific NAM position asking for regulation of internal union affairs might well boomerang and invite the recommendation that industry be subject to even further regulation."[98]

Out of these various proposals from Kennedy, McClellan, and others emerged eventually the Landrum-Griffin Act. The law came out of a torturous process of amendment and compromise in which diverse groups took part. It reflected, therefore, a variety of motives and often quite different understandings of the problem of corruption. Business groups and conservatives argued that union power constituted the main cause of corruption, and therefore real reform involved diminishing the power of unions.[99] Provisions in Landrum-Griffin that put new limitations on organizational picketing and tightened restrictions on secondary boycotts reflected that perspective. Insofar as such restrictions would make new organizing campaigns much more difficult, legislators from the South supported the law as a way to protect their region's lower-waged, non-union status and thus maintain the South's appeal to northern industries looking to relocate.[100]

Not all of the bill's supporters, however, were antilabor. Senator Kennedy had fought to make it less harmful to labor's interests, but he strongly supported its regulation of union government. Similarly, some of the concerns embodied in the bill's language on union democracy had been expressed first by the American Civil Liberties Union.[101] The Byzantine legislative process had even brought some real benefits to organized labor. For instance, the law exempted construction unions from preexisting and particularly burdensome restrictions on picketing.[102]

In the end, Landrum-Griffin combined new restrictions on union organizing activities with a host of provisions that set new standards for union governance. Drawn to correct many of the issues highlighted during the McClellan hearings, these union governance provisions can be grouped in three broad categories involving the conduct of officers, transparency in union affairs, and guarantees for union democracy. Addressing issues raised by Beck's conduct, Landrum-Griffin specified that union officers occupied a position of fiduciary trust with regard to their membership. Actions that violated such trust, for example, engaging in conflicts of interest or misusing union funds, now became violations of federal law. The law imposed new restrictions on who could hold office. Individuals found guilty of various crimes, including extortion, assault, and murder, became ineligible to hold union office for thirteen years from the date of conviction. Reflecting the connections the committee had drawn between the conspiracies of organized crime and the communists, this provision also banned anyone "who is or has been a member of the Communist Party." Union members repeatedly had complained that their officers told them nothing about the finances of their organizations. In response, the new law made union finances transparent. It required unions to file public reports on their internal finances, including details about officers' salaries, expense accounts, investments, and income from dues. Finally, a number of safeguards were installed to protect union democracy. The law set up guidelines to regulate the conduct of union elections, including provisions for appeal in cases of apparent fraud and intimidation. A "Bill of Rights of Members of Labor Organizations" guaranteed members the freedom to speak out about union affairs and protected them from unfair disciplinary action.[103]

The union governance provisions make it difficult to categorize the law itself as antilabor. Since its passage, union members have found these provisions essential in discovering and opposing misconduct on the part of their leaders. Concerns that the law would undercut the stability of union governments have not been borne out. If anything, critics suggest that the law offers too little help to insurgent movements within unions.[104] Thus McClellan's hope that the democratic environment created by the law would be the undoing of ambitious, power-hungry union leaders like Hoffa went unfulfilled. Hoffa himself suffered few inconveniences because of these sections of the law.

Yet the new restrictions on picketing and secondary boycotts made organizing more difficult for all unions. Those provisions of Landrum-Griffin clearly had been intended to undercut the power of organized labor. The Teamsters, who had long made secondary boycotts an important part of their organizing strategy, found it impossible to continue using them.[105] The new restrictions came into place in the midst of a renewed employer counteroffensive, the effects of which unions are still feeling. Since 1959 the proportion of American workers belonging to unions has steadily declined in the United States, with the percentage falling every year after 1958.[106]

The passage of the Landrum-Griffin Act thus marks a moment of victory for the anti-union movement in the United States and the beginning of a trend. It also represents a decisive turning point in the political fortunes of organized labor, an outcome that seemed quite unlikely only two years earlier. In 1957 U.S. labor unions were at their all-time peak in popularity. If a third of the workforce belonged to unions, 76 percent of Americans approved of them, a rate of approval that exceeded the heady days of the New Deal.[107] To all appearances, organized labor had proved its political popularity in 1958. That year Republican support for right-to-work legislation in several state contests, including California, had backfired. The proposals went down in defeat, and, as union members mobilized to vote, Democrats scored major gains over their Republican rivals in Congress. Following the election, Republican Party leaders and business groups expressed their sense of despair.[108]

The McClellan Committee helped to change all that. The committee raised the issue of corruption, gave it unprecedented publicity, and depicted it as a problem growing out of union actions. Union leaders became the villains and businessmen the perennial victims. Union power itself was tagged as a form of corruption—indeed, committee members portrayed it as the most important form of corruption. The presence of organized crime, described as a centrally directed conspiracy that endangered national security, added an extra sense of menace to the threat of corruption. Through news stories, magazine pieces, and televised hearings the spectacle of corruption dramatically touched the American public.

By the fall of 1957, three-quarters of all Americans, when asked, responded that they were familiar with the congressional investigation of union corruption.[109] During those same months, public approval of labor unions underwent a precipitous decline. From February to September 1957 the percentage of Americans who went on record as approving of unions fell from 76 percent to 64 percent.[110] The decline was unmatched in the history of the Gallup Poll on this subject; previous variations had been usually around two or three percentage points. Sensing the change in public mood, Democratic members of Congress elected with union support in 1958 found it impossible to vote against an anti-union corruption measure, even if that meant voting for legislation harmful to organized labor.[111] Thus the committee's ability to make Hoffa's Teamsters appear a threat to national safety helped transform the political landscape for organized labor in general. The law to get Jimmy Hoffa left him untouched but directly affected the rest of the union movement.

10. Reform in the Age of Hoffa

The McClellan Committee's hearings stirred a range of reactions by members of the Teamsters Union. While Dave Beck's political fortunes collapsed under the weight of the committee's revelations, Jimmy Hoffa apparently enjoyed a kind of political immunity. Elected to the union's presidency in 1957 in defiance of the McClellan Committee's efforts to discredit him, Hoffa went on to win unanimous reelection at the union's convention in 1961. He received vociferous support from other Teamster leaders and from much of the rank and file, but he faced stubborn opposition as well. A reform movement emerged in the late 1950s fed by the scandals uncovered by the McClellan Committee and by rank-and-file anger at the misconduct of some of the local leaders Hoffa supported. Although most accounts of Hoffa's career have overlooked this movement, for a time it presented him with a significant threat to his leadership. Hoffa's ability to defeat these reformers marked a turning point in the union's history. Henceforth, internal reform efforts could no longer depend upon the tactics of secession and electoral opposition, and as a result insurgents became increasingly dependent upon the intervention of the state.

The reformers of the late 1950s and early 1960s were more than ambitious would-be office-holders. As opponents to Hoffa's leadership they offered a comprehensive critique of his administration. They disagreed with his alliance to members of organized crime and his willingness to overlook the misconduct of particular local leaders. But they also offered a different vision of the union's role, one that stressed democracy over professionalism and localism over centralization. Like past generations of reformers within the union, they tended to justify both their complaints and their proposals for change by referring to the notion of dignity. As in the past, the term *dignity* often involved references to manliness, especially to a man's ability to fulfill his patriarchal duty.

These reformers mounted the last major secession movement within the Teamsters. Their decision to use this tactic followed a familiar pattern. The union's convention had always provided an inhospitable environment in which to mount an insurgent campaign, and that remained true under Hoffa. In this era, however, the tactic of secession drew additional strength from New Deal labor legislation that provided for government supervision of the collective bargaining process. Thanks to the Wagner Act (1935), secessionists could petition for an election to allow them to serve as the collective bargaining agent for local union members, and the National Labor Relations Board then would oversee the balloting process. The government's presence freed reformers from depending upon the national union to protect the integrity of the vote. It offered them a fair chance to appeal to the membership and win the right of leadership. Thus, a series of local secession movements emerged in the wake of Hoffa's reelection in 1961. These reformers hoped to gain the support of the AFL-CIO and perhaps eventually follow the path taken by the United Teamsters of America against Cornelius Shea. The emergence of a rival Teamsters Union would have forced Hoffa, as it had Shea, to offer some accommodation to his opponents.

In the end, however, Hoffa overcame the insurgency. The critical contest took place in Philadelphia in 1962–63 when a group calling itself the Voice sought to pull the Teamsters' fourth-largest local out of the national union. In defeating the Voice, Hoffa demonstrated that secession no longer provided reformers with strategic leverage.

Defying the McClellan Committee

Although the findings of the McClellan Committee had discredited Dave Beck they produced no similar political defeat for Hoffa, this in spite of the efforts of the committee to repeat the earlier victory. Beck's political fortunes had declined precipitously in the wake of the committee's hearings, and in May 1957 he let it be known that he would not be running for reelection. Hoffa announced his candidacy for the Teamsters' top post in late July.[1] In response, the McClellan Committee held its first set of hearings focusing upon Hoffa that August.[2] After presenting damaging testimony about his financial dealings and his ties to John Dioguardia, the committee's senators denounced Hoffa.[3] Adding weight to this criticism, the AFL-CIO in September 1957 promised to expel the Teamsters if he became the union's president.

The election itself was scheduled to take place at the union's convention in the first week of October, and as that date approached the McClellan Committee held special hearings timed to influence the convention delegates.[4] In spite of all of this pressure, the assembled Teamster delegates voted for Hoffa by a significant margin.[5] This result stemmed from the dynamics of union politics, the suspicion with which many members viewed the McClellan Committee's investigation, and Hoffa's popularity within the union. The same forces ensured that in the years after 1957, in spite of investigations and criminal trials, Hoffa would maintain his grip on union office.

Although he had defied the McClellan Committee, Hoffa had not remained untouched. The hearings did affect his public image within the union, raising concerns about his actions, but Teamster members tended to qualify their expressions of disapproval. In the wake of Hoffa's testimony in August, the *Wall Street Journal* conducted its own survey of two hundred working Teamsters. Members were "impressed by the Senate hearings," but, the *Journal* reported, "some tend to discount them—especially where they relate to Mr. Hoffa." Disapproval was mixed with expressions of indifference and cynicism. One trucker in Pittsburgh said of Hoffa, "He's as good as the next man. He hasn't done anything to hurt us here in Pittsburgh." Other drivers expressed a kind of grudging neutrality. As one put it, "Maybe some of them [Teamster leaders] took money and maybe they didn't, but I'm happy as long as they keep getting contracts as good as the one I'm working under now." Acknowledging such diverse opinions, the *Journal* nevertheless concluded that most Teamsters disapproved of the conduct uncovered by the McClellan Committee. Three-fourths of the members asked about Hoffa "declared they would rather see someone else in the top Teamster job if they had a choice."[6]

The reporters found, however, that most members felt that they had no real input in the union's elections. Articles in the *New York Times* and in *Time* magazine reported similar findings.[7] And in some ways, the membership's view stemmed from a realistic appraisal of the situation. As was the case for many other unions, the Teamsters elected national officers at a regular convention, an event that the vast number of rank and file did not attend. Instead, each local union was to elect delegates to represent the membership, one delegate for each local and another one for each additional 750 members in the local. Although the rules said members should vote on who their delegates would be and could even instruct them on how to vote, in practice the local's officers usually bypassed the membership. Typically, a local's executive board picked the delegates, choosing them from among the local's officers or their surrogates. At times such practices amounted to a kind of autocracy as practiced by local leaders who ignored or defied their member-ship's wishes. Individual members occasionally expressed fear about stand-ing up to their local leaders and objecting to such undemocratic measures, but in many cases the leadership viewed the appointments as a logical result of election to union office. After all, by electing their officers the members had chosen whom they wanted to represent them. Cutting procedural cor-ners did not necessarily mean democracy had been denied. These practices, however, did ensure that in 1957 the union's local officers would choose its president, and Hoffa's political strength in turn reflected their views and concerns.[8]

When these delegates gathered together in early October at the conven-tion's site in Miami Beach, Florida, they had alternatives to voting for Hof-fa. Reform forces coalesced around two candidates, Thomas Haggerty, head of a Chicago Milk Drivers local, and William Lee, president of the Chicago Joint Council. Lee seemed the most tenable rival to Hoffa, but he lacked clear-cut credentials as a reformer. His leadership of the Chicago Joint Council, as well the close friendship he enjoyed with Frank Brewster, an influential West Coast Teamster leader, provided Lee with important political assets. Yet they also tagged him as an insider who heretofore had done nothing to speak out against the union's management. Indeed, Lee had been very close to Beck. Because he waited until the eve of the Teamster convention to declare his candidacy, most observers doubted Lee's chances of convincing the delegates to abandon their earlier commitments to vote for Hoffa.[9]

Such calculations about a candidate's potential for victory weighed heavily in the minds of convention delegates. Voting at the convention took place by public roll call, and local union leaders had good reasons to be wary about standing up and committing themselves to a lost cause. Unions tradition-ally functioned as one-party states, and office-holders often retaliated against their opponents.[10] The Teamsters were no exception to that rule. In mid-Sep-tember the *Wall Street Journal* reported that "truck union insiders say Mr. Hoffa is passing the word to Teamster groups that if they oppose him in the drive for the presidency they can expect reprisals if he wins."[11] In the increas-ingly centralized Teamsters Union, that kind of threat carried much weight. Local union leaders depended upon their conference chiefs for a variety of help, from winning membership grievances to contract negotiations. A na-tional leader bent on retaliation had numerous opportunities for revenge.[12]

Those political considerations necessarily played a role in the decisions made by Teamster delegates, just as they would for officers in any other or-ganization. Journalist Clark Mollenhoff talked to a local leader from Min-neapolis at the start of the convention who admitted that he had not liked what he learned from the McClellan hearings. Yet he still intended to vote for Hoffa. In part his decision stemmed from assistance Hoffa had given his local union in the past, but it also rested on practical considerations. According to Mollenhoff, he explained, "Even if I wanted to object, I can't see where it would do any good. Jimmy has the organization, and he has the votes. I could end up on the outside—and with nothing gained."[13] Hoffa's campaign played on such fears by emphasizing the widespread support and powerful endorsements he had already received.[14]

Still, the political dynamics of the convention do not explain all the support Hoffa received. Many members and many of his fellow union officers had deep appreciation for Hoffa's abilities, and they had an equally strong distrust of the investigation that had been mounted against him. Although critics might stereotype Hoffa's union allies as unscrupulous hacks or gangster flunkies, the reality was that many of his admirers were nothing of the kind. Alois Mueller, a local leader in rural Wisconsin, enjoyed a long and well-respected career in the IBT. When he died in 1992 the Madison *Capital Times* headlined a special column, "Farewell to Al Mueller, A First Class Guy." In August 1957 Mueller wrote to his hometown paper, the *Waukesha Daily Freeman,* to defend Hoffa from criticism that he saw as politically motivated. "Where does Hoffa get his support?" Mueller asked. "From the membership and the officers of the local unions. Why? Because he has done a job for them." Mueller cited Hoffa's role in increasing the size of the bargaining unit and winning better contracts. "It is quite difficult for these drivers to forget about the pensions, insurance benefits, wages and working conditions that were secured under Hoffa's leadership."[15]

In a similar vein, Matt Gelernter, a rank-and-file member from Los Angeles, wrote to Senator McClellan in March 1958, defending Hoffa's leadership. Gelernter charged that Congress wanted to convince Teamsters that Hoffa had betrayed them, but the members who enjoyed high wages in the Southern and Central Conference saw no such betrayal. Like Mueller, Gelernter refused to take the investigators' findings at face value. He pointedly asked the Congressman from Arkansas, "Senator, could it also be that you don't like Brother Hoffa because of the great gains the Teamsters have made through his organizational work in the South?"[16] John F. English, the general secretary-treasurer of the Teamsters, spoke in defense of Hoffa before the AFL-CIO in December 1957. Although Robert Kennedy himself had praised English's honesty, the general secretary-treasurer still balked at the federation's demand that the Teamsters oust Hoffa or face expulsion. English said, "Jimmy Hoffa has done more for our International Union than anybody connected with it including myself, so why in the hell should we kick him out?"[17]

Hoffa's political support in 1957 and later grew out of more than fear or the constraints faced by opposition groups in any union. Looking at Hoffa's record in office, his supporters saw not betrayal but a career marked by solid achievements in organization, wages, and benefits. Moreover, they regarded the motives of the McClellan Committee and the press with suspicion.

Hoffa's Critics within the Union

If many Teamsters viewed Hoffa and the McClellan Committee in the same way as did Alois Mueller, other members reached quite different conclusions. Some rank-and-file members and some local leaders reacted to the revelations of the McClellan Committee with great alarm. They concluded that Hoffa and several other officers allied to him had engaged in patterns of misconduct that betrayed the union's true purpose. These critics often linked their concerns about corruption to a larger view of how the Teamsters Union should be structured, as they envisioned democratically controlled, autonomous locals. In this way they objected to not just corruption but to a union that had become increasingly centralized and dominated by a kind of professional leadership group. The reformers distinguished themselves by their actions from the more opportunistic of Hoffa's opponents. Many who opposed Hoffa at his election in October 1957 put their differences aside as he consolidated his power in the union during the years that followed. A core group of reformers, however, continued to struggle, even after the odds against their success accumulated and the costs of opposition mounted.

A federal court suit that challenged the legitimacy of the 1957 Teamster election galvanized early opposition to Hoffa. A group of thirteen rank-and-file dissidents from New York hired a lawyer and filed suit in September 1957, seeking to block the union's convention that was to be held at the end of the month. The dissidents complained that a large number of convention delegates had been chosen improperly. The Federal Appeals Court refused to grant an injunction to stop the convention, but proceedings on the validity of the dissidents' claims began in late December of that year. The proceedings offered a venue for Hoffa's opponents, a number of whom took the stand to tell about how their opposition had been muzzled by Hoffa's supporters at local-level delegate elections and during the convention.[18]

The suit sought to overturn Hoffa's election. Apparently fearing the worst, Hoffa's lawyers agreed to a settlement that created a board of three monitors who would have the power to investigate and guide the union until a new and fair election could be held. The early reform promise of the board of monitors soon dissipated, however. After an initial period of cooperation, Hoffa stopped complying with their directives, and the union's lawyers mounted the legal equivalent of a war of attrition against the board by peppering the federal judge overseeing the board with endless motions that objected to its conduct. Those objections, combined with other delaying tactics and political divisions that emerged within the board, eventually took their toll. Never able to accomplish much in the way of investigation or oversight, the board's official existence came to an end in 1961 when the courts agreed to a new Teamster election, one that Hoffa won handily.[19] Even as that early reform effort slowly faded, other opponents to Hoffa pursued different avenues of change. In so doing, they drew strength from the findings of the McClellan Committee, which continued to investigate Hoffa's leadership from 1957 to 1959.

Committee hearings in the spring of 1959 focused on Joseph Glimco's leadership of Chicago Taxi Drivers' Local 777. Allegedly a top member of Chicago's Outfit, testimony indicated that Glimco had managed the Mob's efforts to extort money from businessmen who operated in the city's produce market.[20] When he had faced a criminal trial for these activities in 1957, Glimco had used $124,000 of the union's money to pay for his successful legal defense. Local 777 funds had also apparently been used to help Glimco build himself a new house, pay for the country club membership of another officer, and fund a pleasure trip Glimco had taken to California with one of the local's secretaries.[21] Dominic Abata, who had helped organize the local in 1937, testified about how in the 1940s he had been forced to sign over the bulk of his official salary to Glimco until one day in 1951 the Mafioso had told him to resign his position.[22] In spite of these scandalous revelations, the hearings left Hoffa unmoved. Glimco had become an important political supporter for the Teamster president, and Hoffa refused to heed suggestions that Glimco be removed from office and Local 777 be put into a trusteeship.[23]

The members of Local 777, however, did not share Hoffa's sense of equanimity. A couple of weeks after the McClellan Committee held its hearings on Glimco, a rank-and-file reform group became active in the local. One of its leaders was Dominic Abata, who had found testifying before the McClellan Committee an inspiring experience. As he recalled, "When I got back to Chicago after my testimony here, I felt that the cab drivers needed some help. I got myself a committee together to reorganize the cab drivers of Chicago through an independent union."[24] The group Abata helped organize called itself the Democratic Union Organizing Campaign (DUOC). They held their first open meeting on April 2, 1959, and nearly seventy-five cab drivers attended. The members at the gathering sought to have Glimco ousted from office and the financial abuses revealed by the McClellan Committee stopped. They did not believe, however, that working from within the union would bring results. Therefore, they began circulating petitions for the National Labor Relations Board (NLRB) to decertify Local 777 as the bargaining agent for employees of Yellow Cab and Checker Taxi. They aimed to set up a new independent union for taxi company employees.[25]

News accounts indicate that the membership of Local 777 welcomed the reformers' initiative. A poll of the rank and file conducted by the *Chicago Tribune* found that cab drivers overwhelmingly supported the new group.[26] The DUOC provided cab company employees with a way to regain the things they had lost during the years when Glimco controlled their local. Their concerns were both tangible and intangible. On one level, they had lost an effective union; for years it had failed to represent their financial interests or guard their benefits. They had not gotten a raise in more than ten years. Glimco served as the sole trustee of their benefit funds, and he appointed administrators who almost never approved a driver's insurance claim. If a member complained about the fund's actions, he found himself fired. On top of all of that came the embezzlement of union funds that the McClellan Committee had uncovered. As one driver put it, the officers of Local 777 "didn't do anything except steal our money."[27]

Beyond those immediate material issues lay an underlying sense that Glimco, through his total domination of the union and the workplace, had taken away their dignity. As Eleuterio Sepulvda, a twenty-five-year-old driver, told a *Chicago Tribune* reporter, "We have been treated like dogs by Glimco and the business agents. We want to form another union; the one we have is just a racket." Another Local 777 member asked, "What kind of a union is this anyway?" Members feared to stand up for their rights in the workplace and within the union. George Crandall, a driver who attended the April 2 DUOC gathering, said he had gone to one Local 777 meeting and "it stunk. I was afraid to raise my voice against Glimco. I was told in the company garage that I would get in trouble if I spoke up." To get an effective union and regain their dignity, these workers believed they needed to restore democracy. "We want a different union," asserted Horace Neagle, forty-three. "We want a union where we can go to meetings and speak up without getting our heads bashed in." Restoring democracy meant standing up to the fear that had always held them back. "All of us want another union," explained a driver named Jack

Landin. "We have been afraid that we might lose our jobs and get beaten if we stood alone against Glimco and his guys. Now if we all stick together, maybe we can do something."[28]

In the face of physical intimidation, threats, and actual violence, DUOC members gathered enough signatures to call for an NLRB election. In one case a Teamster business agent came up from behind DUOC organizer Everett Clark while he waited in the cab line at Northwestern Station. The business agent threw open the door of Clark's cab and smashed his fist into the driver's eye. Three stitches later closed the cut, but all the other drivers could see Clark's bloodied face as he left the station to go to the doctor's. Other attacks followed a similar pattern, singling out DUOC members for retribution in public places where other drivers could see. Two weeks after the assault on Clark, another DUOC organizer, Louis Linzer, suffered an attack while waiting in a cab line. This time the assailant calmly walked up and asked whether his name was Linzer. When Linzer replied yes, the man punched him through the cab's open window. As Linzer tried to get out of the cab the attacker went at him with a lead pipe.[29] Other DUOC members faced threats. Glimco warned one man, "I have got ways of taking care of guys like you." Then he inquired about the man's children.[30] Nor were reprisals always physical. Drivers active in the reform organization often found themselves fired from their jobs on one pretext or another.[31] Sensing the nature of the opposition they would face, DUOC organizers had planned a very quick petition drive. They apparently caught the leaders of Local 777 by surprise and gathered the signatures necessary for a NLRB election in just ten days—before the full force of Glimco's campaign of intimidation came into effect.[32]

After receiving the petitions, the Labor Board considered the case for more than a year, debating the outlines of the appropriate bargaining group and whether the election could occur during the length of an existing Teamster contract.[33] Meanwhile, DUOC members busied themselves putting out a regular newsletter in which they spelled out their complaints about Local 777 and their ideas about how the union should be run. The DUOC's program emphasized both matters of dollars and cents and the issue of dignity. Organizers assured drivers that they would push for a significant pay increase and that pension and welfare benefits could be improved by changing the management of the union's funds. Garage mechanics would also get a raise, and the DUOC would perform duties that a union was supposed to undertake, duties upon which Local 777 had never felt compelled to expend effort. A system of active and informed shop stewards would be set up, with one steward placed in each cab garage. Those stewards would help the membership see to it that the provisions of the union's contract actually were enforced. The petty tyrannies of company supervisors, who took bribes to assign drivers decent cabs, could not survive the pressure of effective stewards. Similarly, the DUOC promised cab drivers that their administration would provide cabbies with legal representation in traffic court. Drivers usually paid off corrupt police officers rather than trying to fight unjust traffic citations. The DUOC also planned a credit union, which, they hoped, would allow members to avoid dealing with the loan sharks that ran a brisk trade in the cab garages.[34]

The sum and total of these proposals amounted to changing the union from an organization that controlled the members and existed for the sake of collecting their dues to one that represented them and guarded their interests. An article entitled "Glimco and Dignity," which appeared in the December edition of the DUOC's newsletter, exemplified that message:

> When asked why they are trying to prevent a fair election under the NLRB, spokesmen for the Glimco Mob say: "These drivers are *our* drivers, and besides we do not want to *dignify* Abata, and the DUOC." To this we reply: "Union officials *do not own* their members. Rather they should represent the members . . . they should *regard* themselves as instruments to carry out the will and desires of the members." . . . In trying to prevent our election, the Glimco Mob has used the threat, the attempt to bribe, constant harassment, assaults, etc. Were these acts committed in the name of dignity?[35]

An earlier DUOC flier summed up the issue more directly: "Cab Drivers!! Do You Want—Respect For Yourself, For Your Job; For Your Union?"[36] The DUOC promised to transform Local 777 members from chattel to citizens. In doing so it would give them back their dignity.

The NLRB finally scheduled an election for July 1961. Hoffa, who had just been reelected president of the national union, offered Glimco his complete support. He came to Chicago to campaign on Glimco's behalf, but in spite of his efforts the DUOC won the election. By a vote of 2,122 to 1,760, Local 777's members decided to secede and join the independent union formed by the DUOC. Observers noted that Hoffa's personal involvement in the contest meant that the loss represented a significant defeat for him. Indeed, Local 777 members linked their votes for the DUOC with their disapproval of Hoffa. As one Chicago cab driver explained, "This loss sure might hurt Hoffa. He may be okay for some people, but not for me. He's for himself, not the little fellow." Members also emphasized the importance of having the vote conducted by an impartial authority, the NLRB. One driver told a reporter, "It just shows what a secret ballot can do. If that election had been held in our union hall, there wouldn't have been 10 votes for Abata [the DUOC leader]."[37]

The victory of the DUOC in Local 777 proved the viability of reform via this new method of secession. It was not long before another group of Teamster reformers followed suit. In August 1961 some four thousand members in four separate locals in Cincinnati, Ohio, voted to disaffiliate from the IBT. These Teamsters followed the lead of a local official named James Luken, who had opposed Hoffa since the early 1950s. The Cincinnati Teamsters were motivated to pull out not so much by the victory of the DUOC but by Hoffa's reelection in early July. The IBT's convention marked the formal end of the court-appointed monitors. The convention had also rewritten the national union's constitution in ways that granted Hoffa considerably more power. The possibilities for loyal opposition in the Teamsters Union always had been tenuous, and now, to these Cincinnati Teamsters, they seemed nonexistent. As one explained to a reporter, "Now that Hoffa's been elected again and the monitors are gone, we're in bad shape. Hoffa's going to try to get us. He's got the power to do it. Why should we be waiting around for him to murder us?"[38]

As had been the case in Chicago, opposition to Hoffa in Cincinnati stemmed in large part from his links to a particular local leader, in this case William Presser, head of the Ohio Conference of Teamsters. Labeled the "Juke Box King of Ohio" by the newspapers, Presser led a local of vending machine workers in Cleveland and was involved in a web of collusive agreements in that city.[39] A close ally of Hoffa, Presser also had strong ties to the Cleveland Mafia. He allegedly had a number of business partnerships with various Cleveland Mafia leaders and was generally considered their representative in the Teamsters Union.[40] Nicknamed "the Plug" because of his stout appearance, Presser had raised the ire of Cincinnati Teamsters in 1953 when he sought to expand his jukebox racket to that city. Luken and other Cincinnati Teamsters saw this as an opening wedge for Cleveland organized crime and actively opposed it.[41]

Although Hoffa liked to deride his opponents as uninformed rank-and-filers or unrealistic outsiders, Luken was an articulate critic whose opposition stemmed from long experience as a local leader.[42] Testifying before the McClellan Committee, Luken explained his opposition to Hoffa as far more than a clash of personalities. It came down, he said, to different philosophies about how a union should be run. Luken was a realist and had years of practical experience as a union leader. He admitted that for all practical purposes political opposition within a union would always be problematic. "You do not have a basic, two-party set up," he explained. "There is no active minority. An active minority is always subject to criticism that they may be working against the best interests of the local. You do not have two political machines. You have only one." Moreover, union government had no system of checks and balances. "Mr. Hoffa and his group end up being not only the administrative, legislative, and judicial, but they end up being all of them." In other words, they wrote the laws of the union and enforced and interpreted them. As a local union leader, this state of affairs might not have bothered Luken. The same political dynamic that benefited Hoffa also played to Luken's advantage within his own local union. Everything worked to make union leadership into a kind of "benevolent dictatorship." Members, like corporate stockholders, tended to ignore their union as long as things ran smoothly and steady wage gains were achieved. Luken was even willing to admit that "to some extent the best form of government is a benevolent dictatorship." It could get things done quickly and efficiently. But, as he quickly pointed out, "The only thing wrong with it is who in the world is going to control when he [the union leader] will be benevolent and when he will not be benevolent?" In encounters with Presser and Hoffa, Luken said, he had learned firsthand the ways that unchecked power could be abused.[43]

Luken tried to practice what he called "membership-up unionism." He worked assiduously to keep members coming to their local union meetings and to make those meetings free and open forums for discussion. The membership took part in contract negotiations and ratified every agreement with employers. Luken resisted the idea of having his local join one of the larger collective bargaining units like the Ohio Conference or Hoffa's brainchild, the Central State's Conference. Luken felt that when bargaining occurred at that broader level it took control of the union's affairs too far away from the local membership. "I believe," he once stated, "that the control of the local union should be vested within its membership . . . power should not be taken too far away from them." Luken thought that Hoffa, in contrast, practiced "top-down control." The Teamster president had accumulated control at the expense of local leaders and at the expense of the membership itself.[44]

From 1957 on, Luken was one of the most prominent leaders in the Teamsters to oppose Hoffa.[45] It was an increasingly lonely role. Others who had fought Hoffa in 1957 when he first ran for president of the national union found various reasons to drop their opposition. At the 1961 Teamster Convention Luken nominated the only candidate to challenge the incumbent Hoffa but acknowledged, "I recognized it was a futile gesture."[46] Few other delegates saw any reason to make such a risky gesture. By the time the convention roll call had reached the halfway point of a thousand delegates, only fifteen had voted against Hoffa. The opposing candidate, Luken's nominee, moved to end the roll call and asked to have the vote declared unanimous.[47]

Luken's opposition to Hoffa had already drawn retribution, but now he had reason to fear even more forceful reprisals. In preceding years Hoffa and Presser had worked to encourage dissension within the Cincinnati locals. They had sent in an outside organizer to offer employers attractive side deals if they would refuse to bargain with Luken. The Cincinnati Teamster leader received anonymous threats, telephone calls warning him to get out of town. At one point an undertaker was told to come pick up Luken's body at his house, and to complete the symbolic warning funeral flowers were sent to his home.[48]

In the wake of the 1961 convention, with the monitors gone and Hoffa's position consolidated, Luken expected Hoffa to impose a trusteeship over his local union. Once imposed, a Hoffa-appointed trustee could remove Luken from office and restructure the local union in any way Hoffa saw fit. There would be no appeal against this process, Luken explained, "except right back to Mr. Hoffa and right back to a committee appointed by him."[49] Luken decided to pull his people out of the IBT before Hoffa had a chance to impose such a trusteeship. In mid-August, a few weeks after Hoffa's reelection, four Cincinnati local unions, with about four thousand members, met and voted to disaffiliate from the Teamsters.[50]

Hoffa responded by traveling to Cincinnati with a large number of organizers and a well-financed media campaign to try and convince the members not to go. His campaign cited the many benefits of staying with a large and wealthy national union like the Teamsters. He and Luken even participated in a public debate, broadcast by a local radio station. Having heard both sides of the issue, the members got a second chance to vote, this time outside the local union hall. The NLRB ran a secret ballot election at its own polling stations, and Luken's people won these contests by landslide proportions. In the large dairy workers' bargaining unit, for example, the vote was 1,664 to 12 to leave the Teamsters.[51] As had been the case in Chicago, the NLRB offered an impartial venue for achieving the goal of secession. Once again, reformers sought a safe base of operations by setting up an independent rival organization.

Turning Point in Philadelphia

Although Hoffa focused much energy on the dissidents in Chicago and Cincinnati, accounts of the Teamsters Union usually have overlooked the reform efforts that occurred in this period. The *New York Times* asserted in 1961, "Most Teamsters seem perfectly content to ride along with Mr. Hoffa in his cynical conviction that anything goes so long as he keeps delivering higher wages and fatter benefits to his members."[52] Later observers have echoed that sentiment.[53] A biography of Hoffa by Arthur Sloane assures readers that no significant opposition to Hoffa—in fact, no significant rank-and-file dissent—existed in the union by the 1960s. Of Hoffa Sloan observes, "When he was almost anyplace within the domain of the 1.6 million-member labor organization, he was among rabid partisans."[54]

In fact, the situation in the early 1960s was far less placid. By the end of 1961, in spite of his solid reelection victory at the at the IBT's convention, Hoffa appeared vulnerable. Dissidents in Chicago and Cincinnati had pulled out, and other groups of cab drivers in Detroit, St. Louis, and San Diego were moving to secede.[55] Further victories by insurgents raised the possibility of another danger. The AFL-CIO had responded to the revelations of the McClellan Committee by expelling the Teamsters in 1957. In other cases where it expelled an organization for corruption, the federation had followed that action by chartering a rival union to supplant the ousted and corrupt organization. Fearing a difficult battle with the Teamsters, the labor federation had not thus far sponsored a rival organization, but it might do so if further evidence of dissent emerged.[56] If the trucking locals, the strategic center of the Teamsters Union, began to secede, then the danger of an effective rival union, a latter-day UTA supported by the AFL-CIO, could become serious.

Given this context, events in Philadelphia became a turning point for reform. In January 1962 a group of insurgents in Philadelphia's Local 107, following the advice of James Luken, began to push for secession. Unlike the locals that had previously seceded, Local 107 was a trucking local; in fact, it was the fourth-largest local union in the IBT.[57] Secession here might well have led to the emergence of a rival union. Moreover, the insurgents of Philadelphia developed a set of tactics that seemed to reverse the traditional power dynamics that constrained rank-and-file dissent. Drawing on their roots in Philadelphia's working-class neighborhoods, the reformers overcame the organizational barriers that daunted most would-be insurgents. In so doing, they championed a particular vision of the union, one that emphasized autonomous local leaders kept closely accountable to a well-informed and active membership. Their descriptions of this kind of union's goals emphasized the themes of dignity, decency, and democracy. For a time, in spite of intimidation, in spite of violence, and in spite of Hoffa's personal commitment to the contest, it seemed the reformers might win. The contest marked the zenith of reform efforts. Their eventual defeat spelled the end of this period of insurgency and pointed out the limitations of secession as a viable reform strategy.

Rank-and-file reform emerged in Local 107 out of opposition to the local's leadership, especially the local's secretary-treasurer, Raymond Cohen. Opposition to Cohen had grown within the local since 1958, when the McClellan Committee held a series of hearings on his management of the local. The committee found irregularities in how Cohen was elected and also uncovered fraud involving the union's finances. Evidence presented during the hearings, and later used to convict Cohen in a criminal trial, indicated that he regularly dipped into union funds to buy himself a variety of luxury items, from tasteful, charcoal-gray suits to medium-sized yachts. Other testimony indicated that he had negotiated more lenient contracts in return for a payoff from a large employer.[58]

Initially, it appeared that the Senate's allegations presented no great threat to Cohen. Hoffa refused to take any significant action in response to the evidence of his improprieties. In fact, as was the case with Glimco and other similar individuals, Hoffa supported Cohen against local opponents. He even backed him for higher office in the national union.[59]

Nor did Cohen's position with local members seem in immediate jeopardy. At a Local 107 meeting held in the wake of the Senate hearings, the assembled members hanged Senator McClellan in effigy. Seven months later Cohen and the rest of his slate of officers won reelection in a regular election. His 5 to 1 margin of victory seemed to be a personal vindication. Outside observers saw the reelection as yet another example of Teamster apathy and cynicism. The *Philadelphia Evening Bulletin* explained, "What the election appeared to tell Cohen was: keep bringing home the bacon: we don't care about the corruption charges."[60]

Watching what seemed to be a familiar pattern of Teamster toleration for corruption, most observers failed to see that an opposition movement had emerged within the local. Responding to the hearings, a group calling itself the Teamster Betterment Committee printed bulletins calling for Cohen's ouster.[61] After his reelection in 1958, the same group raised public complaints about how the election had been conducted. They charged that Cohen's slate had posted strong-arm men beside the union's ballot boxes and forced members to display their ballots before casting them.[62]

Dissent apparently continued below the surface, breaking out again in the spring of 1961 when a group calling itself the Voice of Teamsters Local No. 107 emerged to contest delegate elections to the IBT convention. Defeated, they called for the upcoming elections for Local 107 officers to be monitored by an outside agency. When Cohen's group refused that reform and no help from the national office of the union appeared likely, the Voice called for secession and gathered enough signatures from Local 107 members to have the NLRB hold a decertification election. If the Voice won that vote, then most members of Local 107 would become members of a new independent union: the Voice.[63]

Although they targeted the local's leadership, the Voice also formed part of a larger opposition movement directed at Hoffa's administration. Holding the Teamster president responsible for allowing corruption to occur in Philadelphia, the dissidents made it clear that they opposed both Cohen and Hoffa. At Voice meetings a mock coffin was displayed near the stage, and a sign above it read "Reserved for Hoffa." They drew on the support and guidance of Teamster reformers elsewhere who had proven the practicality of secession. James Luken spoke at one of the Voice's early meetings in November 1961, soon after he had pulled his own local union out of the IBT. In time both he and Abata of the Chicago cab drivers came to play advisory roles in the Philadelphia struggle. Significantly, the leaders of the Voice also met with officials from the AFL-CIO about the possibilities of secession.[64] Eventually, the federation granted the group a union charter, a move that at least indirectly endorsed their breakaway efforts.[65] Still, the campaign of the Voice remained very much a rank-and-file effort. Leadership within the group came to center on a thirty-five-year-old truck driver named Charlie Meyer whose highest office in the union had been shop steward.[66]

In choosing to become involved in dissent Meyer and other members of the Voice put their jobs and their safety at risk, but becoming involved in a struggle against local union leadership did not make them reformers. What, one might ask, distinguished the efforts of the Voice from any ordinary intra-union conflict? Perhaps behind the rhetoric of reform lay simpler, less high-minded motives involving ethnic solidarity, generation divisions, or ambition. On close examination, however, those typical political motivations fail to explain the Voice. The multi-ethnic makeup of the insurgents and the incumbents reveal that ethnicity played no important role. The names of the leadership for both the Voice and Local 107 suggest no clear ethnic divisions between the two groups.[67] Similarly, the signatures filed with the NLRB requesting a decertification election—a sign of some support for the Voice—indicate no pattern of ethnicity.[68] Nor did the Voice seem to represent any particular generation. News reports described younger Voice adherents often taking the lead in fights with Local 107 officials, but Meyer, the leader of the group, was in his mid-thirties. Other Voice activists hospitalized after a violent dispute in mid-August 1962 were thirty-six, thirty-seven, fifty-three, and fifty-eight.[69] This does not seem to have been particularly a young man's game.

Nor does ambition explain the campaign of the Voice. Winning union office likely did appeal to a capable and ambitious rank-and-file member.

After all, it allowed one to earn an easier and more lucrative living than driving a truck. But for the leaders of the Voice there were surely less onerous and less risky ways to advance their careers. As Paul Jacobs, a frequent writer on union affairs in this period, has noted, "If a Teamster member does desire to be a union leader, he rarely pursues his goal through challenging the existing administration. Rather he seeks to become part of the administration and attach himself to a leader in power."[70] For the rank and file of the Voice, ambition is an even more problematic explanation. Only so many people could hope to be officers, but participation in the Voice carried with it great risks for everyone involved. Robert Rispo, a foot soldier in the struggle, remembered how clearly he understood the risks. Back then, he said, he knew that his participation in the Voice would mean that after the election he "couldn't get a job sweeping the floors." Rispo recalled the contest in 1962 as a fight over substantive issues. "It was like a regular campaign between like the Republicans and Democrats. You went around and said what was wrong with the Teamsters and they went around and said what was wrong with The Voice."[71]

More than political opportunists, the members of the Voice developed a thorough critique of the way that their union had been administered. In doing so they put forward their own vision of what that union's appropriate goals should be and how those goals should be achieved. Running through this vision was an emphasis on the notion of dignity, and that word in turn carried connotations of a very traditional masculinity.

The first issue of the dissidents' journal, *Voice of Truth,* placed the connection between a patriarchal masculinity and the issue of dignity literally front and center. In explaining why the group had begun their campaign, the following words appeared on the journal's cover: "To Every Man, There Comes a Day." The text that followed emphasized the connection between masculinity and dignity by explaining that a man needed to "look at himself through the trusting eyes of his children or the adoring eyes of his wife." For a man to keep his dignity, he could not disappoint the expectations of his dependent wife and children. Membership in a blatantly corrupt union, however, undercut that dignity. The group argued that the scandals that plagued the Cohen administration of Local 107 had brought shame upon all the members. *The Voice Handbook for Organizers* asserted, "Local 107's finances have been handled in such a disgraceful manner that even the honest members of the local have been held up to the other workers in Philadelphia as objects of ridicule, and this is something which we must never allow to happen again." Elsewhere, *The Voice Handbook* put the matter simply and directly, "We want to regain our pride and self-respect." The Voice campaigned on a platform that called for an end to union corruption and the leadership of Cohen and Hoffa, but the group also sought a more militant union. They adopted as their slogan "Dignity, Decency, and Democracy." They also argued that a more democratic local would be more honest and that it would do more to properly enforce the terms of the contract.[72] As the Voice's literature explained, what was at stake was more than dollars and cents. It was the ability of members to enjoy a measure of dignity in their working lives.

One issue of the newsletter, for instance, focused on the union's hiring hall. As the Voice explained, the union had drifted away from its earlier militancy on this and other issues. "When the union came to industries that required this type of institution, the employers right to pick and choose and to pay what he chose was stopped, the Union brought to the Hiring Hall three elements that are known as Dignity, Decency and Democracy." But now, the Voice complained, many employers freely violated the terms of the contract and bypassed the hiring hall. Men got jobs by asking for favors, and companies picked pliant workers over those with more seniority. The Voice called for a stricter enforcement of the contract, asserting that a union member, "shouldn't feel that he is the last 'resort' for the employer or that he will have to prostrate himself and his God-given dignity as a human being to curry favor by payoffs or any other method in order to get work to feed his family."[73]

Using similar language, the Voice called for reforms and stricter enforcement in other areas of the union's contracts. They wanted grievances processed more quickly and effectively, work rules better enforced, and elected shop stewards to represent them. In this way the Voice linked the issue of union corruption with a call for a militant union.[74]

The critique offered by the Voice would matter little, however, unless the group overcame the obstacles that usually hamstrung rank-and-file insurgencies. Typically, such rank-and-file efforts dissolved as a result of the dissidents' vulnerability. Isolated individuals could be physically intimidated. In Local 107, any act of opposition drew a quick and often physical reprisal. Those members who handed out the Teamster Betterment Committee's news sheets, for example, were soon caught at a jobsite and beaten up in front of other union members.[75] The representative of the group that had filed an election protest received so many death threats that he was placed under twenty-four-hour police guard.[76]

If the insurgents could rally enough membership support, they could defend each other from acts of intimidation, but generating a critical mass was difficult. Cohen, like other Teamster leaders, could very effectively dampen public opposition. The spaces where members usually expressed such oppo-

sition and sought support were also spaces in which Cohen enjoyed a predominance of power. For instance, dissidents might try to rally support for
their cause at the local's regular monthly meetings. But Cohen or one of his
supporters chaired those meetings and decided who could speak and who
was out of order. Those meetings were also usually packed with shop stewards, business agents, and others who had been appointed by Cohen. Other
members could and did attend but felt themselves to be on Cohen's turf.
Members who sought to voice complaints in the union hall were shouted
down, ruled out of order, and sometimes ambushed on their way out the
door.[77] As a pamphlet by the Voice put it, "We never had any union democracy."[78]

Teamsters Union members faced special obstacles in building an opposition movement. Unlike insurgent factory workers who could have used their
jobsite as an alternative organizing site, Teamsters worked in relatively small
groups at warehouses and truckyards scattered across the city. At each jobsite the steward, often a Cohen appointee, had a powerful restraining influence.[79]

The Voice overcame the hurdles blocking many other Teamster insurgencies because they drew on a strategy that combined federal intervention—
in the form of the NLRB—and local solidarity. As reformers in Chicago and
Cincinnati had proven, secession allowed insurgents to draw the federal government into their cause. By staking the contest on a decertification election,
members of the Voice had found a way to make sure that an outside group,
the NLRB, monitored the fairness of the election process. The strategy also
took the reformers out from under the thumbs of local and national union
leaders.

In Philadelphia, reformers combined this strategy of secession with a
movement that dug deep roots in the community. The Voice based itself securely in the working-class neighborhoods of northeastern Philadelphia,
which provided a safe-zone from which to organize and rally supporters. The
usual dynamics of union opposition were reversed inside this community.
Typically, union members who stood up in opposition at the union hall drew
immediate attention and often swift reprisal. As a result, few people actually
did stand up, and members generally perceived dissidents to be a somewhat
frightened minority. In northeastern Philadelphia neighborhoods, though,
whole crowds could fill the local meeting halls. For the first time, union
members could actually see themselves as part of a larger group that was
dissatisfied with how the union was run.

Philadelphia insurgents consciously drew on this community-based
strength. They sought to root their movement in the neighborhood public-

ly in a number of ways, such as holding meetings at the local Polonia Hall or sponsoring Holy Communion breakfasts for members and their wives at the local Catholic church. Funds were raised by selling raffle tickets at the door of the meetings.[80] In the neighborhoods of Kensington and Frankford, as the *Philadelphia Bulletin* noted, the Voice became a "tight-knit organization" able to mobilize its membership through an "efficient communications grapevine."[81]

Voice members took pains to increase their visibility in these neighborhoods. They wore distinctive yellow and purple windbreakers with "The Voice" emblazoned on the back. Their cars all carried Voice stickers in spite of the fact that such stickers often made the automobiles targets for roving bands of vandals who would slash tires and break windshields. [82]

Perhaps their greatest demonstration of strength and visibility in the community came on the night of August 15, 1962. A march staged by the Voice that night resulted from trouble that had begun a few days earlier. Prominent Voice members had been encountering harassment on the job for some time. When one of the top leaders of the group, Walter Wolf, was fired on August 13 on what was perceived to be only a pretext, the Voice decided to take a stand and posted a picket line around Wolf's employer's truckyard. When other employers fired Voice members who had taken the day off to walk the picket line, the activists struck those firms as well. Eventually, by the August 15, the dispute came to involve sixteen trucking firms.[83]

Violence broke out that night. The Voice held a meeting at Polonia Hall, and Cohen's administration sponsored a dinner at the union's hall a few blocks away. Sometime during the late afternoon Cohen's supporters ambushed a fifty-eight-year-old Voice adherent and worked him over with baseball bats. A series of such attacks against Voice members had occurred over the course of the campaign, but this one particularly enraged the insurgents. When news of the incident reached the Voice meeting the crowd was galvanized. Voice members and supporters stormed out of the meeting hall and marched over to the union's headquarters. Seeing a crowd numbering between three and five hundred people charging up the hill, frightened officers of Local 107 barricaded the building's doors. For the next hour the demonstrators fought to get inside and grapple with their officers. More than a hundred police arrived to separate the contending forces, but the dissidents and their supporters did not leave until fire department water cannons drove them from the area.[84]

The Voice leadership saw this encounter as a great victory. As the group's newspaper later explained, "We displayed the type of unity and solidarity that amazed the goons."[85] The group's attorney offered a more cautionary compliment afterward when he told them, "Any point which you had to prove has been proved."[86] Indeed, they had very visibly established their strength and unity within the community, and in the days that followed the fired Voice members were all reinstated to their jobs.[87]

By the fall of 1962 the Voice had built a powerful insurgent movement within the Teamsters Union. They had combined the tactic of secession with a militant message and a strong local base to create an organization that could overcome obstacles that usually doomed rank-and-file insurgencies. Members of the Voice received beatings, lost their jobs, and had their cars vandalized, but this time none of those tactics stopped the group from attracting support. When the NLRB held its decertfication election in November 1962, the Voice received 3,274 votes, only five hundred fewer than Cohen's Teamsters. Previous opposition efforts within Local 107 had never gathered a significant number of votes. This time, and in spite of all of their advantages and many acts of intimidation, the Teamsters had squeaked through with only 51 percent of the vote.[88] And thanks to the numerous violent incidents that had attended the election campaign, the NLRB ruled that a rerun election would have to be held in April 1963.[89] The November election thus gave the Voice a chance to prove its strength and an opportunity to gather its forces for a final victory in a few months.

In the end, however, the Voice's strength in the neighborhood proved insufficient to win the larger fight. By 1963 secession and community solidarity, as tactics, faced new obstacles for organizing workers in the trucking industry. More and more since the 1930s, trucking had become an interstate enterprise. Firms shipped freight all along the Eastern Corridor and across the country. A local freightyard in northeastern Philadelphia was likely to be part of a network of trailer exchanges that stretched up to Boston and down to Florida. Under the leadership of Hoffa, the Teamsters had capitalized on the interstate and inter-regional nature of the business to build larger and larger contract groups. By 1964 Hoffa would sign the first National Master Freight Agreement, which would cover most truckers and warehouse workers from coast to coast.

In 1963 Hoffa used the changes in the trucking industry to offer the Voice the ultimate challenge. Taking the movement in Philadelphia much more seriously than have most observers since, Hoffa came to the city in January 1963 and rented a suite of rooms in a downtown hotel. He brought along a group of his closest aides and twenty-five organizers from the union's Eastern Conference to help him campaign against the Voice. They all remained in Philadelphia until the rerun election in April, as Hoffa made the city his temporary base of operations.[90] Using the recent developments in the trucking industry to his advantage, Hoffa warned the members of Philadelphia's Local 107 that if the Voice won the coming election in April 1963 he would see to it that the big regional trucking lines bypassed Philadelphia on their routes. Transfer points would be relocated outside Philadelphia, and employment for Philadelphia truckers and loaders would plummet.[91] In addition, Hoffa also offered an incentive. He promised Local 107 members more generous future contract terms and better pensions, and he finally stepped in to force through a number of reforms. Cohen was publicly nudged aside, and something very much like a trusteeship was imposed.[92]

Conclusion

Thanks to a combination of threats and entreaties, the Voice lost the NLRB's rerun election in April by a vote of 4,893 to 2,550.[93] It was a significant loss that shaped the future course of Philadelphia's Local 107 and the Teamsters Union as a national organization. The outcome of the contest spelled the end of a wave of reform efforts. It also offers a chance to assess the attitudes of Teamster members regarding the issue of corruption.

For the Voice, the electoral defeat in April was a fatal blow. In the years that followed it faded from the scene, and a continuing series of violent incidents and criminal scandals dogged Local 107's administration. In 1967 an official from the U.S. Justice Department described the local as "one of the most corrupt unions in the country" and asserted that organized crime wielded influence over it.[94] By the 1980s the former underboss of the Philadelphia Mafia testified that the local had long been firmly under the control of organized crime. Nicodemo Scarfo, who became boss of the Philadelphia Mafia in the early 1980s, reportedly "considered Teamsters Union Local 107 to belong to the Philadelphia Family."[95]

At the national level, reform activity subsided after the Voice's defeat in April 1963. The string of secession movements that had begun in Chicago in 1961 tapered off. Hoffa's problems now centered on a series of criminal trials rather than staving off a reform movement. Even as he suffered two convictions in 1964, one for jury tampering and another for mail fraud involving the pension fund, his political grip on the union remained secure. At the 1966 Teamster convention, with his appeals pending and prison looming, Hoffa ran unopposed for reelection to the union's presidency. Intending to maintain control even should he be sent to prison, he engineered the creation of an official caretaker's post. Delegates approved a resolution to set up a new office of general vice president, someone who temporarily could assume the duties of the general president should he become incapacitated for any reason. Hoffa then made certain that one of his most trusted aides, Frank Fitzsimmons, won election to the new post.[96]

In some ways the defeat of the Voice in April 1963 made all of this possible, and for that reason it is worth considering what the election revealed about the attitudes of rank-and-file Teamster members. In a fair and democratic ballot members voted for Local 107 and all of its corrupt connotations over the reform program of the Voice. They did so by a 2 to 1 margin. Given the notoriety of Cohen's malfeasance, a vote to stay probably reflected a willingness to accept some level of misconduct. Still, assertions about the cynicism and apathy of Teamster members need to be carefully considered, especially in light of the way votes shifted in 1962 and 1963. Local 107 had polled only 3,870 votes against the Voice in November 1962, but it did better in the second election, winning 4,893. The improved showing suggests that Hoffa's energetic campaign in Philadelphia swung quite a few votes. Because his campaign involved both threats of reprisals and promises of reform, however, no simple conclusion can be drawn from the decision of the thousand members who switched sides. Perhaps they did so because they believed that Hoffa truly remained committed to the needs of his members and would now correct the problems in Local 107. Or maybe they feared that he would carry through on his threats and force interstate trucking companies to abandon the city, robbing local members of their jobs. Probably, as with voters everywhere, a mix of concerns shaped the decisions of these Philadelphia workers.

Nor should the defeat of reform obscure the impressive level of commitment to that ideal held by so many of Local 107's members. The decision in April 1963 by 2,500 Teamster members to vote to risk future employment in the interest of a local insurgency demonstrated a fervent belief in reform. The men who voted for the Voice in April 1963 and the people who marched up Spring Garden Street on August 15, 1962, cared intensely about their union. The similar reform movements that existed elsewhere in the Teamsters indicate something quite different than cynicism and indifference. Faced with clear-cut misconduct by local officers and a failure by Hoffa to remedy the situation, significant numbers of local members risked a great deal to demand reform.

Yet the defeat of the Voice did indicate that the tactics insurgents used could not achieve the desired goal. To gain a secure space, dissidents had turned to secession and local organization. Given the interstate nature of the trucking industry, however, a local organization bent on secession found itself vulnerable to effective pressure from the national union. Economic changes and new contract patterns ended the viability of a reform tactic that had long allowed Teamster dissidents to pressure the national union's leadership. Future insurgent movements would have to turn to other tactics.

Conclusion

The end of Hoffa's union career did not bring a close to the Teamsters' notoriety. Hoffa entered federal prison in 1967. Hoping for more lenient consideration from the parole board he resigned from the union's presidency in 1971. That same year he received a presidential commutation of his sentence and promptly began plans to run for union office again. When he disappeared on July 30, 1975, most observers believed that the Mafia had murdered him in order to block his return to the presidency. Members of organized crime, who enjoyed more placid relations with Hoffa's successors in the Teamsters, allegedly viewed his potential candidacy in the union's 1976 election as a threat to their financial interests.[1] His apparent murder attracted more attention to a wave of new scandals that enveloped the union, this time centering on the mismanagement of the union's Central States Pension Fund.[2]

In subsequent years other scandals tarnished the union's image. In 1982 Roy Williams, who had become president of the union the year before, was convicted of federal bribery charges. A few years later he served as a cooperating witness in a series of federal racketeering trials and publicly testified about his longtime connection with the Kansas City Mafia.[3] Williams's successor to the Teamsters presidency, Jackie Presser, was revealed to have been both a close associate of the Cleveland Mafia and an undercover FBI informant for decades.[4] Some reports charged that Presser's successor, William J. McCarthy, had received the support of the New England Mafia.[5] By 1986 the President's Commission on Organized Crime included the Teamsters among a group of the "four international unions most frequently associated with organized crime."[6]

This notoriety continued to have important public policy implications. The apparent failure of the Landrum-Griffin Act to correct recurring union corruption served as justification for a much more intrusive level of government intervention into union affairs. In 1986 the Justice Department began drawing on authority granted to it by Racketeer Influenced and Corrupt Organizations (RICO) Act of 1970 to file civil suits against notoriously corrupt unions. These suits asked federal courts to grant the government trusteeships over unions long notorious for corruption.[7] The first union to be so targeted was Teamsters Local 560 in New Jersey, and by far the most ambitious such effort involved the government's suit to gain control of the International Teamsters' organization, a case originally filed in 1988. The civil RICO case against the Teamsters led to a court-monitored agreement that granted the government a variety of oversight roles in the union and mandated direct elections of the organization's national officers. A decade later the government's oversight role continued in spite of the union's efforts to bring it to a close.[8]

As in the past, some members struggled to reform the union through the democratic process. In 1970 a new tide of reform began with the creation of a national group calling itself Teamsters United Rank and File (TURF). By the mid-1970s TURF had dissolved, but it was succeeded by the Professional Road Drivers Council (PROD) and Teamsters for a Democratic Union (TDU). Those two groups merged their efforts and focused on an electoral campaign against the national leadership. At the TDU convention in 1976, according to the journalist Lester Velie, TDU "delegates had vowed to win at least half of the seats to the Teamster convention, four years away." Faced with the same constraints encountered by earlier reformers who sought to work within the union, the TDU's achievements fell far short of their aspirations. By the time of the 1986 convention, after a decade of effort, the TDU candidate for the union presidency received only 24 delegate votes against 1,729 for Presser.[9]

The TDU's poor showing at conventions, however, did not present a true picture of the membership's attitudes. Rather, it reflected the barriers that insurgent union candidates had always faced, made more difficult by the fact that secession no longer offered a viable alternative. A more accurate picture of the membership's views emerged in 1991 when the government, according to the RICO settlement, conducted the union's first direct election for national officers. Government oversight combined with a factional split among incumbents allowed an insurgent slate, supported by the TDU, to win election in 1991. With a plurality of the membership's votes, Ron Carey, a self-proclaimed reformer, became president of the union.[10]

Over the course of the union's history a set of basic patterns have emerged. These patterns reflect continuities in its organizational history and in its involvement in corruption scandals. But the union's history also reveals long-term changes that have made democracy a more problematic endeavor for it.

As an organization, the Teamsters Union offered a pragmatic response to the needs of its membership, eschewing any larger social mission in favor of an approach that is usually labeled as "business unionism." The occupations of the membership evolved over time. Horse-drawn wagons gave way to motor trucks, and interstate trucking emerged, but the concerns of drivers remained constant. Driving continued to be a demanding job marked by relatively long hours. Drivers in each era have complained of the capricious treatment of employers and the callous attitudes of other workers and the general public. In response, the union offered its membership material benefits, better wages, and shorter hours along with working conditions that granted them more security and perhaps even improved their status. Members and their union leaders described these benefits in terms of dignity and decency. As the union's official journal asserted in 1956, referring to the benefits the union brought to a typical member, "Things were tough for Martin O'Donnell of Philadelphia until 'the union' came, bringing job security, dignity, and contentment."

Focused on building a strong organization that could deliver such results, Teamster leaders pursued an opportunistic course. When it benefited the organization, they overlooked craft distinctions and took in a range of various occupation groups. At times they welcomed leftists and ignored the kinds of racial, ethnic, and gender distinctions that so often shaped the policies of other unions. Yet when Teamster officials saw no tangible benefits to such policies they forsook any principled stand in the name of working-class unity or social justice. Indeed, the leadership often hearkened to conservative rhetoric that likened the union to any other business and, when it suited their purposes, emphasized race and gender divisions. Over time, this pragmatic emphasis encouraged the efforts of Beck and then Hoffa to centralize the organization and promote professionalism at the expense of democracy. The Teamsters became a service provider, one designed to satisfy the needs of members but not necessarily to empower them.

This pattern of opportunism, often described as the "ideology of business unionism," does not, however, explain the union's recurring involvement in corruption scandals. That history of corruption stemmed from two distinct sources. First, the union's jurisdiction included sectors of the economy long marked by collusive practices among employers. In these sectors organized crime came to play an almost natural role, overseeing collusive arrangements and exploiting vulnerable small employers. Any union seeking to organize in such areas found itself enmeshed in various illicit practices. The experience of the opportunistic Teamsters differed little in this respect from its more idealistic union counterparts. Local unions operating in these sectors became involved in long-standing relationships with elements of organized crime, and those relationships encouraged union leaders to engage in acts that violated the trust of their membership, from malfeasance to bribery and extortion.

But corruption scandals often centered less on specific acts of misconduct by Teamster leaders than they did on the concerns of anti-union forces that worried about the growing influence of organized labor. During times of union growth, when organized labor enjoyed political popularity, employers and their allies used the issue of corruption to shift public opinion. In doing so these anti-union forces promoted a political interpretation of corruption that had little to do with the betrayal of union members' interests and instead focused on the question of union power. Investigations into union corruption often provided the means for popularizing this political interpretation of corruption. At the same time, sensationalized news coverage raised public concern about the possible tyranny of organized labor. As a powerful union, and one dogged by local scandals, the Teamsters stood at the center of these repeated crises of corruption. In 1905 in Chicago, during the 1930s, and again in the late 1950s these artificially created crises of corruption played significant roles in the larger political contest over the rights of organized labor. The crises allowed labor's opponents to undercut the political position of unions and to corrode organized labor's legal rights.

Given the way in which labor's opponents often manipulated the issue of union corruption, members quite rightly came to view the crises of corruption with a jaundiced eye. And yet corruption, in the sense of the betrayal of the membership's interests, still mattered a great deal to many Teamsters. Again and again, members took up the cause of reform, doing so at some risk to their careers and at times their safety.

While doing so, members and officers encountered a number of obstacles that hamstrung the possibilities of reform. Efforts to reform the International by ousting national leaders such as Cornelius Shea or Jimmy Hoffa left insurgents vulnerable to various forms of retaliation. The national leaders used their position to dominate the union's convention, where elections for national office took place. Similarly, reformers at the local level had limited opportunities to voice dissent without fear of various repercussions. Nor did national officers seeking to clean up local pockets of corruption enjoy an enviable position. The tools available to national officers—removing local officials, trusteeships, or revoking a charter—frequently proved ineffective in efforts to deal with a local influenced by organized crime.

Yet reformers did score occasional victories, often by developing innovative tactics. Secession offered a way to threaten the national leadership and yet not expose insurgents to the same kinds of retribution that might have occurred had they remained in the organization. Faced with the growing power of the United Teamsters of America in 1907, Shea acceded to a more democratic election and as a result was defeated. Local reformers mobilized members through newsletters and other forums and thus circumvented the leadership's domination of local union meetings. If a local was not enmeshed in a close, collusive relationship with its employers, a mobilized membership could stand up to efforts at intimidation. In the 1930s reformers in Local 807 defied the waterfront gangster John Dunn, and later the Voice proved the continuing potential of rank-and-file reform in Local 107.

Over time, however, the possibilities of reform eroded. The changing nature of the economy undercut the potential of secession, while at the same time the growing power of the national leadership increased the costs to local officials who dared raise their voices in dissent. Thus the heirs to this reform tradition, the TDU, found their efforts stymied until 1991, when government involvement dramatically changed the electoral rules of the game.

Finally, this long history of reform in the Teamsters Union challenges the common understanding of the union's membership. Commenting on Hoffa's reelection in 1961, the *New York Times* summed up this view by charging, "Most Teamsters seem perfectly content to ride along with Mr. Hoffa in his cynical conviction that anything goes so long as he keeps delivering higher wages and fatter benefits to his members."[11] Crass and cynical, according to this common view, the average Teamster chose to ignore corruption, and for that reason the union remained scandal-plagued and dominated by organized crime. Moreover, this shortsighted materialism cast an ugly shadow on the potential of the labor movement at large. In 1958 A. H. Raskin, the labor reporter for the *New York Times,* asserted that the obstinate support of Teamsters for their embattled leaders "holds dismal implications for those who look to increased democracy in unions as the answer to corruption."[12] On the contrary this history demonstrates that time and time again members took strong stands in the name of reform and in defense of what they understood to be the union's true mission. Wages mattered but so, too, did working conditions and the conduct of their officials. No simple, monolithic attitude toward corruption and scandal can be imputed to the members, but here they resembled every other group in American society faced with conflicting imperatives and contradictory versions of events.

Notes

Introduction

1. Typical examples of this kind of study include Harold Seidman, *Labor Czars: A History of Labor Racketeering* (New York: Liveright Publishing, 1938); John Hutchinson, *The Imperfect Union: A History of Corruption in American Trade Unions* (New York: E. P. Dutton, 1970); Gordon L. Hostetter and Thomas Quinn Beesley, *It's a Racket* (Chicago: Les Quin Books, 1929); Edward Dean Sullivan, *This Labor Union Racket* (New York: Hillman-Curl, 1936); and [Wall Street Journal], *A History of Organized Felony and Folly* (New York: Wall Street Journal, 1923). Studies that focus solely or largely on corruption in the Teamsters Union include Walter Sheridan, *The Rise and Fall of Jimmy Hoffa* (New York: Saturday Review Press, 1972); Clark Mollenhoff, *Tentacles of Power: The Story of Jimmy Hoffa* (Cleveland: World Publishing, 1965); James Neff, *Mobbed Up: Jackie Presser's High-Wire Life in the Teamsters, the Mafia, and the FBI* (New York: Dell Publishing, 1989); and Lester Velie, *Desperate Bargain: Why Jimmy Hoffa Had to Die* (New York: Reader's Digest Press, 1977).

2. Daniel T. Rodgers, *Contested Truths: Keywords in American Politics since Independence* (Cambridge: Harvard University Press, 1998), 3–16.

3. Christopher L. Tomlins, *The State and the Unions: Labor Relations, Law, and the Organized Labor Movement in America, 1880–1960* (New York: Cambridge University Press, 1986); Karl Klare, "Judicial Deradicalization of the Wagner Act and the Origins of Modern Legal Consciousness," *Minnesota Law Review* 62 (1978): 265–339; James A. Gross, *Broken Promise: The Subversion of U.S. Labor Relations Policy, 1947–1994* (Philadelphia: Temple University Press, 1995); James Atleson, *Values and Assumptions in American Labor Law* (Amherst: University of Massachusetts Press, 1983); Melvyn Dubofsky, *The State and Labor in Modern America* (Chapel Hill: University of North Carolina Press, 1994); Matthew W. Finkin, "Revisionism in Labor Law," *Maryland Law Review* 43 (1985): 23–92.

4. "A Chauffeur" to Westbrook Pegler, Dec. 29, 1942, box 98, (James) Westbrook Pegler Papers, 1908–69, Herbert Hoover Presidential Library, West Branch, Iowa.

5. Hutchinson, *The Imperfect Union*, 372; Seidman, *Labor Czars*, 254–56.

Chapter 1: Building a Teamsters Union

1. "Constitution and By-Laws of the Brotherhood of Teamsters of San Francisco, California, Organized August 5, 1900, Adopted October 12, 1905," Labor Union Constitutions and By-Laws, Bancroft Library, University of California, Berkeley.

2. John R. Commons, "The Teamsters in Chicago," in *Trade Unionism and Labor Problems*, ed. John R. Commons (New York: Ginn, 1905), 36–64.

3. U.S. Department of Commerce and Labor, Bureau of the Census, *Special Reports: Occupations at the Twelfth Census* (Washington, D.C.: Government Printing Office, 1904), cxiii, iv, li.

4. *Team Owners' Review* 4 (March 1905): 15; *Team Owners' Review* 5 (Jan. 1906): 25; *Team Owners' Review* 7 (May 1908): 36; *Team Owners' Review* 5 (Aug. 1906): 26.

5. "A Teamsters Responsibility," *Team Owners' Review* 4 (May 1905): 18; "The Chicago Strike, by a Teamster," *The Independent,* July 6, 1905, 15.

6. "Driver or Salesman," *Teamsters' National Journal* 1 (Nov. 1902): 11; "A Coal Dealer on His Drivers," *Team Owners' Review* 6 (April 1907): 21; "The Team Owner and the Driver," *Team Owners' Review* 4 (Aug. 1905): 11–12; *Teamster Magazine* 2 (Dec. 1904): 22–23; "Advice to Teamsters," *Team Owners' Review* 7 (Nov. 1908): 27; Commons, "The Teamsters in Chicago," 48–52.

7. "A Teamsters Responsibility," 18.

8. Jean Cowgill, "The Teamsters' Strike," *The Reader Magazine* 6 (1905): 202.

9. Ernest Poole, "How a Labor Machine Held Up Chicago," *The World To-Day* 7 (July 1904): 896.

10. Luke Grant, "The Walking Delegate," *Outlook,* Nov. 10, 1906, 619.

11. *Team Drivers' Journal* 1 (April 1901): 1–2; "Barn Rules," *Team Owners' Review* 3 (May 1904): 22; "The Chicago Strike, by a Teamster," 15–16; Commons, "The Teamsters in Chicago," 42–48.

12. In the eight southern cities that had populations exceeding fifty thousand in 1900, African Americans on average made up 74 percent of the teamster workforce. Taking the sixteen northern cities that had more than two thousand working teamsters, first- and second-generation immigrants made up an average of 69 percent of the teamster workforce. U.S. Department of Commerce and Labor, Bureau of the Census, *Special Reports: Occupations at the Twelfth Census,* cxiv, 64–65, 480–763.

13. *Proceedings of the Joint Convention of the Team Drivers' International Union and the Teamsters National Union and Proceedings of the Convention of International Brotherhood of Teamsters, Niagara Falls, N. Y., August 3–13, 1903* (Indianapolis: Cheltenham Press, 1903), 44.

14. Timothy Messer-Kruse, "The Best-Dressed Workers in New York City: Liveried Coachmen of the Gilded Age," *Labor History* 37 (Winter 1995–96): 12, 22.

15. U.S. Senate, 48th Congress, *Report of the Committee of the Senate upon the Relations between Labor and Capital, and Testimony Taken by the Committee,* vol. 1: *Testimony,* (Washington, D.C.: Government Printing Office, 1885), 771–73.

16. U.S. Senate, 48th Congress, *Report of the Committee,* 772–73.

17. Hutchins Hapgood, *The Spirit of Labor* (New York: Duffield, 1907), 371.

18. *Proceedings of the Fourth Annual Convention of the International Brotherhood of*

Teamsters (Indianapolis: Cheltenham Press, 1906), 5; Jules Tygiel, *Workingmen in San Francisco, 1880–1901* (New York: Garland Publishing, 1992), 132.

19. Flier enclosed with letter from William H. Ashton to Thomas Hughes, Feb. 4, 1913, Ashton Correspondence File, series 1, box 1, the International Brotherhood of Teamsters, Chauffeurs, Warehousemen and Helpers of America Papers, 1904–52, MSS 9, Wisconsin State Historical Society, Madison (hereafter IBT Papers).

20. *Constitution and By-Laws of the Team Drivers' International Union of America, Adopted at Convention Held at Detroit, Mich., October 23–28, 1899* (Detroit: A. W. Brookes, Printer, 1899), 3.

21. *Team Owners' Review* 4 (March 1905): 14.

22. Messer-Kruse, "The Best-Dressed Workers in New York City," 6, 19.

23. U.S. Department of Commerce and Labor, Bureau of the Census, S. N. D. Norten, *Special Report: Express Business in the United States, 1907* (Washington, D.C.: Government Printing Office, 1908), 10, 15; Noel M. Loomis, *Wells Fargo* (New York: Clarkson N. Potter, 1968), 289; *Team Owners' Review* 8 (Aug. 1909): 5.

24. George W. Briggs to T. L. Hughes, April 3, 1911, Briggs Correspondence File, series 1, box 4, IBT Papers.

25. Tygiel, *Workingmen in San Francisco,* 139; William H. Ashton to Thomas Hughes, June 23, 1915, Ashton Correspondence File, series 1, box 1, IBT Papers; *Team Owners' Review* 4 (April 1905): 14; "Notice for the sale of Acme Local Express Company," *Team Owners' Review* 5 (Jan. 1906): 30.

26. *Team Owners' Review* 4 (May 1905): 18.

27. *Team Owners' Review* 3 (June 1906): 16.

28. *Team Owners' Review* 3 (March 1904): 12.

29. *Team Owners' Review* 4 (March 1905): 14.

30. Philip Taft, *The A.F. of L. in the Time of Gompers* (New York: Harper and Brothers, 1957), 95–123.

31. George Innis to Frank Morrison, April 28, 1902, reel 36, American Federation of Labor Records: The Samuel Gompers Era Microfilm Collection (hereafter AFL Papers: Gompers Era).

32. *The Team Drivers' Journal* 3 (Aug. 1903): 9–10; George Innis to Frank Morrison, Jan. 23, 1899, reel 143, AFL Papers: Gompers Era.

33. *Team Drivers' Journal* 1 (June 1901): 9.

34. *TDIU Constitution and By-laws, 1899,* 4. 4.

35. George Innis to Frank Morrison, July 3, 900, and George Innis to Samuel Gompers, March 16, 1899, both reel 143, AFL Papers: Gompers Era.

36. *Proceedings of the Third Annual Convention of the Team Drivers International Union, Held at Detroit, Michigan, September 10th to 15th, 1900* (Detroit: W. W. Brookes Printer, 1900), 5–7 (microfilm ed.); "Proceedings of the Fifth Annual Convention of the Team Drivers'. . . International Union of America: Toledo, Ohio, September 8th to 13th Inclusive . . . 1902 . . . ," printed as supplement to *Team Drivers' Journal* 2 (Oct. 1902): 15; *Constitution and By-laws of the Team Drivers' International Union of America: Adopted at Convention Held at Toledo, Ohio, September 8–13, 1902* (Detroit: W. W. Brookes, 1902), 6; *Team Drivers' Journal* 2 (March 1902): 1–2.

37. *Proceedings of the Joint Convention of the Team Drivers' International Union and the*

Teamsters National Union and Proceedings of Convention of International Brotherhood of Teamsters, Niagara Falls, N. Y., August 3–13, 1903 (Indianapolis: Cheltenham Press, 1903), 4–9.

38. John B. Andrews, "Nationalisation," in *History of Labour in the United States,* ed. John R. Commons (New York: Augustus M. Kelley, Publishers, 1966), 5:5–15, 44–61.

39. Selig Perlman, "Upheaval and Reorganisation," in *History of Labour in the United States* (New York: Augustus M. Kelley, Publishers, 1966), 2:306–8; Stuart Bruce Kaufman, *Samuel Gompers and the Origins of the American Federation of Labor: 1848–1896* (Westport: Greenwood Press, 1973), 93–100.

40. *Constitution and By-laws of the Team Drivers International Union of America, Adopted at Convention Held in Chicago, Ill., September 9th to 14th Inclusive 1901* (Detroit: W. W. Brookes, 1901), 19–24.

41. *Team Drivers' Journal* 3 (May 1903): 2–3; *Team Drivers' Journal* 3 (June 1903): 2.

42. Sterling D. Spero and Abram L. Harris, *The Black Worker: The Negro and the Labor Movement* (1931, repr. New York: Atheneum, 1974), 57–75.

43. David Witwer, "An Incident at the Statler Hotel: A Black Pittsburgh Teamster Demands Fair Treatment during the Second World War," *Pennsylvania History* 65 (Summer 1998): 350–56.

44. Jean Cowgill, "Labor's Dishonor," *The Reader Magazine* 4 (June 1904): 76–77; Ray Stannard Baker, "Capital and Labor Hunt Together," *McClure's Magazine* 21 (Sept. 1903): 451; Commons, "The Teamsters in Chicago," 36–37; Poole, "How a Labor Machine Held Up Chicago," 897.

45. Cowgill, "Labor's Dishonor," 76–77.

46. Commons, "The Teamsters in Chicago," 39–42; Cowgill, "Labor's Dishonor," 77–78; *By-laws of Teamsters Local No. 704,* 14, Pamphlets in American History, Wisconsin State Historical Society, Madison.

47. Commons, "The Teamsters in Chicago," 38–39, 41; Poole, "How a Labor Machine Held Up Chicago," 897–98; Cowgill, "Labor's Dishonor," 77–78.

48. Tygiel, *Workingmen in San Francisco,* 142–43.

49. William Ashton to Thomas Hughes, Aug. 31, 1913, Ashton Correspondence File, series 1, box 1, IBT Papers; John Devering to Thomas Hughes, July 18, 1925, Devering Correspondence File, series 1, box 26, IBT Papers; Daniel J. Murphy to Daniel Tobin, May 15, 1914, Murphy Correspondence File, series 1, box 38, IBT Papers.

50. Thomas Hughes to Daniel Tobin, Aug. 12, 1911, Thomas Hughes to Daniel Tobin, Nov. 13, 1913, Ed Meyer to Thomas Hughes, Dec. 2, 1913, and Thomas Hughes to Daniel Tobin, Dec. 24, 1913, all in Hughes Correspondence File, series 1, box 34, IBT Papers.

51. Robert D. Leiter, *The Teamsters Union: A Study of Its Economic Impact* (New York: Bookman Associates, 1957), 22.

52. Commons, "The Teamsters in Chicago," 42–48.

53. Ibid., 63–64.

54. Flier enclosed in letter from William Ashton to Thomas Hughes, 4 February 1913, in Ashton Correspondence File, series 1, box 1, IBT Papers.

55. *Proceedings of the Fourth Annual Convention of the International Brotherhood of Teamsters* [1906], 231–33.

56. "The Chicago Strike, by a Teamster," 15–20.

57. *Team Drivers' Journal* 1 (July 1901): 7.

Chapter 2: One Version of Corruption

A previous version of this chapter appeared as an article entitled "Unionized Teamsters and the Struggle over the Streets of the Early-Twentieth-Century City," *Social Science History* 24 (Spring 2000): 183–222.

1. *Chicago Daily News,* Jan. 20, 1907, 1.

2. Daniel T. Rodgers, *Contested Truths: Keywords in American Politics since Independence* (Cambridge: Harvard University Press, 1998), 10.

3. Sidney Fine, *"Without Blare of Trumpets": Walter Drew, the National Erectors' Association, and the Open Shop Movement, 1903–1957* (Ann Arbor: University of Michigan Press, 1995), 6–9, 50–54.

4. Charles William Post, *Controlled by Citizens, Both Labor and Capital Trusts Must Be Governed by the People* (New York: Citizens' Industrial Association of America, n.d.), 4, Wisconsin State Historical Society, Madison.

5. Raymond A. Mohl, *The New City: Urban America in the Industrial Age, 1860–1920* (Arlington Heights: Harlan Davidson, 1985), 27–28.

6. This account of a typical strike action is drawn from a range of accounts on Teamsters strikes in this era. Newspaper accounts of particular strikes in different cities have been used. These include *San Francisco Chronicle,* July 25, 1901, 12, July 26, 1901, 12, July 27, 1901, 12, Aug. 1, 1901, 7; *Boston Herald,* May 1, 1907, 1, May 2, 1907, 2, May 3, 1907, 1–2; *St. Louis Globe-Democrat,* Jan. 30, 1904, 9, Jan. 31, 1904, 1, Feb. 1, 1904, 7, Feb. 3, 1904, 2, Feb. 10, 1904, 16; *Chicago Daily Tribune,* April 8, 1905, 1, April 9, 1905, 1, April 11, 1905, 1, April 12, 1905, 1; and *New York Times,* Aug. 23, 1907, 2, Aug. 24, 1907, 4, Aug. 25, 1907, 2, Aug. 27, 1907, 2, Aug. 28, 1907, 5. Secondary accounts of Teamster strikes in this period include Steven L. Piott, "The Chicago Teamsters' Strike of 1902: A Community Confronts the Beef Trust," *Labor History* 26 (Spring 1985): 250–67; and Tygiel, *Workingmen in San Francisco,* 294–349.

7. John R. Commons, "The Teamsters in Chicago," in *Trade Unionism and Labor Problems,* ed. John R. Commons (New York: Ginn, 1905), 56–57.

8. *New York Times,* Aug. 24, 1907, 4, Aug. 25, 1907, 2; *Boston Herald,* May 1, 1907, 1, May 2, 1907, 2; *Chicago Tribune,* May 1, 1905, 1, May 2, 1905, 2, May 4, 1905, 3.

9. Luke Grant, "Report of Streetcar and Teamster Strike, Indianapolis, Indiana," March 18, 1914, file 0803, reel 15, Files of the United States Commission on Industrial Relations, 1912–18 (microfilm ed.); Peter Burke to Daniel Tobin, Sept. 8, 1910, Burke Correspondence File, series 1, box 11, the International Brotherhood of Teamsters, Chauffeurs, Warehousemen and Helpers of America Papers, 1904–52, MSS 9, Wisconsin State Historical Society, Madison (hereafter IBT Papers).

10. *Minutes of the Second Annual Convention of the International Brotherhood of Teamsters, Convened at Cincinnati, Ohio, August 1, 1904* (Cincinnati: Press of S. Rosenthal, 1904), 76.

11. Commons, "The Teamsters in Chicago," 57.

12. For example in St. Louis, Daniel J. Murphy to Daniel Tobin, May 15, 1914, Daniel J. Murphy to Daniel Tobin, April 3, 1924, Daniel J. Murphy to Daniel Tobin, April 16, 1924, and Daniel J. Murphy to Daniel Tobin, June 2, 1924, all in Murphy Correspondence File, series 1, box 38, IBT Papers.

13. *Minutes of the Second Annual Convention of the IBT* [1904], 22–23.

14. *Chicago Daily Tribune,* July 11, 1902, 1, July 13, 1902, 1, July 14, 1902, 1, July 15, 1902, 1,

July 16, 1902, 1; Ernest Poole, "How a Labor Machine Held Up Chicago," *The World To-Day* 7 (July 1904): 899–900; Commons, "The Teamsters in Chicago," 41–42; Jean Cowgill, "Labor's Dishonor," *The Reader Magazine* 4 (June 1904): 77–80.

15. James R. Barrett, *Work and Community in the Jungle: Chicago's Packinghouse Workers, 1894–1922* (Urbana: University of Illinois Press, 1987), 177–78; Jules Tygiel, *Workingmen in San Francisco, 1880–1901* (New York: Garland Publishing, 1992), 301, 304–5.

16. *New York Times*, May 9, 1903, 3.

17. *Chicago Daily Tribune*, Nov. 12, 1903, 1, Nov. 13, 1903, 1, Nov. 14, 1903, 2, Nov. 15, 1903, 2.

18. *Chicago Daily Tribune*, Nov. 14, 1903, 4.

19. David Montgomery, "Strikes in Nineteenth Century America," *Social Science History* 4 (Feb. 1980): 89–93; David Montgomery, *Workers' Control in America: Studies in the History of Work, Technology, and Labor Struggles* (New York: Cambridge University Press, 1979), 10–26.

20. Melvyn Dubofsky, *Industrialism and the American Worker, 1865–1920* (Arlington Heights: AHM Publishing, 1975), 87.

21. Clarence E. Bonnett, *Employers' Associations in the United States: A Study of Typical Associations* (New York: Macmillan, 1922), 298–302; Philip Taft, *The A.F. of L. in the Time of Gompers* (New York: Harper and Brothers, 1957), 263–64, 275–76; Fine, "*Without Blare of Trumpets*," 1–37.

22. Taft, *A.F. of L. in the Time of Gompers*, 262–63; Selig Perlman and Philip Taft, *History of Labor in the United States*, vol. 4: *Labor Movements* (New York: Macmillan, 1935), 129–30, 133–34; Fine, "*Without Blare of Trumpets*," 4–9.

23. Perlman and Taft, *History of Labor in the United States*, 133.

24. *St. Louis Labor*, Jan. 9, 1904, 8; *St. Louis Post-Dispatch*, Jan. 20, 1904, 1; *St. Louis Globe-Democrat*, Jan. 20, 1904, 1, Feb. 1, 1904, 7. For Grand Rapids, see *Team Owners' Review* 3 (May 1904): 10 and 4 (Jan. 1905): 27, and Fine, "*Without Blare of Trumpets*," 37–38. Regarding Beloit, see Perlman and Taft, *History of Labor in the United States*, 132.

25. Robert D. Leiter, *The Teamsters Union: A Study of Its Economic Impact* (New York: Bookman Associates, 1957), 33; Commons, "The Teamsters in Chicago," 57.

26. Fine, "*Without Blare of Trumpets*," 4; Isaac F. Marcosson, "Labor Met by Its Own Methods," *The World's Work* 7 (Jan. 1904): 4310; Jean Cowgill, "The Teamsters' Strike," *The Reader Magazine* 6 (1905): 205.

27. "A Chicago Organization of Employers," *Iron Age*, Feb. 19, 1903, 3.

28. *Chicago Daily Tribune*, April 6, 1905, 2, April 7, 1905, 5, April 8, 1905, 1.

29. *Chicago Daily Tribune*, April 7, 1905, 5, April 8, 1905, 1, April 11, 1905, 1, April 14, 1905, 3, April 15, 1905, 5, April 26, 1905, 1, May 2, 1905, 2, May 10, 1905, 1, May 23, 1905, 1.

30. *Iron Age*, May 4, 1905, 1471.

31. *Chicago Daily Tribune*, April 17, 1905, 1.

32. *Chicago Record-Herald*, April 29, 1905, 1.

33. *Chicago Daily Tribune*, April 28, 1905, 1, May 3, 1905, 1, May 4, 1905, 3, May 5, 1905, 3, May 6, 1905, 2, May 10, 1905, 1, May 30, 1905, 5, June 4, 1905, 2.

34. Elizabeth Faue, *Community of Suffering and Struggle: Women, Men, and the Labor Movement in Minneapolis, 1915–1945* (Chapel Hill: University of North Carolina Press, 1991), 4–12.

35. Richard Schneirov, *Labor and Urban Politics: Class Conflict and the Origins of Modern Liberalism in Chicago, 1864–1897* (Urbana: University of Illinois Press, 1998), 151–205, 308–15, 353–56; Georg Leidenberger, "Working-Class Progressivism and the Politics of Transportation in Chicago, 1895–1907," Ph.D. diss., University of North Carolina, Chapel Hill, 1995, 46–61.

36. Leidenberger, "Working-Class Progressivism," 61–64.

37. *Labor Advocate,* May 1905, cited in Leidenberger, "Working-Class Progressivism," 170–71.

38. Leidenberger, "Working-Class Progressivism," 141, 113–64; Georg Leidenberger, "'The Public Is the Labor Union': Working-Class Progressivism in Turn-of-the-Century Chicago," *Labor History* 36 (Spring 1995): 187–210; Richard Allen Morton, *Justice and Humanity: Edward F. Dunne, Illinois Progressive* (Carbondale: Southern Illinois University Press, 1997), 9–19.

39. *The Public,* April 15, 1905, 17, 23; *Union Leader,* June 17, 1905, 1.

40. *Chicago Daily Tribune,* May 5, 1905, 1, May 7, 1905, 1, May 11, 1905, 1.

41. *The Public,* May 6, 1905, 70–73, June 3, 1905, 138; *Chicago Daily Tribune,* April 21, 1905, 1.

42. *Chicago Daily Tribune,* April 15, 1905, 3; *Chicago Inter-Ocean,* April 14, 1905, 1.

43. *Chicago Inter-Ocean,* April 25, 1905, 1; *Chicago Daily Tribune,* April 24, 1905, 1, April 25, 1905, 1.

44. *Chicago Daily Tribune,* April 21, 1905, 1.

45. *Chicago Daily Tribune,* June 5, 1905, 1.

46. *Chicago Daily Tribune,* June 13, 1905, 1, June 14, 1905, 1, June 16, 1905, 1.

47. *Chicago Daily Tribune,* June 18, 1905, 1.

48. *Chicago Daily Tribune,* July 2, 1905, 1.

49. *Chicago Inter-Ocean,* April 13, 1905, 1, April 23, 1905, 3; *Chicago Daily Tribune,* April 15, 1905, 3, April 24, 1905, 1.

50. *Chicago Daily Tribune,* June 18, 1905, 1.

51. Luke Grant, "The Rights and Wrongs of the Chicago Strike," *Public Opinion,* June 10, 1905, 887–90.

52. *Chicago Daily Tribune,* June 11, 1905, 5, June 13, 1905, 1.

53. *Chicago Daily Tribune,* June 13, 1905, 1, June 14, 1905, 1, June 15, 1905, 1, June 16, 1905, 1; *Chicago Inter-Ocean,* June 14, 1905, 1, June 15, 1905, 1, June 16, 1905, 2; *Chicago Record-Herald,* June 13, 1905, 1, June 14, 1905, 2, June 15, 1905, 2, June 16, 1905, 1.

54. *Chicago Tribune,* July 3, 1905, 3.

55. *Chicago Record-Herald,* June 20, 1905, 3.

56. *Chicago Daily Tribune,* June 20, 1905, 2.

57. *Chicago Daily Tribune,* June 18, 1905, 1.

58. *Chicago Daily Tribune,* June 13, 1905, 1 (quotation), June 14, 1905, 1, June 15, 1905, 1, June 16, 1905, 1; *Chicago Record-Herald,* June 14, 1905, 2, June 15, 1905, 2, June 16, 1905, 1.

59. *Chicago Daily Tribune,* June 17, 1905, 1, June 19, 1905, 2; *Chicago Inter-Ocean,* June 17, 1905, 2; *Chicago Record-Herald,* June 13, 1905, 1, June 17, 1905, 1.

60. *Chicago Record-Herald,* June 13, 1905, 1; *Chicago Daily Tribune,* June 13, 1905, 1, June 18, 1905, 1.

61. *Chicago Record-Herald,* June 13, 1905, 1.

62. *Chicago Record-Herald,* June 21, 1905, 3.

63. *Chicago Daily Tribune,* July 2, 1905, 1–2.

64. Ibid.

65. See, for example, *Chicago Daily Tribune,* June 17, 1905, 1.

66. Arthur S. Henning, "Cornelius P. Shea, the Teamster 'Boss' of Chicago," *Harpers Weekly,* June 17, 1905, 862–63.

67. *Chicago Daily Tribune,* July 3, 1905, 4.

68. *Chicago Daily Tribune,* May 2, 1905, 1, May 3, 1905, 1, May 27, 1905, 2.

69. Two decades later the *Chicago Daily Tribune* would still recall it as one of the worst strikes in the city's history, *Chicago Daily Tribune,* Jan. 13, 1929, 16.

70. Jane Addams, *Twenty Years at Hull-House* (New York: Macmillan, 1910), 298–99.

71. *Chicago Daily Tribune,* July 21, 1905, 1, July 24, 1905, 2, July 25, 1905, 3, July 28, 1905, 5, July 31, 1905, 3, Aug. 1, 1905, 2; *Union Leader,* Aug. 26, 1905, 6.

72. *Chicago Daily Tribune,* July 21, 1905, 1; *Union Leader,* Aug. 26, 1905, 6.

73. *Official Magazine of the International Brotherhood of Teamsters, Chauffeurs, Stablemen and Helpers* 9 (July 1912): 12.

74. *Chicago Daily Tribune,* July 29, 1905, 2.

75. John Cummings, "The Chicago Teamsters' Strike—A Study in Industrial Democracy," *Journal of Political Economy* (Sept. 1905): 570.

76. Graham Taylor, "Aftermath of the Chicago Teamsters' Strike," *Charities and the Commons,* Sept. 16, 1905, 1088.

77. Leidenberger, "Working Class Progressivism," 191.

78. Cummings, "The Chicago Teamsters' Strike," 568.

Chapter 3: Corruption Viewed through Union Members' Eyes and Reform via Secession

1. John Cummings, "The Chicago Teamsters' Strike: A Study in Industrial Democracy," *Journal of Political Economy* (Sept. 1905): 536–37.

2. Ernest L. Bogart, "The Chicago Building Trades Dispute of 1900," in *Trade Unionism and Labor Problems,* ed. John R. Commons (New York: Ginn, 1905), 119–220; John R. Commons, "The New York Building Trades," in *Trade Unionism and Labor Problems,* ed. John R. Commons (New York: Ginn, 1905), 84–86; Ray Stannard Baker, "The Trusts New Tool: The Labor Boss," *McClure's Magazine* 22 (Nov. 1903): 30–43.

3. Cummings, "The Chicago Teamsters' Strike," 572–73.

4. Hutchins Hapgood, *The Spirit of Labor* (New York: Duffield, 1907), 114, 370–71.

5. Philip Taft, *Corruption and Racketeering in the Labor Movement* (Ithaca: New York State School of Industrial and Labor Relations, Cornell University, 1958), 28, 33–34.

6. *Chicago Daily Tribune,* June 18, 1905, 1.

7. Ernest Poole, "How a Labor Machine Held Up Chicago," *The World To-Day* 7 (July 1904): 896–905; Jean Cowgill, "Labor's Dishonor," *The Reader Magazine* 4 (June 1904): 71–86; Ray Stannard Baker, "Capital and Labor Hunt Together," *McClure's Magazine* 21 (Sept. 1903): 451–63.

8. *Chicago Daily Tribune,* June 2, 1905, 3; *Chicago Record-Herald,* June 2, 1905, 1.

9. *Chicago Record-Herald,* June 2, 1905, 1.

10. Ibid., 2.

11. *Chicago Daily Tribune,* June 22, 1905, 2, June 24, 1905, 1.

12. *Chicago Record-Herald,* July 19, 1908, 4, July 25, 1908, 7.

13. Daniel J. Murphy to Daniel Tobin, April 3, 1924, June 2, 1924, series 1, box 38, the International Brotherhood of Teamsters, Chauffeurs, Warehousemen and Helpers of America Papers, 1904–52, MSS 9, Wisconsin State Historical Society, Madison (hereafter IBT Papers).

14. *Chicago Daily Tribune,* June 21, 1905, 2.

15. Daniel J. Murphy to Daniel Tobin, April 3, 1924, series 1, box 38, IBT Papers.

16. *Chicago Record-Herald,* Aug. 7, 1906, 9.

17. *Chicago Daily Tribune,* Nov. 7, 1903, 1.

18. Evidence Submitted by M. Donnelly and Colleagues of the Stock Yard Unions on J. G. Driscoll, Secretary of the Team Owners Association, July 9, 1903, box 1, folder 1, John Fitzpatrick Papers, Chicago Historical Society; Cowgill, "Labor's Dishonor," 83–84.

19. Evidence Submitted by M. Donnelly and Colleagues; Poole, "How a Labor Machine Held Up Chicago," 902–4.

20. John R. Commons, "The Teamsters in Chicago," in *Trade Unionism and Labor Problems,* ed. John R. Commons (New York: Ginn, 1905), 42.

21. Poole, "How a Labor Machine Held Up Chicago," 901–2; *Chicago Inter-Ocean,* May 21, 1905, 2.

22. Poole, "How a Labor Machine Held Up Chicago," 904; *Chicago Daily Tribune,* April 21, 1904, 3; *Chicago Inter-Ocean,* June 4, 1905, 1, June 20, 1905, 1; Commons, "The Teamsters in Chicago," 62.

23. *Chicago Inter-Ocean,* May 1, 1905, 2.

24. "The Chicago Strike, by a Teamster," *The Independent,* July 6, 1905, 18.

25. *Chicago Daily Tribune,* June 19, 1905, 1; *Union Leader,* June 17, 1905, 8–9.

26. *Chicago Daily Tribune,* July 6, 1905, 3.

27. *Chicago Daily Tribune,* June 15, 1905, 1.

28. "The Chicago Strike, by a Teamster," 18.

29. *Chicago Daily Tribune,* June 15, 1905, 1.

30. *Team Drivers' Journal* 1 (July 1901): 7.

31. Emphasis added. *Constitution and By-Laws of International Brotherhood of Teamsters Adopted at the Convention Held at Cincinnati, Ohio, August 1st to 8th Inclusive, 1904* (Chicago: Moorman and Geller, 1904), 12.

32. Joshua B. Freeman, "Hardhats: Construction Workers, Manliness, and the 1970 Pro-War Demonstrations," *Journal of Social History* 26 (Summer 1993): 725–29; Gail Bederman, *Manliness and Civilization: A Cultural History of Gender and Race in the United States, 1880–1917* (Chicago: University of Chicago Press, 1995), 7–17, 23; Steven Maynard, "Rough Work and Rugged Men: The Social Construction of Masculinity in Working-Class History," *Labour/Le Travail* 23 (Spring 1989): 161–64; E. Anthony Rotundo, *American Manhood: Transformations in Masculinity from the Revolution to the Modern Era* (New York: Basic Books, 1993), 2–5, 223–32.

33. *Chicago Daily Tribune,* May 21, 1905, 1, May 29, 1905, 1, June 4, 1905, 1, June 8, 1905, 4, June 22, 1905, 1.

34. *Chicago Daily Tribune,* May 25, 1905, 2.

35. *Chicago Inter-Ocean,* June 4, 1905, 1.

36. *Chicago Inter-Ocean,* June 9, 1905, 3.

37. *Philadelphia Inquirer,* Aug. 12, 1905, 2; *Chicago Daily Tribune,* Aug. 12, 1905, 1; "Resolution from the Joint Executive Council of San Francisco Teamsters to the Executive Board of the American Federation of Labor, 26 March 1906," Teamsters file, reel 36, American Federation of Labor Records: The Samuel Gompers Era Microfilm Collection (hereafter AFL Papers: Gompers Era).

38. *Chicago Daily Tribune,* Aug. 6, 1905, 2, Aug. 8, 1905, 2, Aug. 11, 1905, 1; *Philadelphia Inquirer,* Aug. 13, 1905, 2; "Teamsters' Weekly Review," *Michigan Union Advocate,* Sept. 8, 1905, 3. No explanation for this term, the "Vaseline Club," was offered at the time. But fifty years later, when the union's official journal was running summaries of past issues, they came across the name of the group and asked the long-time officials at union headquarters about it. They provided the following explanation: "It seems that the Vaseline Club was the result of a political joke. A delegate slipped out and bought a jar of Vaseline, then after the election was over sent it to the defeated clique for the purpose of soothing any soreness on the part of the losers." *International Teamster* 52 (Oct. 1955): 33.

39. *Minutes of Third Annual Convention of International Brotherhood of Teamsters, Convened at Philadelphia, Pennsylvania, August 7, 1905* (Philadelphia: Bradley Printing, 1905), 90–95.

40. *Chicago Inter-Ocean,* Aug. 13, 1905, 1.

41. Victor Soares, "Reforming a Labor Union," *World To-Day* 10 (Jan. 1906): 96.

42. *Minutes of the Third Annual Convention of the IBT* [1905], 95–119.

43. *Chicago Daily Tribune,* Aug. 13, 1905, 1; Soares, "Reforming a Labor Union," 96–97; *Philadelphia Inquirer,* Aug. 16, 1905, 6; *Minutes of the Third Annual Convention of the IBT* [1905], 76–78; "Resolution from the Joint Executive Council of San Francisco Teamsters to the Executive Board of the American Federation of Labor, March 26, 1906."

44. *Michigan Union Advocate,* Aug. 15, 1905, 6, Sept. 1, 1905, 3, Sept. 8, 1905, 1.

45. *Chicago Record-Herald,* Sept. 8, 1905, 2.

46. "Teamsters' Weekly Review," *Michigan Union Advocate,* Sept. 8, 1905, 3.

47. Ibid.; *Chicago Record-Herald,* Sept. 8, 1905, 2.

48. *Chicago Record-Herald,* Sept. 11, 1905, 4.

49. *Chicago Record-Herald,* Sept. 23, 1905, 4; *Teamster Magazine* 3 (Nov. 1905): 13.

50. Cornelius Shea to Samuel Gompers, Nov. 11, 1905, reel 35, AFL Papers: Gompers Era.

51. *Chicago Record-Herald,* Sept. 11, 1905, 4.

52. "Teamsters' Weekly Review," *Michigan Union Advocate,* Oct. 6, 1905, 2.

53. "Teamsters' Weekly Review," *Michigan Union Advocate,* Sept. 22, 1905, 3; *Chicago Record-Herald,* Sept. 19, 1905, 7, Sept. 23, 1905, 4; *Teamster Magazine* 3 (Nov. 1905): 13.

54. The last issue of the *Teamsters' Weekly Review* appeared on October 13, 1905.

55. *Proceedings of the Sixth Annual Convention of the International Brotherhood of Teamsters* [1906] (Indianapolis: Cheltenham Press, 1906), 159–81, 200–205.

56. Cornelius Shea to Samuel Gompers, Sept. 11, 1905, Jan. 27, 1906, reel 36, AFL Papers: Gompers Era; *Proceedings, IBT Convention,* [1906], 162–64.

57. *Chicago Daily Tribune,* Aug. 7, 1906, 3; *Chicago Record-Herald,* Aug. 7, 1906, 9.

58. *Chicago Daily Tribune,* Aug. 7, 1906, 3; *Chicago Record-Herald,* Aug. 7, 1906, 9; *Proceedings, IBT Convention,* [1906], 61–64, 79–119.

59. Warren R. Van Tine, *The Making of the Labor Bureaucrat: Union Leadership in the United States, 1870–1920* (Amherst: University of Massachusetts Press, 1973), 113–59.

60. *Chicago Record-Herald*, Aug. 7, 1906, 9, Aug. 9, 1906, 5; *Proceedings, IBT Convention*, [1906], 26–32

61. *Chicago Record-Herald*, Aug. 9, 1906, 5.

62. Ibid.

63. *Proceedings, IBT Convention*, [1906], 16–19, 56–59.

64. *Chicago Record-Herald*, Aug. 9, 1906, 5, Aug. 10, 1906, 7.

65. *Chicago Record-Herald*, Aug. 10, 1906, 7.

66. *Chicago Daily Tribune*, Aug. 10, 1906, 3; *Chicago Record-Herald*, Aug. 11, 1906, 10.

67. *Chicago Daily Tribune*, Aug. 23, 1905, 1, Sept. 17, 1906, 5; *Chicago Record-Herald*, Sept. 17, 1906, 3.

68. *Proceedings of the Fifth Annual Convention of the International Brotherhood of Teamsters, Held at Boston, Massachusetts, August Fifth to Thirteenth (inclusive) Nineteen Hundred and Seven* [1907] (Indianapolis: Cheltenham Press, 1907), 43–44, 49.

69. *Teamster Magazine* 4 (Aug. 1907): 29–32; *Proceedings, IBT Convention*, [1907], 58–61, 67–77, 79–97.

70. *Team Owners' Review* 5 (Oct. 1906): 21.

71. Thomas L. Hughes to Frank Morrison, Oct. 30, 1906, reel 36, AFL Papers: Gompers Era; *Proceedings IBT Convention*, [1907], 35–40, 135–40.

72. *The Public*, Jan. 26, 1907, 1020, March 2, 1907, 1138.

73. *Chicago Record-Herald*, Feb. 22, 1907, 1.

74. *Team Owners' Review* 6 (May 1907): 25.

75. *Proceedings, IBT Convention*, [1907], 35–40, 135–40.

76. Ibid., 140–68, 171–72.

77. Ibid., 171–73.

78. Steven Fraser, *Labor Will Rule: Sidney Hillman and the Rise of American Labor* (New York: Macmillan, 1991), 43–44, 88–92, 119.

79. Harold C. Livesay, *Samuel Gompers and Organized Labor in America* (Boston: Little, Brown, 1978), 40–49; Dorothee Schneider, "The New York Cigarmakers Strike of 1877," *Labor History* 26 (Summer 1985): 332–33.

80. *Chicago Daily Tribune*, Aug. 10, 1907, 4; *Boston Herald*, Aug. 5, 1907, 4, Aug. 10, 1907, 3; *New York Times*, Nov. 15, 1955, 33; Gary M. Fink, ed., *Biographical Dictionary of American Labor* (Westport: Greenwood Press, 1984), 551; "The I.B.T.C.W.H. of A.," *Fortune* 23 (May 1941): 135–36, 138.

81. *Chicago Record-Herald*, July 19, 1908, 4, July 25, 1908, 7, Sept. 4, 1908, 7, Sept. 5, 1908, 5; *Teamster Magazine* 6 (Nov. 1908): 25–28.

82. *Proceedings of the Seventh Convention, International Brotherhood of Teamsters, Held at Peoria, Illinois, August 1–6, 1910* (Indianapolis: n.p., 1910), 20–21.

83. Daniel Tobin to Lawrence Grace, Dec. 4, 1908, series 1, box 32, IBT Papers; Daniel Tobin to Frank Morrison, March 5, 1909, reel 36, AFL Papers: Gompers Era.

84. Daniel Tobin to Samuel Gompers, March 1, 1909, reel 36, AFL Papers: Gompers Era; *Teamster Magazine* 6 (Aug. 1909): 22.

85. Daniel Tobin to Frank Morrison, March 5, 1909, reel 36, AFL Papers: Gompers Era; *Teamster Magazine* 6 (March 1909): 4.

86. Daniel Tobin to Lawrence Grace, May 1, 1909, Grace Correspondence File, series 1, box 32, IBT Papers; *Teamster Magazine* 6 (Aug. 1909): 10–16; "Certificate of Incorporation: The International Brotherhood of Teamsters of New York and New Jersey," June 9, 1909, Joseph Forkey Correspondence File, series 1, box 28, IBT Papers.

87. Daniel Tobin to Lawrence Grace, Oct. 28, 1908, Grace Correspondence File, series 1, box 32, IBT Papers.

88. Ibid; Daniel Tobin to Mr. McDermott, Dec. 14, 1908, reel 36, AFL Papers: Gompers Era.

89. Daniel Tobin to Lawrence Grace, July 12, 1909, Grace Correspondence File, series 1, box 32, IBT Papers.

90. *Chicago Record-Herald,* May 23, 1909, 2, July 22, 1909, 9, July 24, 1909, 1.

91. Daniel Tobin to Lawrence Grace, Aug. 9, 1909, Grace Correspondence File, series 1, box 32, IBT Papers; Valentine Hoffman to Daniel Tobin, July 29, 1909, series 1, box 33, IBT Papers.

92. *Proceedings, IBT Convention, 1910,* 24.

Chapter 4: Tobin's Union in a Period of Transition, 1910–40

1. Ralph C. James and Estelle Dinnerstein James, *Hoffa and the Teamsters: A Study of Union Power* (New York: D. Van Nostrand, 1965), 54.

2. "The I.B.T.C.W.H. of A.," *Fortune* 23 (May 1941): 138.

3. *Official Magazine of the International Brotherhood of Teamsters, Chauffeurs, Stablemen and Helpers* 11 (Nov. 1912): 14 (hereafter *Official Magazine*).

4. *Official Magazine* 12 (Feb. 1915): 8.

5. Dave Beck, interview by Mark Nackman, Jan. 26, 1978, tape recording, transcript pp. 51–55, Columbia Oral History Project, Columbia University (hereafter Dave Beck Oral History).

6. *Official Magazine* 26 (March 1929): 11.

7. "Initial Cost Not Vital," *Power Wagon* 79 (June 1911): 34; Harry W. Perry, "The Commercial Motor Trucks vs. the Horse," *Scientific American,* Jan. 14, 1911, 36–37, 50–51; "Jollying the Heavy Horse Breeder," *Power Wagon* 72 (Nov. 1910): 19.

8. *Official Magazine* 9 (July 1912): 6.

9. "Science of Motor Transportation," *Power Wagon* 69 (Aug. 1910): 17.

10. *Official Magazine* 25 (May 1928): 13; Stephen B. Goddard, *Getting There: The Epic Struggle between Road and Rail in the American Century* (Chicago: University of Chicago Press, 1994), 92, 141.

11. American Trucking Associations, *American Trucking Trends, 1949* (Washington, D.C.: American Trucking Associations, 1949), 1.

12. Mark Sullivan, *Our Times: The United States, 1900–1925,* vol. 4: *The War Begins, 1909–1914* (New York: Charles Scribner's Sons, 1946), 269.

13. *Proceedings of the Fourth Annual Convention of the International Brotherhood of Teamsters* [1906] (Indianapolis: Cheltenham Press, 1906), 275–76.

14. *Proceedings of the Seventh Convention, International Brotherhood of Teamsters, Held at Peoria, Illinois, August 1–6, 1910* (Indianapolis: n.p., 1910), 8–10 (third day); *Report of Officers of the International Brotherhood of Teamsters, Chauffeurs, Stablemen and Helpers,*

of America, Eighth Convention, Held in the City of Indianapolis, Indiana, October 7 to 12, 1912, Inclusive (Indianapolis: n.p., 1912), 129–30.

15. *Official Magazine* 10 (Nov. 1913): 5.

16. *Official Magazine* 10 (March 1913):17.

17. *Official Magazine* 10 (Aug. 1913): 17; *Reports of Officers of the International Brotherhood of Teamsters, Chauffeurs, Stablemen and Helpers of America, Tenth Convention, Held in the City of Cleveland, Ohio, Commencing October 4, 1920* (Cleveland: Lezius Printing, 1920), 56–57, 62.

18. "Work of a Five-Ton Coal Truck," *Power Wagon* 72 (Nov. 1910): 23.

19. Harry S. Houpt, "Making Chauffeurs of Teamsters," *Scientific American*, Jan. 6, 1912, 24.

20. "Operating Fifty Five-Ton Gas Trucks (Part 1)," *Power Wagon* 70 (Sept. 1910): 10.

21. "Bonus System for Truck Drivers," *Literary Digest*, Aug. 30, 1913, 334.

22. "Long Distance Freighting," *Power Wagon* 79 (June 1911): 29–30.

23. "Denver to San Francisco by Motor," *Power Wagon* 77 (April 1911): 33; "Rough Overland Journey," *Power Wagon* 78 (May 1911): 51.

24. Goddard, *Getting There*, 87–88, 90–92, 141, 149; Merrill J. Roberts, "The Motor Transportation Revolution," *Business History Review* 30 (March 1956): 55–63.

25. Goddard, *Getting There*, 88–92.

26. Ibid., 154.

27. U.S. President's Research Committee on Social Trends, *Recent Social Trends in the United States* (New York: McGraw-Hill, 1933), 458–60.

28. Roberts, "The Motor Transportation Revolution," 85–92; Harold Barger, *The Transportation Industries 1889–1946: A Study of Output, Employment, and Productivity* (New York: National Bureau of Economic Research, 1951), 236–40.

29. U.S. President's Research Committee on Social Trends, *Recent Social Trends*, 460.

30. Ibid., 458–60; Michael L. Berger, *The Devil Wagon in God's Country: The Automobile and Social Change in Rural America, 1893–1929* (Hamden: Archon Books, 1979), 42–44, 109–14.

31. *Reports of Officers of the International Brotherhood of Teamsters, Chauffeurs, Stablemen and Helpers of America, Twelfth Convention, Held in the City of Cincinnati, Ohio, Commencing September 8, 1930* (Indianapolis: n.p., 1930), 106.

32. *Reports of Officers, IBT Convention* [1930], 93–94, 112–13, 127–28.

33. Tobin's description the temporary and informal nature of these new organizing arrangements can be found in Daniel Tobin to Edward Murphy, Dec. 9, 1937, series 1, box 40, the International Brotherhood of Teamsters, Chauffeurs, Warehousemen and Helpers of America Papers, 1904–52, MSS 9, Wisconsin State Historical Society, Madison (hereafter IBT Papers). For secondary accounts of this emerging conference structure, see Donald Garnel, *The Rise of Teamster Power in the West* (Berkeley: University of California Press, 1972), 77–200. Tobin's suspicious reaction to such new organizing principles can be found in Dave Beck Oral History, 43–47.

34. James and James, *Hoffa and the Teamsters*, 16; Steven Brill, *The Teamsters* (New York: Simon and Schuster, 1978), 362–63.

35. *Constitution and By-laws of International Brotherhood of Teamsters, Adopted at Convention held at Detroit, Mich., Aug. 3 to 8, Inclusive, 1908* (Indianapolis: n.p., 1908); Robert

D. Leiter, *The Teamsters Union: A Study of Its Economic Impact* (New York: Bookman Associates, 1957), 58–80.

36. Until 1920 the national union paid strike benefits of $5 a week, raising them to $10 a week where they stayed until 1952. Leiter, *The Teamsters Union*, 36. Regarding availability and ease of secession, see Daniel Tobin to Thomas Hughes, March 11, 1927, series 1, box 33, IBT Papers; and *Proceedings of the Ninth Convention, International Brotherhood of Teamsters, Chauffeurs, Stablemen and Helpers of America, San Francisco, October 4 to 9, 1915, Reports of Officers* (San Francisco: Shannon, 1915), 13–14.

37. *IBT Constitution and By-laws, 1908*, 16–18.

38. *Reports of the Officers, IBT Convention Proceedings* [1915], 19–20.

39. *Proceedings, IBT Convention,* [1920], 31 (fifth day); *Proceedings, IBT Convention,* [1930], 40 (fifth day); *Proceedings of the Thirteenth Convention International Brotherhood of Teamsters, Chauffeurs, Stablemen and Helpers of America, Held at Portland, Oregon, September 9 to 14, 1935* (Indianapolis: n.p., 1935), 23–24 (fifth day); *Proceedings of the Fourteenth Convention International Brotherhood of Teamsters, Chauffeurs, Stablemen and Helpers of America, Held at Washington, D.C., September 9 to 14, 1940* (Indianapolis: n.p., 1940), 29–33 (fifth day).

40. Dave Beck Oral History, 32–33.

41. See, for example, the activities of George W. Briggs, the traveling auditor, or William H. Ashton, the IBT organizer based in Philadelphia. Thomas Hughes to George W. Briggs, Dec. 30, 1911, and George W. Briggs to Thomas Hughes, Jan. 18, Jan. 23, Feb. 2, 1912, series 1, box 4, IBT Papers; William H. Ashton to Thomas L. Hughes, July 25, July 28, Nov. 15, Nov. 20, 1926, series 1, box 3, IBT Papers.

42. *Official Magazine* 22 (March 1925): 17.

43. *Official Magazine* 32 (Dec. 1934): 8.

44. James and James, *Hoffa and the Teamsters*, 90–96.

45. "Who's Who in the International Union," *Official Magazine* 32 (April 1935): 3.

46. "Who's Who in the International Union," *Official Magazine* 32 (Sept. 1935): 4; Dave Beck Oral History, 37–39.

47. *Constitution and By-laws of the International Brotherhood of Teamsters, Chauffeurs, Warehousemen and Helpers of America, Adopted at the Convention Held in Washington, D.C., September 9th to 14th, Inclusive, 1940* (Indianapolis: n.p., 1940), 15, 20.

48. Daniel Tobin to David Gourlie, Nov. 23, 1937, folder 3, box 6, International Brotherhood of Teamsters, Chauffeurs, Warehousemen and Helpers Local 695 (Madison) Records, 1932–66, MSS 434, State Historical Society of Wisconsin, Madison. Another copy of the same letter, also sent out to a new local, can be found in Daniel Tobin to Dear Sir and Brother, Jan. 16, 1939, folder 1, box 2, Laundry and Dry Cleaning Drivers Local 360 (Milwaukee, Wisconsin) Records, 1936–47, MSS DT, University of Wisconsin at Milwaukee (hereafter IBT Local 360 Records). Farrell Dobbs quotes from the same letter, which was sent to Minneapolis Local 574 in 1930. Farrell Dobbs, *Teamster Rebellion* (New York: Monad Press, 1972), 39.

49. *Official Magazine* 12 (July 1915): 6.

50. Michael Casey to Daniel Tobin, June 9, 1923, and Daniel Tobin to Michael Casey, June 14, 1923, series 1, box 14, IBT Papers.

51. David Brody, *Workers in Industrial America: Essays on the Twentieth-Century Struggle* (New York: Oxford University Press, 1980), 31–32.

52. *Official Magazine* 8 (April 1911): 5. Regarding concern for employers, see *Reports of Officers, IBT Convention,* [1940], 36–37; *Official Magazine* 31 (April 1934): 10.

53. *Reports of Officers, IBT Convention,* 1915, 5, 30; *Official Magazine* 10 (June 1913): 2.

54. *Reports of Officers of the International Brotherhood of Teamsters, Chauffeurs, Stablemen and Helpers of America, Eleventh Convention, Held in the City of Seattle, Washington, September 14 to 19, 1925* (Seattle: Alaska Printing, 1925), 36; *Reports of Officers, IBT Convention,* [1940], 21–22.

55. Leiter, *The Teamsters Union,* 33, 39.

56. *Proceedings of the Fourteenth Convention International Brotherhood of Teamsters, Chauffeurs, Stablemen and Helpers of America, Held at Washington, D.C., September 9 to 14, 1940, Reports of Officers,* (Indianapolis: n.p., 1940), 21–22.

57. *Report of the Proceedings of the Fifty-fourth Annual Convention of the American Federation of Labor, Held at San Francisco, California, October 1 to 12, Inclusive, 1934* (San Francisco: Judd and Detweiler, 1934), 453.

58. Daniel Tobin to Michael Casey, Dec. 3, 1930, series 1, box 16, IBT Papers.

59. *Proceedings, IBT Convention,* [1906], 245–50 (fifth day).

60. *Official Magazine* 16 (May 1919): 1; *Official Magazine* 16 (Jan. 1919): 17.

61. Daniel Tobin to D. J. Murphy, May 18, 1915, series 1, box 38, IBT Papers.

62. *Official Magazine* 26 (Dec. 1919): 17.

63. *Official Magazine* 28 (July 1931): 14–15.

64. Robert McClure Robinson, "A History of Teamsters in San Francisco Bay Area, 1850–1950," Ph.D. diss., University of California, Berkeley, 1951, 147–50.

65. "Coal Teamsters—Boston," *Monthly Labor Review* 16 (June 1923): 167–68.

66. John M. Gillespie to George J. Ritchey, Feb. 13, 1938, folder 4, box 1, IBT Local 360 Records.

67. Daniel Tobin to Frank Morrison, July 11, 1932, series 3, box 8, IBT Papers; *Official Magazine* 28 (Nov. 1931): 9–11.

68. *Official Magazine* 24 (Feb. 1927): 9–10.

69. John L. Devring to Thomas L. Hughes, April 6, 1926, series 1, box 27, IBT Papers; Henry G. Burger to Thomas L. Hughes, May 11, 1932, series 1, box 11, IBT Papers; Daniel J. Tobin to Michael Casey, Sept. 18, 1931, series 1, box 16, IBT Papers; *Official Magazine* 25 (Sept. 1928): 10–11.

70. *Official Magazine* 32 (April 1935): 17.

71. *Reports of Officers, IBT Convention,* [1940], 42–45.

72. *Official Magazine* 22 (Sept. 1925): 2–18; *Official Magazine* 32 (March 1935): 1–2.

73. *Reports of Officers, IBT Convention,* [1940], 5–6, 80.

74. Dave Beck Oral History, 147–50; Leiter, *Teamsters Union,* 104.

75. Stephen Brier, ed., *Who Built America? Working People and the Nation's Economy, Politics, Culture, and Society* (New York: Pantheon Books, 1992), 395–96.

76. William Ashton to Thomas L. Hughes, Jan. 27, 1915, series 1, box 2, IBT Papers.

77. Memorandum of Agreement between the Ice Dealers of Detroit and Local No. 376, International Brotherhood of Teamsters, Chauffeurs, Stablemen and Helpers of Ameri-

ca, May 1, 1919, included in letter from John L. Devring to Thomas L. Hughes, April 25, 1919, series 1, box 24, IBT Papers (hereafter Memorandum of Agreement Local 376); "Ice and Water Teamsters—Cleveland," *Monthly Labor Review* 21 (Aug. 1925): 93–94; Walter R. Sanders, *Ice Delivery: A Complete Treatise on the Subject* (Chicago: Nickerson and Collins, 1922), 11–12, 19, 40, 43, 50–51, 55–61, 74–75, 81–82, 134–35.

78. Memorandum of Agreement Local 376; "Ice and Water Teamsters—Cleveland;" Sanders, *Ice Delivery*, 11–12, 40, 50, 55, 74–75, 134–35.

79. Memorandum of Agreement Local 376; Sanders, *Ice Delivery*, 100–101.

80. Philip Korth, *Minneapolis Teamsters Strike of 1934* (East Lansing: Michigan State University Press, 1995), 28–29.

81. "Union Scale of Wages and Hours of Labor as of May 1925," *Monthly Labor Review* 21 (Nov. 1925): 76–81.

82. Korth, *Minneapolis Teamsters Strike of 1934*, 29.

83. Ibid., 72.

84. Sanders, *Ice Delivery*, 4, 54, 183.

85. *Power Wagon* 76 (March 1911): 71; "The Warner Motor Truck Speed Indicator," *Power Wagon* 77 (April 1911): 8; Sanders, *Ice Delivery*, 233.

86. Korth, *Minneapolis Teamsters Strike*, 71–73.

87. James R. Hoffa as told to Oscar Fraley, *Hoffa: The Real Story* (New York: Stein and Day, 1975), 31.

88. *Official Magazine* 11 (Dec. 1913): 10.

89. *Official Magazine* 24 (Jan. 1927): 15–16.

90. "Union Scale of Wages and Hours of Labor as of May 1925," 80.

91. "Chauffeurs—St. Louis," *Monthly Labor Review* 18 (March 1924): 103–4.

92. Memorandum of Agreement Local 376.

93. *Reports of Officers, IBT Convention* [1940], 44.

94. *Reports of Officers, IBT Convention* [1912], 12.

95. "Who's Who in the International Union," *Official Magazine* 32 (April 1935): 2–3; "Who's Who in the International Union," *Official Magazine* 32 (May 1935) 6–7; "Who's Who in the International Union," *Official Magazine* 32 (June 1935): 2–3; "Who's Who in the International Union," *Official Magazine* 32 (July 1935): 6–7.

96. *Official Magazine* 33 (Jan. 1936): 3–4.

Chapter 5: "The Most Racketeer-Ridden Union in the United States"

1. Harold Seidman, *Labor Czars: A History of Labor Racketeering* (New York: Liveright Publishing, 1938), 254.

2. President's Commission on Organized Crime, *The Edge: Organized Crime, Business, and Labor Unions: Report to the President and the Attorney General* (Washington, D.C.: The Commission, 1986), 4.

3. Seidman, *Labor Czars*, 106–24. See also Irving Bernstein, *The Lean Years: A History of the American Worker, 1920–1933* (Boston: Houghton Mifflin, 1960), 338–41; Stephen Fox, *Blood and Power: Organized Crime in Twentieth Century America* (New York: Penguin Books, 1989), 174–75; and John Hutchinson, *The Imperfect Union: A History of Corruption in American Trade Unions* (New York: E. P. Dutton, 1970), 68.

4. Steven Brill, *The Teamsters* (New York: Simon and Schuster, 1978), 360.

5. Fox, *Blood and Power*, 191–92, 198–200.

6. Hutchinson, *The Imperfect Union*, 372.

7. Daniel Bell, *The End of Ideology: On the Exhaustion of Political Ideals in the Fifties* (Glencoe: The Free Press, 1960), 152, 159–61. Similar structural arguments include Howard Kimeldorf, *Reds or Rackets? The Making of Radical and Conservative Unions on the Waterfront* (Berkeley: University of California Press, 1988); and Philip Taft, *Corruption and Racketeering in the Labor Movement* (Ithaca: New York State School of Industrial and Labor Relations, Cornell University, 1958).

8. U.S. National Commission on Law Observance and Enforcement (Wickersham Commission), *Report on the Cost of Crime* (Washington, D.C.: Government Printing Office, 1931), 407.

9. U.S. National Commission on Law Observance and Enforcement, *Report on the Cost of Crime*, 407–408.

10. Ibid., 411.

11. "Why Stand for Racketeers," *Saturday Evening Post*, Aug. 1, 1931, 20.

12. Mark H. Haller, "Illegal Enterprise: A Theoretical and Historical Interpretation," *Criminology* 28 (May 1990): 209–14; Howard Abadinsky, *Organized Crime* (Chicago: Nelson-Hall Publishers, 1994), 106–15, 158–68; Humbert S. Nelli, *The Business of Crime: Italians and Syndicate Crime in the United States* (New York: Oxford University Press, 1976), 101–34; Albert Fried, *The Rise and Fall of the Jewish Gangster in America* (New York: Holt, Rinehart and Winston, 1980), 26–41, 62–64; Jenna Weissman Joselit, *Our Gang: Jewish Crime and the New York Jewish Community, 1900–1940* (Bloomington: Indiana University Press, 1983), 26–28, 42–53; Peter A. Lupsha, "Organized Crime in the United States," in *Organized Crime: A Global Perspective*, ed. Robert J. Kelly (Totowa: Rowman and Littlefield, 1986), 42–44; Lawrence M. Friedman, *Crime and Punishment in American History* (New York: Basic Books, 1993), 226–28.

13. Alan Block, *East Side–West Side: Organizing Crime in New York, 1930–1950* (Swansea, Wales: University College of Cardiff, 1980), 12–13, 129–61; Abadinsky, *Organized Crime*, 111–21, 171–90; Lupsha, "Organized Crime in the United States," 44–48; Nelli, *The Business of Crime*, 143–78; Fried, *The Rise and Fall of the Jewish Gangster*, 89–128; Thomas C. Schelling, "What Is the Business of Organized Crime?" *American Scholar* 40 (Autumn 1971): 643–52.

14. Malcolm W. Klein, *The American Street Gang: Its Nature, Prevalence, and Control* (New York: Oxford University Press, 1995), 40–49, 57–64, 131–35; Jerome Skolnick, Theodore Correl, Elizabeth Navarro, and Roger Rabb, "The Social Structure of Street Drug Dealing," *American Journal of Police* 9 (1990): 1–41; Fried, *The Rise and Fall of the Jewish Gangster*, 25–41, 92–109, 114–74; Joselit, *Our Gang*, 26–28, 92–97, 119–29; Nelli, *The Business of Crime*, 101–9, 134–40, 148–57, 162–74, 179–212; Abadinsky, *Organized Crime*, 112–56, 168–98; Lupsha, "Organized Crime in the United States," 45–53; Peter Maas, *The Valachi Papers* (New York: G. P. Putnam's Sons, 1968), 84–120; Joseph Bonanno with Sergio Lalli, *A Man of Honor: The Autobiography of Joseph Bonanno* (New York: Simon and Schuster, 1983), 122–26, 136–52; Robert T. Anderson, "From Mafia to Cosa Nostra," *American Journal of Sociology* 71 (Nov. 1965): 302–10.

15. Bonanno, *A Man of Honor*, 161–65; Howard Abadinsky, "The McDonald's-ization of the Mafia," in *Organized Crime in America: Concepts and Controversies*, ed. Timothy S.

Bynum (Monsey: Willow Tree Press, 1987), 43–54; Nelli, *The Business of Crime,* 207–12; Fried, *The Rise and Fall of the Jewish Gangster,* 141–74, 201–5, 232–40; Block, *East Side–West Side,* 219–35.

16. *Chicago Tribune,* June 7, 1932, 1, Nov. 3, 1932, 1, Jan. 25, 1934, 3, Nov. 24, 1936, 1, March 26, 1943, 1; Fred D. Pasley, *Muscling In* (New York: Washburn Publishers, 1931), 1–15.

17. Pasley, *Muscling In,* 56–59; *Chicago Tribune,* Sept. 2, 1930, 8.

18. Roger Touhy with Ray Brennan, *The Stolen Years* (Cleveland: Pennington Press, 1959), 84–85.

19. *Reports of Officers of the International Brotherhood of Teamsters, Chauffeurs, Stablemen and Helpers of America, Twelth Convention, Held in the City of Cincinnati, Ohio, Commencing September 8, 1930* (Indianapolis: n.p., 1930), 149.

20. D. J. Tobin to Michael Casey, Feb. 20, 1930, D. J. Tobin to Michael Casey, Feb. 21, 1930, and Daniel Tobin to Michael Casey, Feb. 28, 1930, all in series 1, box 16, the International Brotherhood of Teamsters, Chauffeurs, Warehousemen and Helpers of America Papers, 1904–52, MSS 9, Wisconsin State Historical Society, Madison (hereafter IBT Papers).

21. D. J. Tobin to Michael Casey, March 11, 1930, series 1, box 16, IBT Papers.

22. *Chicago Tribune,* July 26, 1931, 1, Nov. 10, 1931, 1, July 22, 1932, 1, May 2, 1933, 1, March 20, 1943, 7, March 22, 1943, 2, March 26, 1943, 1; *Official Magazine of the International Brotherhood of Teamsters, Chauffeurs, Stablemen and Helpers* 28 (Sept. 1931): 12 (hereafter *Official Magazine*); *Chicago Herald and Examiner,* July 22, 1932, 1.

23. *Chicago Herald and Examiner,* July 22, 1932, 1.

24. *Chicago Tribune,* March 22, 1943, 2; *Chicago Daily Tribune,* June 17, 1933, 1; Clarence C. Saelhof to T. L. Hughes, July 1, 1933, Burger Correspondence File, series 1, box 11, IBT Papers.

25. Michael Cashal to Daniel Tobin, June 18, 1931, series 1, box 20, IBT Papers.

26. Pasley, *Muscling In,* 1–15; Hutchinson, *The Imperfect Union,* 116.

27. D. J. Tobin to Michael Casey, March 11, 1930, series 1, box 16, IBT Papers.

28. *Chicago Tribune,* July 22, 1932, 1; *Chicago Herald and Examiner,* July 22, 1932, 1; Touhy, *The Stolen Years,* 83–86.

29. *Chicago Tribune,* Dec. 21, 1930, 31, June 11, 1932, 11, Nov. 29, 1932, 8; D. J. Tobin to Michael Casey, May 24, 1932, series 1, box 16, IBT Papers.

30. D. J. Tobin to Michael Casey, May 24, 1932, series 1, box 16, IBT Papers.

31. *Chicago Tribune,* June 17, 1932, 1, June 18, 1932, 3.

32. *Chicago Tribune,* Dec. 18, 1959, 6.

33. *Chicago Herald and Examiner,* July 22, 1932, 1; *Chicago Tribune,* July 22, 1932, 1, July 24, 1932, 5.

34. Court of Appeals—New York, *The People of the State of New York against Jacob Bernoff, alias Jack Cohen, Thomas McAdam, alias Tommy Moran, Murray Gabaeff, Edward Taylor, Abraham Lichtenstein, alias Augie, Charles Green, Jeremiah Buckley, George Blume, and John Murphy* (1943) (hereafter *People v. Bernoff*), 209–12.

35. U.S. Congress, Temporary National Economic Committee, *Investigation of Concentration of Economic Power: Part 7: Milk Industry, Poultry Industry,* Public Resolution 113, 76th Cong., 1st sess., March 9, 10, 11, May 1, 2, and 3, 1939 (Washington, D.C.: Government Printing Office, 1939), 2763–64, 2975–76, 3032–34; U.S. Federal Trade Commission, *Report of the Federal Trade Commission on the Sale and Distribution of Milk and Milk Products:*

New York Milk Sales Area, 75th Cong., 1st sess., 1937 (Washington, D.C.: Government Printing Office, 1937), 2–7, 56–57; Trial Memorandum of Sam Adler in Samuel Adler File, Milk Racket, box 2683, District Attorney Files, New York County District Attorney Papers, New York City Municipal Archives (hereafter DA Files).

36. U.S. Congress, Temporary National Economic Committee, *Investigation of Concentration of Economic Power,* 2975–76, 2997–98, 3047–48, 3087–88.

37. *New York Times,* March 28, 1926, 25, July 2, 1926, 10, July 13, 1926, 34, Sept. 14, 1926, 31.

38. *New York Times,* Sept. 13, 1929, 1 (quotation), Aug. 19, 1930, 1, Jan. 2, 1933, 1; Craig Thompson and Allen Raymond, *Gang Rule in New York: The Story of a Lawless Era* (New York: Dial Press, 1940), 35–42, 289–92.

39. *New York Times,* Aug. 19, 1930, 1.

40. *New York Times,* Jan. 2, 1933, 1.

41. Michael Cashal to Daniel Tobin, March 27, 1933, series 1, box 20, IBT Papers.

42. *People v. Bernoff,* 499–557.

43. Ibid., 558–61, 564–66. Regarding Bernoff's history and alleged affiliations, see *New York Times,* Jan. 3, 1941, 1, and New York *Herald-Tribune,* July 1, 1941, and *Sun,* June 30, 1941, reel 19, Thomas Dewey Scrapbooks, microfilm ed., University of Rochester, Rochester, New York (hereafter Dewey Scrapbooks).

44. *People v. Bernoff,* 1670–72.

45. Ibid., 566–76.

46. Ibid., 583–87, 596–602.

47. *Daily Food News and Food Magazine,* Aug. 24, 1935, 1.

48. A copy of *Daily Food News and Food Magazine,* Aug. 26, 1935, 1, and Dept. of Health, Report from Supervisor Abraham Lichterman to Confidential Food Investigator, Subject: Council of Independent Milk Dealers, Inc., Sept. 12, 1935, are both in Milk 1934, folder 3, reel 132, Fiorello La Guardia Papers, microfilm ed., New York Municipal Archives (hereafter La Guardia Subject Files).

49. Trial brief for Barnet Metzger, 8, box 2683, DA Files.

50. *People v. Bernoff,* 614–15.

51. *New York Daily News,* July 1, 1941; New York *Herald-Tribune,* July 1, 1941, reel 19, Dewey Scrapbooks.

52. William H. Brownell Grand Jury testimony, May 7, 1941, 11, transcript in Brownell file, box 2683, DA Files.

53. Trial brief for Max Sacks, 3, Eastern Farms file, box 2683, DA Files.

54. Frederick Beers Grand Jury testimony, Feb. 21, 1941, transcript in Fred Beers file, box 2683, DA Files.

55. *People v. Bernoff,* 617–24, 1680–81.

56. Ibid., 690–94.

57. Ibid., 695–96.

58. Ibid., 696–700.

59. Abadinsky, *Organized Crime,* 294–99; Schelling, "What Is the Business of Organized Crime?" 643–52.

60. Mary M. Stolberg, *Fighting Organized Crime: Politics, Justice, and the Legacy of Thomas E. Dewey* (Boston: Northeastern University Press, 1995), 65–98, 162–92; Block, *East Side–West Side,* 63–93.

61. Barbara Wayne Newell, *Chicago and the Labor Movement: Metropolitan Unionism in the 1930s* (Urbana: University of Illinois Press, 1961), 92–93.

62. Seidman, *Labor Czars*, 254–56.

63. "The I.B.T.C.W.H. of A.," *Fortune* 23 (May 1941): 136.

64. Hutchinson, *The Imperfect Union*, 91–92.

65. Steven Fraser, *Labor Will Rule: Sidney Hillman and the Rise of American Labor* (New York: Macmillan, 1991), 251–54.

66. "Why Stand for Racketeers," *Saturday Evening Post*, Aug. 1, 1931, 20.

67. Gordon L. Hostetter and Thomas Quinn Beesley, *It's a Racket* (Chicago: Les Quin Books, 1929), ix; Edward Dean Sullivan, *Chicago Surrenders* (New York: Vanguard Press, 1930), xii–xiii.

68. Frank Dalton O'Sullivan, *Enemies of Industry* (Chicago: O'Sullivan, 1933), 34.

69. Erich Goode and Nachman Ben-Yehuda, *Moral Panics: The Social Construction of Deviance* (Cambridge: Blackwell Publishers, 1994), 11; Stanley Cohen, *Folk Devils and Moral Panics: The Creation of the Mods and Rockers* (Oxford: Martin Robertson, 1980), 9.

70. U.S. Bureau of the Census, *Historical Statistics of the United States, Colonial Times to 1970, Bicentennial Edition* (Washington, D.C.: Government Printing Office, 1975), 414, 420.

71. Samuel Crowther, "Invisible Government: What Racketeering Costs the Home," *Ladies Home Journal* 48 (Feb. 1931): 3, 59.

72. Joel Kovel, *Red Hunting in the Promised Land: Anti-Communism in the Making of America* (New York: Basic Books, 1994), 118–231; Stephen J. Whitfield, *The Culture of the Cold War* (Baltimore: Johns Hopkins University Press, 1996), 27–51.

73. Hostetter and Beesley, *It's a Racket*, 171.

74. O'Sullivan, *Enemies of Industry*, 12–13. In a magazine account of a "typical gang of racketeers" the author thought it important to note, "All, when in public, are quiet and well behaved. Some of them have families, with whom they live in apparent respectability in a peaceful outlying neighborhood." R. L. Duffus, "The Function of the Racketeer," *New Republic*, March 27, 1929, 166.

75. Edward Dean Sullivan, *This Labor Union Racket* (New York: Hillman-Curl, 1936), 49.

76. *New York Times*, May 25, 1931, 4, quoted in Pasley, *Muscling In,* 257.

77. Sullivan, *This Labor Union Racket*, 7–8.

78. Robert Isham Randolph, "Business Fights Crime in Chicago," *Saturday Evening Post*, Aug. 16, 1930, 141; Pasley, *Muscling In,* 256.

79. *Official Magazine* 31 (Oct. 1934): 15.

80. Daniel Tobin to Michael Casey, Dec. 13, 1932, series 1, box 16, IBT Papers.

81. U.S. Bureau of the Census, *Historical Statistics of the United States,* 178.

82. Robert D. Leiter, *The Teamsters Union: A Study of Its Economic Impact* (New York: Bookman Associates, 1957), 33, 39.

83. Robert H. Zieger, *The CIO, 1935–1955* (Chapel Hill: University of North Carolina Press, 1995), 116–17, 162–63; Melvyn Dubofsky, *The State and Labor in Modern America* (Chapel Hill: University of North Carolina Press, 1994), 146–67, 173–75.

84. George H. Gallup, *The Gallup Poll: Public Opinion, 1935–1971,* vol. 1: *1935–1948* (New York: Random House, 1972), 277–78.

85. Pasley, *Muscling In,* 233–34.

86. Oliver Pilat, *Pegler: Angry Man of the Press* (Boston: Beacon Press, 1963), 178–79.

87. William Z. Foster, *Misleaders of Labor* (Chicago: Trade Union Educational League, 1927).

88. Seidman, *Labor Czars,* 288–303.

89. Walter Chambers, *Labor Unions and the Public* (New York: Howard-McCann Inc., 1936), 143–87, 201–8.

90. Sullivan, *This Labor Union Racket,* 102–3, 256–58.

91. Hostetter and Beesley, *It's a Racket,* 215–42.

92. Thompson and Raymond, *Gang Rule in New York,* 220.

93. Chambers, *Labor Unions and the Public,* 112.

94. Hostetter and Beesley, *It's a Racket,* 205.

95. Sullivan, *This Labor Union Racket,* 32, 69–71.

96. "The I.B.T.C.W.H. of A.," *Fortune,* 96–100.

97. Sullivan, *This Labor Union Racket,* 122.

98. Columns appearing on March 16, 1937, March 30, 1937, and June 26, 1937, box 118, (James) Westbrook Pegler Papers, 1908–69, Herbert Hoover Presidential Library, West Branch, Iowa (hereafter Pegler Papers).

99. For mention of rampant corruption, see columns of Aug. 15, 1939, and Sept. 7, 1939; quotation from column of Feb. 7, 1940, all in boxes 119–20, Pegler Papers.

100. Column appeared on Feb. 7, 1940, box 120, Pegler Papers.

101. Column appeared on May 22, 1940, box 120, Pegler Papers.

102. "Supergovernment," Oct. 12, 1939, box 119, Pegler Papers; "peculiar power," June 25, 1941, box 120, Pegler Papers.

103. Column appeared on June 26, 1941, box 120, Pegler Papers.

104. Column appeared on May 1, 1941, box 120, Pegler Papers.

105. Columns appearing on April 1, 1938, July 13, July 26, Aug. 8, 1939, Jan. 6, Jan. 12, April 6, April 13, April 25, June 7, July 11, Nov. 19, 1940, all in boxes 119 and 120, Pegler Papers.

106. *New York Times,* May 6, 1941, 16; Pilat, *Pegler,* 177.

107. Indictment 102–395, May 31, 1938, U.S. District Court, Southern District of New York, box 67, accession 0627, Papers of Thurman W. Arnold, American Heritage Center, University of Wyoming, Laramie; *New York Times,* June 1, 1938, 1, June 8, 1938, 13.

108. Thurman W. Arnold, *The Bottlenecks of Business* (New York: Reynal and Hitchcock, 1940), 240–42, 245–46, 247–52; Ellis W. Hawley, *The New Deal and the Problem of Monopoly: A Study in Economic Ambivalence* (New York: Fordham University Press, 1995), 431–38; Alan Brinkley, *The End of Reform: New Deal Liberalism in Recession and War* (New York: Vintage, 1996), 106–22.

109. *New York Times,* May 25, 1940, 19, June 20, 1940, 25.

110. *IBT News,* Dec. 8, 1937, 6, Jan. 15, 1938, 1; testimony of Joseph Padway quoted in "Pro and Con Discussion: Should Congress Pass the Hobbs Bill to Outlaw Labor Racketeering?" *Congressional Digest* 22 (June–July 1943): 187.

111. Testimony of James Gaughan in *U.S. v. Local 807 of the International Brotherhood of Teamsters, Chauffeurs, Stablemen and Helpers of America,* U.S. District Court, Southern District of New York, case 102–394 (1940), 2004–6, accession 021-57A–136, FRC Location Number 29455, Federal Records Center, Bayonne, N.J.

112. *Daily Worker,* May 19, 1940, 5.

113. *New York Times,* June 20, 1940, 25.

114. *Official Magazine* 35 (May 1938): 13.

115. *Official Magazine* 35 (June 1938): front cover.

116. *Official Magazine* 34 (July 1937): 12.

117. Daniel Tobin to Michael Casey, May 24, 1932, series 1, box 15, IBT Papers.

118. Harry Cohen to Thomas E. Flynn, Feb. 9, 1942, series 2B, box 111, IBT Papers.

119. Alois Mueller to H. Herman Rauch, Sept. 7, 1937, folder 3, box 1, and Resolution [ante June 21, 1938], folder 4, box 1, Laundry and Dry Cleaning Drivers Local 360 (Milwaukee, Wisconsin) Records, 1936–47, MSS DT, University of Wisconsin, Milwaukee (hereafter IBT Local 360 Records). Regarding the strike, see *Milwaukee Leader,* April 20, 1937, 2, June 18, 1937, 1, June 22, 1937, 2.

120. Alois Mueller to E. E. Wagner, Oct. 7, 1937, box 1, IBT Local 360 Records.

121. *Chicago Tribune,* Nov. 17, 1928, 1.

122. *Official Magazine* 26 (Jan. 1929), 11–12, 14–16.

123. *Chicago Tribune,* Nov. 18, 1928, 5.

Chapter 6: The Possibilities and Limitations of Union Reform in the 1930s

1. Mary M. Stolberg, *Fighting Organized Crime: Politics, Justice, and the Legacy of Thomas E. Dewey* (Boston: Northeastern University Press, 1995), 168–71; Richard Norton Smith, *Thomas E. Dewey and His Times* (New York: Simon and Schuster, 1982), 163–64, 229–34.

2. Thomas Kessner, *Fiorello H. La Guardia and the Making of Modern New York* (New York: McGraw-Hill, 1989), 342–43, 353–55.

3. Smith, *Thomas E. Dewey and His Times,* 232–33.

4. Stephen Fox, *Blood and Power: Organized Crime in Twentieth Century America* (New York: Penguin Books, 1989), 191.

5. Ralph C. James and Estelle Dinnerstein James, *Hoffa and the Teamsters: A Study of Union Power* (New York: D. Van Nostrand, 1965), 16, 67.

6. "The I.B.T.C.W.H. of A.," *Fortune* 23 (May 1941): 136.

7. *Official Magazine of the International Brotherhood of Teamsters, Chauffeurs, Stablemen and Helpers* 34 (May 1937): 17 (hereafter *Official Magazine*).

8. Harold Seidman, *Labor Czars: A History of Labor Racketeering* (New York: Liveright Publishing, 1938), 254; *Proceedings of the Fourteenth Convention International Brotherhood of Teamsters, Chauffeurs, Stablemen, and Helpers of America, Held at Washington, D.C. September 9 to 14, 1940, Reports of Officers* (Indianapolis: n.p., 1940), 86–87.

9. Daniel Tobin to Westbrook Pegler, June 25, 1941, June 27, 1941, series 1, box 11, the International Brotherhood of Teamsters, Chauffeurs, Warehousemen and Helpers of America Papers, 1904–52, MSS 9, Wisconsin State Historical Society, Madison (hereafter IBT Papers).

10. *Proceedings of the Ninth Convention, International Brotherhood of Teamsters, Chauffeurs, Stablemen and Helpers of America, San Francisco, October 4 to 9, 1915, Reports of Officers* (San Francisco: Shannon, 1915), 25–26.

11. Daniel Tobin to Thomas Hughes, Dec. 7, 1916, series 1, box 34, IBT Papers.

12. *Constitution and By-laws of International Brotherhood of Teamsters, Adopted at Convention held at Detroit, Mich., Aug. 3 to 8, Inclusive, 1908* (Indianapolis: n.p., 1908), 14.

13. *Reports of Officers of the International Brotherhood of Teamsters, Chauffeurs, Stablemen and Helpers of America, Tenth Convention, Held in the City of Cleveland, Ohio, Commencing October 4, 1920* (Cleveland: Lezius Printing, 1920), 33, 147–98.

14. G. W. Briggs to T. L. Hughes, Nov. 28, 1911, series 1, box 4, IBT Papers.

15. *Reports of Officers, IBT Convention, 1920*, 71.

16. *Reports of Officers of the International Brotherhood of Teamsters, Chauffeurs, Stablemen and Helpers of America, Eleventh Convention, Held in the City of Seattle, Washington, September 14 to 19, 1925* (Seattle: Alaska Printing, 1925), 192–93.

17. In 1915 the IBT general secretary-treasurer estimated that in a year Briggs could audit about 125 sets of local books and records, and the IBT had between five and six hundred local unions. *Reports of Officers, IBT Convention, 1915*, 3–4, 20–24. For the changes made after Briggs's death, see *Reports of Officers of the International Brotherhood of Teamsters, Chauffeurs, Stablemen and Helpers of America, Twelfth Convention, Held in the City of Cincinnati, Ohio, Commencing September 8, 1930* (Indianapolis: n.p., 1930), 35–36 (third day). The activities of the organizers can be sampled in Henry Burger to Thomas L. Hughes, Feb. 9, 1932, March 21, 1932, April 27, 1932, March 31, 1936, Nov. 29, 1936, series 1, box 11, IBT Papers.

18. *Reports of Officers, IBT Convention, 1925*, 65–70, 139–40.

19. Daniel Tobin to Michael Cashal, March 4, 1941, series 1, box 21, IBT Papers.

20. *Constitution and By-laws of the International Brotherhood of Teamsters, Chauffeurs, Stablemen and Helpers of America, Adopted at the Convention Held in Portland, Oregon, September 9th to 13th, Inclusive, 1935* (Indianapolis: n.p., 1935), 20–24.

21. Michael Cashal to Daniel Tobin, March 16, 1935, series 1, box 20, IBT Papers; *International Teamster* 48 (Sept. 1951): 5; *New York Times*, Aug. 21, 1951, 27.

22. *Official Magazine* 32 (April 1935): 2.

23. Daniel Tobin to Members of the General Executive Board and Organizers of the International Union, March 8, 1921, New York Teamster Organization File, series 4, box 7, IBT Papers; Michael Cashal to Daniel Tobin, Feb. 9, 1921, June 3, 1921, series 1, box 18, IBT Papers.

24. Michael Cashal to Daniel Tobin, July 16, 1921, series 1, box 18, IBT Papers.

25. Michael Cashal to Daniel Tobin, Feb. 6, 1922, series 1, box 18, IBT Papers.

26. Michael Cashal to Daniel Tobin, March 10, June 3, 1921, and Daniel Tobin to Michael Cashal, Feb. 11, 1921, June 2, 1921, series 1, box 18, IBT Papers.

27. *International Teamster* 48 (Sept. 1951): 5.

28. Michael Cashal to Daniel Tobin, June 18, 1931, series 1, box 20, IBT Papers.

29. Michael Cashal to Daniel Tobin, March 27, 1933, series 1, box 20, IBT Papers.

30. Ibid.

31. Michael Cashal to Daniel Tobin, July 13, 1935, series 1, box 20, IBT Papers.

32. New York City Department of Markets, *Report Concerning the Live Poultry Industry in Greater New York* (New York: City of New York, 1935), 26–27, 48–88, 120–24; Harold P. Gastwirt, *Fraud, Corruption, and Holiness: The Controversy over the Supervision of Jewish Dietary Practice in New York City, 1881–1940* (Port Washington: National University Publications, Kennikat Press, 1974), 46–53.

33. Trial transcript of *People of the State of New York against Arthur Herbert, alias "Tootsie" Herbert, David Diamondstone, and Harry Frankel* (March 12, 1937), 871–74, in-

dictment 215820, 1937, box 314, Samuel Adler File, Milk Racket, box 2683, District Attorney Files, New York County District Attorney Papers, New York City Municipal Archives (hereafter DA Files); Craig Thompson and Allen Raymond, *Gang Rule in New York: The Story of a Lawless Era* (New York: Dial Press, 1940), 273–77.

34. Michael Cashal to D. J. Tobin, July 13, 1935, series 1, box 20, IBT Papers.

35. *New York Times,* Jan. 9, 1937, 34, July 28, 1937, 14, July 30, 1937, 38, Aug. 1, 1937, 24, Aug. 3, 1937, 7.

36. *Reports of Officers, 1920 IBT Convention,* 166, 175.

37. Daniel Tobin to Michael Cashal, Nov. 23, 1933, series 1, box 20, IBT Papers.

38. Michael Cashal to Daniel Tobin, March 19, 1934, and Daniel Tobin to Michael Cashal, Dec. 31, 1932, Jan. 4, 1933, series 1, box 20, IBT Papers.

39. *New York Times,* April 5, 1938; *New York Sun,* April 5, 1938; *Journal American,* July 13, 1938, July 18, 1938, reel 14, Thomas Dewey Scrapbooks, microfilm ed., University of Rochester, Rochester, New York (hereafter Dewey Scrapbooks).

40. *IBT Constitution and By-Laws, 1935,* 20–21; *Proceedings of the Fourteenth Convention International Brotherhood of Teamsters, Chauffeurs, Stablemen and Helpers of America, Held at Washington, D.C., September 9 to 14, 1940* (Indianapolis: n.p., 1940), 45–51 (fifth day).

41. Probation Report included in testimony in Court of Appeals—New York, *People of the State of New York against Louis Buchalter, Max Silverman, Harold Silverman* (1940), 2107–9; Alan Block, *East Side–West Side: Organizing Crime in New York, 1930–1950* (Swansea, Wales: University College of Cardiff, 1980), 70–73, 176–82, 220–35; *New York Times,* Nov. 21, 1940, 31, Jan. 9, 1941, 23.

42. Michael Cashal to John Gillespie, May 14, 1940, series 1, box 20, IBT Papers.

43. *New York Times,* May 26, 1939, 46; Burton B. Turkus and Sid Feder, *Murder, Inc.: The Story of "the Syndicate"* (New York: Farrar, Straus and Giroux, 1951), 404–7.

44. Michael Cashal to Daniel Tobin, Dec. 10, 1941, series 1, box 21, IBT Papers.

45. Michael Cashal to Daniel Tobin, Dec. 9, 1940, series 1, box 21, IBT Papers; William Green to Daniel Tobin, Dec. 10, 1940, Local 863 Correspondence, series 2, box 89, IBT Papers.

46. Daniel Tobin to Members of Local 863, Feb. 25, 1941, Local 863 Correspondence File, series 2, box 89, IBT Papers.

47. Daniel Tobin to Michael Cashal, March 4, 1941, series 1, box 21, IBT Papers; J. Edgar Hoover to Daniel Tobin, March 19, 1941, Justice Department Correspondence File, series 5, box 19, IBT Papers.

48. Daniel Tobin to M. J. Cashal, Dec. 11, 1940, series 1, box 21, IBT Papers.

49. Michael Cashal to D. J. Tobin, Mar. 10, 1941, Daniel Tobin to M. J. Cashal, April 1, 1941, April 9, 1941, all in series 1, box 21, IBT Papers.

50. See, for example, Tobin's actions in regard to Local 805 in Daniel Tobin to Michael Cashal, April 14, April 21, 1941; and Michael Cashal to Daniel Tobin, April 23, 1941, series 1, box 21, IBT Papers.

51. David Dubinsky to Daniel Tobin, June 21, 1940, series 4, box 5, IBT Papers.

52. *PM,* Sept. 11, 1946, 2–3.

53. *IBT News,* Dec. 8, 1937, 2, 6; *PM,* Sept. 5, 1946, 6; *Daily Worker,* Dec. 14, 1936, 1.

54. Malcolm Johnson, *Crime on the Labor Front* (New York: McGraw-Hill, 1950), 165–67.

55. Daniel Bell, *The End of Ideology: On the Exhaustion of Political Ideals in the Fifties* (Glencoe: The Free Press, 1960), 184–87; Johnson, *Crime on Labor Front,* 104–32, 165–67.

56. *New York Sun,* Dec. 12, 1938, reel 17, Dewey Scrapbooks; New York State Crime Commission, *Public Hearings (No. 5) Conducted by the New York State Crime Commission Pursuant to the Governor's Executive Orders of March 29, 1951 and November 13, 1952* (Albany: New York State, 1952), 4:2608–11.

57. Michael Cashal to John M. Gillespie, Aug. 16, 1940, series 1, box 31, IBT Papers.

58. Thomas Hickey to Daniel Tobin, Nov. 25, 1942, series 2, box 83, IBT Papers.

59. Ibid.

60. Thomas Hickey to Daniel Tobin, Dec. 24, 1942, series 2, box 83, IBT Papers.

61. *New York Times,* July 3, 1963, 27.

62. *Daily News,* Dec. 10, 1938, 6; U.S. Congress, House of Representatives, Subcommittee 3, Committee on the Judiciary, *Injunctions against Illegitimate Labor Practices and Outlawing Racketeering,* House Resolutions 5218, 6752, 6872, 7067, 77th Cong., 2d sess., April 2, 17, 20, 22, 24, 28, and May 1, 1942, 200.

63. U.S. Congress, House of Representatives, Special Subcommittee of the Committee on Education and Labor, *Labor Practices in the Food Industry,* House Resolution 111, 80th Cong., 1st sess., July 11 and 12, 1947, 22; *People v. Nick Elia et al.,* indictment 222450, Samuel Cohen Grand Jury testimony, Feb. 14, 1940, transcript in box 2483, DA Files.

64. George Hurowitz Grand Jury testimony, Nov. 9, 1939, 7, transcript in box 2485, DA Files.

65. William Hochman witness statement and Albert Sadowsky Grand Jury testimony, Nov. 8, 1939, 16–20, transcripts in box 2485, DA Files.

66. *IBT News* (Nov. 1938): 1.

67. *Daily Worker,* Dec. 7, 1938, 4, Dec. 11, 1938, 2, Dec. 15, 1938, 2; news clipping dated Dec. 12, 1938, reel 242, Fiorello La Guardia Papers, microfilm ed., New York Municipal Archive (hereafter La Guardia Subject Files).

68. News clipping dated Dec. 12, 1938; *Daily News,* Dec. 10, 1938, 6, Dec. 12, 1938, 2; *Daily Worker,* Dec. 10, 1938, 3, Dec. 14, 1938, 4; *New York Times,* Dec. 5, 1938, 4, Dec. 11, 1938, 6.

69. *New York Times,* June 17, 1939, 7, Dec. 1, 1939, 1.

70. *New York Times,* Jan. 18, 1941, 17.

71. *IBT News* (April 1940): 6.

72. *IBT News* (July 1940): 4.

73. U.S. Congress, House of Representatives, Subcommittee 3, Committee on the Judiciary, *Injunctions against Illegitimate Labor Practices,* 193.

74. New York State Crime Commission, *Public Hearings,* 4:2631–43, 4:2664–704, 4:2705–45, 4:2792–837, 4:2871–932.

75. Thomas Hickey to Dave Beck, Jan. 12, 1953, Teamster General Correspondence file, MSS 233, David Kaplan Papers, Wisconsin State Historical Society, Madison (hereafter Kaplan Papers).

76. George Hurowitz Grand Jury testimony, Nov. 9, 1939, transcript in box 2485, DA Files.

77. *IBT News* (April 1940): 6.

78. *Daily Worker,* Dec. 13, 1938, 4; *IBT News* (Jan. 1940): 1.

79. U.S. Congress, House of Representatives, Special Subcommittee of the Committee on Education and Labor, *Labor Practices in the Food Industry,* 24.

80. *IBT News* (June 1940), 5.

81. Ibid.

82. *IBT News* (July 1940), 1, 8; *IBT News* (Sept. 1940): 2.

83. U.S. Congress, House of Representatives, Special Subcommittee of the Committee on Education and Labor, *Labor Practices in the Food Industry,* 22, 59.

84. Papa told a congressional committee: "With the kind of organization we have, and the commodity over which we have jurisdiction, you know a strike wouldn't last very long, would it? No, these people would have to capitulate, wouldn't they? Yes. If we wanted a hundred dollars a week, they would have to go along." Ibid., 58.

85. "Statements of Hyman Panich," Nov. 20, 1939, 1–4, complaint 220786, *People of the State of New York against Albert Manganaro,* box 2420, DA Files.

86. *IBT News* (June 1940): 5.

87. *IBT News,* Jan. 15, 1938, 4.

88. *IBT News* (June 1940): 8; "The Boys" to Daniel J. Tobin, Dec. 18, 1950, Kaplan Papers.

89. *New York Times,* Sept. 14, 1946, 1, Oct. 19, 1946, 1, Nov. 22, 1946, 2; *PM,* Sept. 6, 1946, 9.

90. *New York Times,* Sept. 27, 1938, 1, Sept. 28, 1938, 1, Sept. 29, 1938, 1.

91. *New York Times,* Sept. 1, 1946, 1.

92. *Daily Worker,* Dec. 23, 1937, 3.

93. *U.S. v. Local 807 of the International Brotherhood of Teamsters, Chauffeurs, Stablemen and Helpers of America,* U.S. District Court, Southern District of New York, case 102–394 (1940), 2004–6, 2095–96, accession 021-57A–136, FRC Location Number 29455, Federal Records Center, Bayonne, N.J.

94. "Report of the Teamster Strike September 16, 1938 to September 22, 1938," reel 230, La Guardia Subject Files; *New York Times,* Sept. 21, 1938, 12, Sept. 22, 1938, 1.

95. U.S. Congress, House of Representatives, Subcommittee 3, Committee on the Judiciary, *Injunctions against Illegitimate Labor Practices,* 200–201.

96. U.S. Congress, House of Representatives, Special Subcommittee of the Committee on Education and Labor, *Labor Practices in the Food Industry,* 27.

97. Ibid., 53, 75.

98. New York City Department of Markets, *Report on the Live Poultry Industry,* 88.

99. Ibid., 82–3; *New York World Telegraph,* Oct. 16, 1937, reel 12, Dewey Scrapbooks.

100. U.S. Congress, Temporary National Economic Committee, *Investigation of Concentration of Economic Power;* part 7: *Milk Industry, Poultry Industry,* Public Resolution 113, 76th Cong., 1st sess., March 9, 10, 11 and May 1, 2, and 3, 1939 (Washington, D.C.: Government Printing Office, 1939), 2875.

101. U.S. Congress, Temporary National Economic Committee, *Investigation of Concentration of Economic Power,* 2876.

102. Ibid., 2877.

103. *New York Times,* July 20, 1937, 7.

104. *The People of the State of New York against Arthur Herbert, alias "Tootsie" Herbert, David Diamondstone, and Harry Frankel,* March 12, 1937, 881–82; 906–7, DA Files (hereafter *People v. Herbert*).

105. *New York Times,* Nov. 13, 1937, 4, Nov. 14, 1937, 39.

106. *People v. Herbert,* 907.

107. Ibid., 902.

108. *IBT News* (Sept. 1940): 2.

109. Michael Cashal to Daniel Tobin, Dec. 16, 1941, series 1, box 21, IBT Papers; minutes from Executive Board Meeting of Joint Council 15, International Brotherhood of Teamsters, Hotel New Yorker, March 5, 1942, series 2, box 105, IBT Papers; *IBT News* (Feb. 1941): 3.

110. Howard Kimeldorf, *Reds or Rackets? The Making of Radical and Conservative Unions on the Waterfront* (Berkeley: University of California Press, 1988), 75, 55–67.

111. Kimeldorf, *Reds or Rackets?* 80–98, 120–26.

112. Ibid., 37–47, 120–24.

Chapter 7: "It's a Business with Me"

1. Dave Beck, interview by Mark Nackman, Jan. 26, 1978, tape recording, transcript pp. 18–19, Columbia Oral History Project, Columbia University (hereafter Dave Beck Oral History).

2. John Bartlow Martin, "The Making of a Labor Boss," *Saturday Evening Post,* July 4, 1959, 27.

3. Steven Fraser, *Labor Will Rule: Sidney Hillman and the Rise of American Labor* (New York: Macmillan, 1991), 12–25; Robert H. Zieger, *The CIO, 1935–1955* (Chapel Hill: University of North Carolina Press, 1995), 73, 396; Nelson Lichtenstein, *The Most Dangerous Man in Detroit: Walter Reuther and the Fate of American Labor* (New York: Basic Books, 1995), 25–46.

4. Dave Beck Oral History, 175.

5. Ibid., 169–79, 185–86; Donald Garnel, *The Rise of Teamster Power in the West* (Berkeley: University of California Press, 1972), 64–65; John D. McCallum, *Dave Beck* (Mercer Island: The Writing Works, 1978), 46–48, 55–56; Jonathan Dembo, "Dave Beck and the Transportation Revolution in the Pacific," in *Experiences in a Promised Land: Essays in Pacific Northwest History,* ed. G. Thomas Edwards and Carlos A. Schwantes (Seattle: University of Washington Press, 1986), 343–44; A. H. Raskin, "Union Leader—and Big Business Man," *New York Times Magazine,* Nov. 15, 1953, 13; "Teamsters' Dave Beck," *Fortune* 38 (Dec. 1948): 192; Joe Miller, "Dave Beck Comes Out of the West," *The Reporter,* Dec. 22, 1953, 20–21.

6. "Teamsters' Dave Beck," 192–93; Miller, "Dave Beck Comes Out of the West," 20–21; Garnel, *The Rise of Teamster Power in the West,* 64–71; Robert D. Leiter, *The Teamsters Union: A Study of Its Economic Impact* (New York: Bookman Associates, 1957), 48–51; McCallum, *Dave Beck,* 69–70, 84–86; Richard L. Neuberger, *Our Promised Land* (New York: Macmillan, 1938), 193, 197–200; Murray Morgan, *Skid Road: An Informal Portrait of Seattle* (Seattle: University of Washington Press, 1982), 222–24, 247–49, 256–61; Dembo, "Dave Beck and the Transportation Revolution," 344–46, 350; Charles Waite Romney, "The Business of Unionism: Race, Politics, Capitalism, and the West Coast Teamsters, 1940–1952," Ph.D. diss., University of California, Los Angeles, 1996, 23–24.

7. William R. Childs, *Trucking and the Public Interest: The Emergence of Federal Regulation 1914–1940* (Knoxville: University of Tennessee Press, 1985), 40–43, 101–81; Charles

R. Perry, *Deregulation and the Decline of the Unionized Trucking Industry* (Philadelphia: University of Pennsylvania, Industrial Research Unit, 1986), 9–30.

8. Garnel, *The Rise of Teamster Power in the West*, 77–91; Dave Beck Oral History, 40–42; Leiter, *The Teamsters Union*, 50–51; Dembo, "Dave Beck and the Transportation Revolution," 346–48.

9. Garnel, *The Rise of Teamster Power in the West*, 81–85; Leiter, *The Teamsters Union*, 48–51.

10. Dave Beck Oral History, 80–81.

11. Garnel, *The Rise of Teamster Power in the West*, 77–91; Romney, "The Business of Unionism," 24–28; Dembo, "Dave Beck and the Transportation Revolution," 346–49.

12. Garnel, *The Rise of Teamster Power in the West*, 102, 160–68.

13. Ibid., 169–200; Leiter, *The Teamsters Union*, 50–51; "Teamster's Dave Beck," 194; Dave Beck Oral History, 41–47; Dembo, "Dave Beck and the Transportation Revolution," 349.

14. *Proceedings of the Fourteenth Convention International Brotherhood of Teamsters, Chauffeurs, Stablemen and Helpers of America, Held at Washington, D.C., September 9 to 14, 1940, Reports of Officers* (Indianapolis: n.p., 1940), 5–6, 80.

15. Romney, "The Business of Unionism," 202–3, 220–21; Dave Beck Oral History, 147–50; *International Teamster* 41 (March 1944): 24–25.

16. *International Teamster* 43 (April 1946): 22.

17. *International Teamster* 43 (May 1946): 9.

18. Thomas Flynn to Dave Beck, Nov. 2, 1945, Dave Beck to Thomas Flynn, Nov. 9, 1945, Patrick Gorman to Dave Beck, Oct. 29, 1945, Dave Beck to Patrick Gorman, Nov. 9, 1945, all in series 1, box 3, International Brotherhood of Teamsters, Chauffeurs, Warehousemen and Helpers of America, Papers, 1904–52, MSS 9, Wisconsin State Historical Society, Madison (hereafter IBT Papers); Leiter, *The Teamsters Union*, 95–96.

19. Dave Beck Oral History, 147–50; Garnel, *The Rise of Teamster Power in the West*, 87–88. The quotation is from Miller, "Dave Beck Comes Out of the West," 21.

20. Miller, "Dave Beck Comes Out of the West," 21; Leiter, *The Teamsters Union*, 21, 51.

21. Garnel, *The Rise of Teamster Power in the West*, 200; Dave Beck Oral History, 74–77.

22. Garnel, *The Rise of Teamster Power in the West*, 282–92; Paul Jacobs, *The State of the Unions* (New York: Atheneum, 1963), 11–13, 294–95; Ralph C. James and Estelle Dinnerstein James, *Hoffa and the Teamsters: A Study of Union Power* (New York: D. Van Nostrand, 1965), 16, 89–102; Farrell Dobbs, *Teamster Power* (New York: Monad Press, 1973), passim; Farrell Dobbs, *Teamster Politics* (New York: Monad Press, 1975), 241–49; Farrell Dobbs, *Teamster Bureaucracy* (New York: Monad Press, 1977), 73–97; Arthur A. Sloane, *Hoffa* (Cambridge: MIT Press, 1991), 18–22.

23. Dobbs, *Teamster Power*, 183, 242–50; Dobbs, *Teamster Bureaucracy*, 40–55; James and James, *Hoffa and the Teamsters*, 95–96.

24. McCallum, *Dave Beck*, 31.

25. "Playboy Interview: Jimmy Hoffa," *Playboy* (Nov. 1963): 35.

26. Sloane, *Hoffa*, 3–6; Martin, "The Making of a Labor Boss," 54; Thaddeus Russell, "Restore Teamster Power: Democracy, Militancy, and the IBT," presented at the annual meeting of the American Historical Association, Pacific Coast Branch, Aug. 1998; James R. Hoffa as told to Oscar Fraley, *Hoffa: The Real Story* (New York: Stein and Day, 1975), 28–29.

27. Sloane, *Hoffa*, 6–8; Martin, "The Making of a Labor Boss," 54; Russell, "Restore Teamster Power"; Hoffa as told to Fraley, *Hoffa: The Real Story*, 30–31.

28. Dan E. Moldea, *The Hoffa Wars: Teamsters, Rebels, Politicians, and the Mob* (New York: Charter Books, 1978), 23.

29. Hoffa as told to Fraley, *Hoffa: The Real Story*, 31–33; James and James, *Hoffa and the Teamsters*, 69–70; Martin, "The Making of a Labor Boss," 54; Sloane, *Hoffa*, 4–10; Russell, "Restore Teamster Power."

30. James and James, *Hoffa and the Teamsters*, 70–86; Russell, "Restore Teamster Power"; Sloane, *Hoffa*, 14–18, 35–36; U.S. Congress, House of Representatives, Special Subcommittee of the Committee on Education and Labor, *Investigation of Welfare Funds and Racketeering*, 83rd Cong., 1st sess., Nov. 23, 24, 25, and 27, 1953 (Washington, D.C.: Government Printing Office, 1954), 479–80.

31. James and James, *Hoffa and the Teamsters*, 82.

32. Sloane, *Hoffa*, 21–22, 36–38; James and James, *Hoffa and the Teamsters*, 117–27.

33. Dave Beck Oral History, 73–74; Martin, "The Making of a Labor Boss," 54; Irwin Ross, "Millionaire Labor Boss," *The Progressive* 18 (Sept. 1954): 22; Jacobs, *The State of the Unions*, 15–19, Sloane, *Hoffa*, 36–40; Leiter, *The Teamsters Union*, 53; Sam Romer, *The International Brotherhood of Teamsters: Its Government and Structure* (New York: John Wiley and Sons, 1962), 35–36; wire service copy, seven-part profile on Jimmy Hoffa by Clark Mollenhoff, Nov. 7, 1955, Nov. 8, 1955, Nov. 10, 1955, Nov. 11, 1955, Nov. 14, 1955, Nov. 22, 1955, all in folder 10, box 10, Clark Mollenhoff Papers, Wisconsin State Historical Society, Madison (hereafter Mollenhoff Papers, Wisconsin); "Beck's Big Wheels," *Fortune* 48 (Aug. 1953): 62, 64; Lester Velie, "Riddle in the Middle of America's Most Powerful Union," *Reader's Digest* 67 (Dec. 1955): 91–96.

34. Dave Beck to Daniel Tobin, May 9, 1949, series 1, box 3, IBT Papers.

35. Dave Beck, "The Challenge of Organization," *International Teamster* 50 (Oct. 1953): 2–3; Garnel, *The Rise of Teamster Power in the West*, 185–86.

36. Jacobs, *The State of the Unions*, 38.

37. Romer, *The International Brotherhood of Teamsters*, 35, 141.

38. Dave Beck to Secretaries of All Locals, and Joint Councils of Central States Area, April 11, 1953, Dave Beck to All Trade Division Officers, Alois Mueller, June 2, 1953, and Harold Gibbons to Secretary Treasurers of All Local Unions, June 11, 1953, all in box 8, folder 8, International Brotherhood of Teamsters, Chauffeurs, Warehousemen, and Helpers Local 695 (Madison) Records, 1932–66, MSS 434, State Historical Society of Wisconsin, Madison (hereafter Local 695 Papers); Garnel, *The Rise of Teamster Power in the West*, 174–82; Romer, *The International Brotherhood of Teamsters*, 84–96; Leiter, *The Teamsters Union*, 69–73; Miles E. Hoffman, *International Brotherhood of Teamsters, Chauffeurs, Warehousemen and Helpers of America: Development, Structure, Functions* (Philadelphia: Temple University, School of Business Administration, 1964), 9–11; *Proceedings of the Fifteenth Convention, International Brotherhood of Teamsters, Chauffeurs, Warehousemen and Helpers of America, Held at San Francisco, California, August 11 to 15, 1947* (Indianapolis: n.p., 1947), 293–94, 315–16; *Proceedings of the Sixteenth Convention, International Brotherhood of Teamsters, Chauffeurs, Warehousemen and Helpers of America, October 13–17, [1952], Los Angeles, Calif.* (n.p., 1952), 134–35, 314–15; *Proceedings of the Seventeenth [1957] Convention, International Brotherhood of Teamsters, Chauffeurs, Warehousemen and Help-*

ers of America, Miami Beach, Florida (Washington, D.C.: n.p., 1957), 388–98; *International Teamster* 45 (March 1948): 31; Beck, "The Challenge of Organization."

39. Garnel, *The Rise of Teamster Power in the West,* 174–83; Romer, *The International Brotherhood of Teamsters,* 89. For examples of this process of professionalization at work in terms of comparison and common identity, see, for example, Minutes of Meeting of Southern Conference of Teamsters, Held in New Orleans, Louisiana, New Orleans Hotel, November 20–21, 1944, series 2C, box 114, IBT Papers, and Minutes of Meeting of Southern Conference of Teamsters, Held in Memphis, Tennessee, Peabody Hotel, March 19–20, 1945, series 2C, box 115, IBT Papers. For examples of the new oversight role, see, R. E. Woodall to Thomas E. Flynn, Feb. 20, 1946, series 2C, box 115, IBT Papers, and Thomas Flynn to Henry G. White, Oct. 3, 1944, Local 552 Correspondence File, series 2A, box 46, IBT Papers; G. A. Kelly to Harold Gibbons, June 16, 1953, folder 8, box 8, Local 695 Papers.

40. Sloane, *Hoffa,* 19–24, 193–215, 288–92; James and James, *Hoffa and the Teamsters,* 89–101, 117–40; Hoffman, *International Brotherhood of Teamsters,* 20–21; Leiter, *The Teamsters Union,* 172–73; Romer, *The International Brotherhood of Teamsters,* 37–38, 85–86, 91.

41. Leiter, *The Teamsters Union,* 110; Hoffman, *International Brotherhood of Teamsters,* 21–22.

42. *Proceedings, IBT Convention,* [1952], 191–202; Romney, "The Business of Unionism," 253–67; Leiter, *The Teamsters Union,* 124–25; James and James, *Hoffa and the Teamsters,* 165–66, 194–97; Sloane, *Hoffa,* 208–10.

43. U.S. Congress, Senate, Select Committee on Improper Activities in the Labor or Management Field, *Investigation of Improper Activities in the Labor or Management Field,* 85th Cong., 1st sess., July 1, 6, 7, 8, and 9, 1959 (Washington, D.C.: Government Printing Office, 1959), part 55, 1993 (hereafter McClellan Committee, *Hearings*); James and James, *Hoffa and the Teamsters,* 167–85; Clyde Summers, "Teamster Joint Grievance Committees: Grievance Disposal without Adjudication," reprinted from, *The Proceedings of the Thirty-seventh Annual Meeting of the National Academy of Arbitrators* (Washington, D.C.: Bureau of National Affairs, 1985).

44. *Proceedings, IBT Convention,* [1952], 201.

45. Garnel, *The Rise of Teamster Power in the West,* 182.

46. Jimmy Hoffa on *Tomorrow with Tom Snyder,* NBC-TV, Feb. 25, 1975, tape B41551, Library Archives, the Museum of Television and Radio, New York.

47. Dave Beck Oral History, 129–30, 135–39; Garnel, *The Rise of Teamster Power in the West,* 164–67.

48. Newspaper report read into record in U.S. Congress, House of Representatives, Special Subcommittees of the Committee on Government Operations and Education and Labor, *Investigation of Racketeering,* 83d Cong., 1st sess., June 8, 11, 12, and 13, 1953 (Washington, D.C.: Government Printing Office, 1954), 76–77.

49. Romer, *The International Brotherhood of Teamsters,* 114–15. By 1955 almost 12 percent of all IBT locals were in trusteeship (105 out of 897). Jacobs, *The State of the Unions,* 15.

50. *Proceedings, IBT Convention,* [1957], 20, 43, 489–90, 506–7; Romer, *The International Brotherhood of Teamsters,* 3–4, 35; Leiter, *The Teamsters Union,* 39.

51. "A New Era Begins at Ward's," *International Teamster* 52:5 (May 1955): 6–7, 32; Leiter, *The Teamsters Union,* 176–79.

52. Lon W. Smith, "An Experiment in Trade Union Democracy: Harold Gibbons and the Formation of Teamsters Local 688, 1937–1957," Ph.D. diss., Illinois State University, 1993, 130–34.

53. McClellan Committee, *Hearings, Part 41*, 15641–42.

54. The IBT was bucking a trend that emerged by the late 1950s as most unions saw their membership declining. Membership in organized labor peaked in 1956 and 1957 and then began falling. Among the ten largest unions in the country, the Teamsters' growth was even more outstanding. From 1953 to 1962 the UAW lost 343,000 members, the Steel Workers fell by 222,000, and the Carpenters declined by 152,000. The Teamsters, however, gained 167,000 members. Only the IBEW came close to matching them, gaining 141,000 members in the same period. Leo Troy, *Trade Union Membership, 1897–1962* (New York: National Bureau of Economic Research, 1965), 4–7.

55. Raskin, "Union Leader—and Big Business Man," 13.

56. Romney, "The Business of Unionism," 92, 194–95, 245; Dembo, "Dave Beck and the Transportation Revolution," 350–51; Garnel, *The Rise of Teamster Power in the West*, 76–77; Romer, *The International Brotherhood of Teamsters*, 100; Miller, "Dave Beck Comes Out of the West,"21; "Teamsters' Dave Beck," *Fortune* 38 (Dec. 1948): 197; Raskin, "Union Leader—and Big Business Man," 13, 30; Morgan, *Skid Road*, 249–60; Neuberger, *Our Promised Land*, 194–200. The quote is from Notes on Interview with Dave Kaplan, 25 October 1948, box 15, Daniel Bell Papers, Tamiment Library, New York University, New York.

57. Martin, "The Making of a Labor Boss," 53.

58. Dudley W. Buffa, *Union Power and American Democracy: The UAW and the Democratic Party, 1935–1972* (Ann Arbor: University of Michigan Press, 1984), 16–19; U.S. Congress, House of Representatives, Special Subcommittees of the Committee on Government Operations and Education and Labor, *Investigation of Racketeering*, 314–15; Sloane, *Hoffa*, 45–47; Wire service copy, profile of Hoffa's political role in Michigan politics, by Clark Mollenhoff, Nov. 8, 1955, folder 2, box 52, Mollenhoff Papers, Wisconsin.

59. Romer, *The International Brotherhood of Teamsters*, 137–38.

60. U.S. Congress, Senate, Subcommittee to Investigate the Administration of the Internal Security Act and Other Internal Security Laws of the Committee on the Judiciary, *Relationship between Teamsters Union and Mine, Mill and Smelter Workers*, 87th Cong., 1st sess., October 13, 1961 (Washington, D.C.: Government Printing Office, 1962), 29.

61. Vicki L. Ruiz, *Cannery Women, Cannery Lives: Mexican Women, Unionization, and the California Food Processing Industry, 1930–1950* (Albuquerque: University of New Mexico Press, 1987); Waite, "Business of Unionism," 194–238.

62. Dobbs, *Teamster Bureaucracy*, 73–263; Moldea, *The Hoffa Wars*, 32–33; Sloane, *Hoffa*, 28–30; James and James, *Hoffa and the Teamsters*, 102–11; and Jacobs, *The State of the Unions*, 4, 12–13.

63. Hoffman, *International Brotherhood of Teamsters*, 37.

64. J. A. Swearingen to Thomas Flynn, Jan. 21, 1944, Local 667 Correspondence File, series 2A, box 64, IBT Papers.

65. Dexter Lewis to Thomas Flynn, Feb. 27, 1945, Local 667 Correspondence File, series 2A, box 64, IBT Papers.

66. In 1942 Tobin claimed, "We have a few local unions—not very many—consisting

entirely of Negroes. The Negroes want this condition, but gradually we are trying to overcome this and we have succeeded substantially." "No Color Line in Teamsters Union," *International Teamster* 40 (Dec. 1942): 10. Evidence of the national union's efforts in this regard, and the apparent resistance of both black and white members, can be found in the following letters: Leo B. Carter to John A. Bassemier, Aug. 19, 1946, Leo B. Carter to Thomas Flynn, Aug. 2, 1946, Leo B. Carter to Thomas Flynn, Aug. 19, 1946, and Albert Boyer to Thomas Flynn, Oct. 8, 1946, all in series 2A, box 34, IBT Papers.

67. "JC58: The South Texas Story," *International Teamster* 51 (Feb. 1954): 8.

68. In 1966 Harold Gibbons, a top aide of Hoffa, asserted that after Hoffa had become president in 1957 he moved to end the existence of the remaining all-black, "Jim Crow" locals in the South. Richard D. Leone, *The Negro in the Trucking Industry* (Philadelphia: Industrial Research Unit, Department of Industry, Wharton School of Finance and Commerce, University of Pennsylvania, 1970), 65.

69. Romney, "The Business of Unionism," 97–194.

70. "Letter from General President Dave Beck," *International Teamster* 52 (June 1955): 3.

71. Stephen J. Whitfield, *A Death in the Delta: The Story of Emmett Till* (Baltimore: Johns Hopkins University Press, 1998), 71–74.

72. Leone, *The Negro in the Trucking Industry,* 65; James and James, *Hoffa and the Teamsters,* 277. The donation came in the wake of the murder of Viola Liuzzo, wife of a Detroit Teamster official, who had volunteered to help in the demonstrations in Selma. *New York Times,* March 27, 1965, 10.

73. Magazine scrapbook, John L. McClellan Papers, Ouachita Baptist University, Arkadelphia, Ark. (hereafter McClellan Papers).

74. Leone, *The Negro in the Trucking Industry,* 1–2, 33–67.

75. Ibid., 65, 88.

76. Kevin Boyle, "'There Are No Union Sorrows That the Union Can't Heal': The Struggle for Racial Equality in the United Automobile Workers, 1940–1960," *Labor History* 36 (Winter 1995): 5–23.

77. Hoffman, *International Brotherhood of Teamsters,* 3.

78. "What Are Good Unions Made Of?" *International Teamster* 52 (July 1955): 12–15.

79. "Southern Conference Is Praised," *International Teamster* 43 (April 1946): 2–3.

80. J. R. Braddock, Jr., to Thomas E. Flynn, March 6, 1943, Local 613 Correspondence File, series 2A, box 55, IBT Papers.

81. Leah Vosko and David Witwer, "'Not a Man's Union': Women Teamsters in the United States during the 1940s and 1950s," *Journal of Women's History* 13 (Autumn 2001): 177–84.

82. Dorothy Sue Cobble, "Recapturing Working-Class Feminism: Union Women in the Postwar Era," in *Not June Cleaver: Women and Gender in Postwar America, 1945–1960,* ed. Joanne Meyerowitz (Philadelphia: Temple University Press, 1994), 58.

83. *Proceedings, IBT Convention, 1947,* 226.

84. U.S. Congress, Senate, Subcommittee on Domestic Land and Water Transportation of the Committee on Interstate and Foreign Commerce, *Study of Domestic Land and Water Transportation,* 81st Cong., 2d sess., April 4, 1950 (Washington, D.C.: Government Printing Office, 1950), 1213.

85. *Chicago Tribune*, May 20, 1992, sec. 5, 3.

86. *The Name Is Hoffa* (St. Louis: Teamsters Joint Council 13, 1956), 12.

87. M. Murphy, "Over the Road Legal," *New Yorker*, Nov. 19, 1949, 78, 83–84.

88. Murphy, "Over the Road Legal," 82–93.

89. Studs Terkel, *Working* (New York: Avon Books, 1974), 281–82, 284.

90. Testimony of J. W. Dildine in *U.S. v. Local 560 of the International Brotherhood of Teamsters*, U.S. District Court, District of New Jersey, civil no. 82–689 (April 11, 1983), 4960–61, 4970–71.

91. *Proceedings of the Joint Convention of the Team Drivers' International Union and the Teamsters National Union and Proceedings of the Convention of the International Brotherhood of Teamsters* (Indianapolis: Cheltenham Press, 1903), 44.

92. Terkel, *Working*, 286–87.

93. "Slurs on Truck Drivers Resented," *International Teamster* 44 (Dec. 1946): 22–23.

94. U.S. Bureau of Labor Statistics, *Monthly Labor Review* 70 (Jan. 1950): 36–39.

95. U.S. Department of Labor, Bureau of Labor Statistics, *Union Wages and Hours: Local Truckdrivers and Helpers, July 1, 1975*, bulletin 1917 (Washington, D.C.: Government Printing Office, 1976), 5.

96. U.S. Bureau of the Census, *U.S. Census of Population: 1950*, vol. 4: *Special Reports, Part 1, Chapter D, Industrial Characteristics* (Washington, D.C.: Government Printing Office, 1955), 1D-66 to 1D-67.

97. Leiter, *The Teamsters Union*, 183; James and James, *Hoffa and the Teamsters*, 361–64.

98. Leiter, *The Teamsters Union*, 175.

99. Alfred Maund, "Peons on Wheels: The Long Haul Trucker," *The Nation*, Nov. 14, 1953, 393–94; U.S. Congress, Senate, Subcommittee on Domestic Land and Water Transportation of the Committee on Interstate and Foreign Commerce, *Study of Domestic Land and Water Transportation*, 1242–43.

100. James Higgins, "Why We Don't Act So Polite," *New Republic*, July 21, 1947, 19.

101. Al Weiss, "National Survey of Teamster Progress: Wages, Hours, and Working Conditions," *International Teamster* 52 (Nov. 1955): 6–12.

102. For an example of the importance members attached to this provision, see Elleers Guiss to John L. McClellan, Feb. 6, 1957, Opinion File folder Indiana, file 21, drawer E, McClellan Papers.

103. "Suggestions for Union Stewards and Shop Committee Chairmans, and Committee Members," n.d., folder 13, box 14, Local 695 Papers.

104. Minutes of shop meeting held at Steffke Freight Company, Beaver Dam, Wis., Jan. 3, 1953, Nov. 7, 1953, and Dec. 12, 1953, and Monthly Craft Meeting Report, Beaver Dam, Nov. 11, 1954, all in folder 6, box 54, Local 695 Papers.

105. Arnold M. Rose, *Union Solidarity: The Internal Cohesion of a Labor Union* (Minneapolis: University of Minnesota Press, 1952), 62.

106. "One Taxi Driver's Success Story," *International Teamster* 53:2 (February 1956): 16–17.

107. Earl A. Quigley, Otto H. Frobe, and Earl D. Weller to Westbrook Pegler, July 15, 1947, box 99, (James) Westbrook Pegler Papers, 1908–69, Herbert Hoover Presidential Library, West Branch, Iowa.

108. Dan La Botz, *Rank and File Rebellion: Teamsters for a Democratic Union* (New York:

Verso Press, 1990), 114–39; Romney, "The Business of Unionism," 1–11, 315–21; Brill, *The Teamsters*, 392–99; Samuel R. Friedman, *Teamster Rank and File: Power, Bureaucracy, and Rebellion at Work and in a Union* (New York: Columbia University Press, 1982), 2–33.

Chapter 8: The Revelations of the McClellan Committee

1. Robert F. Kennedy, *The Enemy Within* (New York: Harper and Brothers, 1960), 160–61.

2. George H. Gallup, *The Gallup Poll: Public Opinion, 1935–1971*, vol. 3: *1959–1971* (New York: Random House, 1972), 1595.

3. U.S. Senate, Select Committee on Improper Activities in the Labor or Management Field, *Index to Hearings: Part 1* (Washington, D.C.: Government Printing Office, 1960), 3–5.

4. John Hutchinson, *The Imperfect Union: A History of Corruption in American Trade Unions* (New York: E. P. Dutton, 1970), 141–69; Clark Mollenhoff, *Tentacles of Power: The Story of Jimmy Hoffa* (Cleveland: World Publishing, 1965), 10–121; Anthony V. Baltakis, "Agendas of Investigation: The McClellan Committee, 1957–1958," Ph.D. diss., University of Akron, 1997, 10–20.

5. A. H. Raskin, "Union Leader—and Big Business Man," *New York Times Magazine,* Nov. 15, 1953, 13, 30, 32, 34; Irwin Ross, "Millionaire Labor Boss," *The Progressive* 18 (Sept. 1954): 19–22; Joe Miller, "Dave Beck Comes Out of the West," *The Reporter,* Dec. 22, 1953, 20–23; Mollenhoff, *Tentacles of Power,* 165.

6. U.S. Congress, Senate, *Interim Report of the Select Committee on Improper Activities in the Labor or Management Field Pursuant to S. Res. 74 and 221 85th Congress together with Individual Views,* 85th Cong., 2d sess., Report 1417, March 24, 1958 (Washington, D.C.: Government Printing Office, 1958), 60–86 (hereafter McClellen Committee, *Interim Report*); Mollenhoff, *Tentacles of Power,* 77–78, 88–89, 98–100, 104–5; *New York Times,* Feb. 5, 1969, 45; John D. McCallum, *Dave Beck* (Mercer Island: The Writing Works, 1978), 110–11, 121–23, 126.

7. U.S. Congress, Senate, Select Committee on Improper Activities in the Labor or Management Field, *Investigation of Improper Activities in the Labor or Management Field,* 85th Cong., 1st sess., July 1, 6, 7, 8, and 9, 1959 (Washington, D.C.: Government Printing Office, 1959), 1993 (hereafter McClellan Committee, *Hearings*), part 5, 15994–619; McClellan Committee, *Interim Report,* no. 1417, 60–87.

8. *New York Times,* Jan. 23, 1957, 1, Feb. 3, 1957, 9, March 29, 1957, 10, March 30, 1957, 1; Archie Robinson, *George Meany and His Times: A Biography* (New York: Simon and Schuster, 1981), 191–96; Joseph C. Goulden, *Meany* (New York: Atheneum, 1972), 231–40; Hutchinson, *The Imperfect Union,* 287–334, 431–54; Baltakis, "Agendas of Investigation," 129–42.

9. *New York Times,* March 30, 1957, 40, April 4, 1957, 17, 25, May 5, 1957, 62, May 12, 1957, 1, 55, May 15, 1957, 27, May 18, 1957, 10, May 19, 1957, 76, May 23, 1957, 26, May 26, 1957, 1, 47.

10. John Bartlow Martin, "The Struggle to Get Hoffa: Part One: Kennedy Sets a Snare," *Saturday Evening Post,* June 27, 1959, 93–94.

11. Kennedy, *The Enemy Within,* 44–48, 61–62; Mollenhoff, *Tentacles of Power,* 152–56.

12. John Bartlow Martin, "The Labor Boss Leaves a Baffling Trail," *Saturday Evening Post*, July 11, 1959, 27; Walter Sheridan, *The Rise and Fall of Jimmy Hoffa* (New York: Saturday Review Press, 1972), 32–36.

13. Mollenhoff, *Tentacles of Power*, 39; James and James, *Hoffa and the Teamsters*, 62–64; Martin, "The Labor Boss Leaves a Baffling Trail," 81–82; John Bartlow Martin, "The Making of a Labor Boss," *Saturday Evening Post*, July 4, 1959, 53 (quotation); Dan E. Moldea, *The Hoffa Wars: Teamsters, Rebels, Politicians, and the Mob* (New York: Charter Books, 1978), 143.

14. A. H. Raskin, "Reuther vs. Hoffa," *New York Times Magazine*, Sept. 22, 1957, 71; Paul Jacobs, *The State of the Unions* (New York: Atheneum, 1963), 64; Martin, "The Making of a Labor Boss," 54.

15. John Bartlow Martin, "Hoffa Takes the Stand," *Saturday Evening Post*, July 18, 1959, 103.

16. McClellan Committee, *Hearings, Part 13*, 4938–51, 4966–71, 5073–75; McClellan Committee, *Interim Report*, no. 1417, 229–33.

17. McClellan Committee, *Hearings, Part 13*, 4990–93, 5008–12; McClellan Committee, *Interim Report*, no. 1417, 224–27.

18. McClellan Committee, *Hearings, Part 13*, 5058–59; McClellan Committee, *Interim Report*, no. 1417, 237–39; Kennedy, *The Enemy Within*, 128–31.

19. McClellan Committee, *Hearings, Part 13*, 4951.

20. Ibid., 5009, 5011 (quotation), 5058–59.

21. *Tenth Annual Report of the Temporary Commission of Investigation of the State of New York to the Governor and the Legislature of the State of New York* (Albany: State of New York, March 1968), 52; McClellan Committee, *Interim Report*, no. 1417, 162–64; *New York Times*, Jan. 16, 1979, B6; Peter Maas, *The Valachi Papers* (New York: G. P. Putnam's Sons, 1968), 170–71.

22. McClellan Committee, *Interim Report*, no. 1417, 162–221; McClellan, *Hearings: Part 12*, 4600–617; McClellan Committee, *Hearings: Part 10*, 3603–23, 3757–65, 3770–76, 3781–837.

23. McClellan Committee, *Interim Report*, no. 1417, 162–221; Moldea, *The Hoffa Wars*, 25–39; Arthur A. Sloane, *Hoffa* (Cambridge: MIT Press, 1991), 86–88.

24. The friendship claim is in "Playboy Interview: Jimmy Hoffa," *Playboy* (Nov. 1963): 36. For Dioguardia's alleged involvement in the Riesel attack, see *New York Times*, April 6, 1956, 1, Aug. 18, 1956, 1, Aug. 29, 1956, 1, May 21, 1957, 1.

25. McClellan Committee, *Hearings: Part 13*, 5241; U.S. Senate, Permanent Subcommittee on Investigations, *James R. Hoffa and Continued Underworld Control of New York Teamster Local 239*, 87th Cong., 2d sess., Senate Report 1784 (Washington, D.C.: Government Printing Office, 1962), 2–4.

26. U.S. Senate, Permanent Subcommittee on Investigations, *James R. Hoffa and Continued Underworld Control of New York Teamster Local 239*, 5–15.

27. McClellan Committee, *Hearings, Part 49*, 17749–57; *Chicago Tribune*, Sept. 5, 1954, 1.

28. U.S. Congress, Senate, Permanent Subcommittee on Investigations, *Organized Crime and Illicit Traffic in Narcotics: Hearings, Part 2*, 88th Cong., 1st sess., Oct. 10, 11, 15, and 16, 1963 (Washington, D.C.: Government Printing Office, 1963), 508–11.

29. *Chicago Tribune,* Sept. 3, 1954, 2.

30. For the union's inactivity, see *Chicago Tribune,* Sept. 1, 1954, 2, and *Chicago Tribune,* March 29, 1962, both in Scrapbook, vol. 10, Seafarers International Union Archives, Harry Lundberg School for Seamanship, Piney Point, Md. (hereafter SIU Scrapbook). For Glimco and extortion, see *Chicago Tribune,* Sept. 4, 1954, 1.

31. U.S. Congress, Senate, Select Committee on Improper Activities in the Labor or Management Field, *Final Report, Part 3,* 86th Cong., 2d sess., Senate Report 1139, Feb. 26, 1960 (Washington, D.C.: Government Printing Office, 1960), 514–30, 548–50, 564–69 (hereafter McClellen Committee, *Final Report*).

32. *Chicago Tribune,* July 8, 1961, 5, July 11, 1961, 15, July 13, 1961, 10, July 15, 1961, 4, July 17, 1961, 5, July 18, 1961, 3, July 19, 1961, 1.

33. Sloane, *Hoffa,* 186.

34. James, *Hoffa and the Teamsters,* 64.

35. Jacobs, *The State of the Unions,* 48.

36. Firsthand accounts include the testimony of Angelo Lonardo, former underboss of the Cleveland Mafia, and Vincent Cafaro, a member of the Genovese crime family in New York City, in U.S. Senate, Permanent Subcommittee on Investigations, *Organized Crime: Twenty-five Years after Valachi,* 100th Cong., 2d sess., April 11, 15, 21, 22, 29, 1988 (Washington, D.C.: Government Printing Office, 1988), 86–94, 223–25, 529–32; Maas, *The Valachi Papers,* 95–99; testimony of James Aladena Fratianno, in *U.S. v. Carl Angelo DeLuna et al.,* U.S. District Court for the Western District of Missouri, Western Division, case 83-00124-01/15-CR-W-8, 8–15, vol. 16 (Oct. 22, 1985); and *U.S. v. Anthony Salerno et al.,* U.S. District Court, Southern District of New York, case 86 CR 245, May 14, 1987, 3182–89. Secondary material includes Humbert S. Nelli, *The Business of Crime: Italians and Syndicate Crime in the United States* (New York: Oxford University Press, 1976), 3–23, 29–140, 254–57; Stephen Fox, *Blood and Power: Organized Crime in Twentieth Century America* (New York: Penguin Books, 1989), 11–76; Howard Abadinsky, *The Mafia in America: An Oral History* (New York: Praeger, 1981), 11–28; Robert T. Anderson, "From Mafia to Cosa Nostra," *American Journal of Sociology* 71 (Nov. 1965): 302–10; Annelise Graebner Anderson, *The Business of Organized Crime: A Cosa Nostra Family* (Stanford: Hoover Institution Press, 1979), 15–17, 34–40; and Howard Abadinsky, *Organized Crime* (Chicago: Nelson-Hall Publishers, 1994), 129–212.

37. For firsthand accounts, see U.S. Senate, Permanent Subcommittee on Investigations, *Organized Crime: Twenty-five Years after Valachi,* 223–61, 529–38; Fratianno in *U.S. v. Anthony Salerno et al.,* 3177–283; Lonardo in *U.S. v. Anthony Salerno et al.,* 382–476; Abadinsky, *The Mafia in America,* 52–114; Joseph Bonanno with Sergio Lalli, *A Man of Honor: The Autobiography of Joseph Bonanno* (New York: Simon and Schuster, 1983), 151–58; Maas, *The Valachi Papers,* passim; and Ovid Demaris, *The Last Mafioso: The Treacherous World of Jimmy Fratianno* (New York: Times Books, 1980), passim. See also Anderson, *The Business of Organized Crime,* 35–46, 74–102; Howard Abadinsky, "The McDonald's-ization of the Mafia," in *Organized Crime in America: Concepts and Controversies,* ed. Timothy S. Bynum (Monsey: Willow Tree Press, 1987), 43–54; Mark H. Haller, "Illegal Enterprise: A Theoretical and Historical Interpretation," *Criminology* 28 (May 1990): 215–29; and Abadinsky, *Organized Crime,* 28–40.

38. U.S. Senate, Permanent Subcommittee on Investigations, *Organized Crime: Twenty-*

five Years after Valachi, 88–90, 250–53, 311–15; Lonardo testimony in *U.S. v. Anthony Salerno et al.,* 436–98; deposition of Jimmy Fratianno in *U.S. v. International Brotherhood of Teamsters, Chauffeurs, Warehousemen and Helpers of America, AFL-CIO et al.,* U.S. District Court, Southern District of New York, case 88 CV 4486 (Jan. 6, 1989), 104–6, 132–37, 140–56, 192–203; Anderson, *The Business of Organized Crime,* 16–33; Bonanno, *A Man of Honor,* 147–216; Abadinsky, *Organized Crime,* 37–47.

39. The standard sources for this account include Moldea, *The Hoffa Wars,* 25–39, and Sloane, *Hoffa,* 29–34. A more dramatic account that dates the beginning of the relationship in the early 1930s is in Lester Velie, *Desperate Bargain: Why Jimmy Hoffa Had to Die* (New York: Reader's Digest Press, 1977), 3–5. By contrast, Steven Brill places the beginnings of Hoffa's mob involvement in 1949, when he became familiar with Paul Dorfman, a close associate of Anthony Accordo, one of the leaders of the Chicago Outfit. Steven Brill, *The Teamsters* (New York: Simon and Schuster, 1978), 202–3.

40. Moldea, *The Hoffa Wars,* 37.

41. U.S. Congress, Senate, Select Committee on Improper Activities in the Labor or Management Field, *Second Interim Report,* 86th Cong., 1st sess., Senate Report 621 (Washington D.C.: Government Printing Office, 1959), 677; Victor G. Reuther, *The Brothers Reuther and the Story of the UAW: A Memoir by Victor G. Reuther* (Boston: Houghton Mifflin, 1976), 269–303; Nelson Lichtenstein, *The Most Dangerous Man in Detroit: Walter Reuther and the Fate of American Labor* (New York: Basic Books, 1995), 271–76.

42. Quoted in Sloane, *Hoffa,* 33.

43. *Detroit Free Press,* Jan. 12, 1969, 3A, Sept. 17, 1972, 19a; *Detroit News,* June 16, 1969, 1b; U.S. Senate, Permanent Subcommittee on Investigations, *Organized Crime and Illicit Traffic in Narcotics,* 38–41.

44. *Detroit News,* Aug. 2, 1976, 1.

45. The FBI placed an illegal bug in Giacalone's office at a company he owned, Home Juice Co. The bug was in place from 1961 to 1964. In addition, the FBI placed a bug in the apartment of Sylvia Paris, with whom Giacalone was having an affair. As with other such illegal devices placed by the FBI at this time, the goal was to collect intelligence about organized crime affairs. Because it was gathered illegally, none of the information could be officially used in court. The FBI has never chosen to officially release this material, although transcripts have found their way into the hands of journalists over the years, and retired FBI agents have drawn on the transcripts in writing books. The transcripts from Detroit were referred to as "Home Juice." I have reviewed three volumes of these transcripts, covering several months in 1963, and I have reviewed a set of the intelligence reports, labeled "airtels" but commonly referred to as "302s," which spanned the entire period of the listening device. Those reports allowed the FBI in Detroit to circulate what they saw as key transcripts to other offices across the country. Because this material is not yet publicly available, I have chosen to base my account of what the Home Juice transcripts reveal on a series of newspaper articles that appeared in the *Detroit News* in early August 1976. These lengthy articles were written by three experienced crime reporters who had been given full access to the complete set of FBI Home Juice transcripts. I have checked their findings against the material to which I had access in order to ensure its accuracy. In order to allow others to verify my information and not merely cite my account of Hoffa's Mafia ties by referring to a confidential source, I have cited the *Detroit News* arti-

cles here and not the actual Home Juice transcripts or the FBI airtels. The full set of these articles are found in Seth Kantor, Robert Pavich, and Michael Wendland, "Tapes Tie Mob to Hoffa Plot," *Detroit News,* Aug. 1, 1976, 1; Seth Kantor, Robert Pavich, and Michael Wendland, "'Tony' and 'Jack' Once Talked of Killing Top Detroit Cops," *Detroit News,* Aug. 2, 1976, 1; and Seth Kantor, Robert Pavich, and Michael Wendland, "Life in Mob: Plots, Payoffs—and Power," *Detroit News,* Aug. 3, 1976, 1.

46. Kantor, Pavic, and Wendland, "Tapes Tie Mob to Hoffa Plot," 1.

47. Ibid., 15A.

48. Ibid., 1.

49. Ibid., 1.

50. Brill, *The Teamsters,* 52–56, 59–60, 69–71.

51. *Detroit News,* Aug. 1, 1976, 1.

52. *Daily Star-Journal* [Warrensburg, Mo.], Jan. 3, 1989, 1; *New York Times,* April 28, 1989, 10; *St. Louis Globe-Democrat,* May 22, 1981; *Kansas City Times,* April 29, 1989, A23; President's Commission on Organized Crime, *The Edge: Organized Crime, Business, and Labor Unions, Appendix* (Washington, D.C.: The Commission, 1985), 105–7; deposition of Roy L. Williams in *U.S. v. International Brotherhood of Teamsters, Chauffeurs, Warehousemen and Helpers of America, AFL-CIO et al.* (Dec. 1, 1988), 14–18, 82–84 (hereafter Deposition of Roy Williams).

53. The quotations are from the Deposition of Roy Williams, 491–92. For other accounts Williams offered of this period, see President's Commission on Organized Crime, *The Edge: Appendix,* 77–80, and Williams's testimony, Oct. 30, 1985, in *U.S. v. Carl Angelo DeLuna et al.,* vol. 22, pt. 2, 51–54.

54. Deposition of Roy Williams, 90–94. Williams's account seems both dramatic and convenient. It was independently confirmed, however, through the reports of one of Williams's union associates from the period, Floyd Hayes, who—unbeknown to Williams—was providing information to the FBI in 1963 and 1964. According to FBI reports from that time, Williams gave an almost exactly similar account of his kidnapping to Hayes in the late 1950s, soon after it happened. *U.S. v. Roy L. Williams, Joseph Lombardo, Thomas F. O'Malley, and Andrew G. Massa,* U.S. District Court, Northern District of Illinois, Eastern Division, case 81 CR 269 (Feb. 16, 1983), 867–71.

55. Deposition of Roy Williams, 94–97.

56. *U.S. v. Carl Angelo Deluna et al.,* 53.

57. Deposition of Roy Williams, 156–57, 204–6, 220–28; *U.S. v. Carl Angelo DeLuna et al.,* 105–7, 181–86, 215–18.

58. The quotation is from an FBI transcript of an overheard conversation between Nick Civella and Joseph Lombardo, a Chicago Mafia figure. The conversation took place on March 25, 1979, and the transcript was read into the record subsequently at several criminal trials. *U.S. v. Carl Angelo DeLuna et al.,* 10.

59. Deposition of Roy Williams, 104.

60. Lon W. Smith, "An Experiment in Trade Union Democracy: Harold Gibbons and the Formation of Teamsters Local 688, 1937–1957," Ph.D. diss., Illinois State University, 1993, 63–143, 156–69, 171–83; "An Experiment in Health Care," *International Teamster* 47 (Nov. 1950): 22–24, 30; Brill, *The Teamsters,* 354–59, 366; *St. Louis Post-Dispatch,* Nov. 21,

1982, 2C; *How Community Action Succeeds in St. Louis: A Report from Local 688* (n.p., March 1956), Taniment-Wagner Labor Archives, New York University, New York.

61. Brill, *The Teamsters,* 365.

62. Smith, "An Experiment in Trade Union Democracy," 209–10; McClellan Committee, *Hearings, Part 32,* 12439–453; *St. Louis Post-Dispatch,* Sept. 18, 1980, 18A; McClellan Committee, *Hearings, Part 46,* 16580–81.

63. McClellan Committee, *Hearings, Part 46,* 16536–538.

64. Smith, "An Experiment in Trade Union Democracy," 115–21, 211–12; Gary Mormino, "A Still on the Hill: Prohibition and Cottage Industry," *Gateway Heritage* 7 (Fall 1986): 6–7.

65. McClellan Committee, *Hearings, Part 38,* 14258–59; McClellan Committee, *Hearings, Part 37,* 14015–17.

66. McClellan Committee, *Hearings, Part 39,* 14646–49; Smith, "An Experiment in Trade Union Democracy," 211–14; Brill, *The Teamsters,* 365.

67. Brill, *The Teamsters,* 365.

68. Smith, "An Experiment in Trade Union Democracy," 211–15; Brill, *The Teamsters,* 365–68; McClellan Committee, *Hearings, Part 37,* 13969–81, 13986–87, 14008–20, 14076; McClellan Committee, *Hearings, Part 38,* 14400–407; "Joint Council 13 in Trusteeship," *International Teamster* 50 (April 1953), 23; "Joint Council 13," *International Teamster* 52 (Oct. 1955): 16–20.

69. *St. Louis Post-Dispatch,* April 26, 1981, A17.

70. The informant was Jackie Presser. See ALPRO File 159–4733–28, Oct. 1977, 6, and ALPRO File 159–4733–6, March 1977, both in *U.S. International Brotherhood of Teamsters, Chauffeurs, Warehousemen and Helpers of America, AFL-CIO et al.* Presser alleged that Gibbons followed the lead of Allen Dorfman in Teamsters affairs, and Dorfman in turn had long represented the interests of the Chicago Outfit. For further confirmation of Gibbons's ties to Dorfman, see the conversation recorded in Dorfman's office, 1:20 P.M., Dec. 21, 1979, *U.S. v. Carl Angelo Deluna et al.,* exhibit P406a.

71. *Chicago Tribune,* Sept. 5, 1954, 3.

72. "Teamster Seeks Chicago Mayorship," *International Teamster* 52 (Feb. 1955): 32; Ovid Demaris, *Captive City* (New York: Lyle Stuart, 1969), 30.

73. Lichtenstein, *The Most Dangerous Man in Detroit,* 275–76.

74. Williams Deposition, 234–36.

75. Brill, *The Teamsters,* 369–70; *St. Louis Post-Dispatch,* Nov. 21, 1982, 2C.

76. Brill, *The Teamsters,* 201–5; Moldea, *The Hoffa Wars,* 49–50; McClellan Committee, *Hearings, Part 43,* 16082–85.

77. McClellan Committe, *Hearings, Part 43,* 15989–6005.

78. Brill, *The Teamsters,* 200–204.

79. Government Exhibit S-106-T, recording made May 22, 1979, *U.S. v. Williams et al.*

80. Robert D. Leiter, *The Teamsters Union: A Study of Its Economic Impact* (New York: Bookman Associates, 1957), 204–20; James, *Hoffa and the Teamsters,* 215–317.

81. William F. Roemer, Jr., *Accardo: The Genuine Godfather* (New York: Donald I. Fine, 1995), 171–74; testimony of Carl Thomas, *U.S. v. Carl Angelo DeLuna et al.,* 13–75; President's Commission on Organized Crime, *Organized Crime and Gambling: Record of Hear-*

ing VII, June 24–26, 1985, New York (Washington, D.C.: Government Printing Office, 1985), 472–486; Brill, *The Teamsters,* 210–11.

82. Sheridan, *The Rise and Fall of Jimmy Hoffa,* 359–82; Sloane, *Hoffa,* 303–12.

83. *New York Times,* Nov. 4, 1970, 16.

84. Sheridan, *The Rise and Fall of Jimmy Hoffa,* 365–77.

85. *New York Times,* June 24, 1976, 1, June 18, 1975, 32; Brill, *The Teamsters,* 236–37; Velie, *Desperate Bargain,* 12–13.

86. Government Exhibit S-106-T, recording made May 22, 1979, *U.S. v. Williams.*

87. "Playboy Interview: Jimmy Hoffa," *Playboy* (Dec. 1975): 74.

88. *St. Louis Post-Dispatch,* March 26, 1995, 1A.

89. *International Teamster* 55 (Dec. 1958): 12.

90. Kennedy, *The Enemy Within,* 75–94, 118, 308–10.

91. The officials who had been subjects of McClellan Committee revelations were: John J. Conlin, vice president; John O'Rourke, vice president; Owen Brennan, vice president; and Ray Cohen, a trustee. Regarding O'Rourke's ties to Robert Kennedy, which included supporting his run for senator from New York, see Edwin Guthman, *We Band of Brothers* (New York: Harper and Row, 1964), 47–48.

92. Kennedy, *The Enemy Within,* 17, 120; John F. English, "Best System in the Country," *International Teamster* 56 (Jan. 1959): 26–36.

93. A case frequently cited by Kennedy and the committee involved Glenn Smith and several other Tennessee Teamster officials charged with committing acts of violence during the course of organizing campaigns in that state. Kennedy, *The Enemy Within,* 72–73; McClellan Committee, *Final Report, Part 3,* 708–9.

94. Clyde Crosby, a Portland Teamsters official, was tried on charges of lying to the committee about his contact with a vice operator in the city. At trial, a federal judge dismissed the charges. Similarly, when Harold Gibbons and two other Teamster officials were tried on charges of making illegal campaign contributions the trial judge stopped the trial and ordered a verdict of acquittal. On Crosby, see *New York Times,* Nov. 5, 1958, 16, Feb. 3, 1959, 25, and Feb. 4, 1959, 15. On Gibbons, see *New York Times,* Oct. 4, 1960, 58, Oct. 21, 1960, 14, and Oct. 27, 1960, 73.

95. Miles E. Hoffman, *International Brotherhood of Teamsters, Chauffeurs, Warehousemen and Helpers of America: Development, Structure, Functions* (Philadelphia: Temple University, School of Business Administration, 1964), 7–8.

96. The quotation is from Robert F. Kennedy, "An Urgent Reform Plan," *Life,* June 1, 1959, 114.

97. For the committee's investigation of endemic corruption in the garbage industry, see McClellan Committee, *Hearings, Part 17;* on laundry, *Hearings, Parts 35–36;* on vending machine distribution, *Hearings, Parts 46–48, 53 and 57;* on construction, *Hearings, Parts 42 and 44;* on collusion among newspaper and magazine distributors in New York City, *Hearings, Part 51.*

98. U.S. Congress, House, Committee on Ways and Means, *Central States Teamsters Fund,* 95 Cong., 2d sess., March 22, 1978 (Washington, D.C.: Government Printing Office, 1978); U.S. Congress, House, Select Committee on Aging, *Fraud and Abuse in Pensions and Related Employee Benefit Plans,* 97th Cong., 1st sess., Nov. 4, 1981 (Washington, D.C.: Government Printing Office, 1982), 81–101; *Wall Street Journal,* July 22, 1975, 1, July 23, 1975, 1;

"Behind the Crackdown on a Huge Teamster Pension Plan," *U.S. News and World Report,* July 12, 1976, 73–75; Brill, *The Teamsters,* 200–260.

Chapter 9: Raising the Specter of Hoffa

1. Robert H. Zieger, *The CIO, 1935–1955* (Chapel Hill: University of North Carolina Press, 1995), 359–60; John Hutchinson, *The Imperfect Union: A History of Corruption in American Trade Unions* (New York: E. P. Dutton, 1970), 295.

2. Hutchinson, *The Imperfect Union,* 295–303; Daniel Bell, *The End of Ideology: On the Exhaustion of Political Ideals in the Fifties* (Glencoe: The Free Press, 1960), 183–87.

3. *New York Times,* Jan. 30, 1957, 1; Hutchinson, *The Imperfect Union,* 305–6; Anthony V. Baltakis, "Agendas of Investigation: The McClellan Committee, 1957–1958," Ph.D. diss., University of Akron, 1997, 29–34.

4. A description of how one reporter used the committee to build a story on Barney Baker is in Clark Mollenhoff to Bram Cavin, Aug. 13, 1965, folder 10, box 10, Clark Mollenhoff Papers, Wisconsin State Historical Society, Madison (hereafter Mollenhoff Papers, Wisconsin); undated, untitled notes in box 131, Clark Mollenhoff Papers, Herbert Hoover Presidential Library, West Branch, Iowa; Clark Mollenhoff, *Tentacles of Power: The Story of Jimmy Hoffa* (Cleveland: World Publishing, 1965), 291.

5. Edwin Guthman, *We Band of Brothers* (New York: Harper and Row, 1971), 2–7, 57–58.

6. Guthman, *We Band of Brothers,* 57; Baltakis, "Agendas of Investigation," 110–13.

7. Robert F. Kennedy, *The Enemy Within* (New York: Harper and Brothers, 1960), 175, 287–89.

8. Clark Mollenhoff to Richard Wilson, n.d., folder 2, box 73, Mollenhoff Papers, Wisconsin.

9. John L. McClellan, "What We Learned about Labor Gangsters," *Saturday Evening Post,* May 3, 1958, 22–23, 64–67, and May 10, 1958, 35, 142, 144, 146. Robert F. Kennedy, "Hoffa's Unholy Alliance," *Look,* Sept. 2, 1958, 31–32.

10. John Dos Passos, "What Union Members Have Been Writing Senator McClellan," *Reader's Digest* 73 (Sept. 1958): 25–32. These letters of complaint were sprinkled throughout McClellan's papers from the labor investigation period, and in addition two thick manila folders were marked, "Derogatory File (Union)" for 1957 and 1958, file 20, drawer B, John L. McClellan Papers, Ouachita Baptist University, Arkadelphia, Ark. (hereafter McClellan Papers).

11. Charles Morrow Wilson to John L. McClellan, Feb. 9, 1959, Hobart Lewis to John L. McClellan, March 10, 1959, and Hobart Lewis to John L. McClellan, April 15, 1959, all in *Reader's Digest* article folder, file 30, drawer D, McClellan Papers. The article that resulted was Charles M. Wilson, "Corruption, the Committee, Senator McClellan," *Reader's Digest* 74 (June 1959): 85–90.

12. John L. McClellan, *Crime without Punishment* (New York: Duell, Sloan and Pearce, 1962) 20.

13. *Legislative History of the Labor-Management Reporting and Disclosure Act of 1959* (Washington, D.C.: Government Printing Office, 1959), 2:1096–97.

14. Lee Edwards, *Goldwater: The Man Who Made a Revolution* (Washington, D.C.: Regnery Publishing, 1995), 73, 75.

15. Carl T. Curtis to John H. Bundy, Oct. 31, 1957, Investigate Improper Activities in Labor + Management folder, box 82, Carl T. Curtis Papers, Nebraska State Historical Society, Lincoln (hereafter Curtis Papers).

16. Carl T. Curtis to Wilford I. King, Oct. 28, 1957, Investigate Improper Activities in Labor + Management folder, 1957, Curtis Papers.

17. Baltakis, "Agendas of Investigation," 37–67, 118–22, 223–43, 275–76.

18. Robert Kennedy on *The Jack Paar Show* [excerpt], NBC-TV, July 23, 1959, tape T85:0127, Library Archives, the Museum of Television and Radio, New York.

19. Address of Sen. John L. McClellan to the Annual convention of the American Institute of Supply Associations, Sept. 18, 1957, box 82, Investigate Improper Activities in Labor + Management folder, 1957, Curtis Papers.

20. U.S. Congress, Senate, Select Committee on Improper Activities in the Labor or Management Field, *Investigation of Improper Activities in the Labor or Management Field,* 85th Cong., 1st sess., July 1, 6, 7, 8, and 9, 1959 (Washington, D.C.: Government Printing Office, 1959), part 16, 1993 (hereafter McClellan Committee, *Hearings*).

21. Discussions of the possible agenda among committee members can be found in Barry Goldwater to John L. McClellan, June 11, 1957, Carl T. Curtis to John L. McClellan, June 13, 1957, and John L. McClellan to Carl T. Curtis, June 22, 1957, all in Investigate Improper Activities in Labor + Management folder, 1957, Curtis Papers. For a narrative account of these meetings, see Baltakis, "Agendas of Investigation," 143–46.

22. This was the official list of priorities McClellan sent to the Senate leadership as part of his report on the committee's activities. John L. McClellan to Thomas C. Hennings, Jr., Aug. 12, 1957, Investigate Improper Activities in Labor + Management folder, 1957, Curtis Papers. For his more complete explanation of these priorities, see Address of Sen. John L. McClellan to Annual Convention of the American Institute of Supply Associations, Sept. 18, 1957, Curtis Papers.

23. Untitled [Organizational Plan], July 10, 1957, Investigate Improper Activities in Labor + Management folder, 1957, Curtis Papers.

24. McClellan to Thomas C. Hennings, Jr., Aug. 12, 1957, Investigate Improper Activities in Labor + Management folder, 1957, Curtis Papers.

25. McClellan Committee, *Hearings, Part 36,* 13297–365, 13385–89.

26. Kennedy, *The Enemy Within,* 96–104.

27. McClellan Committee, *Hearings, Part 36,* 13297–357; the quotations are from 13299, 13334, and 13342.

28. Ibid., 13315–16.

29. Ibid., 13321.

30. Ibid., 13297–365.

31. *New York Times,* Aug. 6, 1958, 1.

32. *Chicago Tribune,* Aug. 6, 1958, 6.

33. The Associated Press story is drawn from the *Newark Evening News,* Aug. 5, 1958, 1.

34. "The Senate Hearings on Racketeering," *Management Record* 19 (July 1957): 240.

35. Karl Mundt to Raymond Moley, June 8, 1957, reel 125, microfilm, record group 3, Legislation: Improper Activities in the Labor or Management Field, Karl E. Mundt Papers, Karl E. Mundt Archival Library, Dakota State University, Madison, South Dakota.

36. Quoted in Alan K. McAdams, *Power and Politics in Labor Legislation* (New York: Columbia University Press, 1964), 79.

37. The quotation is from the tape of *The Jack Paar Show*.

38. McAdams, *Power and Politics*, 68–69.

39. Memorandum from Robert F. Kennedy to Sen. Carl T. Curtis, Oct. 19, 1957, Investigate Improper Activities in Labor + Management folder, 1957, Curtis Papers; McClellan Committee, *Hearings, Part 41*, 15625–46, 15675–96, 15727–28.

40. Ralph C. James and Estelle Dinnerstein James, *Hoffa and the Teamsters: A Study of Union Power* (New York: D. Van Nostrand, 1965), 144–48.

41. Memorandum from Robert F. Kennedy to Sen. Carl T. Curtis, Oct. 19, 1957; McClellan Committee, *Hearings, Part 41*, 15626–40, 15675–96.

42. McClellan Committee, *Hearings, Part 41*, 15632.

43. For Kennedy's acknowledgment of this fact and his discussion of the way that congressional questioners could misuse a witness's Fifth Amendment required answers, see Kennedy, *The Enemy Within*, 297–300.

44. McClellan Committee, *Hearings, Part 41*, 15700–704.

45. Ibid., 15641–42.

46. "Can the Labor Racketeer Be Stopped?" *U.S. News and World Report*, Oct. 10, 1958, 52–57.

47. McClellan, *Crime without Punishment*, 268–69.

48. Sylvester Petro, *Power Unlimited: The Corruption of Union Leadership* (New York: Ronald Press, 1959), 199, 5, 17, vi.

49. Mollenhoff, *Tentacles of Power*, 408–11.

50. *Chicago Daily News*, July 10, 1958, 8.

51. *Cincinnati Enquirer*, Aug. 13, 1957, 4.

52. "'I'm the Boss of an Outfit That Wins,' Tough Jimmy's Union: The Power and the Danger," *Life*, May 18, 1959, 31–39.

53. "Is Congress Boss, or Hoffa?" *Life*, June 1, 1959, 30.

54. *New York Times*, July 8, 1961, 18.

55. *Louisville Courier-Journal*, July 6, 1961, and (Portland) *Oregon Journal*, July 8, 1961, in Hoffa Cartoons, 1957–61 folder, Hoffa Clippings, State Historical Society of Wisconsin, Madison.

56. *Wall Street Journal*, July 22, 1959, 12.

57. McClellan Committee, *Hearings, Part 32*, 12201–15, 12319–21.

58. Arthur M. Schlesinger, Jr., *Robert Kennedy and His Times* (Boston: Houghton Mifflin, 1978), 167–69; McClellan, *Crime without Punishment*, 122.

59. McClellan Committee, *Hearings, Part 32*, 12192–93, 12232, 12487.

60. This account is drawn from the testimony offered in three separate hearings on the Detroit jukebox industry along with the lengthy grand jury transcripts from 1946 that were inserted into the Kefauver Committee hearings in 1951. U.S. Congress, Senate, Special Committee to Investigate Organized Crime in Interstate Commerce, *Investigation of Organized Crime in Interstate Commerce*, 82d Cong., 1st sess., Feb. 8, 9, and 19, 1951 (Washington, D.C.: Government Printing Office, 1951), 185–91, 751–1031; U.S. Congress, House of Representatives, Special Subcommittee of the Committee on Government Operations and Education and Labor, *Investigation of Racketeering*, 83d Cong., 1st sess., June 8, 11, 12, and 13, 1953 (Washington, D.C.: Government Printing Office, 1954), 7–49, 85–104, 115–68, 185–227, 271–91; McClellan Committee, *Hearings, Part 48*, 17405–679. The quotation "to get together with the Italian syndicate" is from *Investigation of Racketeering*, 15.

61. The Associated Press used similar language. *Philadelphia Inquirer,* April 8, 1959, 3, April 9, 1959, 3.

62. U.S. Senate, Select Committee on Improper Activities in the Labor or Management Field, *Final Report, Part 4,* 86th Cong., 2d sess., Senate Report 1139 (Washington, D.C.: Government Printing Office, 1960), 741.

63. Transcript of John L. McClellan's concluding comments to *Sound of Violence,* (TV) broadcast, April 29, 1959, July 8, 1959, *Armstrong Circle Theater* folder, file 30, drawer D, McClellan Papers.

64. David Meerse to John L. McClellan, Nov. 22, 1959, John L. McClellan to David Meerse, Dec. 21, 1959, Labor Committee Out of State folder, file 25, drawer B, McClellan Papers.

65. McClellan Committee, *Hearings, Part 32,* 12428.

66. Associated Press, July 4, 1958; *Philadelphia Inquirer,* Aug. 10, 1957, McClellan Scrapbook, McClellan Papers.

67. McClellan Committee, *Hearings, Part 32,* 12226.

68. Ibid., 12219–29.

69. McClellan, *Crime without Punishment,* 114.

70. McClellan Committee, *Hearings, Part 32,* 12262–63, 12356–69, 12363.

71. "Where Terror Begins," *Life,* March 2, 1959, McClellan Scrapbook, McClellan Papers.

72. *Congressional Record-Senate,* Aug. 27, 1957, 14625–30, clipping in Investigate Improper Activities in Labor + Management folder, 1957, Curtis Papers.

73. U.S. Senate, Select Committee on Improper Activities in the Labor or Management Field, *Second Interim Report,* 86th Cong., 1st sess., Report 621 (Washington, D.C.: Government Printing Office, 1959), 110.

74. McClellan, *Crime without Punishment,* 60–61.

75. *Congressional Record-Senate,* Aug. 27, 1957, 14625–30.

76. *New York Herald Tribune,* July 1, 1958, McClellan Scrapbook, McClellan Papers.

77. "Where Terror Begins."

78. Irving Bauer to Sen. John L. McClellan, July 11, 1958, and Frances C. Wells to John L. McClellan, Aug. 13, 1958, both in Labor Committee, Out of State folder, file 24, drawer E, McClellan Papers.

79. Stephen J. Whitfield, *The Culture of the Cold War* (Baltimore: Johns Hopkins University Press, 1991), 1–26; Tom Engelhardt, *The End of Victory Culture: Cold War America and the Disillusioning of a Generation* (New York: Basic Books, 1995), Michael S. Sherry, *In the Shadow of War: The United States since the 1930s* (New Haven: Yale University Press, 1995), 6–10, 171–77, 214–17.

80. Speech before the American Trucking Association, Washington, D.C., Oct. 20, 1959, reprinted in *RFK: Collected Speeches,* ed. Edwin O. Guthman and Richard C. Allen (New York: Viking, 1993), 34–38.

81. Speech before University of Georgia Law School, Athens, May 6, 1961, in *RFK: Collected Speeches,* ed. Guthman and Allen, 47–54.

82. Kennedy, *The Enemy Within,* 306–7.

83. Kennedy on *The Jack Paar Show.*

84. *Congressional Record-Senate,* Jan. 20, 1959, 816.

85. U.S. Bureau of the Census, *Historical Statistics of the United States, Colonial Times to 1970, Bicentennial Edition: Part 1* (Washington, D.C.: Government Printing Office, 1975), 176–78.

86. Leo Troy, *Trade Union Membership, 1897–1962* (New York: Columbia University Press, 1965), A11, A14, A19, A24, A27.

87. Elizabeth A. Fones-Wolf, *Selling Free Enterprise: The Business Assault on Labor and Liberalism, 1945–1960* (Urbana: University of Illinois Press, 1994), 257–58; Gilbert J. Gall, *The Politics of Right to Work: The Labor Federations as Special Interests, 1943–1979* (New York: Greenwood Press, 1988), 73; Melvyn Dubofsky, *The State and Labor in Modern America* (Chapel Hill: University of North Carolina Press, 1994), 217; Zieger, *The CIO, 1935–1955*, 360–69.

88. 1956 Public Relations Program for NAM Campaign against Labor Monopoly Abuses, folder 2, box 851.1, accession 1411, National Association of Manufacturers Papers, Hagley Museum and Library, Wilmington, Del. (hereafter NAM Papers).

89. Fones-Wolf, *Selling Free Enterprise*, 271; William H. Miernyk, *Trade Unions in the Age of Affluence* (New York: Random House, 1965), 112–23; *New York Times*, May 5, 1957, 62.

90. Gall, *The Politics of Right to Work,* 35–36, 72.

91. Philip M. Talbot to John L. McClellan, Nov. 25, 1957, Labor Committee, Out of State folder, file 25, drawer B, McClellan Papers; 1956 Public Relations Program for NAM Campaign against Labor Monopoly Abuses, NAM Papers; Fones-Wolf, *Selling Free Enterprise,* 258–61; McAdams, *Power and Politics,* 52–54, 68–71; Miernyk, *Trade Unions in the Age of Affluence,* 13–14, 69; Baltakis, "Agendas of Investigation," 114–18.

92. Fones-Wolf, *Selling Free Enterprise,* 271; Baltakis, "Agendas of Investigation," 392–94; McAdams, *Power and Politics,* 71–75, 78–80; R. Alton Lee, *Eisenhower and Landrum-Griffin: A Study in Labor-Management Politics* (Lexington: University Press of Kentucky, 1990), 18–44; Edwards, *Goldwater,* 63–67, 73–81, 98–101.

93. McAdams, *Power and Politics,* 69–70.

94. Ibid., 5–6, 43–66, 84–99; Lee, *Eisenhower and Landrum-Griffin,* 74–116; Fones-Wolf, *Selling Free Enterprise,* 274–76; Dubofsky, *The State and Labor,* 219–21; Baltakis, "Agendas of Investigation," 363–96.

95. *Legislative History of the Labor-Management Reporting and Disclosure Act of 1959* (Washington, D.C.: Government Printing Office, 1959), 2:1098.

96. Transcript of interview with Senator McClellan by Ted Yates, Jr., Sept. 4, 1957, Radio-TV folder, file 18, drawer E, McClellan Papers; McClellan, *Crime without Punishment,* 271–72; McClellan, "What We Learned about Labor Gangsters."

97. *Legislative History of the Labor-Management Reporting and Disclosure Act of 1959,* 2:1098–100.

98. Charles R. Sligh, Jr., and Sybil S. Patterson, "Recommendations of Subcommittee on Labor Disputes and Collective Bargaining," Sept. 12, 1957, NAM Papers; for the Chamber of Commerce, Philipp M. Talbott to John L. McClellan, Nov. 25, 1957, Labor Committee, Out of State folder, file 25, drawer B, McClellan Papers.

99. Baltakis, "Agendas of Investigation," 389–94.

100. McAdams, *Power and Politics,* 212–13.

101. American Civil Liberties Union, *Democracy in Trade Unions: A Survey, with a Pro-*

gram of Action (New York: American Civil Liberties Union, 1943); Clyde W. Summers, *Democracy in Labor Unions: A Report and Statement of Policy* (New York: American Civil Liberties Union, 1952).

102. McAdams, *Power and Politics,* 166–67; Dubofsky, *The State and Labor,* 219–20.

103. Martin H. Malin and Lorraine A. Schmall, *Individual Rights within Unions* (Washington, D.C.: Bureau of National Affairs, 1988), 33–345; James R. Bellace and Alan D. Berkowitz, *The Landrum-Griffin Act: Twenty Years of Federal Protection of Union Members' Rights* (Philadelphia: Industrial Research Unit, The Wharton School, University of Pennsylvania, 1979); Philip Taft, *Rights of Union Members and the Government* (Westport: Greenwood Press, 1975), 18–286.

104. Michael Goldberg, "An Overview and Assessment of the Law Regulating Internal Union Affairs," presented at the Conference on Union Governance and Democracy, Georgia State University, Atlanta, May 1999; Clyde Summers, "Democracy in a One-Party State: Perspectives from Landrum-Griffin," *Maryland Law Review* 43 (1984): 93–117; Edgar N. James, "Union Democracy and the LMRDA: Autocracy and Insurgency in National Union Elections," *Harvard Civil Rights–Civil Liberties Law Review* 13 (Spring 1978): 325–58.

105. James and James, *Hoffa and the Teamsters,* 149–52.

106. U.S. Bureau of the Census, *Historical Statistics of the United States,* 178.

107. Seymour Martin Lipset and William Schneider, *The Confidence Gap: Business, Labor, and Government in the Public Mind* (Baltimore: Johns Hopkins University Press, 1987), 203.

108. McAdams, *Power and Politics,* 2–4; Lee, *Eisenhower and Landrum-Griffin,* 90–94; Fones-Wolf, *Selling Free Enterprise,* 271–74.

109. George H. Gallup, *The Gallup Poll: Public Opinion, 1935–1971,* vol. 2: *1949–1958* (New York: Random House, 1972), 1516.

110. Lipset and Schneider, *The Confidence Gap,* 203.

111. McAdams, *Power and Politics,* 152–73, 232–33, 267–76; Dubofsky, *The State and Labor,* 219–22.

Chapter 10: Reform in the Age of Hoffa

1. *New York Times,* May 26, 1957, 1, July 17, 1957, 1.

2. John Bartlow Martin, "The Labor Boss Leaves a Baffling Trail," *Saturday Evening Post,* July 11, 1959, 27; Walter Sheridan, *The Rise and Fall of Jimmy Hoffa* (New York: Saturday Review Press, 1972), 32–36.

3. *New York Times,* Aug. 24, 1957, 6, Sept. 29, 1957, 1.

4. *New York Times,* Sept. 17, 1957, 1, Sept. 24, 1957, 27, Sept. 30, 1957, 1.

5. The results of the final convention roll-call vote gave Hoffa 1,208 delegate votes compared to 313 votes for William Lee and 140 votes for Thomas Haggerty. *Proceedings of the Seventeenth [1957] Convention, International Brotherhood of Teamsters, Chauffeurs, Warehousemen and Helpers of America, Miami Beach, Florida* (Washington, D.C.: n.p., 1957), 388.

6. *Wall Street Journal,* Sept. 6, 1957, 1.

7. Ibid.; *New York Times,* Aug. 25, 1957, 2; "The Engine Inside the Hood," *Time,* Sept. 9, 1957, 30.

8. Sam Romer, *The International Brotherhood of Teamsters: Its Government and Structure* (New York: John Wiley and Sons, 1962), 12–16; *New York Times,* Aug. 25, 1957, 2.

9. *New York Times,* Sept. 1, 1957, 56, Sept. 2, 1957, 1, Sept. 30, 1957, 1.

10. Clyde Summers, "Democracy in a One-Party State: Perspectives from Landrum-Griffin," *Maryland Law Review* 43 (1984): 93–99; Edgar N. James, "Union Democracy and the LMRDA: Autocracy and Insurgency in National Union Elections," *Harvard Civil Rights–Civil Liberties Law Review* 13 (Spring 1978): 247–66; Paul Jacobs, *The State of the Unions* (New York: Atheneum, 1963), 274–76.

11. *Wall Street Journal,* Sept. 16, 1957, 4.

12. Ralph C. James and Estelle Dinnerstein James, *Hoffa and the Teamsters: A Study of Union Power* (New York: D. Van Nostrand, 1965), 178–85; Romer, *The International Brotherhood of Teamsters,* 84–96; Clyde Summers, "Teamster Joint Grievance Committees: Grievance Disposal without Adjudication," reprinted from, *The Proceedings of the Thirty-seventh Annual Meeting of the National Academy of Arbitrators* (Washington, D.C.: Bureau of National Affairs, 1985), 323–30.

13. Clark Mollenhoff, *Tentacles of Power: The Story of Jimmy Hoffa* (Cleveland: World Publishing, 1965), 225.

14. See, for example, Hoffa's campaign newsletter, *Grass Rooter,* Oct. 3, 1957, 1, in Portraits Unsorted Items folder, box 16, Daniel Bell Papers, Taniment-Wagner Labor Archives, New York University (hereafter Bell Papers).

15. *Capital Times,* Nov. 13, 1992; A. E. Mueller to The Editor, *Waukesha Daily Freeman,* Aug. 13, 1957, folder 14, box 9, International Brotherhood of Teamsters, Chauffeurs, Warehousemen and Helpers Local 695 (Madison) Records, 1932–66, MSS 434, State Historical Society of Wisconsin, Madison (hereafter Local 695 Papers).

16. Matt Gelernter to Senator McClellan, March 26, 1958, Select Labor Committee folder, file 24, drawer D, John L. McClellan Papers, Ouachita Baptist University, Arkadelphia, Ark.

17. Address of John F. English before the American Federation of Labor–Congress of Industrial Organizations in Atlantic City, Dec. 6, 1957, folder 9, box 8, Local 695 Papers.

18. *New York Times,* Sept. 20, 1957, 1, Sept. 22, 1957, 78, Oct. 12, 1957, 1, Oct. 14, 1957, 28, Oct. 15, 1957, 1, Oct. 31, 1957, 1, Dec. 3, 1957, 39, Dec. 7, 1957, 13, Dec. 11, 1957, 23, Dec. 14, 1957, 30, Dec. 17, 1957, 39, Dec. 19, 1957, 35, Jan. 9, 1958, 37, Jan. 11, 1958, 11, Jan. 14, 1958, 39.

19. Michael J. Goldberg, "The Teamsters' Board of Monitors: An Experiment in Union Reform Litigation," *Labor History* 30 (Fall 1989): 563–84; Sam Romer, "The Teamster Monitors and the Administration of the International Union," *Labor Law Journal* 12 (July 1961): 604–13.

20. *Chicago Tribune,* Aug. 29, 1954, 1, Aug. 30, 1954, 1, Aug. 31, 1954, 3, Sept. 1, 1954, 2, Sept. 2, 1954, 2, Sept. 3, 1954, 2; U.S. Congress, Senate, Select Committee on Improper Activities in the Labor or Management Field, *Final Report, Part 3,* 86th Cong., 2d sess., Senate Report 1139, Feb. 26, 1960 (Washington, D.C.: Government Printing Office, 1960), 514–16 (hereafter McClellan Committee, *Final Report*); *Organized Crime and Illicit Traffic in Narcotics: Hearings, Part 2,* 88th Cong., 1st sess., Oct. 10, 11, 15, and 16, 1963 (Washington, D.C.: Government Printing Office, 1963), 508–11; McClellan Committee, *Hearings, Part 49,* 17731–748, 17762–777.

21. McClellan Committee, *Final Report, Part 3,* 514–30, 548–54, 564–69; Chicago Crime

Commission, *A Report on Chicago Crime for 1968* (Chicago: Chicago Crime Commission, 1969), 99; McClellan Committee, *Hearings, Part 49*, 17736–737.

22. McClellan Committee, *Hearings, Part 49*, 17749–58.

23. *New York Times,* Sept. 3, 1959, 1, Sept. 29, 1959, 33; Sheridan, *The Rise and Fall of Jimmy Hoffa,* 135–36.

24. McClellan Committee, *Hearings, Part 55,* 19276.

25. *Chicago Tribune,* April 3, 1959, 1; *Chicago Sun-Times,* April 3, 1959, 6.

26. *Chicago Tribune,* April 4, 1959, 1.

27. *Chicago Tribune,* April 3, 1959, 1, April 4, 1959, 1 (quotation); *Chicago Sun-Times,* April 3, 1959, 6.

28. Ibid.

29. Freedom of Information Act request materials from the National Labor Relations Board, case file 13-CA-3022, Checker Taxi Company Inc. et al., testimony in General Counsel's Brief to the Trial Examiner, 48–49, 92–93 (hereafter FOIA NLRB, General Counsel's Brief); *Chicago Tribune,* May 5, 1959, 1, May 12, 1959, 5, May 17, 1959, 8.

30. The quotation is from FOIA NLRB General Counsel's Brief, 85; other examples of the threats can be found in FOIA NLRB General Counsel's Brief, 84–85, 93–94, 101–3; *Chicago Tribune,* June 28, 1959, 8.

31. FOIA NLRB, General Counsel's Brief, 27–55, 74–80, 101–3; *Chicago Tribune,* May 14, 1959, 1; *Chicago Sun-Times,* May 14, 1959, 2.

32. Irving Friedman, interview by author, July 10, 1991, Chicago.

33. *Chicago Tribune,* May 15, 1959, F9, June 25, 1959, 1, June 26, 1959, 2; interview with Irving Friedman; Dominic Abata to Frank McCulloch, March 23, 1961, FOIA NLRB case file.

34. Freedom of Information Act request materials from the National Labor Relations Board, case file 13–CA-3022, Checker Taxi Company Inc. et al., General Counsel exhibit file, vol. 2, Exhibits GC-19 to GC-25 (hereafter FOIA NLRB GC Exhibit File); interview with Irving Friedman; *Chicago Tribune,* Dec. 25, 1958, 1.

35. FOIA NLRB, GC exhibit file, vol. 2, exhibit GC-24, emphasis in the original.

36. Ibid., exhibit GC-17.

37. *Chicago Tribune,* July 8, 1961, 5, July 1, 1961, 15, July 13, 1961, 10, July 15, 1961, 4, July 17, 1961, 5, July 18, 1961, 3, July 19, 1961, 1; Ed Bunin, *Hack 777* (Evanston: Regency Books, 1963), 121–22. The quotations are from the *Wall Street Journal,* Aug. 1, 1961, Scrapbook, vol. 10, Seafarers International Union Archives, Harry Lundberg School for Seamanship, Piney Point, Md. (hereafter SIU Scrapbook).

38. *Cincinnati Enquirer,* Aug. 1, 1961, 1.

39. James Neff, *Mobbed Up: Jackie Presser's High-Wire Life in the Teamsters, the Mafia, and the FBI* (New York: Dell Publishing, 1989), 16–70; U.S. Congress, Senate, Special Committee to Investigate Organized Crime in Interstate Commerce, *Investigation of Organized Crime in Interstate Commerce,* 82d Cong., 1st sess., Feb. 8, 9, and 19, 1951 (Washington, D.C.: Government Printing Office, 1951), 752–795, 801–92, 999–1000.

40. See the testimony of the former underboss of the Cleveland Mafia, Angelo Lonardo, in *U.S. v. Carl Angelo DeLuna et al.,* U.S. District Court for the Western District of Missouri, Western Division, case 83-124-01/15-CR-W-8 (Nov. 22, 1985), 30–32; and U.S. Senate, Permanent Subcommittee on Investigations, *Organized Crime: Twenty-five Years*

after Valachi, 100th Cong., 2d sess., April 11, 15, 21, 22, 29, 1988 (Washington, D.C.: Government Printing Office, 1988), 88, 90–91, 94–95. See also deposition of Roy Williams in *U.S. v. International Brotherhood of Teamsters, Chauffeurs, Warehousemen and Helpers of America, AFL-CIO et al.* (Dec. 1, 1988), 102–4; deposition of Jimmy Fratianno, Jan. 6, 1989, in *U.S. v. International Brotherhood of Teamsters, Chauffeurs, Warehousemen and Helpers of America, AFL-CIO et al.,* U.S. District Court, Southern District of New York, case 88 CV 4486 (Jan. 6, 1989), 157–58, 168–69; and Neff, *Mobbed Up,* 16–26, 29–33, 37–43, 50–52.

41. Neff, *Mobbed Up,* 63–66; *Cincinnati Enquirer,* Dec. 7, 1957, 12, Aug. 21, 1961, 16, Aug. 28, 1961, 1.

42. *Philadelphia Inquirer,* April 7, 1963, SIU Scrapbook; notes of interview with Jimmy Hoffa, Dec. 26, 1957, folder 9, box 68, Clark Mollenhoff Papers, Wisconsin State Historical Society, Madison.

43. McClellan Committee, *Hearings, Part 55,* 19355–94; quotation on 19361–62.

44. The quotation is from a cassette recording of a radio broadcast debate between Hoffa and Luken on August 27, 1961; the tape was provided by Steven Luken. McClellan Committee, *Hearings, Part 55,* 19361–66.

45. *Cincinnati Enquirer,* Aug. 30, 1957, 1, Sept. 21, 1957, 3, Oct. 4, 1957, 1, Dec. 7, 1957, 12.

46. *Cincinnati Enquirer,* July 8, 1961, 1.

47. Ibid.; Arthur A. Sloane, *Hoffa* (Cambridge: MIT Press, 1991), 180–81; *Proceedings, Eighteenth* [1961] *Convention, International Brotherhood of Teamsters, Chauffeurs, Warehousemen, and Helpers of America, Miami Beach, Florida* (Washington, D.C.: n.p., 1961), 26–44 (fifth day).

48. McClellan Committee, *Hearings, Part 55,* 19378–84; Steven Luken, telephone interview by author, May 2, 1991; William Luken, telephone interview by author, April 18, 1991.

49. Recording of debate between Hoffa and Luken; *Proceedings, IBT Convention,* [July 5, 1961], 21–22, 39–46 (third day).

50. *Cincinnati Enquirer,* Aug. 16, 1961, 1, Aug. 21, 1961, 16.

51. *Cincinnati Enquirer,* Aug. 21, 1961, 1, Aug. 25, 1961, 1, 8, 11, Aug. 28, 1961, 1, Oct. 18, 1961, 1, Oct. 21, 1961, 1, Nov. 7, 1961, 6, Dec. 22, 1961, 10, Dec. 24, 1961, 2A; recording of debate between Hoffa and Luken.

52. *New York Times,* July 8, 1961, 18.

53. See for instance, Steven Brill, *The Teamsters* (New York: Simon and Schuster, 1978), 397–99.

54. Sloane, *Hoffa,* 316.

55. *New York Times,* Feb. 25, 1965; *AFL-CIO News,* Nov. 7, 1964; *Baltimore Evening Sun,* Feb. 12, 1962, all in SIU Scrapbook.

56. *Wall Street Journal,* April 22, 1963. This news article is from an unorganized newspaper clipping collection held at the Seafarers' International Union Archives, Piney Point, Md. (hereafter SIU Clipping Files). Philip Taft, "The Response of the Bakers, Longshoremen and Teamsters to Public Exposure," *Quarterly Journal of Economics* /4 (Aug. 1960): 393–412; John Hutchinson, *The Imperfect Union: A History of Corruption in American Trade Unions* (New York: E. P. Dutton, 1970), 287–41. Regarding the cautious attitude of the AFL-CIO, see Archie Robinson, *George Meany and His Times: A Biography* (New York: Simon and Schuster, 1981), 186–202, and Joseph C. Goulden, *Meany* (New York: Athenaeum, 1972), 253–62.

57. *Philadelphia Evening Bulletin,* Jan. 15, June 18, 1962, SIU Clipping Files.

58. McClellan Committee, *Hearings, Parts 27 and 28.* The trial testimony on union finances, the yacht, and the payoff is in *Philadelphia Evening Bulletin,* April 6, April 11, April 15, April 16, 1963, *Philadelphia Daily News,* April 11, April 15, April 17, 1963, and *Philadelphia Inquirer,* April 11, April 16, 1963, all in SIU Clipping Files. For Cohen's conviction, see *Philadelphia Evening Bulletin,* July 15, 1963, *Philadelphia Evening Bulletin* Clipping Files, Temple University Archives, Philadelphia (hereafter *Bulletin* Clipping Files).

59. *Philadelphia Evening Bulletin,* Feb. 22, June 11, Aug. 27, Sept. 19, Nov. 29, Dec. 6, 1959, *Bulletin* Clipping Files; "Teamster Notes," box 15, Bell Papers.

60. *Philadelphia Inquirer,* April 21, 1958, 1; *Philadelphia Evening Bulletin,* Dec. 5, 1958, 1.

61. *107 Teamsters Record,* Aug. and Sept. 1959, in the files of the Association for Union Democracy, Brooklyn, N.Y. (hereafter AUD Files)

62. *Philadelphia Inquirer,* Dec. 9, 1958, 24.

63. *Philadelphia Evening Bulletin,* June 25, Sept. 14, Oct. 14, 1962, *Bulletin* Clipping Files; *The Voice Handbook for Organizers* and *Philadelphia Inquirer,* Aug. 19, 1962, SIU Clipping Files; *Dictatorial Unionism or Democratic Unionism,* Voice flier from fall 1961, in MTLR: Investigation of Objections file, box 1248, file 2, case file 4 RC 5059, NLRB, National Archives, Suitland, Md. (hereafter NLRB Local 107 Files).

64. *Philadelphia Evening Bulletin,* Sept. 14, Nov. 19, 1962, and *Philadelphia Daily News,* March 6, 1963, June 18, 1962, all in SIU Clipping Files; *Philadelphia Evening Bulletin,* Jan. 10, 1962; *New York Times,* Dec. 6, 1961, clippings in AUD Files; John Bunker, "The Philadelphia Story," *Seafarers' Log* 45 (Jan. 1983): 34–35; John Bunker, "The Chicago Cab Story," *Seafarers' Log* 44 (Dec. 1982): 36–37; "The Lonely Insurgents," *The Nation,* May 16, 1959, 439; interview with Irving Friedman.

65. *Philadelphia Inquirer,* Jan. 28, 1963, SIU Clipping Files.

66. *Philadelphia Inquirer,* Aug. 19, 1962, SIU Clipping Files; *Voice of Truth* 1 (Sept. 1962): 2–4, Taniment-Wagner Labor Archives, New York University, New York.

67. The names on the two main leadership lists for the Voice included Charles Meyer, Gerald Dunn, John Clark, Francis Arnold, Andrew Kozak, Patrick O'Donnell, Frank Amoroso, and William Wickert. The top officials at Local 107 included Raymond Cohen, Edward Walker, Joseph Grace, Edward Battisfiore, and Michael Hession. *Voice of Truth* 1 (July 1962): 1–3, SIU Clipping Files; *Philadelphia Evening Bulletin,* Dec. 13, 1962, April 6, April 9, 1963, *Bulletin* Clipping Files.

68. The family names of members of the Voice who wrote to complain to the NLRB about Teamster harassment suggest a mix of ethnic backgrounds. A review of the decertification petitions shows the same mix. See the list of sixty-six affidavits contained in Investigation of Objections, file 1, box 1248, and petition lists in Voice List of Cards file, box 1249, both in NLRB Local 107 Files.

69. *Philadelphia Evening Bulletin,* Aug. 13, 1962, *Philadelphia Daily News,* Aug. 16, 1962, and *Philadelphia Inquirer,* Aug. 19, 1962, all in SIU Clipping Files.

70. Jacobs, *The State of the Unions,* 60.

71. Deposition of Robert Rispo in *U.S. v. International Brotherhood of Teamsters, Chauffeurs, Warehousemen and Helpers of America, AFL-CIO et al.,* U.S. District Court, Southern District of New York, case 88 CV 4486, Jan. 19, 1989, 118, 120.

72. *Voice of Truth* 1 (May 1962), and *The Voice Handbook for Organizers,* 6, 8, both in SIU Clipping Files.

73. "The Hiring Hall as It Should Be Run," *The Voice of Truth* 1 (July 1962): 2, in NLRB Files.

74. *The Voice Handbook for Organizers,* SIU Clipping Files.

75. *Philadelphia Evening Bulletin,* Sept. 14, 1959, *Bulletin* Clipping Files.

76. *Philadelphia Inquirer,* April 22, 1959, 1, April 24, 1958, 4.

77. McClellan Committee, *Hearings, Part 27,* 10403–36. For unions in general, see Warren R. Van Tine, *The Making of the Labor Bureaucrat: Union Leadership in the United States, 1870–1920* (Amherst: University of Massachusetts Press, 1973), 33–56; Will Herbert, "Bureaucracy and Democracy in Labor Unions," *Antioch Review* 3 (Fall 1943): 405–17; and Leonard R. Sayles and George Strauss, *The Local Union: Its Place in the Industrial Plant* (New York: Harper and Brothers, 1953), 167–89, 244–49.

78. *The Voice Handbook for Organizers,* 2. Another description of a Local 107 meeting can be found in *A Voice of Truth Extra!! Report on the Local 107 Meeting,* SIU Clipping Files.

79. *Philadelphia Evening Bulletin,* April 14, 1963, *Bulletin* Clipping Files.

80. *Voice of Truth* 1 (May 1962): 4, SIU Clipping Files.

81. *Philadelphia Evening Bulletin,* Nov. 23, 1962, *Bulletin* Clipping Files.

82. *Philadelphia Evening Bulletin,* Aug. 13, 1962, and *Philadelphia Inquirer,* Aug. 19, Nov. 10, 1962, both in SIU Clipping Files; Report and Recommendations on Objections to Election, case 4-RC-5059, dated Jan. 24, 1963, no. 1 file, box 1249, NLRB Files.

83. *Philadelphia Inquirer,* Aug. 14, 16, 17, 1962, and *Philadelphia Daily News,* Aug. 14, 16 1962, all in SIU Clipping Files.

84. Affidavit of John Fuest, Dec. 6, 1962, Investigation of Objections, file 1, box 1248, NLRB Files; see also *Philadelphia Inquirer,* Aug. 16, 1962, *Philadelphia Evening Bulletin,* Aug. 16, 17, 1962, and *Philadelphia Daily News,* Aug. 16, 1962, all in SIU Clipping Files.

85. *Voice of Truth* 1 (Sept. 1962): 1, SIU Clipping Files.

86. *Philadelphia Evening Bulletin,* Aug. 17, 1962, *Bulletin* Clipping Files.

87. *Philadelphia Evening Bulletin,* Aug. 18, 19, 1962, *Philadelphia Inquirer,* Aug. 18, 1962, and *Philadelphia Daily News,* Aug. 18, 1962, all in SIU Clipping Files.

88. *Philadelphia Evening Bulletin,* Nov. 19, 1962. Regarding finances, it later came out that Hoffa and the national union had given Cohen a "blank check" to win the fight and had pumped more than $180,000 into this election battle. *Evening Bulletin,* May 7, 1963, *Bulletin* Clipping Files.

89. *Philadelphia Evening Bulletin,* March 28, 1963, *Bulletin* Clipping Files.

90. *Evening Bulletin,* Feb. 11, 1963, SIU Clipping Files.

91. *Philadelphia Daily News,* Feb. 27, 1963, *Philadelphia Inquirer,* Feb. 27, 1963, and *Philadelphia Evening Bulletin,* Feb. 26, 1963, all in SIU Clipping Files.

92. *Philadelphia Inquirer,* March 20, April 10, April 14, 1963, and *Philadelphia Evening Bulletin,* March 20, 1963, all in SIU Clipping Files; James and James, *Hoffa and the Teamsters,* 204–9.

93. *Philadelphia Inquirer,* April 30, 1963, and *Philadelphia Evening Bulletin,* April 28, 1963, both in SIU Clipping Files.

94. Pennsylvania Crime Commission, *A Decade of Organized Crime: 1980 Report* (St. Davids: Commonwealth of Pennsylvania, 1980), 81–84; U.S. Congress, Senate, Permanent Subcommittee on Investigations, *Profile of Organized Crime: Mid-Atlantic Region,* 98th Cong., 1st sess., Feb. 15, 23, 24, 1983 (Washington, D.C.: Government Printing Office, 1983), 390–94, quotation on 390.

95. Statement of Philip Leonetti, July 23, 1990, and statement of Nicholas Caramandi, Aug. 16, 1990, both in the charge file of *Investigations Officer v. Joseph Cimino, Jr.*, Aug. 30, 1990, an internal charge filed according to the consent decree in *U.S. v. IBT,* case 88 CIV. 4486 (DNE).

96. Sloane, *Hoffa,* 288–330; James and James, *Hoffa and the Teamsters,* 375; *Constitution International Brotherhood of Teamsters, Chauffeurs, Warehousemen and Helpers of America, Adopted by the Miami Beach, Florida, Convention, July 4–7, 1966* (Washington, D.C.: n.p., 1966), 38–39.

Conclusion

1. James R. Hoffa as told to Oscar Fraley, *Hoffa: The Real Story* (New York: Stein and Day, 1975), 11–24, 233–42; Arthur A. Sloane, *Hoffa* (Cambridge: MIT Press, 1991), 350–99; Steven Brill, *The Teamsters* (New York: Simon and Schuster, 1978), 43–89, 100–110. Other works that provide alternative explanations but still focus upon the Mafia include Dan E. Moldea, *The Hoffa Wars: Teamsters, Rebels, Politicians, and the Mob* (New York: Charter Books, 1978), 277–421; and Lester Velie, *Desperate Bargain: Why Jimmy Hoffa Had to Die* (New York: Reader's Digest Press, 1977), 3–195.

2. *Time,* Aug. 11, 1975, 7–8; *Time,* Aug. 18, 1975, 14, 17–18; P. Owens, "Teamster Mess: Jimmy, Fitz and the Money Machine," *The Nation,* Oct. 18, 1975, 363–66; "Behind the Crackdown on a Huge Teamster Pension Plan: Central States Fund," *U.S. News and World Report,* July 12, 1976, 73–75.

3. *New York Times,* April 29, 1989; *Washington Post,* April 29, 1989.

4. James Neff, *Mobbed Up: Jackie Presser's High-Wire Life in the Teamsters, the Mafia, and the FBI* (New York: Dell Publishing, 1989).

5. *New York Times,* March 17, 1989, A1; *Los Angeles Times,* July 28, 1988, 1, Oct. 11, 1988, 1; Neff, *Mobbed Up,* 473–75.

6. President's Commission on Organized Crime, *The Edge: Organized Crime, Business, and Labor Unions: Report to the President and the Attorney General* (Washington, D.C.: The Commission, 1986), 4–5.

7. *New York Times,* Nov. 22, 1986, 1.

8. Scholarly overviews of government trusteeship efforts include Michael J. Goldberg, "Cleaning Labor's House: Institutional Reform Litigation in the Labor Movement," *Duke Law Journal* 4 (Sept. 1989): 965–83, and Clyde W. Summers, "Union Trusteeships and Union Democracy," *University of Michigan Journal of Law Reform* 24 (Spring–Summer 1991): 691–707. For more recent efforts of the current leadership to end the government's oversight role, see *New York Times,* Aug. 14, 1999, A1.

9. Lester Velie, "Can the Rank and File Clean Up the Teamsters?" *Reader's Digest* (Jan. 1977): 57–58; Jerry Bornstein, "Transforming the Teamsters," *The Progressive* 40 (Dec. 1976): 47–48; Steve Early, "Teaming Up for Reform," *The Progressive* 47 (Dec. 1983): 17–18; Kenneth C. Crowe, *Collision: How the Rank and File Took Back the Teamsters Union* (New York: Charles Scribner's Sons, 1993), 46–64; Dan La Botz, *Rank and File Rebellion: Teamsters for a Democratic Union* (New York: Verso Press, 1990), 19–82, 143–94.

10. Crowe, *Collision,* 254–63, 287–88.

11. *New York Times,* July 8, 1961, 18.

12. A. H. Raskin, "Why They Cheer for Hoffa," *New York Times Magazine,* Nov. 9, 1958, 18.

Index

DAVID WITWER is an associate professor of history at Lycoming College in Williamsport, Pennsylvania, and is the author of articles in journals such as *Labor History*, the *Journal of Social History*, and the *Journal of Women's History*. A graduate of DePauw and Brown universities, he has also worked in the offices of the New York County district attorney and the U.S. attorney, Southern District of New York, and been a visiting fellow at the Shelby Cullom Davis Center for Historical Studies at Princeton University.

The Working Class in American History

The University of Illinois Press
is a founding member of the
Association of American University Presses.

Composed in 10.5/13 Adobe Minion
at the University of Illinois Press
Manufactured by Thomson-Shore, Inc.

University of Illinois Press
1325 South Oak Street
Champaign, IL 61820–6903
www.press.uillinois.edu